Parts of Speech

Benjamins Current Topics

Special issues of established journals tend to circulate within the orbit of the subscribers of those journals. For the Benjamins Current Topics series a number of special issues have been selected containing salient topics of research with the aim to widen the readership and to give this interesting material an additional lease of life in book format.

Volume 25

Parts of Speech. Empirical and theoretical advances
Edited by Umberto Ansaldo, Jan Don and Roland Pfau

These materials were previously published in *Studies in Language* 32:3 (2008).

Parts of Speech

Empirical and theoretical advances

Edited by

Umberto Ansaldo
University of Hong Kong

Jan Don
Roland Pfau
University of Amsterdam

John Benjamins Publishing Company
Amsterdam / Philadelphia

The paper used in this publication meets the minimum requirements of American National Standard for Information Sciences – Permanence of Paper for Printed Library Materials, ANSI Z39.48-1984.

Library of Congress Cataloging-in-Publication Data

Parts of speech : empirical and theoretical advances / edited by Umberto Ansaldo, Jan Don and Roland Pfau.

p. cm. (Benjamins Current Topics, ISSN 1874-0081 ; v. 25)

Includes bibliographical references and index.

1. Parts of speech. 2. Grammar, Comparative and general--Grammatical categories. 3. Linguistic universals I. Ansaldo, Umberto. II. Don, Jan, 1963- III. Pfau, Roland.

P270.P37 2010

415--dc22 2010030034

ISBN 978 90 272 2255 8 (Hb ; alk. paper)

ISBN 978 90 272 8771 7 (Eb)

John Benjamins Publishing Co. · P.O. Box 36224 · 1020 ME Amsterdam · The Netherlands

John Benjamins North America · P.O. Box 27519 · Philadelphia PA 19118-0519 · USA

Table of contents

Parts of Speech

Particulars, universals and theoretical constructs

Umberto Ansaldo, Jan Don and Roland Pfau
University of Amsterdam

1. Introduction

This volume collates a selection of studies first presented at a conference on Parts of Speech (PoS) held at the University of Amsterdam in June 2006. The aim of that conference was to bring together approaches as different as possible, from the theoretical to the descriptive, the synchronic to the diachronic, variation and language contact to acquisition. The studies introduced below reflect the current concerns within the field in different domains: theoretical concerns regarding the status of PoS; descriptive puzzles in the application of PoS to a range of diverse languages; and elaborations of models for PoS.

Since the earliest studies of human language, it has been recognized that the elements that together make a sentence come in different types. It was first recognized by Plato (*Cratylus*) that a sentence is built from a nominal part (*onoma*) and a verbal part (*rhema*). Later, Dionysius Thrax in his *Techne Grammatike* developed a theory in which eight different word-classes were distinguished. In order to make the relevant distinctions, a combination of morphological, syntactic and semantic criteria was applied.

It seems safe to say that actual practice in present-day linguistics does not differ much from that of two millennia ago where a set of categories is distinguished, among which the 'lexical' categories *noun*, *verb* and *adjective*, and that morphological, semantic and syntactic criteria all help us make the relevant distinctions. Verbs are roughly those elements that typically express actions, come with tense, aspect and mood markers, and are the heads of predicates. In contrast, nouns typically refer to objects, come with case and number markers, and are heads of arguments. Adjectives most typically are modifying elements that often show agreement with the modified element.

However, as shown in the approaches to PoS presented in this volume, it is not true that categorial assignment is completely unproblematic; far from it. Different descriptive traditions, as well as different linguistic theories, may assume different sets of categories, applying different criteria to set them apart. In fact, one of the most interesting questions is whether PoS should be treated as descriptive tools or whether there is actually a core set of PoS that can be postulated as universal constructs. A related question is whether essentially these alleged universal PoS should be defined semantically, syntactically, or otherwise.

The diversity encountered in the study of PoS, the contrasting perspectives that arise from different theories and the methodological choices implied in selecting a syntactic, semantic or other analysis have led Haspelmath (2007) to suggest that it would be impossible in principle to come up with any cross-linguistically valid formal category, because categories of language structure are ultimately language-specific. According to this view there are no pre-established cross-linguistic categories that linguists can choose from in their descriptions, and therefore, they have no other choice than to "adopt the Boasian approach of positing special language-particular categories for each language, unless they do not mind Anglo-centric or Dyirbalo-centric descriptions that give a distorted picture of their language" (Haspelmath 2007: 121). In this sense, he suggests that, as long as the evidence for universal categories is more negative than positive, we need to be careful about the generalizations we derive on the nature of PoS in linguistic analyses.

Structural analyses of PoS often lead to controversial category assignment which, according to Haspelmath (2007), is futile if the categories under discussion are not cross-linguistically compatible in the first place. A semantically-based classification may be somewhat more promising, because semantically-based categories do not need to match identically but should simply match in communicative function, in terms of overall 'translatability' (Haspelmath 2007: 128). However, as pointed out by Newmeyer (2007), many linguists have successfully made comparisons between syntactic categories in different languages and have come up with explanations for their different behavior in those very languages. How would this be possible in the alleged absence of formal cross-linguistic categories?

2. Overview of the volume

The first paper in this volume presents a fresh take on PoS in sign languages, and offers a thorough methodological study on how to identify PoS in the first place, something often taken for granted in other linguistic domains. In comparing *Deutsche Gebärdensprache* (German Sign Language) with Kata Kolok, a Balinese community sign language, Schwager and Zeshan opt for a basic language-specific assignment of PoS based on cross-linguistically valid criteria, thus avoiding the imposition of pre-established categories in linguistic analysis. This serves as a useful reminder that broad generalizations across PoS systems may achieve the overarching goal of producing taxonomies of languages, but do not necessarily lead to a deeper understanding of what is specific and what is universal cross-linguistically. This issue is taken up in the second paper, in which Lehmann puts forward a strong statement against the universal categoriality of roots. In his view, postulating universal categories is misleading; this is essentially a claim of an empirical-theoretical dichotomy which, if accepted, questions whether theory-building can actually explain language-specific properties of language. When we shift our attention away from the familiar ground of Indo-European structure, it becomes obvious that our notions of PoS are still heavily based on the study of Greek and Latin grammars, and that one often assumes too much about the alleged universality of the linguistic categories derived from such observation. This is clear in the analysis of PoS in Late Archaic Chinese (LAC) discussed by Bisang in the third paper in this volume. LAC is a precategorial language, i.e. a language in which there is no assignment of categoriality in the lexicon, the result of loss of morphosyntactic material over time. N and V are interpreted based solely on argument structure, as the meaning of lexical items is derived from the specific construction in which they appear. This strict formal requirement for PoS assignment, according to Bisang, argues against universality of PoS in the lexicon.

In the two following contributions, we are offered new perspectives on a class of words with a very tricky status: adjectives. Based on the analysis of Tukang Besi, an Austronesian language of Indonesia, Donohue shows that the semantic prototypes that can be identified as 'adjectives' in fact lack a distinctive morphosyntax, but pattern with either N or V depending on their discourse function, and must therefore be assigned variable categorial status. The study of the Miyako-Hirara dialect of the Ryukyu Islands (Japan) likewise presents us with a 'split' status in the adjectival domain: the language, treated as switch-adjective by Koloskova and Ohori, codes adjectives as either N or V depending on information structure. What is furthermore of interest is that this is the result of morphosyntactic loss, which suggests that PoS distinction at the lexical level is no robust property of language (see also Bisang, this volume). It may indeed be the case that only very few of the many PoS observed cross-linguistically have universal status, perhaps as few as two. This is argued for in the paper by Gil, which offers yet another dimension of the syntax of Jakarta Indonesian, where only two syntactic categories can be distinguished: N and V. The paper looks at children's acquisition of categories within constructionist approaches and suggests that categorization starts at a very broad level and gets more specific over time.

It is obvious that, if universal aspects of linguistic categorization can be uncovered, the acquisitional domain is in need of further investigation. With this in mind, Don and Erkelens look at another dimension of acquisition, namely phonological cues in adults' classification. Their study shows that phonological cues matter in the classification of Dutch nouns, and proposes that children, too, may use phonology in assigning categorial membership to lexemes.

Yet another domain in need of much more investigation is language contact, for the potential it holds of revealing degrees of compatibility between PoS systems of different languages. As shown in Nichols' contribution, the grammatical complexity of Zuni noun roots poses constraints on borrowability, leaving some hope of identifying borrowability constraints that have so far eluded us.

Three papers in this volume look at the nature of PoS within functional theory-construction, in particular within the approach known as the 'Amsterdam Model' (Anward 2004). Salazar-Garcia offers an evaluation of the strengths and the weaknesses of the model, in particular in arguing for a constituent-based, rather than language-based taxonomy of PoS. A specific claim of this paper relates to Spanish quantifiers, the analysis of which leads the author to claim that degree words are lexical, rather than morphosyntactic. Rijkhoff discusses the dichotomy between flexible and rigid PoS and proposes a more sophisticated yet very challenging definition of nouns: rather than one unified category, he argues, we may have to postulate at least four different categories, based on semantic and syntactic criteria. In the final study, Hengeveld and van Lier present a cross-linguistic investigation of 23 varieties and set out to map the correlation between lexical and clausal constructs based on their comparable functional properties. In doing so, their study moves the Amsterdam Model into a new domain of grammatical theory, Functional Discourse Grammar (Hengeveld and Mackenzie 2008).

3. Final remarks

In collating a set of diverse approaches to PoS we wish to present the reader with a combination of explorations in language-specific aspects of PoS, novel conceptualization as well as elaborations of existing theories, which is representative of the current concerns, challenges and potential solutions to one of the oldest and most fundamental aspect of linguistic enquiry. Since PoS often constitute the tools with which we approach the earliest stages of linguistic analysis, we can never be too careful about how precisely we think we understand them.

References

Anward, Jan. 2000. A dynamic model of part-of-speech differentiation. *Approaches to the typology of word classes*, Petra M. Vogel & Bernard Comrie (eds.), 3–45. Berlin: Mouton de Gruyter.

Haspelmath, Martin. 2007. Pre-established categories don't exist: Consequences for language description and typology. *Linguistic Typology* 11: 119–132.

Hengeveld, Kees and Lachlan J. Mackenzie. 2008. *Functional discourse grammar: A typologically based theory of language structure*. Oxford: Oxford University Press.

Newmeyer, Frederick J. 2007. Linguistic typology requires crosslinguistic formal categories. *Linguistic Typology* 11: 133–157.

Word classes in sign languages

Criteria and classifications

Waldemar Schwager and Ulrike Zeshan
University of Hamburg, Germany / University of Central Lancashire, Preston, UK

The topic of word classes remains curiously under-represented in the sign language literature due to many theoretical and methodological problems in sign linguistics. This article focuses on language-specific classifications of signs into word classes in two different sign languages: German Sign Language and Kata Kolok, the sign language of a village community in Bali.

The article discusses semantic and structural criteria for identifying word classes in the target sign languages. On the basis of a data set of signs, these criteria are systematically tested out as a first step towards an inductive classification of signs. Approaches and analyses relating to the problem of word classes in linguistic typology are used for shedding new light on the issue of word class distinctions in sign languages.

1. Introduction

This article reports on in-progress research on word class typology across sign languages, which is based on data from two different sign languages: German Sign Language and Kata Kolok, the sign language of a village community in Bali. The goal of this research project is to investigate the parts of speech (PoS) systems in the target sign languages in a way that produces descriptively adequate results for each of the languages, while at the same time developing a cross-linguistically applicable methodology. This is a very challenging task with few precedents in the research literature on sign language linguistics. Not only have there been very few attempts at identifying word classes in individual sign languages, there are also serious theoretical problems that need to be resolved along the way.

Summarising some initial methodological approaches and empirical results, we explore semantic, syntactic and morphological criteria and classifications that enter into a multi-factor analysis of parts of speech systems in sign languages. Although a number of further stages of analysis will be necessary until actual PoS classifications can be proposed for the target languages, the theoretical and methodological principles of the approach can already be demonstrated, as well as the kinds of interesting insights, though far from exhaustive, that can be gained along the way. Eventually, further research aims at testing the approach on a wider data set comparing 250 signs from each of the target languages against an exhaustive set of semantic, morphological and syntactic criteria.

This article consists of two main parts: Section 2 summarises a number of theoretical issues that arise when we consider PoS systems in sign languages, and gives a brief overview of previous work on the topic. Section 3 focuses on the comparative study of the two target sign languages, where criteria and classifications are tested against actual sign language data. We discuss the semantic, the syntactic, and the morphological levels of analysis, all of which enter into a comprehensive perspective on PoS classification in sign languages.

2. Theoretical issues and previous work on PoS systems in sign languages

2.1 Sign languages and sign language data

Sign languages are visual-gestural languages that use the hands and arms as well as non-manual means such as facial expressions, head movements, and body postures to convey linguistic messages. Research over the past decades has demonstrated that sign languages are natural human languages with a complex organisation of their lexicon and grammar. Moreover, the structure of each sign language is independent of the structure of the surrounding spoken language(s). For instance, the sign language used in the German deaf community is lexically, grammatically and typologically very different from spoken German. Most known sign languages are predominantly used by deaf communities in urban settings and exist as minority languages among the majority spoken and written languages used by hearing people. Another, lesser-known situation where sign languages are used concerns village communities with a history of hereditary deafness and a local sign language that is used by deaf and hearing people alike. Both types of sign languages feature in the research that this article reports on.

There is no satisfactory way of recording the dynamic, three-dimensional properties of sign language utterances on paper. In the absence of multi-media publications with integrated video files, authors in sign language linguistics therefore resort to a more or less standardised transcription, which may be enriched by illustrations for added clarity. The transcriptions consist of multi-line, vertically aligned text not unlike interlinear transcriptions in spoken language linguistics. However, the central transcription line consists not of a representation of the signs themselves, but instead employs small-caps glosses as stand-ins for the signs. Glosses are often in English, but may be in another relevant written language. In this article, we generally use German glosses for German Sign Language signs and English glosses for Kata Kolok signs.[1] The transcriptions allow the reader to reconstruct the word order in a signed utterance and the internal morphology of signs, but do not give any indication of what the utterance actually looks like. A number of abbreviations are used in the transcriptions, which are listed in the appendix to the article.

2.2 The word unit in sign languages

In order to provide some background to the discussions in Section 3, particularly for the benefit of non-specialists in sign language linguistics, this section characterises the word unit in sign languages and briefly touches on theoretical issues associated with this topic. A number of terms and concepts specific to sign language linguistics are also introduced.

Previous work on sign languages has made considerable progress in identifying and characterising the word unit. Although sign language linguists generally speak of 'signs' rather than 'words', both essentially denote the same kind of entity. Zeshan (2002) argues that for signers, the cultural and psycholinguistic validity of signs is equivalent to that of words in spoken languages, and shows that it is possible to identify grammatical and phonological words, as well as clitics and affixes in sign languages. Sandler (1999) explores the sign unit in terms of a number of constraints that typically apply to monomorphemic signs, thus characterising a canonical sign unit. This includes constraints for the canonical sign to be monosyllabic, that is, having a single movement contour, and to use only one set of selected fingers in its handshape configuration.

A serious theoretical problem at the sub-lexical level is due to the fact that sign languages are much more iconic than spoken languages, with many signs "looking like" what they mean to some degree. In fact, sign languages can be characterised as languages with a very high degree of phonosymbolism (Zeshan 2002).[2] When a sign

Figure 1. BAUM ('tree') in German Sign Language.

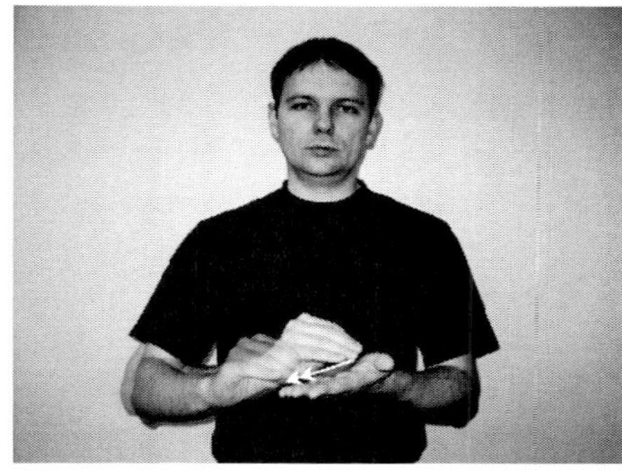

Figure 2. SCHREIB ('write') in German Sign Language.

meaning 'tree' or 'write' (see Figures 1 and 2) visually represents parts of the concept on the hands — for instance, the tree trunk by the lower arm and the tree branches by the fingers, or the paper to write on by the palm of one hand over which the other hand moves as if to write on it — this can cause confusion because these parts of the signs would be minimal meaningful units, but would otherwise be regarded as phonemes rather than morphemes.

Usually, a sign is considered to consist of several formational units, its phonemes or phonological parameters: handshape, movement, place of articulation, hand orientation, and sometimes a non-manual component. The sign in Figure 1 therefore has a handshape phoneme (all fingers extended), a movement phoneme (wrist twisting), a place of articulation phoneme (space in front of the signer), and so on. However, it is also clear at the same time that the fingers of the hand represent the branches of the tree, and signers can exploit this iconic potential. For instance, the branches (fingers) could be made to sway in the wind, or the other hand, representing a bird, could make contact with the first hand to perch on a branch (e.g. the little finger) of the tree. The handshape is then clearly meaningful in such signs while, at the same time, continuing to function as a building block of the sign at the phonological level. This overlap between formational and meaningful functions of sub-lexical parts of signs causes theoretical problems in distinguishing phonemes from morphemes in sign languages, which has led some authors to coin new terms such as "phonomorphemes" or "ion-morphs" (Fernald and Napoli 2000). On the other hand, Zwitserlood (2003) argues that signs such as the ones discussed here should indeed be regarded as morphologically complex.

At the current stage of research, there is no widely accepted overt definition of the morpheme unit in sign languages, although it is clear that the traditional notion of morphemes as being "minimal meaningful units" is problematic to apply to sign languages. In the absence of such a definition, it is methodologically preferable to start by investigating morphological processes, which are relatively straightforward to identify. This is the approach used in this article, particularly in Section 3.5.

While we normally have little difficulty to identify the words/signs in signed utterances, there are cases where this is problematic. In particular, this concerns certain types of spatial-iconic signs that are usually called "classifiers" in the sign language linguistics literature (cf. Schembri 2003).[3] The analytical problem is most conspicuous in a sub-type where particular handshapes represent classes of similar referents. For instance, in German Sign Language an upright index finger PERSON-CL is used for human referents, whereas a horizontal flat hand can represent vehicles (Figures 3 and 4).

Since both hands can be used simultaneously for signing, it is also possible to combine these two signs into one, with the entity in the class of vehicles (e.g. a car) represented on the right hand and an entity in the class of human referents (e.g. a man) represented on the left hand. The movement and location of the classifier hands iconically map onto the movement and location of their referent entities, and these constructions can be used very productively. For example, the right hand could well be

Figure 3. PERSON-CL in German Sign Language.

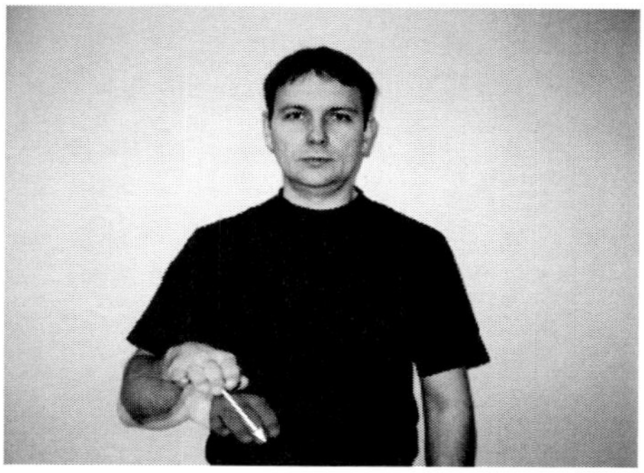

Figure 4. VEHICLE-CL in German Sign Language.

"approaching" from one side and then "crash into" the other hand, as in the man being run over by the car. It is very difficult to decide how many signs/words such a sequence should be segmented into. Is each hand a word, and both occur simultaneously? Would the "approaching" part of the hand's movement be a separate word from the "collision" part of the movement? Is the whole proposition contained in a single sign/word, or is it just difficult to identify the word boundaries in such an utterance? To then give a convincing account of the internal morphological structure of such formations is even more difficult, and they have long resisted a convincing morphological analysis in sign language research (cf. Emmorey 2003 for an overview). For the purpose of this article, classifier signs are not considered in the analysis, but it should be kept in mind that parts of the lexicon in sign languages are theoretically challenging to deal with and eventually will have to be included in a comprehensive word class analysis.

We also find a substantial amount of systematic ambiguity or vagueness in many sign languages. For instance, in Indo-Pakistani Sign Language (IPSL) many signs tend to have rather general meanings that are narrowed down by the context of the utterance, and since many grammatical categories can remain unmarked, a sequence of signs can be difficult to categorise structurally, although its meaning is entirely clear semantically. For example, an IPSL utterance such as in example (1) can have three related, but structurally different interpretations, as given in (2). Note that in IPSL, a personal pronoun can function as a possessive pronoun and nominal plurals need not be marked in any way. Personal pronouns in sign languages are indexical signs (therefore glossed as INDEX) that are oriented towards a location in the signing space, most commonly realised as pointing with the index finger.

IPSL

(1) INDEX_1 WORK A-LOT

(2) a. 'I work a lot.'
b. 'My work is a lot.'
c. 'I have a lot of things to do (works).'

Although the utterance in (1) is systematically ambiguous as far as the relationship of the individual signs to each other is concerned, this does not mean that the signs in such utterances are thrown together in an ad hoc fashion and lack structural restrictions. In fact, changing the word order as in example (3) results in an ungrammatical utterance:

IPSL
(3) *INDEX$_1$ A-LOT WORK

The problem with respect to a PoS analysis is that even where we can observe syntactic restrictions in sign languages, it is often far from clear how exactly such regularities relate to word classes, or are criterial for determining the PoS system. Thus the above data from IPSL do not provide clear clues as to whether the sign WORK has a nominal or a verbal character, and similar problems are encountered in many other sign languages as well.

Where morphological marking occurs in sign languages, it is similarly often difficult to understand how it may relate to or be criterial for establishing word classes. Morphological processes are often inapplicable for phonological reasons, that is, because of the physical form of the sign. For instance, if a morphological process requires a sign to be repeated at several locations in space rather than being signed only once in its neutral location, the process by definition cannot apply to signs that must be made on a particular part of the body, such as signs touching the head or the chest area. The types of morphology that we commonly find in sign languages are uncommon in most spoken languages (cf. Section 3.5), and their restrictions can operate in ways that do not obviously relate to criteria for word classes.

2.3 Previous approaches to PoS classification in sign languages

In the description of undocumented spoken languages, determining the word classes and their properties is typically one of the first tasks. By contrast, sign language linguistics has been quite shockingly neglectful of this fundamental issue. Generally, signs are either labelled as "adjectives", "nouns" etc. on the basis of a translation of the sign's meaning into a relevant spoken language — DEAF in British Sign Language must be an adjective because *deaf* in English is an adjective — or the PoS system of American Sign Language (ASL), the most extensively documented sign language, is uncritically applied to a lesser-described sign language. Both approaches are, of course, neither methodologically nor theoretically viable.

Principled attempts at PoS classification in sign languages are few and far between. An early influential study on ASL discusses the distinction between related pairs of nouns and verbs (Supalla and Newport 1978). In ASL, there are subtle differences in movement patterns between sign pairs such as AIRPLANE and FLY-BY-AIRPLANE, SCISSORS and CUT-WITH-SCISSORS, DOOR and OPEN-DOOR, and the like. The handshape, hand orientation and place of articulation are the same in both signs of each pair, but the movement patterns differ, with nouns (AIRPLANE, SCISSORS, DOOR) being characterised by smaller and repeated movements. This distinction holds for instruments and related actions only, such as in SCISSORS and CUT-WITH-SCISSORS, and does not apply to all nouns and verbs in ASL. Johnston (2001) investigates whether the same process applies in Australian Sign Language as well. Padden's (1988) seminal study on ASL discusses a number of diagnostic tests and argues for a PoS system including nouns, adjectives, and three sub-classes of verbs. In simplified terms, the main criteria are the following (note the starred ungrammatical examples in (4)–(6) below): Nouns can be modified by quantifiers, as is exemplified by TREE in (4a), which is quanitified by the sign FOUR. By contrast, a verb such as RUN cannot be combined with a quantifier. Adjectives are defined by being able to inflect for intensive aspect. The form of a sign such as RED can be formationally modified and then means 'very red' (5a). By contrast, TREE cannot be modified in this way (5b). Finally, verbs cannot be pre-modifiers of other signs, so whereas the adjective BIG is modifying SHOE in (6a), the verb RUN is ungrammatical in the same modifier slot (6b).

ASL

(4) a. FOUR TREE
b. *FOUR RUN

(5) a. RED#INTS
b. *TREE#INTS

(6) a. BIG SHOE
b. *RUN SHOE

Without going into the details of the analysis here, it is significant to point out that the class of verbs is defined negatively only, through inability to pre-modify other signs. No convincing set of criteria is discussed that would positively identify all sub-classes of verbs, and they in fact have quite different morphological properties (for further details on verb sub-classes, see Sections 3.4.1 and 3.5). Moreover, it is doubtful whether the criteria really apply across the board to all signs that are intended to be members of each category, since they are not systematically tested against a wide variety of lexemes in ASL.

Although the above criteria are clearly language-specific to ASL, they have often been transferred to other sign languages. By contrast, Zeshan (2000) is an attempt at identifying both open and closed word classes in IPSL in a different way, since diagnostic tests employed by Padden (1988) generally do not work for IPSL. The proposed PoS system for IPSL is quite different from Padden's, classifying signs from open word classes in terms of their spatial behaviour. Thus signs are either unable to take any spatial modification, for instance because they must always be made on a particular part of the body, or the place of articulation of a sign can be moved in space, for instance by placing the hand on one side of the signer rather than in front, or the sign moves between two grammatically relevant locations. The third class of signs has verbal properties (cf. the discussion of directional/agreement signs in Section 3.5). The PoS classification for IPSL also includes closed word classes such as signs with classifier handshapes and indexical signs. Finally, Erlenkamp (2000) proposes a PoS classification for German Sign Language. We will deal with her proposal in more detail below, since this article also considers German Sign Language as one of its target languages.

In summary, the main problem in all previous PoS analyses of sign languages is that there is no principled way of identifying criteria for PoS differentiation. Criteria seem ad hoc and generally lack theoretical justification, a problem which is aggravated by the fact that semantic, morphological and syntactic criteria may themselves lead to conflicting results (cf. Sasse 1993). While a detailed study of PoS systems in sign languages will need to go beyond traditional categorisations, the alternatives that would lead to descriptively adequate, methodologically sound and theoretically interesting analyses have not been worked out yet.

3. Towards unified criteria for PoS differentiation in sign languages

3.1 Sign language data

In order to systematically approach some of the theoretically and methodologically challenging issues addressed in the first part of this article, we mainly use data from two unrelated sign languages: German Sign Language (Deutsche Gebärdensprache, henceforth abbreviated DGS), the language of the German deaf community, and Kata Kolok (henceforth abbreviated KK), a sign language used in a village community in northern Bali, Indonesia. These sign languages are not only geographically and genetically unrelated to each other and have never been in contact with one another, they are also typologically dissimilar and exist in quite different socio-linguistic settings. Such a cross-linguistic perspective is important and integral to the approach if there is to be any chance of obtaining insights that are applicable to more than one particular sign language. In addition to these theoretical considerations, the choice of our data has also been motivated by the availability of suitable sign language corpora.

DGS is used as a first language by more than 80,000 deaf sign language users in Germany, as well as about 300,000 people who are hard of hearing. The German deaf community is a linguistic and cultural minority which is in a language contact situation with the surrounding dominant language, spoken/written German. Prior to the language's official recognition in 2002, DGS faced a long period of linguistic oppression, but is now reasonably well documented, including the availability of educational materials for teaching the language. Heßmann (2001) recorded spontaneous signed texts in DGS and transcribed one hour of these data, though in a semantically-based way and without any reference to the part-of-speech assignment of individual signs in this corpus. By contrast, Erlenkamp (2000) is an explicit attempt at characterising the word class system of DGS in a typological framework. However, this contribution remains preliminary and has not been widely absorbed in the research community. It has also been criticised for methodological and theoretical shortcomings by Keller, Pfau and Steinbach (2002).

Unlike DGS in its largely urban context, Kata Kolok (literally "deaf language") is the sign language of a small village community in northern Bali. The village has a high incidence of hereditary deafness, with currently 50 deaf people in a total population of about 2,500.[4] According to oral history, village records and local myths, KK has existed in the village for 800 years (Marsaja 2008). KK is used by both deaf and hearing people in the village, with the deaf being monolingual users of KK and most hearing people growing up bilingually (or rather, multilingually) with competence in both the sign language and a number of spoken languages used in the village. The KK data corpus was gathered during two field trips as part of the "Sign Language Typology" research project, and the data are archived at the Max Planck Institute for Psycholinguistics (MPI) in the Netherlands and at the University of Central Lancashire in the UK. Out of this extensive corpus of spontaneously produced sign language data, four hours of transcribed data are available for the purpose of our comparative parts of speech analysis. Unlike for DGS, there is no research into word classes in KK yet, and its linguistic documentation has only just begun. Previous publications on KK (e.g. Branson, Miller and Marsaja 1996) focus on its socio-cultural setting and do not include information about its linguistic structures.

In Section 3.5, we will use data from a third sign language, Russian Sign Language (RSL), for further comparison. RSL data are also part of the MPI sign language corpora, and the language has been analysed at the morphological level in Schwager (2004). However, RSL data play a limited role within the scope of this work because DGS and RSL are typologically similar to each other, both being in contrast with KK. Parts of speech analyses of the three sign languages function as a pilot project, and it is expected that the resulting framework will be applied to other sign languages in the future.

3.2 Theoretical background on semantic and structural criteria

All lexical units of a language have a number of features that characterise them. Words with the same, similar, or equivalent characteristic features can be assigned to the same word class. Therefore, in order to determine the word classes in any given sign language, we also need to study the individual features that characterise its words/signs. In principle, there are unlimited possibilities of assigning lexical units to classes. Among these possibilities, some are sensible choices and many others are not. How many classes are to be posited depends on the constellation of criteria that are potentially available for the purpose of PoS classification in a particular language, and ultimately depends on the explanatory goal of the analysis itself.

In this article, we adopt a theoretical framework according to which word class assignment in any given sign language has to be done language-specifically, yet should be based on cross-linguistically applicable criteria. This is an important theoretical decision, which is particularly suitable for comparing typologically diverse languages (cf. Croft 2001). Rather than just imposing ready-made traditional labels such as "noun", "verb", etc., as has been common practice in much of the earlier sign language research literature, it is important to find a principled standard of comparison and apply this consistently across the target languages. Logically, this analysis is done in two stages: 1. establishing the same, similar, or equivalent distinguishing criteria that are potentially relevant to PoS systems in DGS and KK, and 2. working towards a comparative analysis of PoS distinctions in DGS and KK on the basis of these criteria.

In the process of positing features that are criterial for word class assignment in sign languages, we choose features that are relevant not only for sign languages, but also for spoken languages. The parts of speech analyses generally draw on theoretical work by Sasse (1993) and Anward (2001). Sasse (1993) states that (lexical) categories are language-specific bundles of features which have both formal and conceptual aspects. Therefore, semantic, morphological and syntactic levels of word units are distinguished and enter into a parts of speech analysis in sign languages.

For the semantic level, new semantic feature bundles have been compiled and refined for each concept class (see Section 3.3.2), largely following approaches in Löbner (2002), Sasse (1993) and Anward (2000, 2001). The syntactic level relies on Hengeveld (1992) and Anward (2000), and on the morphological level, criteria were created on the basis of the existing sign linguistics literature, in particular Sandler and Lillo-Martin (2006) (see Section 3.5).

When discussing the assignment of signs to classes, it is important to always be precise about which of these levels is relevant at the time. All too often the morphological level is confused with the semantic or the syntactic level. In order to avoid confusing definitions, classes should only be defined using features that belong to one and the same level. Moreover, it will be preferable for all distinguishing features to be binary. Such binary distinguishing features should not only be posited as such, but should also be structured hierarchically within a particular feature bundle of a class, as is exemplified in Section 3.3.2 below. For PoS differentiation in signed/spoken languages, the following priority of levels is assumed: 1. Semantic criteria should be determined language-independently and are used as a first step towards PoS differentiation. 2. Syntactic, morphological, and discourse-pragmatic criteria should be determined language-specifically.

It has long been recognised that semantic criteria are problematic as a starting point for assigning words to parts of speech. Thus, Evans (2000) argues that synonyms may be mapped onto different word classes in different languages, so that two words from different languages which essentially express the same meaning may belong to distinct word classes in each language. In fact, such cases are also found in sign languages, as we illustrate with examples in Section 3.4.2. However, this line of argumentation only focuses on the lexical level, not on the level of minimal semantic features. Semantic mapping of individual lexical units is of course language-specific, and also sometimes culturally determined, but the minimal semantic features such as [human], [concrete], [individuated], etc., are cognitive-linguistically and, so to speak, pre-categorically based, and can therefore be taken to be language-independent. Thus, they constitute a good point of departure for defining the membership of parts of speech across languages.

Since for sign languages, in particular previously undocumented ones such as KK, the issue of PoS distinctions is severely understudied, it is preferable to begin our pilot study by relying on the widest possible range of criteria, certainly including structural criteria from both syntax and morphology. The ad hoc application of both syntactic and morphological criteria for PoS differentiation in sign languages has proved equally problematic or has produced ambiguous results in one way or another in previous studies. For instance, one of the findings in both Erlenkamp (2000) and Zeshan (2000) is that most signs in DGS and in IPSL can appear either in an argument or in a predicate slot, without any formal marking. In many spoken languages, nouns and adjectives can function as predicates without any verb or copula needed in the sentence, and this is also the case in sign languages. By and large, it has not been easy to identify workable syntactic tests for sign languages, given that they often have relatively free word order and some of their sentence structures are unfamiliar from a spoken language background, including spatial syntax and simultaneous constructions. We still do not know enough about the syntactic behaviour of sign languages to rely on syntactic criteria exclusively.

Distinguishing word classes on the basis of morphological criteria is possible only for languages that have appropriate processes of inflection and/or agglutination. For isolating languages such as Chinese, PoS-classes cannot be posited on the basis of morphological criteria. Sign languages also have a large number of such non-inflecting lexemes, as noted in Erlenkamp (2000) for DGS. Moreover, morphological criteria are always language-specific and may be impossible to apply across sign languages in their entirety if a certain morphological process occurs in one sign language but is absent in another sign language (see examples from DGS and KK in Section 3.5). Morphological processes by themselves do not constitute reliable criteria for word class assignment in sign languages.[5]

In the remainder of this article, we posit syntactic and morphological criteria in combination with semantic criteria, and then test the viability of this approach against examples from the sign languages in our corpus, mainly focusing on Kata Kolok and German Sign Language.

3.3 Semantic criteria for PoS differentiation

3.3.1 *A semantic metalanguage*

Given that semantic criteria are taken as a starting point in our approach, the next question to deal with is which semantic criteria should be identified to establish the intended semantic metalanguage. The concepts of our cognitive world fall into various classes, yet such semantic classification is not random across languages because of a degree of language-independent, cognitive-linguistic determination. Similar concepts can be grouped together in a class, which is called a concept class. In Sasse's terms (1993: 202): "Eine Konzeptklasse ist ein Bündel verwandter Konzepte, das durch ein übergeordnetes Merkmal (gewöhnlich ein „Hyperonym") definiert werden kann."[6] Such classes, by virtue of their semantic features, often figure in lexical-grammatical restrictions related to parts of speech in a given language. At the semantic level, concept classes such as concrete entities, abstract entities, properties, states, actions, etc, can be posited. Expanding on Stassen (1997), Anward (2000, 2001) defines a total of eight semantic classes: person/thing,[7] event, property, place, time, relation, quantity and situation. However, in order to approach a characterisation of lexical meanings that can be used cross-linguistically as a starting point for our analysis, we need to take another step and also consider bundles of minimal semantic features that characterise a semantic class, as well as inherent properties of the semantic features (which may themselves be either categorical or gradual).

According to Löbner (2002), distinguishing features of concept classes should always be binary. In this regard, it is important to note that not all features are applicable to all concept classes. For example, a binary feature [±dynamic] that defines an aspectual differentiation between 'dynamic' and 'static', is fully compatible with the semantic class of events, but is not really applicable to the entity class. Therefore, in tabulating the minimal semantic features of concept classes, the feature [dynamic] can be positive or negative within the concept class of events, but is zero, that is, inapplicable, within the concept class of entities (cf. Table 1 in Section 3.3.2).

Moreover, semantic classes characterised by bundles of distinguishing features should not show fuzzy boundaries. Following Löbner (2002), we assume that semantic classes or categories have an internal structure, with better and less good (in other words: more or less 'prototypical') members of a category, and that sign/word meaning can in addition be flexible/vague. However, the boundaries of a given semantic category cannot be fuzzy and membership of lexical items in semantic categories is not gradient, but binary. In other words, semantic classes/categories have variable, but not fuzzy boundaries. Finally, defining a structured hierarchy for the minimal semantic features is crucial for well-formed semantic categorisation. For instance, it is logically impossible for a feature [human] to be higher than a feature [animate]. Section 3.3.2 provides examples of such feature hierarchies.

Within the framework of this semantic metalanguage, the fact that there are better and less good members of a concept class is not unexpected, and may be explained with reference to diachronic reasons, such as grammaticalisation and lexicalisation. Such units may partially adopt new features of a concept class but still preserve some previous features of another class. Thus, semantic change may, for certain lexical items, cause semantic "interference" with a purely synchronic classification of a language, but does not jeopardise the approach in general.

As is detailed in the following section, semantic features and concept classes have been posited with a view towards being cross-linguistically valid, so that a typological comparison of languages at the semantic level in terms of same, similar or equivalent units becomes possible. Although the aim of establishing the hierarchical semantic features as such is to obtain a valid cross-linguistic basis, this does not mean that all features have to be present in all languages. Rather, certain features can be lexico-grammatically relevant in one language, but irrelevant, and therefore absent, in another language. For instance, the distinction between what is traditionally known as "mass nouns" and "count nouns" is grammatically relevant in English and in American Sign Language (Padden 1988), but not in Indo-Pakistani Sign Language (Zeshan 2000) and in many spoken languages. Similarly, Wilbur (2008) claims that the semantic feature of telicity is reflected in formational aspects of signs in American Sign Language, but this is unlikely to hold in all sign languages.[8]

In principle, a language-specific, synchronically adequate system of semantic features can be deduced from the general, language-independent semantic metalanguage, although for the purpose of this article this has not actually been done yet. Rather, we explicate selected parts of the semantic feature system regarding the concept classes of entity, event and property. The event class is itself subdivided into (sub)classes of action, process and state. There are further concept classes to be identified which do not enter into the discussion here, such as: time class (e.g. 'tomorrow'), place class (e.g. 'here'), quantity class (e.g. 'three', 'much'), and some synsemantic classes (such as deictics, classifiers, etc.).

3.3.2 *Semantic feature systems for entity, event, and property classes*

To exemplify a concrete instantiation of the theoretical considerations explained in the previous section, this section proposes partial semantic feature hierarchies for the event and the entity classes, as well as the more problematic property class. We then take a look at a number of semantically equivalent signs from DGS and KK to test how the semantic metalanguage functions in the cross-linguistic comparison of signs.

Figure 5 shows a feature hierarchy for the entity concept class. The feature system partly follows the traditional practice of ontological classification known since the time of Aristotle and Dionysius Thrax (cf. Lehmann and Moravcsik 2000), but also includes some new, refined features in the hierarchy. A systematic matrix of hierarchically structured semantic features, as given in Figure 5 for the entity class, and also in

Figure 6 for the event class, is not commonly found in the literature. While many of the labels are well-known, they have been re-arranged into comprehensive matrices of semantic features. Lehmann and Moravcsik (2000) group nouns into subclasses with a view towards their morphosyntactic behaviour, and their subclasses include categories such as mass nouns vs. count nouns, collective vs. individual nouns, and the like. In Figure 5, however, these and other additional categorisations are reinterpreted and cast in terms of minimal semantic features.

In Figure 5, the feature [±proper] first divides this class into common names, designating a concept, and proper names, designating an individual (cf. Lehmann and Moravcsik 2000). Proper names are further subdivided into subclasses by features [±animate] and [±human], yielding classes for person names, individual names for animals, and proper names for things. Under the category of proper names, person names include items such as *John, Mary, Gandhi,* etc. By contrast, the category of human names (persons) is classified under common names and consists of items such as *student, president, baby, dwarf, foreigner,* etc.

Using a further feature [±local], proper names for things may be subdivided into geographic names (e.g. *Siberia, Berlin*) and individual names for objects (e.g. *Eiffel Tower, Crown Jewels*). As detailed below, place names are particularly interesting with respect to the cross-linguistic comparison of DGS and KK. Whereas the 'proper' class always has the values [+concrete], [0 homogeneous], [+individuated], and [−count], these features are differentiated in the 'common' class. For example, the 'mass' class consists of a sortal subclass (e.g. *wine*, which has a plural *wines*) and a material subclass (e.g. *air, rice*), which are differentiated by a feature [±count].

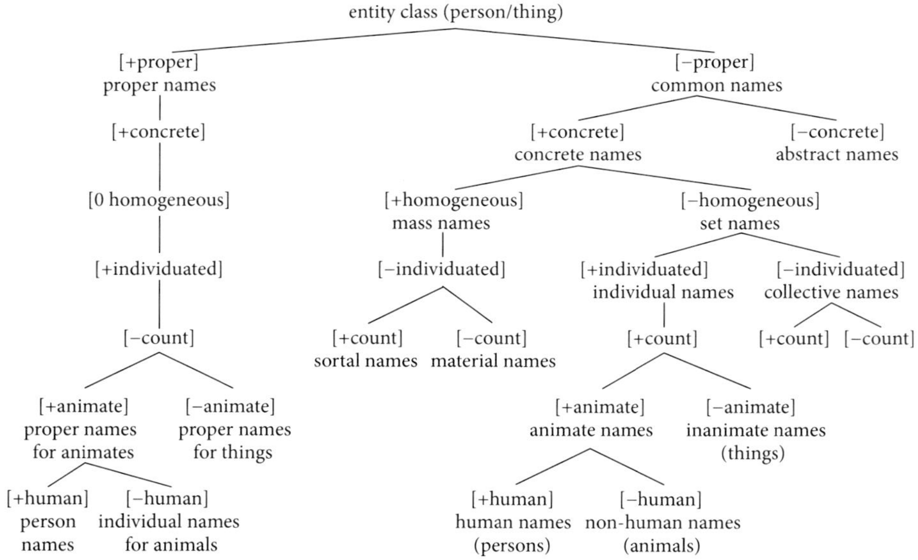

Figure 5. Hierarchy of semantic features for entity class.

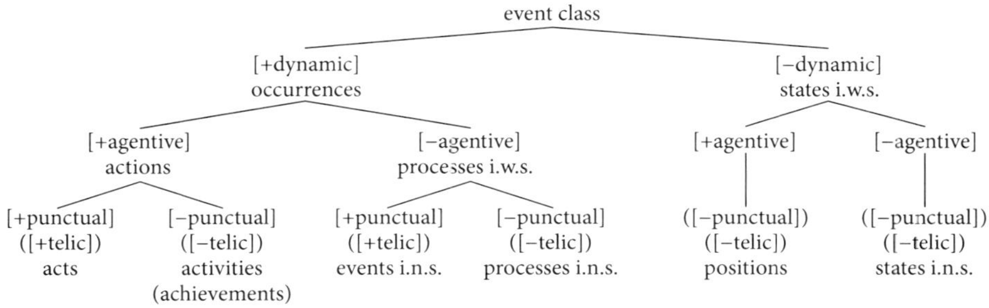

Figure 6. Hierarchy of semantic features for event class.

The event class is subdivided into the (sub)classes of state, action, and process by the features [±dynamic] and [±agentive] (cf. Figure 6). Other features used in the event domain focus on telicity and on *Aktionsart*, drawing on previous theoretical frameworks, in particular Vendler (1967) and Van Valin (2001). Using the additional features of [±telic] and [±punctual], we can characterise signs from our data as belonging to one of the lowest-level sub-classes. The following examples are from DGS:[9]

	DGS	
(7)	act	GEB ('give')
	activity	ARBEIT ('work')
	event i.n.s.	FALL ('fall')
	process i.n.s.	REGEN ('rain')
	position	ZWEIBEINIG-CL:'person standing upright'
	state i.n.s.	WISS ('know')

Note that in the previous literature, there is some conceptual overlap between the aspectual feature pair 'static' vs. 'dynamic' on the one hand and the temporal feature pair 'time-stable'/'persistent' vs. 'temporary'/'transitory' on the other hand (e.g. Lehmann and Moravcsik 2000). However, both of these feature pairs are distinct from each other in that the former basically refers to the presence or absence of a change, such as movement or development, in an event concept (cf. also Comrie 1976; Bybee 2000), whereas the latter can refer to the temporal characteristics of any concept class, be it an entity, property, event or any other concept class (cf. Stassen 1997). Thus, the scale of dynamicity may partially overlap with the scale of time-stability inasmuch as the latter applies to event concepts only.

It is more difficult to posit minimal semantic features in the domain of property concepts. The property class can partially be defined on the basis of Dixon's (1982) pioneering work on adjectives inasmuch as there are more or less prototypical semantic types designating properties. Dixon (1982) identifies the following, listed here with DGS signs instantiating each of the types:

DGS

(8)	dimension	GROSS ('large')
	value	GUT ('good')
	colour	ROT ('red')
	age	NEU ('new')
	physical property	KALT ('cold')
	human propensity	FRECH ('cheeky')
	speed	SCHNELL ('fast')

However, to abstractly define 'property' in terms of basic semantic features is very problematic. For the purpose of this article, a non-aspectual feature [±qualitative] is used to preliminarily distinguish the property class from other classes. This feature applies positively to a property concept but always negatively to any concept from another concept class. In contrast with the conceptual class of states, the property class is, for logical reasons, not easily compatible with aspectual features such as [dynamic] or [punctual], which helps to distinguish the two classes. A further feature [±gradable] subdivides the property class into gradable/polar and non-gradable/absolute property subclasses.

Compiling the abovementioned features of entity, event, and property classes into a single feature matrix, the semantic distribution of features across these three main classes can be read off Table 1. As mentioned before, a 'zero' value means that a feature is not logically compatible with a concept class. This usually means that the feature can be neglected in further analysis because we do not expect it to have any lexical or grammatical relevance for the concept (class) in question.

Table 1. Distribution of semantic features across entity, event, and property classes.

binary semantic features	**entity**	**event**			**property**
		action	process	state	
[proper]	±	0	0	0	0
[concrete]	±	0 / –	0 / –	0 / –	0 / –
[homogeneous]	± / 0	0	0	0	0
[individuated]	±	0	0	0	0
[countable]	±	0	0	0	0
[animate]	±	0	0	0	0
[human]	±	0	0	0	0
[dynamic]	0	+	+	–	0 / –
[agentive]	0	+	–	±	0 / –
[punctual]	0	±	±	–	0
[qualitative]	–	–	–	–	+
[gradable]	–	±	±	±	±

3.3.3 *Application of semantic criteria to DGS and KK*

The minimal features in Table 1 are complementarily distributed over the three main semantic classes, and this semantic distribution of the main concept classes tests successfully on data from both DGS and KK. Thus, the featural mapping provides a good point of departure for defining word classes across signed (and potentially also spoken) languages.

Methodologically, one of the main reasons for proceeding via a semantic metalanguage on the way towards our word class typology across sign languages is to facilitate the creation of the basic 250-word data sets mentioned in the introduction. In deriving the lexical items that will go into each of the data sets, it is important a) to cover all the main conceptual categories, including those not discussed in detail in this article, and b) to choose, as far as possible, signs with similar or equivalent semantic content from all target sign languages. The semantic classifications discussed in this section make it possible to establish data sets that fulfill these two criteria in a principled way.

Though testing the semantic features on signs from DGS and KK has not been done comprehensively for the purpose of this article, a preliminary survey reveals many parallels, but also some interesting differences. Without prejudice to culturally-based semantic differences of lexical meanings in both sign languages, many entity, event and property concepts do overlap in the two languages, as in these examples:

(9)		DGS	KK	
	entity	GEHÖRLOS	DEAF	(see Figures 7 and 8)
		FRAU	FEMALE	
		HUND	DOG	

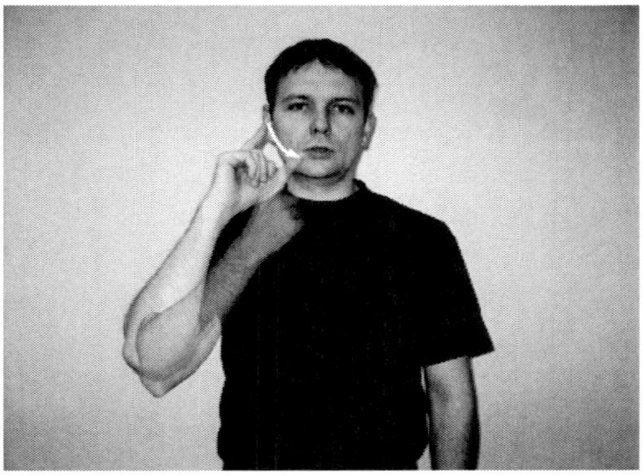

Figure 7. GEHÖRLOS ('deaf') in German Sign Language.

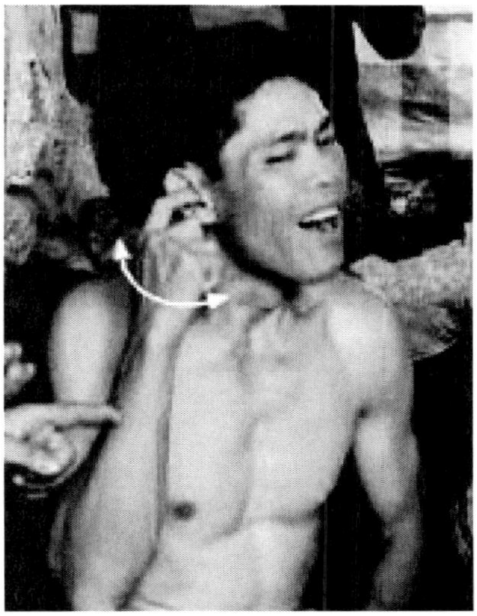

Figure 8. DEAF in Kata Kolok.

	REIS	RICE
event	ARBEIT	WORK
	ESS	EAT
	STERB	DIE
	GEBÄRD	SIGN-TALK
property	SCHLECHT	BAD
	GROSS	BIG
	SCHWARZ	BLACK
	SCHÖN	BEAUTIFUL

So far, it seems that differences occur both at the level of individual lexemes and at the level of sub-classes. For instance, the sign DEAF in KK always refers to a 'deaf person' and is an entity concept only. In DGS, the equivalent sign GEHÖRLOS ('deaf') refers to either a person or a property of a person and is therefore used both with an entity and as a property meaning. Consequently, the DGS corpus (Heßmann 2001) includes utterances such as GEHÖRLOS FRAU ('deaf woman'), with GEHÖRLOS being used to refer to a property of an individual. Despite the very frequent occurrence of the sign DEAF in the KK corpus, equivalent expressions are entirely absent, and DEAF in KK is used to refer to the entity 'deaf person' only. The fact that GEHÖRLOS ('deaf') has two meanings belonging to two different concept classes makes it difficult to categorise. When the sign is used in context, the syntactic slot serves to disambiguate between the two interpretations (see similar examples (29a) and (29b) in Section 3.4.2). However, considered in isolation, the meaning of GEHÖRLOS could either be vague/polysemous, or there could be two homophonous signs, meaning 'deaf' (as a property) and 'deaf person' respectively.

This theoretical debate is familiar from the PoS literature on spoken languages (e.g. Croft 2001) and cannot be resolved within the limited scope of this article. However, for a comprehensive PoS analysis, it will be helpful to distinguish between signs with several meanings from different concept classes, such as GEHÖRLOS, and signs with several related meanings from one and the same concept class. The latter situation commonly occurs in KK. The degree of lexical specificity often differs in DGS and KK, particularly with respect to event concepts. Where KK often has a single sign with a wide range of meaning depending on the context of the utterance, DGS employs several lexically differentiated items, such as in this example:

(10)	KK	DGS
	WRITE	SCHREIB ('write')
		UNTERSCHREIB ('sign')
		BESTÄTIG ('certify')
		ENTSCHEID ('decide')
		AUSBILD ('educate')
		etc.

Figure 9. A pointing sign in Kata Kolok.

When the KK sign WRITE is used with reference to children, it can have the meaning 'learn, study in school', but in relation to an adult, it would mean 'teach'. However, all meanings of WRITE are semantically related and belong to the same main concept class, so there is no motivation for considering an analysis in terms of more than one lexical item.

Another interesting difference in the lexical organisation of DGS and KK is the almost total absence of place names in the latter. Place names are characterised by the semantic features [+proper, +concrete, 0 homogeneous, +individuated, −count, −animate, +local], and there are many such signs in DGS denoting countries (e.g. DEUTSCHLAND 'Germany'), cities (e.g. FRANKFURT), etc. However, KK has only a handful of place names at most. Usually, places are referred to by using a system of absolute spatial reference, which involves pointing to the exact direction of the target location (Marsaja 2008). This includes pointing behind oneself and pointing with fully outstretched arms (see Figure 9), both of which are unusual forms in DGS and other urban sign languages. It is uncommon in the local situation to talk about unfamiliar places, for instance in Europe, and obviously, it would be difficult to expand the system of absolute spatial reference beyond known locations. However, there are strategies around this problem if the need arises and which have not been fully investigated. For instance, signers may point to the direction of the nearest airport in order to refer to an unfamiliar place overseas, or to foreigners from overseas, signing, for instance, WHITE-FOREIGNER $\text{INDEX}_{\text{airport}}$ to refer to a European researcher visiting the village.

Clearly, the lexical and grammatical organisation of KK interface here in ways which are absent from DGS. The principle of absolute spatial reference through pointing makes lexical items in the category of place names unnecessary in KK. The grammar of pointing in KK is very complex, since there needs to be a way of specifying distance as well as direction, but the system has not been described in detail yet.[10] In DGS, there is no such grammaticalised system of pointing, and therefore, the function of referring to place names must be handled by the lexicon.

When working comparatively across several sign languages, both the language-independent semantic metalanguage and language-specific concept classification come into play.[11] A more comprehensive investigation over larger data sets, testing systematically for a large number of semantic and structural features, can then yield principled results in the word class typology of sign languages. The next sections deal with criteria and classifications on the structural levels of syntax and morphology.

3.4 Syntactic criteria for PoS differentiation

3.4.1 *Criteria and classification on the syntactic level*

As pointed out by Anward (2001), there seems to be a basic characteristic mapping of semantic classes onto syntactic functions across languages (cf. similarly Croft 2001, which is based on substantial cross-linguistic evidence). Given the three major concept classes posited in the previous section, prototypical combinations of semantic class and syntactic function may be lexicalized in terms of 'traditional' parts of speech. The combination of entity class and argument function is lexicalized as nouns (11a), event class and predicate function as verbs (11b). The combinations of property class and modifier function are lexicalized by adjectives in argument modifier (attributive) function (11c) and by adverbs in predicate modifier (adverbial) function (11d) (cf. Anward 2001).

(11)	a.	[entity; argument]	Noun
	b.	[event; predicate]	Verb
	c.	[property; argument modifier]	Adjective
	d.	[property; predicate modifier]	Adverb

Hengeveld (1992) argues that there is a lot of variation in part-of-speech differentiation across (spoken) languages in that, on the one hand, a language does not obligatorily use all syntactic functions, lacking, for instance, one or both modifier functions. On the other hand, a language may lexicalise any combination of semantic class and syntactic function other than the prototypical ones listed in (11) above. Consequently, concept classes may also be multiply lexicalized in non-prototypical syntactic functions (cf. Anward 2001).

In order to investigate which concepts of concept classes can be lexicalized in which syntactic functions, the part-of-speech definitions in Hengeveld (1992), given in a slightly modified form in (12), are useful as an initial point of reference.

(12)	a.	predicate use (p):	items can, without special marking, be used as a predicate,
	b.	argument use (a):	items can, without special marking, be used as an argument,
	c.	argument modifier use (am):	items can, without special marking, be used as an argument modifier,

d. predicate modifier use (pm): items can, without special marking, be used as a modifier of a predicate or of another modifier.

Whether [entity; argument] and [event; predicate] need to be separately lexicalized in DGS and KK is first and foremost an empirical question. For DGS, Erlenkamp (2000) argues that the noun-verb distinction is neutralised because of the absence of a noun category. In her approach, the DGS lexicon is divided into three categories instead of the traditional parts of speech. There is a small class of 'directional verbs' comprising 13 signs, and another small group of signs in the class of 'classificatory verbs'. As in IPSL (cf. Section 2.3), directional verbs in DGS move between two grammatically significant spatial locations; this phenomenon is explained in more detail in Section 3.5. Classificatory verbs have a classifier handshape and include signs such as those in the examples in Figures 3 and 4 in Section 2.2. All other DGS signs belong to a large group of 'multifunctional signs' in Erlenkamp's analysis. The resulting correlation between lexical and syntactic categories in DGS can be represented in a simplified way as in Figure 10:

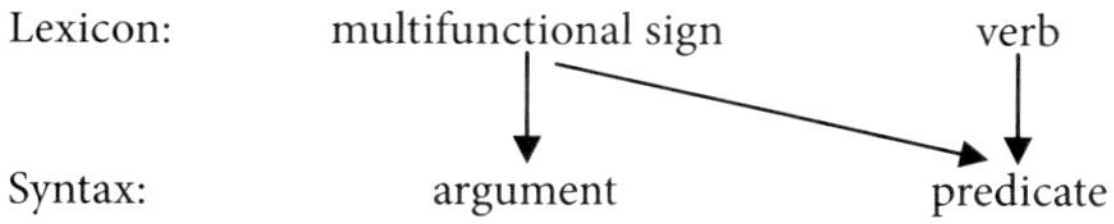

Figure 10. Correlation between lexical and syntactic categories in DGS according to Erlenkamp (2000).

However, this approach has been criticised in Keller, Pfau and Steinbach (2002) for its idiosyncratic selection of criteria defining the word classes. These include: 1. reference, 2. morphological distribution (of plural or local marking), 3. reduplication (e.g. intensity or duration of action), 4. valency, and 5. occurrence of lexical items in certain syntactic slots, such as in argument or predicate function. It is therefore difficult to use this approach as a basis of comparison for typological studies on word classes in other sign languages.

3.4.2 *Application of syntactic criteria to DGS and KK*

For the purpose of this article and until more detailed data become available, we discuss selected representatives from each one of the three main concept classes in this section and briefly point out tendencies for the two target sign languages which emerge from the preliminary findings.

On the basis of these criteria, signs can be mapped onto their syntactic functions as in Table 2. For this first pilot investigation, a small number of signs were chosen on the basis of a) being reasonably frequent in the data corpora, so that substantiated generalisations can be made, and b) having reasonably close semantic matches in both sign languages. Table 2 summarises a few illustrative examples. Some items in DGS

(QUESTION in the entity class, and DEAF and HEARING in the property class) do not have equivalents in KK and the corresponding slots are therefore empty in the table. A question mark, which also occurs with a few KK items, means that despite the sign's relatively frequent occurrence, no conclusive evidence could be found yet in the data as to its semantics and/or structural status in utterances. For instance, it is not clear whether the sign FRIEND in KK, made with two intertwined index fingers in a to-and-fro movement, designates an entity or an event, and how the sign maps onto syntactic functions in the sentence. An utterance such as (13) could have several different interpretations. Interpretations (14a) and (14c) would assign FRIEND to an argument function, whereas in interpretation (14b), FRIEND would be in a predicate slot (cf. similar sentences in examples (22) to (24) below). Further tests are needed to conclusively decide the status of the KK sign FRIEND, and a number of other signs which are marked by question marks in Table 2.

KK

(13) INDEX_1 FRIEND GOOD

(14) a. 'My friend is good/nice.'
b. 'I am befriending (someone), that is good.'
c. 'I have a friend.'

The DGS signs DEAF and HEARING occur twice in the table because their semantic content maps onto two different major concept classes, as already discussed. The DGS sign QUESTION is similar and formationally related to ASK, but the latter has obligatory verb agreement. In KK, there is a more general term SIGN-TALK (see Figure 11), which means 'communicate (in sign language)' and includes all kinds of communicative acts, such as telling, discussing, asking, and so forth.

As the table shows, there are striking differences with respect to the occurrence of concepts and concept classes in syntactic slots in both sign languages. Members of the

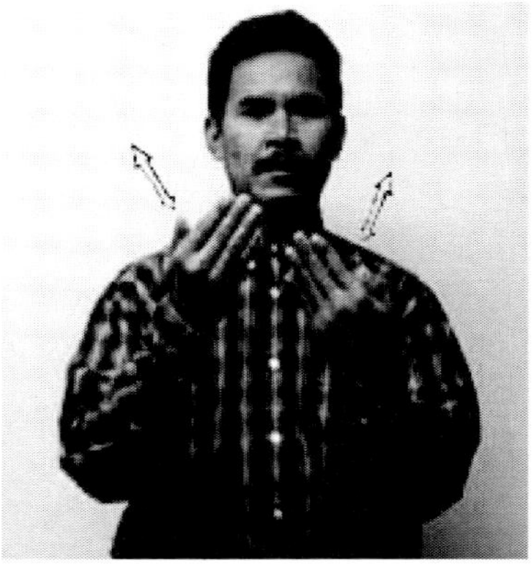

Figure 11. SIGN-TALK in Kata Kolok.

Table 2. Occurrences of entity, event, and property concepts in syntactic functions.

semantic classes	sign examples	DGS				Kata Kolok			
		p	a	am	pm	p	a	am	pm
entity	DEAF / HEARING	+	+			+	+		
	FEMALE	+	+				+		
	CAR		+				+		
	FRIEND	+	+				?		
	QUESTION		+						
	FOOD		+				?		
event	SIGN-TALK	+				+			
	ASK/REQUEST	+				+			
	STAY	+				+			
	DIE	+				+			
	CAR-DRIVE	+				+			
	EAT	+				+			
	WORK	+	+			+			
property	DEAF / HEARING			+					
	SMALL	+		+		+		?	
	BAD / GOOD	+		+	+	+			
	BLACK	+		+		+			

entity concept class in DGS can also be used predicatively, but this is almost never the case in KK. Instead, KK seems to be closer to the prototypical mapping for nouns as the combination [entity; argument], as in (12a). Further characteristics of a putative "noun" category in KK would need to be checked against the entity class as a whole.

Interestingly, the DGS lexicon includes an abstract entity concept FRAGE ('question') (15a), which occurs in argument function without the obligatory verb agreement morphology of its verbal counterpart FRAG ('ask') (15b).[12] Whereas DGS has lexicalised both [event; predicate] and [entity; argument] for this concept (see Figures 12–14), the same concept in KK only occurs as [event; predicate], and there is no entity-like abstraction.

DGS

(15) a. POSS$_2$ QUESTION INDEX$_1$ REALLY UNDERSTAND^NEG
'I really do not understand your question.'

b. POSS$_1$ FRIEND $_3$ASK$_1$
'My friend asks me.'

In contrast to Indo-European languages, both sign languages primarily lexicalise the concept 'deaf' as a prototypical noun [entity; argument], which can also be used predicatively. This illustrates that any lexicalisation is culturally determined as well. DGS has further lexicalised a property concept 'deaf' in attributive use, probably through language contact with German. The following examples illustrate the use of DEAF in DGS and KK. (16b) shows the ungrammaticality of using DEAF as a modifier in KK.

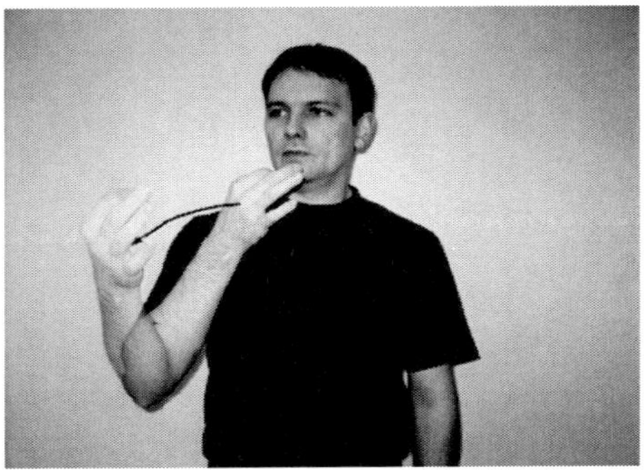

Figure 12. DGS $_1$FRAG$_3$ ('I ask someone').

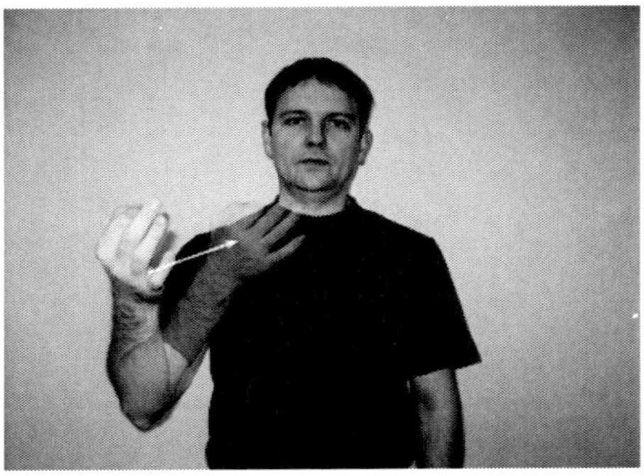

Figure 13. DGS $_3$FRAG$_1$ ('someone asks me').

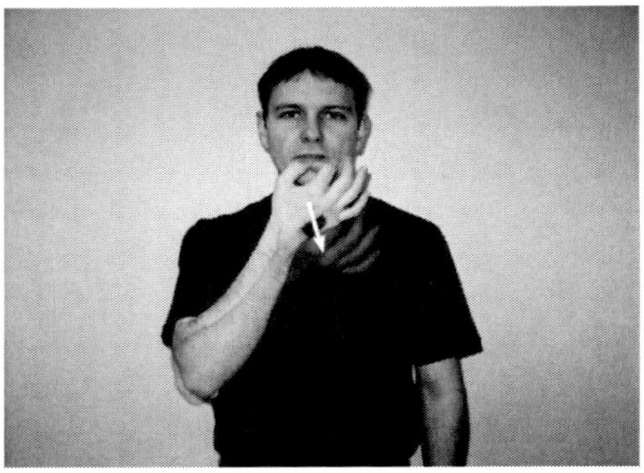

Figure 14. DGS FRAGE ('question').

KK

(16) a. DEAF COME
'A deaf person came.'
b. * FEMALE DEAF COME
'A deaf woman came.'

DGS

(17) DEAF FRIEND $_x$PERSON-CL$_y$:'one comes here'
'A deaf friend comes to me.'

The syntactic use of property concepts in KK is also much more restrictive than that in DGS. Property concepts in KK seem to be used as predicates only, as illustrated in the following examples:

KK

(18) a. CHICKEN INDEX$_x$ SMALL, DEAD
'There was a chicken there, which was small. It was dead.'
b. * SMALL CHICKEN DEAD
'A small chicken is dead.'

DGS

(19) BIRD SMALL DEAD
'A small bird is dead.'

In addition to their use in predicate function, the DGS property signs GUT ('good') and SCHLECHT ('bad') can be used as both argument and predicate modifiers (examples (20) and (21)), whereas the semantic equivalents in KK are used in predicate function only, often following a whole phrase/sentence functioning as the argument (22).

DGS

(20) POSS_1 WIFE WORK GOOD
'My wife works well.'

DGS

(21) INDEX_1 BEEN GOOD RESTAURANT $_1\text{VISIT}_x$
'I have been to a good restaurant.'

KK

(22) INDEX_1 DEAF GATHER, GOOD
'It is nice when I get together with deaf people.'

The KK sign GOOD is also used in a possessive construction in the predicate slot and then has a possessive meaning. In possessive constructions in KK, the sign GOOD has become grammaticalised and does not necessarily have a literal meaning. While example (23) is ambiguous between the lexical and the grammatical function of GOOD, the context in an utterance such as (24) clearly indicates that GOOD has lost its lexical meaning and is functioning in a possessive reading only.

KK

(23) INDEX_1 FEMALE MARRY GOOD
'I have a wife, (which is good).'

(24) INDEX_1 FEMALE MARRY GOOD, CRAZY
'I have a wife. She is crazy.'

However, KK does not completely lack signs that can be used as modifiers. For instance, in (25) MUCH is used as predicate modifier. Moreover, the morphology of KK includes processes of marking the comparative in entity concepts (see Section 3.5).

KK

(25) INDEX_1 GO-AWAY WORK MUCH COME GIVE MONEY, GOOD#INTS
'I go and work a lot to bring money (to my family), and that is great.'

In DGS, the sign ARBEIT ('work') can occur in argument function in addition to the prototypical predicate slot:

DGS
(26) WORK FIND DIFFICULT#INTS
'It is very difficult to find a job.'

In such a context, it is worthwhile asking whether ARBEIT retains its original event semantics or has become an abstract entity. It seems that ARBEIT occurs in the combinations [event; predicate] and [event; argument] only, without any special marking differentiating between the two usages. Similar cases can also be found in English, as in the examples in (27), where (27b) acts as a bridge context. The re-arrangement of categories here proceeds in two stages, where [event; argument] is intermediate between the two prototypical assignments.

(27) a. It is so stressful to work nowadays. (work$_V$ [event; predicate])
b. Work is so stressful nowadays. (work$_N$ [event; argument])
c. I showed my work to my boss, but he didn't like it. (work$_N$ [entity; argument])

In DGS, ARBEIT ('work') does not seem to occur in contexts where it has clearly lost its event semantics and is conceptualised as an entity. Further evidence for the event character of the sign ARBEIT when used in an argument slot comes from the fact that, unlike other entity concepts, it is not compatible with possessive pronouns (examples 28a-b). Instead, a personal pronoun is used (28c).

DGS
(28) a. POSS$_2$ CAR GOOD
'Your car is good.'
b. *POSS$_2$ WORK GOOD
c. INDEX$_2$ WORK GOOD
'Your work is good./You work well.'

Whereas ARBEIT ('work') in DGS always has an event meaning no matter in which semantic slot it occurs, the sign GEHÖRLOS ('deaf') can have either an entity meaning ('deaf person') or a property meaning, the latter particularly when used in a modifier slot, as in (29a). In predicative use, GEHÖRLOS has an entity meaning only (29b).

DGS
(29) a. DEAF FRIEND
'a deaf friend'
*'a deaf person, a friend'
b. INDEX$_x$ DEAF
'S/he is a deaf person.'

As mentioned in the discussion in 3.3.3, it is difficult to decide here on theoretical grounds whether the sign GEHÖRLOS ('deaf') is polysemous, or whether there are two homophonous signs, each with its own meaning.

In the limited context of this article, we do not go into details of which lexical categories are lexicalised and mapped onto which syntactic functions in DGS and KK. This would necessitate an extensive analysis on the basis of a large data corpus from both languages, which is yet to be undertaken.

3.5 Criteria and classification on the morphological level

Languages obviously differ greatly from one another at the morphological level, and therefore, morphological criteria for word class assignment must be determined language-specifically for each language. The degree to which sign languages can differ from one another at the morphological (and also the syntactic) level has not been properly recognised even in the sign language linguistics literature, mainly because there is very little information about non-Western, and also non-urban, sign languages. The better-documented urban sign languages in industrialised countries have been found to have many morphological processes in common (e.g. expression of agreement, aspectual marking, cf. Aronoff et al. 2005). In particular, the morphology of these sign languages is largely simultaneous rather than sequential, and involves modulations in signing space typical of the sign language modality. However, comparing a wider range of typologically dissimilar sign languages does reveal a larger degree of cross-linguistic differentiation (cf. Zeshan 2005, 2006).

In this section, we consider morphological properties of DGS, RSL and KK, also drawing on Schwager (2004) for the discussion of the morphology of RSL as well as the morphological typology of sign languages in general (see Kimmelman (2009) for further discussion of the noun-verb distinction in RSL). With respect to the morphological level within the topic of parts of speech, the approach used here is different from earlier approaches such as Zeshan (2000) and Erlenkamp (2000) in that we first establish an extensive inventory of morphological processes, exploring a full range of theoretically possible and cross-linguistically instantiated types of morphology. This inventory is then tested against sign language data from typologically diverse sign languages, observing the morphological behaviour of a substantial number of semantically equivalent signs.

Sign languages have complex morphologies, but many of their morphological processes are uncommon, unattested or even logically impossible in spoken languages. Since it would go far beyond the scope of this article to explain the various kinds of sign language morphology in detail, we can only attempt a very general overview and give a few illustrative examples in order to demonstrate how morphological criteria bear on parts of speech categorisations in sign languages.

A particularly striking example of different categorisation for DGS/RSL and KK at the morphological level concerns the category of directional verbs, also known as agreement verbs. These verbs, already mentioned in Section 3.4.1, have been discussed extensively in the sign linguistics literature (e.g. Meir 1998; Mathur 2000; Padden 1990). Directional verbs in DGS and RSL inflect for subject and object in one of

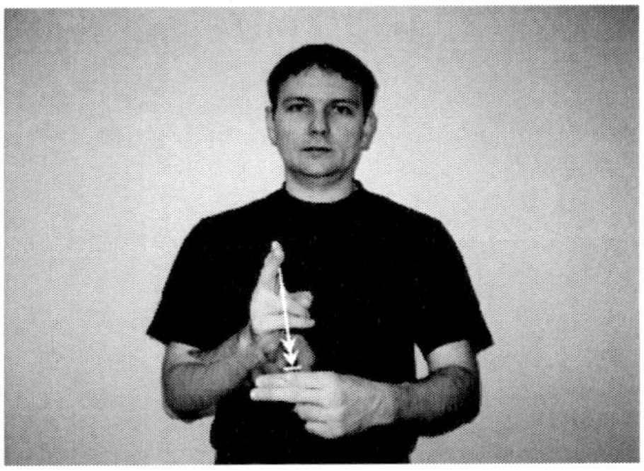

Figure 15. RSL $_{1}$DISTURB$_{2}$ ('I disturb you').

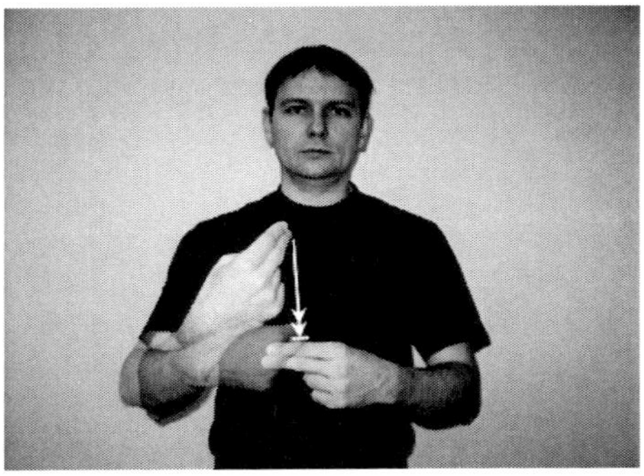

Figure 16. RSL $_{2}$DISTURB$_{1}$ ('you disturb me').

two ways: they either take subject agreement prefixes and indirect object agreement suffixes which consist of spatial locations at the beginning and the end point of the predicate sign's movement respectively (see Figures 12 and 13 in Section 3.4.2), or they inflect internally through featural alteration, changing only the orientation of the hand in terms of which way the palm and/or fingertips are facing (see Figures 15 and 16).

Thus the number and role of arguments that a verb may take, that is, the verb's valency, is overtly expressed through subject/object affixation in DGS. If an [event; predicate] in DGS is used transitively, the spatial subject/object affixes must be added if this option is available for the particular sign. However, many semantically transitive signs in DGS do not participate in this kind of morphology and do not allow the addition of agreement affixes. Therefore, if a transitive [event; predicate] cannot apply the spatial agreement morphology, it requires an auxiliary verb called PAM (person agreement marker, Rathmann (2000), see Figure 17). The PAM auxiliary then takes on valency-induced agreement morphology, as in example (30) below.

DGS
(30) MOST DEAF HATE#INTS PAM$_{3}$ TEACHER
'Most deaf people hate teachers (at deaf schools) very much.'

Figure 17. $_{1}$PAM$_{3}$ in German Sign Language.

While valency is lexically inherent in both DGS and KK signs, it can be morphologically marked in DGS only. In KK, there is no class of directional/agreement verbs and no auxiliary, so that the transitivity of [event; predicate] cannot be expressed overtly at the morphological level. Events in predicate use may be used as transitive or intransitive without any morphological changes in KK.[13] For instance, ASK/REQUEST [event; predicate] in KK is transitive and requires a subject and an object, but the sign's transitivity/valency does not have consequences at the morphological level. Figure 18 shows the transitive predicate sign ASK/REQUEST used in example (31). The form of the sign does not vary according to who is the subject or the object of the sentence, since no process of adding a directional movement to the sign exists to express transitivity in KK. Unlike ASK/REQUEST in KK, the semantically equivalent sign in DGS does have a directional movement, as indicated by the subscript in the transcription of example (32).[14]

KK
(31) PAST-TIME INDEX$_1$ MONEY ASK/REQUEST NEG
'I did not ask (someone) for money.'

DGS
(32) INDEX$_1$ MONEY BEG#DISTR$_3$ NEVER
'I never went around begging for money.'

Without going into details of sign language morphology here, Table 3 lists a substantial number of morphological processes, comparing data from DGS, RSL and KK. Similarly to the link between semantic classes and syntactic slots in Section 3.4.2, Table 3 links semantic classes and morphological processes. The classification of morphological processes in the third column of the table assumes that there is a typology of phonological representation of morphology in sign languages, whereby sign language morphology is

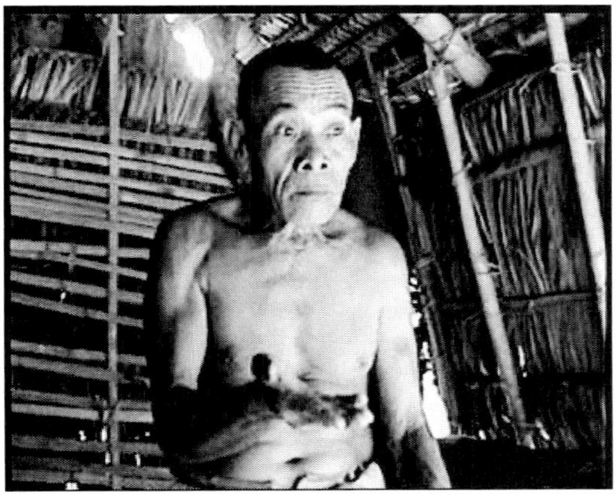

Figure 18. ASK/REQUEST in Kata Kolok.

Table 3. Outline of morphological criteria in DGS, RSL, and KK.

concept classes	grammatical categories	morphological processes	DGS	RSL	KK
event	subj./obj. agreement	(1) affixation	+	+	–
		(2) featural alteration	+	+	–
	distributive	(3) reduplication	+	+	–
	reciprocal	(4) reduplication	+	+	–
	negation	(5) affixation	+	+	–
		(6) suprafixation	+	-	–
	aspect	(7) reduplication	+	+	–
		(8) affixation	–	+	–
		(9) featural alteration	–	–	–
	intensive	(10) featural alteration	+	+	+
	diminutive	(11) featural alteration	?	+	?
	mood	(12) suprafixation	+	+	+
	class agreement	(13) affixation	+	+	+
entity	number	(14) reduplication	+	+	?
	locus (agreement)	(15) affixation	+	+	–
property	comparative	(16) featural alteration	+	+	+
		(17) suprafixation	+	+	+

subdivided into intrasegmental, suprasegmental, and segmental morphology, the latter again subdivided into sequential (or concatenative) and simultaneous morphology (cf. Schwager 2004). Sign languages have both form-building morphology for grammatical categories such as subject/object agreement and aspect/aktionsart marking, and sign-building morphology which creates new signs, for instance by way of compounding.[15] Only the former is represented in Table 3.

The types of morphological processes represented in Table 3 include affixation (1, 5, 8, 13 and 15 in the third column), featural alteration (2, 9, 10, 11 and 16), reduplication (3, 4, 7 and 14) and suprafixation (6, 12, 17). They relate to the three levels of phonological representation of sign language morphology mentioned above in the following way:

(33) a. Featural alteration is an intrasegmental morphological process.
b. Suprafixation is a suprasegmental morphological process.
c. Reduplication and affixation are segmental morphological processes; they can be simultaneous or sequential.

An example of featural alteration has already been discussed in connection with the category of agreement verbs (cf. no. 2 in Table 3). Since the orientation of palm and fingers can be considered a feature of the handshape in such a sign, changing this orientation is equivalent to an intrasegmental feature alteration, much like the *umlaut* found in some Germanic languages. For class agreement (no. 13 in the table), the handshape representing the referent class, such as the human and vehicle referents in Figures 3 and 4, is a bound morpheme that is combined with morphemes of location and movement in an affixation process, whereby a complex multimorphemic sign is created. Suprafixation occurs when manual signs are combined with non-manual signals, which can spread over more than one sign. For instance, in many sign languages a side-to-side headshake signalling negation combines with the predicate sign and can then spread over other signs, maximally co-occurring with the entire utterance (Zeshan 2004). As has been argued by Pfau (2002), the headshake can be considered affixal to the verb in such cases, but behaves like a suprasegmental, "intonational" feature at the formational, phonological level (cf. no. 6 in the table).

In a few cases, it is not clear from the data yet whether a morphological process occurs systematically. For instance, this is the case for diminutive marking of event concepts in DGS and KK (no. 11 in the table). The diminutive is the counterpart of the intensive marking and denotes a weak instantiation of an event. For instance, the sign CRY in RSL can receive an intensive marking to mean something like 'cry one's eyes out, weep bitterly', or a diminutive marking meaning 'cry a little, shed a few tears'. In both cases, there is a slight internal difference in the movement component of the sign (featural alteration in the movement phoneme), and there is an additional non-manual marking (suprafixation) which has not been included in the simplified Table 3. The diminutive occurs with a number of event lexemes in RSL (though by no means with all of them), but it is not clear whether an equivalent process exists systematically in DGS and KK.

In spoken languages, affixation and reduplication are sequential processes adding morphemes either before or after a stem. While this occurs in sign languages as well, it is more common for segmental morphology in sign languages to be simultaneous. For instance, a one-handed sign can be reduplicated by mirroring its movement on the second hand at the same time, which is used to express dual and reciprocal categories in many sign languages (cf. no. 4 in the table and Figure 19). When the spatial location of a sign is changed for grammatical purposes, such as signing HOUSE not in the neutral location in front of the signer, but on the far right-hand side, for instance, the

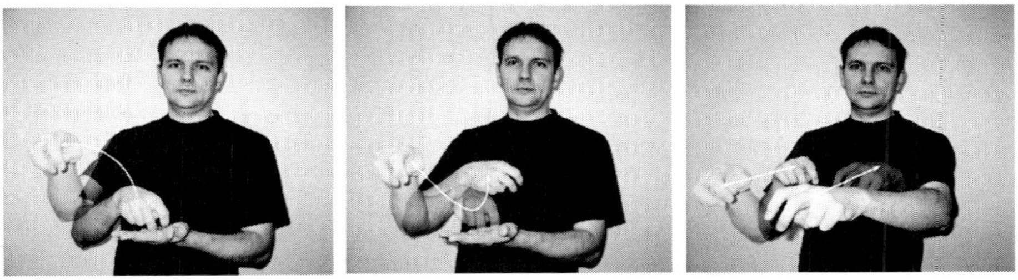

a. b. c.

Figure 19. RSL sign $_1$SEND-LETTER$_3$ (19a), reduplicated sequentially (19b) and simultaneously (19c).

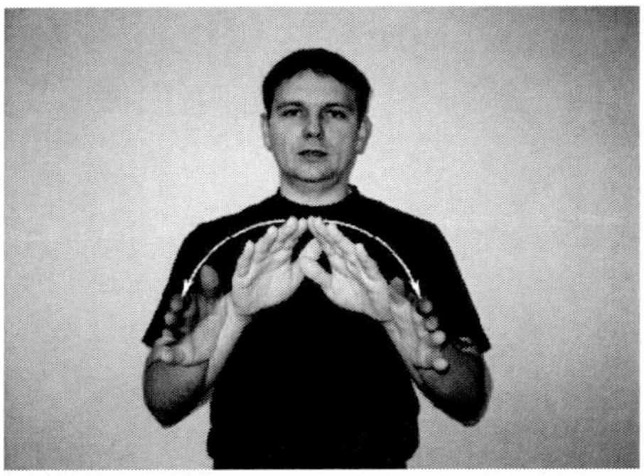

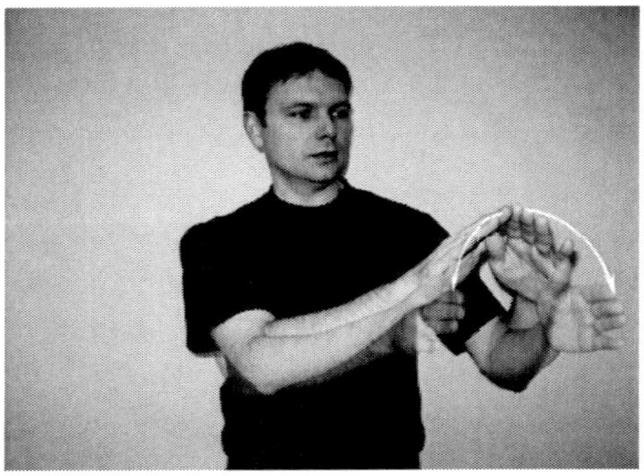

a. b.

Figure 20. DGS sign HOUSE in neutral location (20a) and with locus affix (20b).

grammatically significant spatial location on the right side can be regarded as an affix signaling locus agreement, which is produced simultaneously with the sign HOUSE itself (cf. no. 15 in the table and Figure 20).

Comparing the kinds of morphological processes that are found in DGS, RSL and KK, a number of general tendencies appear at first sight. The morphologies of DGS and RSL are much more similar to one another than to KK, with only a few different values for DGS and RSL. This is in line with the previous findings of sign language linguistics which argue for a lot of morphological similarities across sign languages, chiefly on the basis of data from North American and European sign languages. Secondly, by far the largest number of morphological processes relates to events, but KK expresses far fewer grammatical categories at the morphological level than DGS and RSL. Morphology relating to the entity concept class is also largely absent in KK, with only one questionable category (no. 14 in the table). Finally, it is of interest that property concepts have associated morphology in all three sign languages and thus behave identically in this domain, although the actual set of signs falling into the property class is not the same across the target sign languages (cf. Section 3.3.3). KK signs for property concepts participate in the same kinds of morphological processes for marking the grammatical category of comparative as DGS signs for property concepts (no. 16 and 17 in the table), but unlike in DGS, the KK signs tend not to appear in the syntactic positions of either argument or predicate modifier (cf. Section 3.4.2).

At this stage of research, it is too early to demonstrate conclusively how the morphological differences between DGS, RSL and KK relate to their respective PoS systems. A much more extensive survey based on a much larger data set will be necessary to consolidate the initial results. In general, the above findings suggest that morphological operations may play a greater role in distinguishing between different word classes in sign languages like DGS and RSL, which have a larger array of morphological processes to draw on. This is exemplified, for instance, by the class of agreement verbs in DGS and RSL. Moreover, the fact that KK is a more "isolating" language than DGS and RSL is a real typological difference and has a direct bearing on the search for word class categories in KK, where morphological criteria will play a much lesser role in word class assignment. Whatever further investigation may reveal, the present study certainly demonstrates the importance and the methodological viability of looking at a comprehensive range of morphological processes rather than arbitrarily choosing only a limited set of morphological criteria.

4. Conclusion

This article has explored a unified approach studying PoS systems across typologically diverse sign languages. Both language-independent semantic features and language-specific morphosyntactic criteria play an important role in this undertaking. Rather than having an ad hoc mix of criteria at various levels, a shortcoming that previous attempts have suffered from, the present approach allows for a principled way of approaching the lexical categorisations inherent in diverse sign languages. At the same time, the data upon which the emerging generalisations are based are taken directly from large transcribed corpora of spontaneously produced sign language data, thus keeping the theoretical work close to the primary data. Since there is so little established tradition and consolidated knowledge related to parts of speech systems in sign languages, this aspect of the approach is particularly important.

Further research that will build upon the preliminary results presented in this article is already inherent in the methodological and theoretical issues addressed in Section 2 of this article. First of all, the complete 250-word data sets should be compiled for all three target sign languages and checked against the large number of features that have been detailed above. Secondly, "difficult" sign types, such as the notoriously complicated classifier signs mentioned in Section 2.2, also need to be included in the analysis, as well as closed lexical classes in addition to the open classes discussed here. If the analysis tools prove fruitful for the initial three sign languages, the same methodology could then be used to investigate aspects of PoS systems in other sign languages. Over time, it should be possible to achieve coherent PoS characterisations compiling information from all relevant levels, semantic, syntactic and morphological. Comparing these to PoS systems in spoken languages will then be of great potential interest for the study of linguistic typology and language universals.

Abbreviations

$_{x}$PERSON-CL$_{y}$:'…'	human classifier, with locus marking and meaning between quotes
INDEX$_{1}$	personal pronominal marker in first person
INDEX$_{x}$	indexical marker, with locus marking
INTS	intensifier
DIST	distributive

NEG	negative
PAM_3	person agreement marker, with locus marking in third person
POSS_1	possessive pronominal, with first person marking
POSS_2	possessive pronominal, with second person marking
$_3\text{GLOSS}_1$	directional sign with subject agreement prefix in third person and object agreement suffix in first person
GLOSS-GLOSS	multi-word gloss representing a single sign
GLOSS^GLOSS	sequential morphemes
GLOSS#GLOSS	simultaneous morphemes

Acknowledgements

We are indebted to Roland Pfau and to an anonymous reviewer for useful comments on the first draft of this article. We would also like to express our deep gratitude to the Kata Kolok using village community in Bali for allowing us to do research in their village and to make use of their video data in publications. This study is part of a larger research project on "Sign Language Typology — The Cross-Linguistic Study of Sign Languages", which is supported by the German Research Council (Deutsche Forschungsgemeinschaft, DFG), grant no. ZE507/1–3.

Notes

1. It is a common convention in much of the literature on German Sign Language to use glosses in German. Where no such convention exists, as is the case for Kata Kolok as well as some other sign languages discussed in this article, English glosses are generally used. For convenience, however, we also use English glosses for examples of German Sign Language sentences in Sections 3.4 and 3.5.

2. Spoken languages also have words that "sound like" what they mean, but these sound-symbolic words, such as *roar, rumble, swish, beep*, etc. in English, are marginal in the lexicon. In sign languages, a major part of the lexicon consists of such words, and they cannot therefore be ignored as marginal cases.

3. The term "classifier" is widely used in sign language linguistics, although the phenomena it covers are different from the use of the same term in spoken language linguistics.

4. Statistically and without the genetic factor, a community of this size would be expected to have only one or two deaf people.

5. For the purpose of this article, we are not considering additional possible factors at the phonological and the discourse levels. For example, it has been suggested that in DGS, the silent mouth movements derived from spoken German words play a role in distinguishing between nouns and verbs (see Boyes-Braem and Sutton-Spence (2001) for details about mouth movements in various sign languages). Discourse pragmatic features could be relevant, for instance, in connection with indexical signs, where there is a difference between the physical presence or absence of referents in the signing environment.

6. "A concept class is a bundle of interrelated concepts that can be defined by a superordinate feature (usually a hyperonym)."

7. We use the term 'entity' as a concept class instead, with a semantic range including person/animal/plant/thing as well as abstract entities.

8. Wilbur (in press) even goes further by arguing that the formational aspects of ASL signs that reflect semantic telicity should actually be regarded as morphemes.

9. Note that for want of better terms, some terms occur at two different levels, once in a wider sense (i.w.s.) and once in a narrower sense (i.n.s.).

10. Decoding the complex system of pointing in KK is the central theme of a current research project on KK at the Max Planck Institute for Psycholinguistics.

11. This applies to closed classes of 'function words' as well as open classes. For instance, not all sign languages differentiate between a basic clause negator 'not' and more specific negators with aspectual meanings, such as 'not yet', 'not any more' (Zeshan 2004).

12. Verb agreement morphology is explained in more detail in Section 3.5.

13. KK does have one pair of formationally related signs generally denoting 'giving' or 'taking', which seem to have a directional movement. However, we cannot say with certainty at this stage whether these signs are morphologically complex or simply constitute two different lexical entries.

14. In this example, the verb agrees with the object (third person distributive) only.

15. Form-building morphology includes all processes of inflection, whereas sign-building morphology refers to processes that create new lexical items, such as derivation and compounding.

References

Anward, J. 2000. A dynamic model of part-of-speech differentiation. *Approaches to the typology of word classes*, Bernard Comrie & Petra Vogel (eds.), 3–45. Berlin: Mouton de Gruyter.

Anward, J. 2001. Parts of speech. *Language typology and language universals: An international handbook*. Vol. 1, Martin Haspelmath; Ekkehard König; Wulf Oesterreicher & Wolfgang Raible (eds.), 726–735. Berlin: Mouton de Gruyter.

Aronoff, Mark; Irit Meir & Wendy Sandler. 2005. The paradox of sign language morphology. *Language* 81(2): 301–344.

Boyes Braem, Penny & Rachel Sutton-Spence (eds.). 2001. *The hands are the head of the mouth: The mouth as articulator in sign languages*. Hamburg: Signum.

Branson, Jan; Don Miller; Gede Marsaja & Wayan Negara. 1996. Everyone here speaks sign language, too: A deaf village in Bali, Indonesia. *Multicultural aspects of sociolinguistics in deaf communities*, Ceil Lucas (ed.), 39–57. Washington, DC: Gallaudet University Press.

Bybee, Joan. 2000. Verb. *Morphology: An international handbook on inflection and word-formation*. Vol. 1, Geert Booij; Christian Lehmann & Joachim Mugdan (eds.), 794–808. Berlin: Mouton de Gruyter.

Comrie, Bernard. 1976. *Aspect*. Cambridge: Cambridge University Press.

Croft, William. 2001. *Radical construction grammar. Syntactic theory in typological perspective.* Oxford: Oxford University Press.

Dixon, Robert M.W. 1982. Where have all the adjectives gone? *Where Have All the Adjectives Gone? and other essays in Semantics and Syntax*, Robert Dixon, 1–62. Berlin: Mouton Publishers.

Emmorey, Karen (ed.). 2003. *Perspectives on classifier constructions in sign languages*. Mahwah, NJ: Lawrence Erlbaum.

Erlenkamp, Sonja. 2000. *Syntaktische Kategorien und lexikalische Klassen: Typologische Aspekte der Deutschen Gebärdensprache*. München: Lincom.

Evans, Nicholas. 2000. Word class in the world's languages. *Morphology: An international handbook on inflection and word-formation*. Vol. 1, Geert Booij; Christian Lehmann & Joachim Mugdan (eds.), 674–732. Berlin: Mouton de Gruyter.

Fernald, Theodore B. & Donna J. Napoli. 2000. Exploitation of morphological possibilities in signed languages: Comparison of American Sign Language with English. *Sign Language & Linguistics* 3(1): 3–58.

Hengeveld, Kees. 1992. Parts of speech. *Layered structure and reference in a functional perspective*, Michael Fortescue; Peter Harder & Lars Kristoffersen (eds.), 29–56. Amsterdam: John Benjamins.

Heßmann, Jens. 2001. *GEHÖRLOS SO!: Materialien zur Gebärdensprache*. Hamburg: Signum.

Johnston, Trevor. 2001. Nouns and verbs in Auslan (Australian Sign Language): an open or shut case? *Journal of Deaf Studies and Deaf Education* 6(4): 235–257.

Keller, Jörg; Roland Pfau & Markus Steinbach. 2002. Book review: Sonja Erlenkamp, Syntaktische Kategorien und lexikalische Klassen: Typologische Aspekte der Deutschen Gebärdensprache. Lincom Europa, 2000. *Sign Language & Linguistics* 5(2): 247–253.

Kimmelman, Vadim. 2009. Parts of speech in Russian Sign Language: the role of iconicity and economy. *Sign Language & Linguistics* 12(2): 161–186.

Lehmann, Christian & Edith Moravcsik. 2000. Noun. *Morphology: An international handbook on inflection and word-formation*. Vol. 1, Geert Booij; Christian Lehmann & Joachim Mugdan (eds.), 732–757. Berlin: Mouton de Gruyter.

Löbner, Sebastian. 2002. *Understanding semantics*. London: Arnold [Understanding Language Series]. (German edition: Sebastian Löbner. 2003. *Semantik. Eine Einführung*. Berlin: Mouton de Gruyter).

Marsaja, Gede. 2008. *Kata Kolok — A deaf village and its sign language in Bali, Indonesia*. Nijmegen: Ishara Press.

Mathur, Gaurav. 2000. *Verb agreement as alignment in sign languages*. PhD thesis, MIT (MIT Working Papers in Linguistics).

Meir, Irit. 1998. Syntactic-semantic interaction in Israeli Sign Language verbs: The case of backwards verbs. *Sign Language & Linguistics* 1(1): 3–37.

Padden, Carol. 1988. *Interaction of morphology and syntax in American Sign Language*. New York, NY: Garland Publishing.

Padden, Carol. 1990. The relation between space and grammar in ASL verb morphology. *Sign language research: theoretical issues*, Ceil Lucas (ed.), 118–132. Washington, DC: Gallaudet University Press.

Pfau, Roland. 2002. Applying morphosyntactic and phonological readjustment rules in natural language negation. *Modality and structure in signed and spoken languages*, Richard P. Meier, Kearsy A. Cormier & David G. Quinto-Pozos (eds.), 263–295. Cambridge: Cambridge University Press.

Rathmann, Christian. 2000. Does the presence of a person agreement marker predict word order in sign languages? Paper presented at the *7th International Conference on Theoretical Issues in Sign Language Research*. July 2000, Amsterdam, Manuscript.

Sandler, Wendy. 1999. Cliticization and prosodic words in a sign language. *Studies on the phonological word*, Tracy A. Hall & Ursula Kleinhenz (eds.), 223–254. Amsterdam: John Benjamins.

Sandler, Wendy & Diane Lillo-Martin. 2006. *Sign language and linguistic universals*. Cambridge: Cambridge University Press.

Sasse, Hans-Jürgen. 1993. Das Nomen — eine universale Kategorie? *Sprachtypologie und Universalienforschung* 46: 187–221.

Schembri, Adam. 2003. Rethinking 'classifiers' in signed languages. *Perspectives on classifier constructions in sign languages*, Karen Emmorey (ed.), 3–34. Mahwah, NJ: Lawrence Erlbaum.

Schwager, Waldemar. 2004. *Polymorphemische Gebärden in der Russischen Gebärdensprache*. MA thesis, University of Amsterdam.

Stassen, Leon. 1997. *Intransitive predication*. Oxford: Oxford University Press.

Supalla, Ted & Elissa L. Newport. 1978. How many seats in a chair? The derivation of nouns and verbs in American Sign Language. *Understanding language through sign language research*, Patricia Siple (ed.), 91–132. New York, NY: Academic Press.

Van Valin, Robert. 2001. *Syntax*. Cambridge: Cambridge University Press.

Vendler, Zeno. 1967. *Linguistics in philosophy*. Ithaca, NY: Cornell University Press.

Wilbur, Ronnie B. 2008. Complex predicates involving events, time and aspect: Is this why sign languages look so similar? *Signs of the time. Selected papers from TISLR 2004*, Josep Quer (ed.), 217–250. Hamburg: Signum.

Zeshan, Ulrike. 2000. *Gebärdensprachen des indischen Subkontinents*. München: Lincom.

Zeshan, Ulrike. 2002. Towards a notion of 'word' in sign languages. *Word: A cross-linguistic typology*, Robert M.W. Dixon & Alexandra Y. Aikhenvald (eds.), 153–179. Cambridge: Cambridge University Press.

Zeshan, Ulrike. 2004. Hand, Head and Face — Negative Constructions in Sign Languages. *Linguistic Typology* 8(1): 1–58.

Zeshan, Ulrike. 2005. Sign languages. *The world atlas of language structures*, Martin Haspelmath; Matthew S. Dryer; David Gil & Bernard Comrie (eds.), 558–567. Oxford: Oxford University Press.

Zeshan, Ulrike (ed.). 2006. *Interrogative and negative constructions in sign languages*. Nijmegen: Ishara Press.

Zwitserlood, Inge. 2003. *Classifiying hand configurations in Nederlandse Gebarentaal*. Utrecht: LOT.

Authors' address

Ulrike Zeshan
International Centre for Sign Languages and Deaf Studies
Livesey House LH212
University of Central Lancashire
Preston PR1 2HE UK
United Kingdom

uzeshan@uclan.ac.uk, Waldemar.Schwager@t-online.de

Roots, stems and word classes

Christian Lehmann
University of Erfurt

The assignment of a linguistic sign to a word class is an operation that must be seen as part of the overall transformation of extralinguistic substance into linguistic form. In this, it is comparable to such processes as the transitivization of a verbal base, which further specifies a relatively rough categorization. Languages differ both in the extent to which they structure the material by purely grammatical criteria and in the level at which they do this. The root and the stem are the lowest levels at which a linguistic sign can be categorized in terms of language-specific structure. Further categorization is then achieved at the level of the syntagm.

An empirical investigation comparing the categorization of roots and stems in a sample of six languages (English, German, Latin, Spanish, Yucatec Maya, Mandarin Chinese) turns up far-reaching differences. These differences in the amount of categorization that languages apply to linguistic signs at the most basic levels throw into doubt any thesis claiming universal categoriality or acategoriality for roots. Such a static view must be replaced by a dynamic one which asks for the role of categorization in linguistic activity. At the same time, these differences raise the issue of the amount of structure — or of grammar — that is necessary for a human language.[1]

> The great tragedies of science are the slaying of beautiful hypotheses by ugly facts. (Thomas H. Huxley)

1. Introduction

The Modist theory of the parts of speech as laid down by Thomas of Erfurt (14th cent.; cf. Bursill-Hall 1972) goes roughly as follows: Pre-linguistic concepts are like an amorphous substance that gets a linguistic form by being assigned a grammatical category. The most important of these categories are the parts of speech. They have a basis in perception, but do not directly reflect it. Instead, the transfer of a concept into such a category is an operation of the intellect. The notional aspect of the operation is the addition of a *modus significandi* (roughly, the meaning of a grammatical category) to the basic concept. Its formal aspect is the transfer of a *dictio* — roughly, a root — into a *pars orationis* 'part of speech'.

Similarly, Coseriu (1955) considers that the meaning of a lexeme is composed of its lexical meaning ('semanteme') and its categorial meaning ('categoreme'). The former concerns what is signified, the latter concerns how it is signified. Languages differ in the degree of 'autonomy' of the lexical meaning as against the categorial meaning, which essentially means that a given lexical meaning may or may not entail a particular categorial meaning in the language. This autonomy of the lexical meaning is greater in English and Chinese than in Spanish (Coseriu 1955, Section 2.3.2) and 'most Indo-European languages' (Section 5.2.2). To give an example from the data of the present study to illustrate what Coseriu means: The concept 'comfort' is coded in Spanish by the stem *consol-*, which can only be inflected as a transitive verb. That is, given the lexical meaning as paired with a stem, the word class is given, too. The same concept is coded in Mandarin Chinese by the stem *ānwèi*, which can be used as a verb ('to comfort') or as an adjective ('comforting'). Thus, the lexical meaning of the Mandarin stem is more independent from specific word classes than in Spanish. In Coseriu's theory, the categories are not syntactic classes, but categories of speaking, in a sense to be made precise in the next section. In general, however, languages do not contain 'pure' lexical meanings that would be associated with a category only in speaking. For every semanteme, one of its alternate categories is usually primary (p. 39f).

The above are postulates of linguistic theories. As such, they cannot be upheld; we will come back to this in Section 4. In what follows, we will consider them as hypotheses. The central hypothesis in this connection is that roots are precategorial. It will be tested on samples of stems and roots taken from six languages. In Section 2, some basic notions of grammatical categorization are introduced. The central section of the paper is Section 3, which first discusses the methodology to be employed and then presents the results of the analysis. Section 4 draws some theoretical and methodological conclusions from the findings.

2. Grammatical categorization

The question of grammatical categorization in the world's languages has often been analyzed within the confines of word-class systems. It has been observed that languages differ in the number and kinds of word classes that they distinguish and that word-class distinctions seem to be stricter in some languages than in others. In this perspective, it would appear that languages with many different word classes and with sharp boundaries between them fulfill some function neglected by languages with fewer or more fluid word classes. Here we will widen the perspective a bit and view the categorization of lexemes into word classes as one kind of **grammatical categorization**, where 'grammatical' is taken to comprise 'syntactic' and 'morphological'.

It is a theorem of semiotic theory that linguistic expressions must be composed of meaningful elements that belong to categories. This should be deducible from the requirement that there must be compositional rules of forming the meaning of complex expressions, which in turn follows from yet more basic goals of cognition and communication. Taking this for granted, we may ask at which level of grammatical structure such categorization takes place. I am here referring to the **complexity levels** of grammatical structure. The levels relevant for the categorization of units with lexical meaning are the ones of Table 1.

Table 1. Levels of grammatical categorization

phrase
word form
stem
root

Consider (1) for illustration:

(1) The undermining of established theories is forbidden.

- *Mine* is a lexical root that belongs to either of the categories noun or verb.
- *Undermine* is a stem that belongs to the category verb.
- *Undermining* is a word form that belongs to any of the categories noun, adjective or adverb (the latter when heading a gerundial).
- *The undermining of established theories* is a phrase that belongs to the category noun phrase.

(1) refers to what the noun phrase designates and predicates something about it. The propositional operation of reference works with an expression belonging to the category noun phrase. This operation does not care for the category assignments of the lower levels. In this perspective, the traditional name of the categories here at stake, viz. 'parts of speech', is entirely apt because it is at the level of the propositional operations that categorization is needed. Categorization at lower levels, e.g. the level called 'word classes' or 'lexical categories', is required only to the extent that compositional semantic complexity below the level of propositional operations is wanted. That is to say: Speakers certainly need semantic complexity below the level of propositional operations. However, as word-formation shows, it need not be compositional.

A meaningful expression may be categorized at some lower level and then be handed through to the upper levels with its category unchanged, as is the case for the subject of (2) (cp. with the subject of (1)).

(2) War is forbidden.

Assigning an element to a target category or equipping it with such a category is an operation that can take place at various levels. The element may be stored in the inventory under the target category or under a different category or without any category. In the first situation, the operation of categorizing the element has, so to speak, already been done in the language system. The category need not be marked on the element if it is part of the element's identity. For instance, the English stem *war* belongs to the category noun, and that is part of its lexical information; but the fact is not marked on it by any structural means. In the second and third situations, the target category will somehow be coded on the element or in its immediate context (cf. Kuryłowicz 1936). For instance, the assignment of *undermining of established theories* to the category noun phrase is marked by the formative *the* appearing in front of it. These options are available to languages; and they may differ typologically in resorting to one rather than another solution of the categorizing task under different conditions.

The categories we are talking about are **structural categories**. They are, thus, part of the particular language system. They are distinct from the **cognitive categories** into which signs fall. 'Property' is such a cognitive category, and both the adjective *clever* and the noun *cleverness* fall into that category. We will come back to the question of how the cognitive category becomes relevant for the grammatical categorization.

Before a sign reaches the level of the utterance, it may be categorized and recategorized several times. With reference to the levels of Table 1, we may distinguish between the primary and the final categorization of a sign. The **primary categorization** is the one at the lowest level, the **final categorization** is the one at the highest level. Examples of multiple recategorization are not hard to come by; one was already mentioned in (1). For subsequent discussion, it will nevertheless be sufficient to work with the primary and final categorizations as a binary distinction.

In a way to be made precise by linguistic theory, the passage from the lower to the higher levels of grammatical organization up to the text level is associated with the transition from *langue* to *parole*. The latter is a transition from the virtual to the actual and is, therefore, not gradual like the passage from the lowest to the highest level of Table 1. However, as is well known from research on grammaticalization, the language system determines structure more rigidly at the lower levels of Table 1 than at the higher levels. At the highest level, the speaker freely selects and combines linguistic units; the lower the level of complexity, the more he can rely on ready-made units of the language system, which predetermines their structure. Therefore, the primary and the final categorization of linguistic units are determined at different levels, by cognitive and communicative principles of a different nature.

What determines the final categorization of an expression?

The final categorization of a sign is determined by the syntactic function it has to fulfill in the sentence. That, in turn, is determined by the propositional operation (reference, predication, modification; cf. Croft 1991) to be performed on it. In terms of a teleonomic hierarchy, the speaker chooses his means according to his cognitive and communicative goals. Sometimes he has to adapt the means that the system offers him. That is to say, the use of a certain expression in a certain category may necessitate some prior operation of recategorization on it.

What determines the primary categorization of an expression?

While the syntactic function of an expression is the only factor in its final categorization, it cannot be the only factor in the primary categorization, because a lexical concept[2] must be available for different syntactic functions so that the primary categorization cannot foresee the ultimate use that a sign will be put to. Primary categorization has to proceed by a probability calculus of the sort: what will most probably be the syntactic function of this lexical concept? For this decision, there are by definition no other criteria available than the meaning of the sign. Primary categorization of lexical concepts is essentially determined by universal cognitive principles. The best-understood of these rely on the time-stability of a concept (cf. Croft 1991):

- If the concept has a high time-stability, i.e. it is thing-like, then it will be used in referring. The category of a word whose primary use is reference is 'noun'.
- If the concept has a low time-stability, i.e. it is event-like, then it will be used for predication. The category of a word whose primary use is predication is 'verb'.

If the concept is not clearly determined in terms of time-stability, then a couple of other major classes become available. Some of these, above all the adjective and similar categories, are still weakly determined by time-stability, viz. by the medium stability characteristic of properties and states. Here, however, categorization becomes more arbitrary and more language-specific. Little is known, *a fortiori*, about the factors underlying the primary categorization of concepts as adverbs.

In this paper, only the categorization of lexical concepts in terms of parts of speech is dealt with. There is, on the other hand, the set of categories of grammatical formatives, variously called 'secondary grammatical categories' or 'morphological categories'. The assignment of a concept to any such category is a matter of grammaticalization, not to be treated here.

3. Categoriality of roots and stems

What I am presenting here is an interim report on ongoing research. Its point of departure is the pre-theoretical observation that there appear to be substantial differences among languages with regard to category determinacy of roots, i.e. to the extent to which roots are categorized at all. Instead of category determinacy or categorial specificity, we will say 'categoriality' for short. The questions to be answered by empirical investigation are the following:

- What kind of variation is observed in the primary categorization of lexical concepts?
- If there are significant differences among languages, with what do they correlate?[3]

A small convenience sample of six languages was taken, including Latin, Spanish, English, German, Mandarin Chinese and Yucatec Maya. Some of these languages were included because there are long-standing suppositions that they behave specially with respect to the two leading questions;[4] others were included because data were easy to come by. The inclusion of both Latin and Spanish renders the diachronic perspective possible, which will occasionally be taken here.

3.1 Methodology

The object of the present research is, thus, the set of roots of a language, and the task is to determine the range of word classes for these. Since the roots of a language number in the thousands, one may wish to take a sample. One method that would, in principle, suit the goal is to take a random sample from a dictionary. However, since in comparative research on grammar and lexicon, an onomasiological perspective must be taken (cf. Lehmann 2005), the choice method here is the selection of a lexical field. A field is wanted which is liable to present variation in categorization. Variation in two respects is needed: Different word classes should be represented in the field; and average categoriality of items in the field should be low. (These two kinds of variation are expected to correlate.) These conditions rule out lexical fields of physical objects or of destructive acts. In such fields, the cognitive factor determining primary categorization in the sense of Section 2 is relatively strong. That means, most lexical concepts concerning physical objects in any language will be categorized as nouns; and most lexical concepts concerning destructive acts will be coded by transitive verbs. Here universal cognitive principles of categorization prevail, with the result that root categoriality will be relatively high and typological differences among languages have little chance to assert themselves.

A field that would qualify well by these conditions would be sounds and noises. This, however, presents a practical problem of getting data. For lesser-known languages, dictionaries do not suffice in this domain. For living languages, data may be obtained in fieldwork, but the diachronic perspective will be largely excluded, and questions concerning changes in the primary categorization of lexical units could not be posed. I therefore chose the domain of experience, which includes the subdomains characterized in Table 2 (cf. Verhoeven 2007):

Table 2. Conceptual domain of experience

subdomain	definition	subdivision	example root concepts
bodily sensation	feelings related to the experiencer's body	saturation, temperature, irritation, health condition	hunger, tire, itch …
emotion	cognitively based feelings	self-directed, other-directed	happy, angry, fear …
volition	psychological energy determining actions	psycho-physical disposition, intention	want, greed, hope …
cognition	internal experiences based on mental functions	presence or absence of information, conceptual activity, propositional attitudes	know, dream, decide …
perception	input of information through the senses	sight, hearing, touch, taste, smell	see, loud, noise …

I only considered the first four of the five subdomains of Table 2, the reason being again an expectation that in the remaining subdomain, perception, cognitive principles will determine categorization to a large extent.

A set of basic concepts in these subdomains was established on a rather intuitive basis (s. Section 4 for the obvious methodological weakness involved), but exclusively by cognitive, not by structural criteria. In this approach, the English words *clever* and *cleverness* code the same concept. The full set of concepts is enumerated in Table 3.

Table 3. Basic concepts

subdomain	concepts
bodily sensation	feel, rest, hunger, thirst, satisfied, enjoy, refresh, cold, cool, hot, chill, sweat, wake, brisk, sleep, tire, feeble, flabby, sound, intact, recover, sick, ill, suffer, endure, pain, ache, itch, numb, cramp, tickle, wanton, lust, rut, irritate
emotion	temper, calm, happy, bliss, love, proud, comfort, startle, astonish, scare, dread, shudder, terror, timid, shy, fear, anxiety, excite, fury, rage, grudge, wrath, annoy, anger, vex, resent, angry, bother, bore, patient, disgust, sad, grief, sorrow, shame, serious, serene, gay, please, amuse, frenzy, enthuse, charm, hate, envy, pity, move
volition	want, wish, strive, endeavour, effort, instinct, long, yearn, desire, greed, eager, wait, hope, inclined, mood
cognition	mind, soul, think, know, acquaint, presage, understand, decide, puzzle, mad, remember, learn, forget, imagine, dream, respect, honor, believe, trust, agree

These concepts are translated into the target languages. (The data and subsequent analyses are not reproduced here for want of space; a sample is shown in the appendix.) No attempt is made to obtain precise translation equivalents, because that is both impossible and inessential to the task. Instead, to the extent that there is a choice among expressions in a language, preference is given to morphologically simple expressions whose literal meaning is in the lexical field, so that the root itself is an experiential root rather than functioning in an experiential expression by metaphor. The condition of simplicity makes us choose *satisfy* as the English coding of the concept 'satisfied' instead of the participle *satisfied*, and similarly *anger* as the English coding of the concept 'angry'.[5] The condition of literality makes us exclude English *upset* as a coding of 'angry'. Sometimes this condition cannot be satisfied; for instance, *move* is the only straightforward English coding of the concept 'move emotionally' (German *rühren*). If two concepts are rendered by the same stem in the target language, the stem enters the sample only once, and accordingly the sample of stems will be smaller for that language. For instance, I could not find in Spanish a distinction between 'timid' and 'shy'.

Given a concept and a root coding it, then there are often more than one stem that transfer the root into different word classes, as in English *anxi-ous* and *anxi-ety*. If the above criterion of simplicity does not decide it, one of the stems is chosen arbitrarily. If different concepts are represented by different stems based on the same root, as in Latin *senti-* 'feel' and *ad-senti-* 'agree', then these stems are included. Such discretionary decisions do no harm as long as we do not ask for the particular word classes that prevail among the stems in the field; this latter question would indeed require a refinement of the methodology.

Then each expression is analyzed morphologically, and the root is identified. Items based on non-native roots are excluded if there are alternatives. Finally, the set of lexical categories for each root is determined by criteria dealt with in Section 3.2. Here again, the degree of methodological refinement is low. The most important word classes are the same for the six languages, viz. noun (N), verb (V) and adjective (A). The concepts of our field are practically never coded as adverbial or adpositional roots, although roots of these categories may appear in compound stems. Some languages have roots of minor categories. Again, these differences are not important since the epistemic interest is not in the nature of the categories, but in their distinction.

3.2 Analytic decisions

In what follows, some principles that are relevant to the morphological analysis, in particular in the identification and categorization of roots and the distinction between root and stem, are formulated.[6] The methodology involved in identifying the word classes that a given item belongs to will be taken for granted here, although it is currently the object of heated debate (see *Linguistic Typology* 9/3, 2005).

A root is assigned to word class W if it occurs in the contexts that define W. For inflecting systems, that means that the root combines with inflectional morphemes of W. For non-inflecting systems, the context is a syntactic construction. In both cases, it is, of course, required that the root be insertable in its context without further morphological or phonological modification, especially without any derivational morphemes or thematic suffixes. This condition assures, e.g., that German *Wut* 'fury' is only categorized as noun. The verb *wüten* 'rage' has a stem *wüt-*, which differs from the root by metaphony.

By this criterion, a root may belong to more than one word class simultaneously (e.g. Engl. *chill* is A, N or V), or it may belong to no word class (e.g. Engl. *aggress* as in *aggressive*). In the latter case, it is assigned to category X. These decisions presuppose semantic sameness. For instance, 'mind' is *mente* in Spanish. The root is *ment-*. This root cannot directly inflect, i.e. it belongs to category X. The fact that there is a (homonymous) root *ment-* which does directly inflect in *mentir* 'lie' plays no role in this assignment.

A **recurrent morpheme** is an association of a significans with a significatum that recurs in different contexts. By the principle 'once a morpheme — always a morpheme', a stem containing a recurrent morpheme is considered complex, no matter whether the rest is recognizable as a recurrent morpheme. This is relevant in two cases:

- Unproductive derivational operator, as in Yucatec Maya *uk'-ah* (drink-?) 'thirsty'. Such cases present no problem of categorization, since the category of the root can be ascertained in other contexts.
- Unproductive root, as in Yucatec Maya *k'oh-a'n* (?-RSLTV) 'ill'. In such cases, the root is classified as X (despite the fact that in productive formation, the resultative suffix only combines with a verbal base[7]).

A morpheme or paradigm that is used productively to convert stems into category W is or involves a derivational operator; i.e. it is not (merely) an inflectional morpheme or paradigm, even if it also appears on roots that only belong to W. This concerns the Latin **thematic vowels**. These function in transcategorization, e.g. *cal-e-re* 'be hot' as opposed to *cal-idu-s* 'hot'; but they also appear on many verbs and nouns that have no counterpart in another word class, e.g. *par-e-re* 'obey'. Thus, by this principle, the Latin thematic vowels are derivational operators; they form neither part of the root nor part of the inflectional ending.

In many languages, every **adjective** can be used as a noun. Given a root used as an adjective, then its use as a noun is considered an alternate root categorization if it is an abstract noun (e.g. German *stolz* 'proud', *Stolz* 'pride'), but it is considered a recategorization at the syntactic level if the noun designates an object (typically, a person) that the meaning of the adjective applies to (e.g. Engl. *young*). In other words, *stolz* is categorically indeterminate (A/N), but *young* is not (A).[8]

For Spanish nouns, the suffixes *-o*, *-a* and *-e* are considered derivational suffixes, as their Latin predecessors. As a consequence, the root *deleit-* is a verb root (*deleit-ar* 'delight'), but not a noun root (*deleit-e* 'delight' is derived). In the adjectives, instead, the endings *-o* and *-a* are inflectional endings (masculine vs. feminine); consequently, what remains after their subtraction is an adjective stem. Similarly, the thematic vowels of the three conjugation classes (*-a*, *-e*, *-i*) are considered part of the inflectional endings, not as derivational operators. This means that roots like *salv-* 'save, safe' can directly inflect (in two different categories, in this case). These latter analytic decisions differ from the corresponding decisions taken for Latin. This difference makes Spanish appear as a language of a slightly different morphological type than Latin. The decisions themselves are by no means cogent; but as we shall see in Section 3.4.1, they seem to have little influence on the results.

3.3 Calculus

On the basis of the analysis described in the preceding sections, each item — root or stem — in the sample was assigned a numerical value for categoriality, by the following consideration: The lower the number of categories that an item may be used in, the higher its categoriality. Consequently, its categoriality is, in principle, the reciprocal value of the number of its categories (s. Table 4, rows 1–3). Only if the item can be used in no category, its categoriality is stipulated to be 0.[9] The following values were used in the data analysis:

Table 4. Values of categoriality

number of categories	value
1	1
2	0.5
3	0.33
0	0

Moreover, the number of morphs composing a stem was noted. Table 5 is an illustrative section of the table of English stems:

Table 5. Values of some English stems

stem	categoriality		morphs
	categories	value	
re-cover	V	1	2
sick	A	1	1
ill	A	1	1
suffer	V	1	1
en-dure	V	1	2
pain	N/V	0.5	1
ache	N/V	0.5	1
itch	N/V	0.5	1

Here is the corresponding section for the roots appearing in the sample of Table 5:

Table 6. Categoriality of some English root types

root	**categoriality**	
	categories	**value**
cover	X	0
sick	A	1
ill	A	1
suffer	V	1
dure	X	0
pain	N/V	0.5
ache	N/V	0.5
itch	N/V	0.5

As said in Section 3.2, homonymy is paid attention to, so that the morpheme *cover* that appears in *recover* is distinct from the morpheme *cover* 'wrap'. The former is not usable as a stem and therefore receives category X and value 0.

As explained in Section 3.1, the samples of stems of the six languages differ in size. Since in each language sample, each stem appears only once, the number of stem types equals the number of stem tokens. This is not so for the morphs — roots and bound morphs —, since the same morphs may be used in different stems. For instance, *re-* occurs in *resent*, *remember* and *respect*. Therefore, for each language an inventory of the (types of) major class roots appearing in the sample was made.

On the basis of these data, for each language sample figures F1–F5 were computed as integers:

F1. stems
F2. morph tokens
F3. root tokens
F4. root types
F5. non-root tokens: F2 – F3.

The morphological complexity of stems was determined by two figures:

F6. morphs per stem: F2 / F1.
F7. non-roots per stem: F5 / F1.

The average categoriality was computed for stems and for roots of each language as follows:

F8. categoriality of stems: arithmetic mean of categoriality values of stems (a segment of which is illustrated in Table 5, col. 3), i.e. sum total of these categoriality values divided by F1;
F9. categoriality of roots: arithmetic mean of categoriality values of root types (cf. Table 6, col. 3), i.e. the sum total of these categoriality values divided by F4.

For both of these means, the tables below also show the standard deviation. This, however, will not be analyzed since these distributions differ considerably from normal distributions.

3.4 Results

3.4.1 *Categoriality of stems*

Table 7 shows the categoriality of stems (F8) for the six samples:

Table 7. Categoriality of stems

language	stems types = tokens	mean categoriality	standard deviation
Latin	107	0.99	0.068
Spanish	116	0.98	0.102
Yucatec	78	0.96	0.144
German	116	0.86	0.230
Mandarin	112	0.84	0.233
English	116	0.77	0.245
average		0.90	

As appears from Table 7, there are considerable differences among the sample languages in this respect. At one pole of the scale, we have Latin and Spanish, where essentially every stem belongs to just one word class. In Latin, a stem that can be inflected for more than one word class is the exception. Our sample contains two of them, *met-u-* 'fear' and *ir-a-* 'wrath', which may be declined or conjugated. The fact that Spanish is so close to Latin is astonishing given the analytic decision taken in Section 3.2 to the effect that thematic vowels of adjectives and verbs are considered as part of the stem in Latin, but not in Spanish. This may be interpreted to mean that high categoriality of stems is a typological feature of both languages, although they differ in their techniques to achieve it. At the opposite pole, there is English, where roughly every second stem belongs to more than one category. Expectably, Mandarin is close to the lower pole, too, but as has been remarked repeatedly by Sinologists, its stems are not as indeterminate as the English stems are.

For a language such as English, with low stem categoriality, the speaker's task of assigning the words to categories is fully achieved only at the level of syntax. This is done by inserting words into certain syntactic templates which force a syntactic category on them. In a language with high stem categoriality, such as Latin, the syntax contributes nothing to the categorization of words, which means that such templates play a minor role in constructions.

3.4.2 *Categoriality of roots*

Table 8 shows the categoriality of roots (F9 of Section 3.3) for the six samples:

Table 8. Categoriality of roots

language	roots types	mean categoriality	standard deviation
German	117	0.78	0.327
Yucatec	71	0.76	0.404
English	116	0.62	0.381
Mandarin	155	0.60	0.465
Spanish	111	0.59	0.490
Latin	86	0.30	0.462
average		0.61	

This time, the differences among the languages are even more striking. At the upper pole of the continuum, there is German, where roughly every second root comes with a specification of its unique word class. Another language whose root categoriality is well above average is Yucatec Maya. This finding is in consonance with earlier work highlighting the rigid grammatical relationality of Yucatec roots (Lehmann et al. 2000; cf. also Lois & Vapnarsky 2003).[10]

At the lower pole, we have Latin, where the root that may directly be inflected according to a word class is the exception. Relevant examples are *prem-* 'press' and *ang-* 'frighten', which are verb stems, and *felic-* 'happy', which is an adjective stem.[11] Much more commonly, a root is first extended by a thematic vowel before it can inflect.

Although Spanish has the second-lowest value in this sample, Spanish roots are much more category-specific than Latin ones. This difference has nothing to do with the analytic decisions explicated in Section 3.2, since in neither language are the thematic vowels considered to be part of the root. In a diachronic perspective, it may be interpreted to mean that Spanish has been strengthening primary categorization at the lowest levels.

3.4.3 *Categoriality of roots and stems*

If we only look at the languages occupying the poles of the two scales of categoriality (Table 7) and root categoriality (Table 8), there appears to be no connection between the two scales. This changes if we arrange them side by side, as in Table 9:

Table 9. Root and stem categoriality

categoriality language	root	stem	difference
Latin	0.30	0.99	0.69
Spanish	0.59	0.98	0.29
Mandarin	0.60	0.84	0.24
Yucatec	0.76	0.96	0.20
English	0.62	0.77	0.15
German	0.78	0.86	0.08
average	0.61	0.90	0.28

Here it is at once evident that, for each language in the sample, stem categoriality is higher than root categoriality. This is the basic generalization to be made despite the enormous range of variation represented in the last column. This time, the poles are occupied by Latin and German. Latin has productive processes of stem formation, and it uses them essentially in order to categorize roots. German, on the other hand, has no such processes, nor does it need them, because its roots are largely precategorized.

While the universal principle is clear, the question remains whether the enormous cross-linguistic differences are typologically relevant. Does the difference between root categoriality and stem categoriality correlate with anything else? Here I can only hint at a factor that appears to play a role, the morphological complexity of stems. Table 10 shows the languages again arranged according to the difference in categoriality between roots and stems and confronts these values with the ratio of morphs per stem:

Table 10. Categoriality difference and morphs per stem

value language	categoriality difference	morphs per stem
Latin	0.69	2.02
Spanish	0.29	1.54
Mandarin	0.24	1.82
Yucatec	0.20	1.45
English	0.15	1.29
German	0.08	1.27
average	0.28	1.57

It appears there is a flawless correlation between the two values, with the one exception of Mandarin. Now, the exceptional behavior of Mandarin is instructive. Many derivational operators just as stem-forming operators are structural heads, bestowing their category onto the composite whole. In Mandarin, however, complex stems are not formed by such operators, but by compounding, where the structural head of the compound is often less than clear. Here one root is just like the other, i.e. if one root does not suffice to determine the target category, then compounding it with a second root will not help very much. We therefore tabulate the results once more, this time considering not the ratio of morphs per stem, but the ratio of non-root morphs per stem. The result is shown in Table 11.

Table 11. Categoriality difference and non-roots per stem

language / values	categoriality difference	non-roots per stem
Latin	0.69	0.88
Spanish	0.29	0.54
Mandarin	0.24	0.0
Yucatec	0.20	0.32
English	0.15	0.28
German	0.08	0.23
average	0.28	0.375

Again, the two values correlate nicely, and again Mandarin is the only exception. Since the lexemes of the Mandarin sample are composed exclusively of roots, the ratio of non-roots per stem is zero. Despite the absence in Mandarin of operators that could confer a target category onto a base in a regular way, categoriality increases in stems over roots by 0.24, which is almost the cross-linguistic average. In a loose way of speaking, we may say that the increase in categoriality from roots to stems is, in principle, brought about by operators of stem formation, most efficiently by Latin-type thematic formatives. Failing that, sheer morphological complexity raises categoriality, anyway, though less efficiently.[12]

4. Conclusion

The piece of research reported here suffers from lack of methodological rigor in various respects:

- the empirical domain, i.e. the set of stems to be investigated, has to be delimited more exactly,
- decisions concerning inclusion and exclusion of data must be more principled,
- cross-linguistic comparability of data must be secured more systematically,
- morphological analysis must be refined,
- categoriality must be measured in a more formal way.

Future research with better methodology will doubtless modify the results obtained here. It will also be necessary to extend the research to more languages. Another look at Table 7 reveals that the sample, small and biased as it is, contains a language (Latin) that occupies the pole of extreme stem categoriality. On the other hand, the lowest stem categoriality in the sample is 0.77 (English). There are doubtless languages closer to the zero pole. A candidate is Samoan. According to Mosel & Hovdhaugen (1992:73–77), all Samoan words can be used as heads of noun, verb or modifier phrases. As for root categoriality (Table 8), Samoan would again occupy the zero pole.[13] Neither does the sample contain a language close to the pole of high root categoriality (the highest value in Table 8 being 0.78 for German). Here Persian may be a candidate.[14]

Pending such methodological refinements and expansions of the database, I assume that the generalization concerning **staggered level-dependent categoriality** of linguistic signs is likely to survive. For the two lowest levels of Table 1, the stem and the root, the present research has proved that categoriality is consistently higher at the stem level, thus, at the higher level.[15] And we know independently that every syntagm has a unique category at the sentence level. We can therefore safely generalize that categoriality increases with the grammatical levels.[16] This makes sense in view of our initial assumption (Section 2) that if anywhere, then structural categories are needed at the level of the sentence.[17] Therefore, a necessary extension of the research started here would include an analysis of categoriality at higher levels.

Diachronically, roots are lexicalized stems. Engl. *thirst* is originally a derived abstract noun to a Germanic verb meaning 'to dry', and similarly German *Angst* is originally derived from a verb etymologically identical with the Latin verb *angere* 'frighten', which is in the sample, too. In a certain perspective, lexicalization (like grammaticalization) is a reduction process where information is lost. If a stem is lexicalized to a root, that loss may affect different kinds of features. If categorial information is lost, then lexicalization is the diachronic manifestation of the categoriality difference between stems and roots that was ascertained in Section 3.4.3 for each language at the synchronic level. If, however, no categorial information is lost in lexicalization, then the root that is output of the process may inherit the category of the stem that is its input. If that happens on a large scale and if roots had low categoriality at the input stage, then the result of the change will be an increase in overall root categoriality. This is apparently what happened on the way from Latin to Spanish.

There have been 'theories' in the recent literature which claim that universally roots are categorially indeterminate in the lexicon and that it is the syntactic context that determines their category. Thus, Hopper & Thompson (1984:747) argue in a functional-typological framework "that linguistic forms are in principle to be considered as **lacking categoriality** completely unless nounhood or verbhood is forced on them by their discourse functions." In a variant of distributed morphology, Marantz (1997) denies categorial status to roots. Such theories suffer from a methodological and a theoretical misconception. The methodological mistake is that they try to resolve at the theoretical level what is a purely empirical issue. Eugenio Coseriu once wrote (1958:109):

> "La idea de juntar hechos para resolver los problemas teóricos es una idea reaccionaria que implica detener la investigación y no fundarla más sólidamente, como se

> pretende; es, en los casos extremos, una forma típica de misologismo que pretende presentarse como cautela científica."[18]

There is nothing one could reasonably object to this. There is just one thing that should be added:

> The idea to postulate a set of principles in order to solve empirical problems is an escapist idea which only serves to delay research and not — as is often claimed — to provide a more solid foundation; in the extreme cases, it is a typical form of arm-chair linguistics posing as theoretical linguistics.

Sometimes one feels tempted to remind those 'theorists' of Martin Joos's famous dictum "that languages could differ from each other without limit and in unpredictable ways" (Joos (ed.) 1957:96); not because Joos was literally right, but because he formulates the appropriate methodological attitude to empirical issues. Whether or not roots are category-specific is such an empirical question. The methodologically sound position is to be prepared for cross-linguistic variation in every respect that is not of logical necessity invariable.[19]

The theoretical mistake consists in positing universal properties of categories of grammar, in this case the precategoriality of roots. Languages are problem-solving systems. Some of the tasks to be solved are universal. The task of assigning expressions to categories is among these, so it must be incorporated into linguistic theory. However, incorporating one of the possible solutions into linguistic theory fails to recognize that the solution of a problem is dynamic in nature and there are generally alternative ways of solving a problem. The task of universals research is not to stipulate one of the possible solutions as a property of universal grammar, but to analyze the variation encountered in order to identify its principle.

One important result of this empirical investigation is that there are languages, in particular German, with a strong primary categorization of roots.[20] If we had investigated a lexical field such as fruit trees, then a high categoriality of members of the field — most of them beings nouns — would be a rather trivial result of the cognitive principle of grammatical categorization mentioned in Section 2. However, the data adduced are from the field of experience. There are no known cognitive principles that would regulate the grammatical categorization of roots meaning 'calm' or 'dread', and indeed there is wide variation to be found:

- both inside a language and cross-linguistically, roots designating such concepts belong to a wide range of categories,
- and in every language, such roots have relatively low categoriality.

In view of this, it is all the more remarkable that there are languages that apply a primary categorization to most of their roots although it is not so clear what it is needed for. Theoretically, it could suffice to have precategorial roots, to categorize them once at the level of the stem and then assign them their final category at the level of the sentence. Some languages like Latin come close to that model. It is no coincidence that the modists came up with a theory of precategorial roots, since their linguistics was exclusively based on Latin. However, some languages do it differently. Some like German do the bulk of the categorization at the level of the root, with stem formation adding little to that. As we have seen, categorization at the level of the stem is essentially the result of morphological operations. Again, categorization at the syntactic level essentially means inserting the item in a syntactic template. All of this requires structural apparatus; it raises structural complexity. The German position is therefore: Concerning categorization of signs, do at the root-level what can be done at the root-level, and reserve structural complexity for other functions.

Taking up a theoretical consideration introduced in Section 2: The *raison d'être* of a sentence is to serve as an utterance. More generally, the *raison d'être* of (virtual) *langue* is to render (actual) *parole* possible. Consequently, the categorization of units of *langue*, like roots and stems, is, so to speak, a preliminary categorization or precategorization whose purpose is to unburden categorization in *parole*.

On the basis of the data gathered, other kinds of questions may be approached. For instance: For each language, which category prevails in the roots of each of the subdomains? Are there universal tendencies in this respect; are there typologically relevant differences among the languages?[21] However, answers to such questions presuppose that first the methodology be refined as required above.

Notes

1. Thanks are due to three anonymous reviewers for helping me improve this paper.

2. The expression 'lexical concept', though well-established in current linguistics, begs an important theoretical issue: Concepts as such are language-independent; but the assignment of a given concept to either lexicon or grammar is a matter of language-specific structure, more precisely, of the linguistic operations/processes of lexicalization and grammaticalization. There is nothing in the nature of a concept that would make it intrinsically lexical or grammatical.

3. This question has seldom been addressed in the field of word classes, a recent exception being Haig (2006), whose methodology relies on word-formation. The methodological approach taken here partly resembles the one taken in the research on causative and anticausative coding of a set of verbal concepts in various languages as executed in Haspelmath (1993).

4. For instance, Coseriu's (1955) above-mentioned statement on Chinese is part of a century-old debate; cf., e.g., Simon (1937) reacting to a verdict in Misteli (1893) that Chinese did not have word classes.

5. The direction of derivation is determined by purely structural, not by historical, psychological or usage criteria. Thus, for example, the basic term coding the concept 'tired' in English is the verb *tire*, no matter how much other criteria might speak in favor of *tired*.

6. No confusion should arise from the fact that the expressions 'categorization of linguistic units' or 'determination of the category of a linguistic unit' are ambiguous, because they may refer to a theoretical or to a methodological aspect of the object. The theoretical question is what factors in language activity determine the assignment of a linguistic unit to a particular category. This has been discussed briefly in Section 2. The methodological question is how the linguist finds out what category a certain linguistic unit belongs to. That involves methods of structural analysis like those mentioned here. The two questions are entirely independent of each other.

7. Assignment of *k'oh-* to category V would not be based on any independent evidence, but just on analogy. However, since the root is no longer in use, the formation is not a product of today's language system, but of an earlier stage, where *-a'n* may well have combined with bases of different categories. Anyway, as explained at the end of Section 3.1, it does not affect the present research question if such decisions have to be revised.

8. This is not to deny the difference between conversion of an adjectival into a noun phrase at the syntactic level, analyzable as its combination with a zero head, and conversion of the word-class by substantivization of an adjective at the level of word-formation. However, the criteria for such a distinction refer to the use of adjectives in texts, whereas here we are dealing with lexical inventories.

9. This decision is less than satisfactory, since by the logic of the reciprocal value, the categoriality value of an item that can be used in 0 categories should be ∞. This figure, however, would have ruined all of the calculations. Nor would it make sense to say that an item that can be used in no category has a higher categoriality than an item nailed down on one category.

10. Mandarin root categoriality is not so low in this field. Bisang (2006) shows that root categoriality is extremely low in Late Archaic Chinese. It seems plausible that root categoriality has been rising in the history of Chinese. Cf. fn. 4.

11. Lest anybody think that uncategorized roots are created by an artifact of the analysis, viz. by truncating stems, it should be repeated (cf. Section 3.2) that many roots do accept alternate thematic vowels or other derivational suffixes. For instance, from the stem *laeto-* 'merry', we obtain the root *laet-* by subtracting the thematic vowel. Although this root is no stem by itself, it also serves as the basis for the verb stem *laet-a-* 'rejoice', with a different thematic vowel. Similarly, by subtracting the thematic vowel from the stem *ama-* 'love', we obtain the root *am-*, which also serves as the basis for the noun stem *am-or* 'love', with a different derivational suffix. By the above-mentioned principle 'once a morpheme — always a morpheme', the same operation is applied to stems such as *ir-a* 'wrath', although the root *ir-* is otherwise useless.

12. The correlation between categoriality difference and morphological complexity is trivial in two precise cases: In a perfectly isolating language, root equals stem. Here the categoriality difference and morphological complexity are both zero. No language in the world comes even close to this ideal. The most isolating languages, like Archaic Chinese and Vietnamese, are heavily compounding, similarly to Mandarin in my sample. Here stems are morphologically more complex than roots, and the categoriality increases, too. The other case where the correlation is trivial is a language where stems differ from roots by a stem-forming operator. Latin does come close to this type (cf. Haig 2006:6). Even in such a language, however, there is no logical necessity for root categoriality to be lower than stem categoriality.

13. Mosel & Hovdhaugen (1992:77) sometimes refer to "words", sometimes to "roots". If what they say is true for words, then by the principle of Section 3.4.3 above, it would have to hold *a fortiori* for stems.

14. Avazeh Mache (University of Erfurt) translated the concept list into Persian and found that 100% of the roots were uniquely categorized.

15. This fits nicely with Hopper & Thompson's (1984) and Croft's (1991:48) finding that categoriality of a stem decreases if it becomes a component of another stem.

16. A similar claim is made in Haig (2006:49): "If precategoriality is a feature anywhere in a grammar, then in its deepest levels." He suggests a distinction between "early and late categorizing languages" with respect to a passage through T1 from bottom to top. In Hawkins 2007, it is hypothesized that if a language does not do the categorization at the lexical level, it will need more categorizing apparatus at the syntactic level.

17. Another important theoretical issue that I am not resolving here concerns the model character of one level of T1 for categorizations made at another level. The above would invite the inference that higher levels dictate the necessary categories, and categorizations made at lower levels follow that model. On the other hand, there is Dik's (1985) Principle of Formal Adjustment of Derived Constructions, according to which derived constructions are coined on the model of basic constructions. That would seem to entail that categories of lower levels serve as models for categorization at higher levels.

18. The idea to accumulate facts in order to solve theoretical problems is a reactionary idea which only serves to delay research and not — as is often claimed — to provide a more solid foundation; in the extreme cases, it is a typical form of averseness to logic posing as scientific caution.

19. Cf. Lombardi Vallauri (2004) for this position in general, and Haig (2006:41) for precategoriality as a typological parameter rather than a universal, in particular.

20. Don (2004) argues the same for Dutch.

21. Cf. Verhoeven (2007, ch. 5.4.1) for the categorial profile of Yucatec Maya in the domain of experience.

References

Bisang, Walter. 2006. Transcategoriality and syntax-based parts of speech — the case of Late Archaic Chinese. Paper read at 'Universality and Particularity in Parts-of-Speech Systems', Amsterdam, 8–10 June 2006. Mainz: Universität Mainz.

Bursill-Hall, G. L. 1972. *Grammatica speculativa of Thomas of Erfurt*. London: Longman.

Coseriu, Eugenio. 1955. Sobre las categorias verbales ('partes de la oración'). *Revista de Lingüística Aplicada* 10: 7–25. Repr.: Coseriu, Eugenio 1978. *Gramática, semántica, universales. Estudios de lingüística functional*, 50–79. Madrid: Gredos [Biblioteca Románica Hispánica, II/280].

Coseriu, Eugenio. 1973, *Sincronía, diacronía e historia. El problema del cambio lingüístico*. (2nd edn. Madrid: Gredos [Biblioteca románica hispánica, 2,193].

Croft, William. 1991. *Syntactic categories and grammatical relations. The cognitive organization of information*. Chicago IL: Chicago University Press.
Dik, Simon C. 1985. Formal and semantic adjustment of derived constructions. *Predicates and terms in Functional Grammar*, Machtelt A. Bolkestein, et al. (eds.), 1–28. Dordrecht: Foris [Functional Grammar Series, 2].
Don, Jan. 2004. Categories in the lexicon. *Linguistics* 42:931–956.
Haig, Geoffrey. 2006. Word-class distinctions and morphological type: Agglutinating and fusional languages reconsidered. Kiel: Seminar für Sprachwissenschaft der Universität. Ms.
Haspelmath, Martin. 1993. More on the typology of inchoative/causative verb alternations. *Causatives and transitivity*, Bernard Comrie & Maria Polinsky (eds.), 87–120. Amsterdam: John Benjamins [Studies in Language Companion Series, 23].
Hawkins, John A. 2007. Nouns and noun phrases: grammatical variation and language processing. Paper read at the Symposium 'Nouns cross-linguistically', 22–23 June 2007, Università degli Studi del Molise, Campobasso.
Hopper, Paul J. & Thompson, Sandra A. 1984. The discourse basis for lexical categories in universal grammar. *Language* 60: 703–752.
Joos, Martin (ed.). 1957. *Readings in linguistics. The development of descriptive linguistics in America since 1925*. New York, NY: American Council of Learned Societies.
Kuryłowicz, Jerzy. 1936. Dérivation lexicale et dérivation syntaxique (contribution à la théorie des parties du discours). *Bulletin de la Société de Linguistique de Paris* 37: 79–92.
Lehmann, Christian. 2005. Zum Tertium Comparationis im Sprachvergleich., *Beiträge zum romanisch-deutschen und innerromanischen Sprachvergleich. Akten der gleichnamigen internationalen Arbeitstagung (Leipzig, 4.10.-6.10.2003)*. Christian Schmitt & Barbara Wotjak (eds.), 1:157–168. Bonn: Romanistischer Verlag. (2 Vols).
Lehmann, Christian; Shin, Yong-Min & Verhoeven, Elisabeth. 2000. *Person prominence and relation prominence. On the typology of syntactic relations with special reference to Yucatec Maya*. München: lincom [Lincom Studies in Theoretical Linguistics, 17].
Lois, Ximena & Vapnarsky, Valentina. 2003. *Polyvalence of root classes in Yukatekan Mayan languages*. München: Lincom [Lincom Studies in Native American Linguistics, 47].
Lombardi Vallauri, Edoardo. 2004. The relation between mind and language: The innateness hypothesis and the poverty of the stimulus. *The Linguistic Review* 21: 345–387.
Marantz, Alec. 1997. No escape from syntax. Don't try morphological analysis in the privacy of your own lexicon. *Proceedings of the 21st Annual Penn Linguistics Colloquium*, Alexis Dimitriadis, et al. (eds.), 201–225. Philadelphia PA: University of Pennsylvania Press [University of Pennsylvania Working Papers in Linguistics, 4/2].
Misteli, Franz. 1893. *Charakteristik der hauptsächlichsten Typen des Sprachbaues. Neubearbeitung des Werkes von Prof. H. Steinthal (1861)*. Berlin: F. Dümmler [Steinthal, Heymann & Misteli, Franz, *Abriß der Sprachwissenschaft*, Bd. II].
Mosel, Ulrike & Hovdhaugen, Even. 1992. *Samoan reference grammar*. Oslo: Norwegian University Press.
Simon, Walter. 1937. Has the Chinese language parts of speech? *Transactions of the Philological Society* 99–119.
Verhoeven, Elisabeth. 2007. *Experiential constructions in Yucatec Maya. A typologically based analysis of a functional domain in a Mayan language*. Amsterdam: J. Benjamins [Studies in Language Companion Series, 88].

Author's address

Seminar für Sprachwissenschaft
Philosophische Fakultät
Universität
Postf. 90 02 21
99105 Erfurt

Christian.Lehmann@Uni-Erfurt.De

Appendix

One example from each of the four subdomains in the six languages.

language	stem	categories	categoriality	root	categories	categoriality
English	hunger	N/V	0.5	hunger	N/V	0.5
German	Hunger	N/V	0.5	hunger	N/V	0.5
Latin	fame-s	N	1	fam-	X	0
Spanish	hambre	N	1	hambr-	X	0
Mandarin	è	V	1	è	V	1
Yucatec	wi'h	A	1	wi'h	A	1
English	excite	V	1	cite	X	0
German	aufreg-	V	1	reg-	V	1
Latin	concita-	V	1	cit-	X	0
				con-	Adv	1
Spanish	agit	V	1	agit	V	1
Mandarin	jīdòng	V	1	jī	V	1
				dòng	V	1
Yucatec	péek'óol	V	1	peek	V	1
				óol	N	1
English	greed	N	1	greed	N	1
German	Gier	N/V	0.5	Gier	N/V	0,5
Latin	ave	V	1	av	X	0
Spanish	afán	N	1	afán	N	1
Mandarin	tānkán	N/V	0.5	tān	V	1
				kán	X	0
Yucatec	–					
English	imagine	V	1	imagine	V	1
German	vorstell-	V	1	stell	V	1
Latin	cogita	V	1	con	Adv	1
				ag	V	1
Spanish	imagin-	V	1	imagin	V	1
Mandarin	xiǎngxiàng	N/V	0.5	xiǎng	V	1
				xiàng	N/V	0.5
Yucatec	wayáak'	N/V	0.5	wayáak'	N/V	0.5

Precategoriality and syntax-based parts of speech

The case of Late Archaic Chinese

Walter Bisang
University of Mainz

Late Archaic Chinese is a precategorial language, i.e., a language whose lexical items are not preclassified in the lexicon for the syntactic functions of N and V. This will be shown on the basis of structural-conceptual criteria as those developed by Croft (2000) and Sasse (1993b) as well as on the basis of methodological criteria as those suggested by Evans & Osada (2005). As is claimed in Construction Grammar (Goldberg 1995, 2005), the meaning of lexical items is derived by integrating their own lexical meaning with the meaning contributed by the construction. The construction analysed in this paper is the argument structure construction. Linking between lexicon and syntax is subject to stereotypical pragmatic implicatures (Levinson 2000) that follow a version of the animacy hierarchy. As it will turn out, Late Archaic Chinese does not strictly lack parts of speech. In fact, without the distinction of nouns and verbs at the level of syntax it would not be possible to analyse utterances in Late Archaic Chinese. The only thing that Late Archaic Chinese can do without is noun/verb distinction in the lexicon. This typologically remarkable property is due to a process of morphological change. If such a historical process can take place irrespective of parts of speech distinctions, precategoriality in the lexicon cannot be a robust universal feature even if most theoretical approaches take it for granted.

1. Introduction

Most linguistic theories take it for granted that word forms are specified for certain syntactic categories in the lexicon. If a lexical item occurs in the syntactic position of a noun or a verb it is supposed to be lexically preclassified for the nominal or the verbal position, i.e., its assignment to one of these positions must be licensed by lexical preclassification. As will be argued in this paper, this assumption does not hold for all languages and is thus empirically inadequate. In Late Archaic Chinese, the highly prestigeous language of the classical texts of Confucius, Mencius, Laozi and other authors between the 5th and the 3rd centuries BC, lexical items are precategorial in the sense that they are not preclassified for the assignment to a certain syntactic position like N or V. The following three examples with the lexeme *xìn* 'believe/belief, be trustworthy/truth' give a first impression of the precategorial status of lexical items in Late Archaic Chinese:

(1) *xìn* in the position of an intransitive verb (Hanfeizi 47):
修士者未必智，智士者未必信。
xiū shì zhě wèi bì zhì, zhì shì
cultivated knight NML/TOP not.yet must be.wise be.wise knight
zhě wèi bì **xìn**.
NML/TOP not.yet must trustworthy
'A cultivated knight is not necessarily wise, a wise knight is not necessarily trustworthy.'

(2) *xìn* in the position of a transitive verb (Mencius 7A.34):
人皆信之。
rén jiē **xìn** zhī.
man all believe OBJ:3
'People all believed him.'

(3) *xìn* in the position of a noun (Hanfeizi 18):
[Context: 'If a ruler of men is not able to make the laws clear and thus control the authority of the great ministers …]
無道得小人之信也。
wú dào dé [xiǎo rén zhī **xìn**]$_{DP}$ yě.
not.have way get/reach small man ATTR confidence EQ
… [he] has no way of achieving the confidence of the commoners.'

In example (1), *xìn* takes the position of an intransitive verb with the stative meaning of 'be trustworthy', in (2) it occurs in the position of a transitive verb and is thus translated into English as 'believe'. Finally, we find *xìn* in the head position N of a noun phrase in example (3), where it is translated as 'confidence'.

The claim of precategoriality reaches straight to the general architecture of the human language capacity and to the question of how its basic components of the lexicon, syntax, semantics/cognition and pragmatics interact. For that reason, the second section of this paper will show how the interaction of these components creates the phenomenon of parts of speech on the basis of Croft (1991, 2000, 2001) and Sasse (1993a,b) (also cf. Bisang 2010) and on the basis of stereotypical implicatures (Levinson 2000) that determine the relation between syntax and the lexicon. The same section will also deal with the methodological criteria for distinguishing parts of speech suggested by Evans & Osada (2005). Section 3 will test the precategoriality of Late Archaic Chinese lexical items in the argument structure construction. It will particularly deal with object-denoting lexemes in the V-position (§ 3.1) and action-denoting lexemes in different N-positions (§ 3.2). The framework for the test concerning object-denoting lexemes in the V-position will be based on Construction Grammar in terms of Goldberg (1995, 2005) because this approach can consistently explain how an individual lexical item is interpreted by integrating its meaning with the meaning of the construction as a whole. Precategoriality is not limited to words, it extends to bound morphemes. This will be shown in Section 4 which deals with Chinese morphology as reconstructed for the preclassical period, i.e., the time immediately preceding Late Archaic Chinese. The conclusion and the outlook in Section 5 will briefly sketch how the typologically remarkable situation of precategoriality can be accounted for by a very particular historical situation in which the loss of word-class indicating morphology had to be compensated by an increasing relevance of the syntactic structure of the argument structure construction, and the semantics of its positions for the interpretation of lexical items. Based on the notion of "coercion" (Michaelis 2004), it will be argued that the positions of N and V coerced the lexical items of Late Archaic Chinese into a particular semantic interpretation as an object, a property or an action.

2. The architecture of the human language capacity — structural and methodological criteria for the distinction of parts of speech

This section will deal with the interaction of the basic components of the human language capacity that are necessary to account for the situation in Late Archaic Chinese and with the methodological criteria the claim of precategoriality must meet. Subsection 2.1 will introduce the structural prerequisites for distinguishing parts of speech and the basic components these prerequisites are associated with. As will be seen, approaches that define parts of speech exclusively in terms of semantics, pragmatics and morphosyntactic markedness but fail to integrate the interaction between syntax and the lexicon systematically run the risk of being unable to account for precategoriality simply because they don't provide the tools for describing this phenomenon. But even if theories provide the necessary tools they take syntactic preclassification of lexical items at the level of the lexicon for granted. As will be shown in Subsection 2.2, this does not apply to Late Archaic Chinese. In this language, lexical items are linked to the V-position and to the N-position by stereotypical pragmatic implicatures.

While the first two subsections address the basic organization of the human language capacity and the structural criteria relevant for defining parts of speech, the third and last subsection (2.3) will introduce Evans & Osada's (2005) methodological criteria that must apply to a language if it is claimed to lack parts of speech distinctions. These criteria are crucial for the claim of precategoriality made in this paper. Only if they fully and consistently apply to the data can the relevance of precategoriality in Late Archaic Chinese be granted. Otherwise, additional factors may come in that argue against its relevance.

2.1 Structural prerequisites for distinguishing parts of speech

The actual discussion of parts of speech is based on the following four prerequisites for distinguishing word classes (cf. Sasse 1993b: 196–201):

(4) Four prerequisites (Sasse 1993b: 196–201):
- Semantic criteria
- Pragmatic criteria / criteria of discourse function
- Formal criteria (morphosyntactic markedness)
- Distinction between lexical and syntactic levels of analysis

The first three criteria are generally agreed on in one way or another by contemporary linguists. The distinction between the lexical and the syntactic levels is often overlooked in the literature.

Croft (1991, 2000, 2001) is one of the linguists who define parts of speech on the basis of the first three criteria in (4). He creates a conceptual space illustrated in Table 1 below that consists of three pragmatic functions arranged horizontally (reference, modification, predication) and three semantic classes arranged vertically (objects, properties, actions):

Table 1. Croft's conceptual space for parts of speech and function-indicating morphosyntax (adapted from Croft 1991: 53/67, Croft 2000: 89 and Croft 2001: 88/92)

	REFERENCE	MODIFICATION	PREDICATION
OBJECTS	*object reference:* UNMARKED NOUNS	*object modifier:* genitive, adjectivalizations, PP's on nouns	*object predication:* predicate nominals copulas
PROPERTIES	*property reference:* deadjectival nouns	*property modifier:* UNMARKED ADJECTIVES	*property predication:* predicate adjectives copulas
ACTIONS	*action reference:* action nominals, complements, infinitives, gerunds	*action modifier:* participles, relative clauses	*action predication:* UNMARKED VERBS

Each of the nine cells in Table 1 represents a construction which can have different morphosyntactic expression formats in individual languages. The name of the construction is written in italics in the above table, some possible morphosyntactic expression formats are mentioned in normal print. Word classes manifest themselves within the above conceptual space by markedness patterns of function-indicating morphosyntax, i.e., by a morphosyntax that overtly encodes the three pragmatic functions of reference, modification and predication depending on whether the lexemes involved denote objects, properties or actions. Croft understands parts of speech as universals in the sense of "typological prototypes … which should be called noun, verb and adjective" (Croft 2000: 65; 2001: 63). These prototypes are characterized by the following unmarked combinations of pragmatic function and semantic class that universally constitute parts of speech (Croft 2000: 88):

nouns:	reference to an object
adjective:	modification by a property
verb:	predication of an action

Thus an object-denoting lexeme like *car* tends to be relatively less marked in an object-reference construction (*car*) than in an object-modifier construction (*of the car, the car's*) or in an object-predication construction (*is a car*). The same applies to property-denoting lexemes in the property-modifier construction and to action-denoting lexemes in the action-predication construction.

The fourth prerequisite in (4) may be problematic from Croft's (2001) perspective of Radical Construction Grammar under the assumption that there are universal syntactic categories such as N and V, since this theory rejects the existence of universal syntactic categories. Syntactic categories are seen as language specific, ultimately even construction specific. In spite of this, there is no problem for the discussion in this paper, since it is strictly based on the properties of language-specific constructions, i.e., argument structure constructions in Late Archaic Chinese with their specific positions for N and V. But even if one does not adopt Croft's (2001) radical approach to Construction Grammar, it should be possible to integrate his conceptual space and the markedness patterns it evokes to theories based on the existence of universal syntactic categories of N and V. For that purpose, it is necessary to look at the markedness of the lexemes occurring in the N-position or in the V-position under the pragmatically and semantically defined structures represented in Table 1. Even in a theory with universal syntactic categories the lexical items in the N-position and the V-position are subject to the markedness pattern predicted by Croft's conceptual space for parts of speech.

Another reason why the fourth prerequisite is often neglected has to do with the fact that most theories take the one-to-one correlation between lexical categories and syntactic categories for granted. However, it is self-evident that the existence of languages in which items are not preclassified for syntactic categories like N and V can only be discovered if the fourth prerequisite is taken seriously. Broschart (1997) showed that Tongan is such a language. As will be argued in this paper, Late Archaic Chinese is another language whose lexical items are precategorial.

2.2 The role of pragmatics for the linking from the lexicon to syntax

If lexical items are precategorial in Late Archaic Chinese it is to be expected that all of them can occur in the V-position as well as in the N-position without any difference in marking (cf. the criterion of exhaustiveness in Subsection 2.3). Although this seems to be true it is remarkable that the frequency with which individual lexical items occur in the V-position or in the N-position varies considerably. Some words occur in both positions with more or less the same frequency, others show strong preferences. Thus, lexemes like *xìn* 'believe/belief' in (1) to (3) can take both positions with relative ease. Another word such as *shì* 'N: matter, affair, work; V: serve, work' is found with the same frequency in both functions in Mencius (cf. Kennedy 1964: 323). A large proportion of other lexemes like person-denoting lexemes or instrument-denoting lexemes prefer the N-position (but cf. (14) and (15) on person-denoting lexemes in the V-position and (17) to (19) on instrument-denoting lexemes in the V-position). As will be argued in the rest of this section, the reason for this situation is based on pragmatics or, to be more precise, on stereotypical implicatures. The relevance of pragmatics is discussed in some more detail in Bisang (2008).

The assignment of lexical items to the syntactic positions of N and V is based on the following implicature: Lexemes denoting concrete objects **stereotypically imply** the occurrence in an N-position. Lexemes denoting abstract objects are more or less open to both V and N. This correlation is expressed by the following formula, where '>' means 'implies stronger N-inference than':

(5) Concrete Objects > Abstract Objects

The hierarchy in (5) can be further refined to the following version of the animacy hierarchy:

(6) 1st/2nd person > proper names > human > nonhuman > abstracts[1]

In the present argumentation, this hierarchy is understood as the basis of **I-implicatures (Inference of stereotype)** as defined by Levinson (2000), who states that "stereotypes are connotations associated with meanings, but not part of them, which nevertheless play a role in interpretation". The higher the position of a lexeme is in hierarchy (6), the more likely is the stereotypical implicature that it belongs to the cognitive category of object and has to fit into an N-position. If a lexeme situated in a high position of the animacy hierarchy is used in the V-position, this produces a flouting effect (Grice 1975), which can be used for rhetoric purposes.

The rhetoric use of flouting the stereotypical implicature inherent to the animacy hierarchy in (6) is illustrated by example (7) from Han Yu (768–842 AD). The sentence in (7) is uttered in a particular context that addresses the conditions under which barbarians may be treated like Chinese. Han Yu, who was one of the most prominent and brilliant advocates of the "Old-Style" movement (*gǔwén* movement), reacts to this problem by going back to the simplicity and to the expressive power of the literary style of the classical period, i.e., he puts the lexemes concerning the ethnicities involved (*Zhōngguó* 'China' and *Yí* 'Yi-barbarians') into the V-position and thus flouts a stereotypical implicature that was valid in the classical period and was most likely still in use among the literati of his time. The interpretation of *Zhōngguó* 'China' and *Yí* 'Yi-barbarians' in the V-position exactly follows the rules presented below in (9b). Thus, the two lexical items in the V-position can be translated as 'treat them like Chinese/Yi-barbarians' or 'consider them to be Chinese/Yi-barbarians':

(7) Han Yu 6.42b:
諸侯用夷禮，則夷之，夷而進於中國，則中國之。
Zhūhóu yòng **Yí** lǐ, zé **Yí** zhī, **Yí** ér jìn
feudal.lords use N:Yi rites then V:Yi OBJ:3 V:Yi in.spite.of enter
yú *Zhōngguó*, zé *Zhōngguó* zhī.
into N:China then V:China OBJ:3
'If the feudal lords followed the rites of the Yi, then [he = Confucius] treated them like Yi[-barbarians], if they joined China in spite of being Yi, [he] treated them like [civilised] Chinese.'

2.3 Methodological criteria

The claim of precategoriality does not only depend on criteria related to basic components of the architecture of the human language capacity, it is also complemented by some methodological criteria. Evans & Osada (2005: 366) formulate "three criteria which must be satisfied before a language can be claimed to be monocategorial". Although their concept of monocategoriality is not limited to instances in which a lexical item can occur in positions of different parts of speech categories, the criteria introduced by them are also relevant for precategoriality because it is precategoriality that provides an important basis for claiming that there is only a single major word class in a language.

The criterion of **compositionality** deals with the semantics of individual lexemes in different word-class indicating constructions. It states that semantic differences of a given lexeme in different syntactic positions (e.g. argument or predicate) must be fully attributable to the functions of these positions (Evans & Osada 2005: 367).

The other two criteria have to do with the distribution of lexical items. According to the criterion of **bidirectionality**, it is not sufficient to say that X can be used in the function of Y, it is also necessary that Y can take the function of X (Evans & Osada 2005: 375). Thus, if an object-denoting lexeme can take the V-position, it should also be possible for an action-denoting lexeme to occur in the N-position. Finally, the criterion of **exhaustiveness** requires that the lack of a noun/verb-distinction needs to hold for all the relevant words of the lexicon. It is not sufficient to find a few lexical items which happen to be able to occur in the V-position and in the N-position.

As will be shown in the course of this paper, each of the three criteria holds for late Archaic Chinese. Compositionality fully applies to the interpretation of lexical items in the V-position of the argument structure construction. As is to be expected from Goldberg's (1995, 2005) version of Construction Grammar, the changes in meaning of an object-denoting lexeme in the V-position can be largely predicted from the meaning of that lexical item itself plus the meaning of the construction (cf. Section 3.1).

Bidirectionality is often difficult to prove because an individual action-denoting lexeme in a N-position allows for alternative syntactic analyses (e.g. as a minimal headless relative clause or as a minimal unmarked complement clause). In spite of this, some unambiguous examples of action-denoting lexemes in a N-position will be presented in examples (23)–(27) of Subsection 3.2.

Although the corpus of Late Archaic Chinese is of considerable length, exhaustiveness cannot be fully proven. Another factor that undermines a rigid proof of exhaustiveness is the fact that the probability with which a lexical item will be assigned to N or V depends on stereotypical implicatures that are based on a hierarchy (i.e., the animacy hierarchy as presented in (6)). Since the lexical items that take a high position in that hierarchy will not occur very frequently in the marked position, it is not possible to conclude from their unattestedness that they are not possible in a given situation. In spite of this, the regularity with which lexical items can be interpreted in different word-class indicating constructions can be taken as a good indicator for the pervasiveness of precategoriality in Late Archaic Chinese.

3. Tests of precategoriality in Late Archaic Chinese

This section will discuss the argument structure construction in Late Archaic Chinese. The V-position and its interaction with object-denoting lexemes will be the topic of Subsection 3.1, action-denoting lexems in the N-position will be discussed in Subsection 3.2. The V-position in the argument structure construction has been described elsewhere in more detail (Bisang 2008a). Thus, Subsection 3.1 will only present the general principles determining the interaction between lexical items and the argument structure construction plus some illustrative examples.

Since Section 3 as a whole will analyse object-denoting lexemes in a verbal position as well as action-denoting lexemes in a nominal position, this section shows that Late Archaic Chinese meets the criterion of bidirectionality.

3.1 The argument structure construction and the V-position

Late Archaic Chinese makes no distinction between the predication of properties and the predication of actions. Thus, it can be characterized as an adjectival-verb language in terms of Schachter (1985). From a wider perspective, the constructions relevant in this subsection are the intransitive argument structure construction (8a) and the transitive argument structure construction (8b). Intransitive verbs have one NP argument (NP_S) which can precede or follow the V-position. Transitive verbs have two argument NPs, an actor (NP_A) and an undergoer (NP_U). If both of their arguments are overt, the actor is in the preverbal position, the undergoer in the postverbal position. If there is no overt actor argument, an overt undergoer argument can occur in either position depending on constraints of information structure.

(8) Argument structure constructions in Late Archaic Chinese:
a. Intransitive: (i) NP_S V *or*:
(ii) V NP_S
b. Transitive: NP_A V NP_U

As is quite remarkable for Late Archaic Chinese (cf. Norman 1988: 91), the transitive construction in (8b) can be used with basically any action-denoting or property-denoting lexeme that has only one argument position. In this case, the transitive argument structure construction contributes causative meaning. For a more precise description, it is necessary to distinguish between intransitive arguments which have control over the predicate [+con] and those which do not [−con]. Non-control intransitive predicates will be interpreted in terms of the operators CAUSE and BECOME, while control predicates will only get the CAUSE operator (9a). In addition, the transitive argument construction can produce putative meaning with non-control intransitive predicates. The term "putative" is traditionally used in grammars of Late Archaic Chinese (cf. e.g. Gabelentz 1881). It stands for an interpretation in the sense of 'consider NP_S to be V' or 'treat NP_S as V' (9b):

(9) Meaning contribution of the transitive argument structure construction (Notation from Role & Reference Grammar, Van Valin & LaPolla 1997):
a. Causative interpretation:
$\mathbf{V}_{\mathbf{intr[-con]}}{}'\ (NP_S) \rightarrow\ NP_A$ [CAUSE [BECOME $\mathbf{V}_{\mathbf{intr[-con]}}{}'\ (NP_{U(S)})$]]
$\mathbf{V}_{\mathbf{intr[+con]}}{}'\ (NP_S) \rightarrow\ NP_A$ [CAUSE $\mathbf{V}_{\mathbf{intr[+con]}}{}'\ (NP_{U(S)})$]
b. Putative interpretation:
$\mathbf{V}_{\mathbf{intr[-con]}}{}'\ (NP_S) \rightarrow\ NP_A$ [CONSIDER/TREAT AS $\mathbf{V}_{\mathbf{intr[-con]}}{}'\ (NP_{U(S)})$]

In example (10), the [+con] verb *lái* 'come' is interpreted causatively in the transitive argument structure construction. The same also applies to the [−con] stative verb *ān* 'be calm, be content, be safe'. The next two examples illustrate how the [−con] verb *xiǎo* 'be small' can be interpreted causatively (11) as well as putatively (12):

(10) A [+con] and a [−con] verb in causative interpretation (Lunyu 16.1):
是故，遠人不服，則修文德以來之，既來之，則安之。
shì gù yuǎn rén bù fú, zé xiū wén dé
this reason far people NEG submit then cultivate civil.culture virtue
yǐ **lái** zhī, jì **lái** zhī, zé **ān** zhī.
in.order.to come OBJ:3 PFV come OBJ:3 then be.content OBJ:3
'If people of far-off [cultures] do not submit, then [the ruler must] cultivate civil culture and virtue to make them come [= attract them] and when he has attracted them, he [must] content them.'

(11) A [−con] verb in causative interpretation (Han Feizi 8.2):
鼻大可小小不可大也。
Bí dà kě **xiǎo**, xiǎo bù kě **dà** yě.
nose big can small small NEG can big EQ
'If a nose is big, one can make it smaller, if it is small, one cannot make it bigger.'

(12) A [−con] verb in putative interpretation (Mencius 7 A 24.1):
孔子登東山而小魯，登太山而小天下。
Kǒng-ze dēng Dōng Shān ér **xiǎo** LØ dēng Tài Shān
Confucius ascend East Mountain and small Lu ascend Tai Shan
ér **xiǎo** tiānxià.
and small beneath.the.heavens/the.world
'Confucius ascended the Eastern Mountain and Lu appeared to him small [and he considered Lu to be small], he ascended the Tai Mountain and all beneath the heavens appeared to him small.'

The V-position in the argument structure construction presented in (9) cannot only take action-denoting and property-denoting lexemes, it can also take object-denoting lexemes. The meaning of object-denoting lexemes is predictable from a combination of the meaning of the lexeme plus the meaning contributed by the construction. For adequately describing the interaction between the meaning of the lexical items and the transitive argument structure construction in detail, it is necessary to distinguish a number of lexical subcategories. In this subsection, I will only discuss (i) lexemes denoting humans and relations between humans (kinship terms or nouns denoting administrative positions) and (ii) instruments. Both of these instances are attested with relative frequency in Late Archaic Chinese texts. Additional subcategories are (iii) lexemes denoting sense organs, (iv) lexemes denoting places and buildings, (v) personal pronouns and (vi) numbers and measure words.

Person-denoting lexemes (PDL) in the V-position of the intransitive argument structure construction are interpreted either in the sense of 'X behaves like the PDL' or 'X becomes a PDL' (cf. (13a)). The interpretation of person-denoting lexemes in the V-position of the transitive argument structure construction follows the same principles as outlined in (9). The details are given in (13b).

(13) Semantics of person-denoting lexemes (PDL) in the V-position:
a. in intransitive argument structure constructions:
(i) NP_S behaves like a PDL, NP_S is a PDL
(ii) NPs becomes a PDL
b. in transitive argument structure constructions:
(i) NP_A CAUSE NP_U to be/behave like a PDL
(ii) NP_A CONSIDER NP_U to be/behave like a PDL

Example (14) illustrates the case of a person-denoting lexeme in the intransitive argument structure construction in the sense of 'X behaves like a PDL' (13a.i). Thus, the lexeme *jūn* 'prince' is interpreted as 'behave like a prince', etc.

(14) PDL in an intransitive argument structure construction (Mencius 5B.3):
[Context: Duke Jǐng of Qí asked Confucius about good government. Confucius replied:]
君君臣臣父父子子·公曰善哉信如君不君臣不臣父不父子不子雖有粟吾得而食諸。
Jūn **jūn**, chén **chén**, fù **fù**,
N:prince V:behave.like.a.prince N:minister V:minister N:father V:father
zǐ **zǐ**. Gōng yuē: shàn zāi! xìn rú jūn
N:son V:son duke say good EXCL believe/indeed if N:prince
bù **jūn**, chén bù **chén**, fù bú **fù**,
NEG V:prince N:minister NEG V:minister N:father NEG V:father
zǐ bù **zǐ**, sūi yfiu sù, wú dé ér shí zhū?
N:son NEG V:son even.if have millet I get and eat OBJ:3.Q
'Let the prince behave like a prince, the minister like a minister, the father like a father and the son like a son. The duke said: How true! If, indeed, the prince does not behave like a prince, the minister does not behave like a minister, the father does not behave like a father and the son does not behave like a son, even if I have millet [i.e. food], shall I manage to eat it?'

Example (15) illustrates the use of the person-denoting lexeme *yǒu* 'friend' in the transitive argument structure construction with the meaning of 'X considers/treats Y as a PDL' (13b.ii):

(15) PDL in a transitive argument structure construction (Mencius 5B.3):
吾於顏般也則友之矣
wú yú Yàn Bǎn yě, zé **yǒu** zhī ye
I PREP Yan Ban be thus V:friend OBJ:3 PF
'What I am to Yan Ban, I treat him/consider him as a friend.'

Instrument-denoting lexemes (IDL) in the V-position of the intransitive argument structure construction are interpreted either in the sense of 'X is an IDL' or 'X is used as an IDL' (cf. 16a). In the V-position of the transitive argument structure construction, instrument-denoting lexemes are either interpreted causatively (16b.i) or applicatively (16b.ii):

(16) Semantics of instrument-denoting lexemes (IDL) in the V-position:
a. In intransitive argument structure constructions:
NP_S is an IDL/is used as an IDL.

b. In transitive argument structure constructions:
   (i) NP_A CAUSE $NP_{U[S]}$ to be IDL: to use something/someone in the function of IDL.
   (ii) NP_A applies IDL on $NP_{U[S]}$: to use the IDL on something/someone

In example (17), the lexeme *qì* 'vessel, instrument, implement' is used intransitively with the meaning of 'be a vessel/instrument/implement' (16a). In (18), the same lexeme is used causatively in the transitive argument structure construction (16b.i). Finally, example (19) illustrates the applicative use of the instrument-denoting lexeme *biān* 'whip' (16b.ii).

(17) *qì* 'vessel, instrument, implement'
君子不器。
jūn-zǐ bú **qì**.
accomplished.scholar NEG vessel/implement
'The accomplished scholar is not an instrument.'/'The gentleman is not an implement.'

(18) *qì* 'vessel, instrument, implement': causative interpretation, to use something/someone in the function of IDL (Lunyu 13.25):
及其使人也器之。
jí qí shǐ rén yě, **qì** zhī.
reach/and POSS:3 employ man EQ/TOP V:instrument OBJ:3
'As for his [i.e. the prince's/ruler's] employment of people, he uses them as instruments [according to their capacities].'

(19) *biān* 'whip': applicative, to use the IDL on s.th./s.o. (Zuo, Xi 23.4):
公子怒欲鞭之。
gōng-zǐ nù yù **biān** zhī.
prince be/get.angry want V:whip OBJ:3
'The prince got angry and wanted to whip him [apply the whip on him].'

3.2 Action denoting lexemes in the N-position

Evans & Osada (2005) postulate bidirectionality as one criterion that must be satisfied in a language whose lexical items are precategorial. As was pointed out in Subsection 2.3, bidirectionality certainly is a valid criterion but grammar does not always operate symmetrically when it comes to the syntactic positions of nouns and verbs. This is particularly true in a language in which the marking of grammatical categories is not compulsory (cf. Bisang 2004 on the lack of obligatory categories in languages of East and mainland Southeast Asia in general). In Late Archaic Chinese, an action-denoting lexeme in the N-position can be interpreted as a noun but it might as well be interpreted as the verbal node of a headless relative clause, as an unmarked complement clause or as an adverbial clause. The following constructed example may give the reader some idea of this problem:

(20) 病不幸
bìng bù xìng.
ill NEG be.fortunate
a. 'Illness is unfortunate'
b. 'The one who is ill is unfortunate.'
c. 'That s/he is ill is unfortunate.'
d. 'If s/he is ill this is unfortunate.'

In example (20), the nominal interpretation of *bìng* 'illness' (20a) is only one possible analysis. In all the other analyses, *bìng* is in a verbal position. In analysis (20b), *bìng* takes the V-position of an unmarked headless relative clause, in (20c) it is the verb of a complement clause whose subject is omitted and in (20d) it is the verb of the protasis of a conditional clause. Of course, Late Archaic Chinese has overt structural means to distinguish each of the above interpretations, but their use is not compulsory.

The following example is from a real text, in which the lexemes *jiàn* 'remonstrate' and *yán* 'say, speak' occur twice in two different functions. In the first instance (21), one may analyse the two lexemes in the underlined text as nouns:

(21) Two lexemes in nominal interpretation (Mencius 4B.3):
諫行言聽，膏澤下於民，有故而去，則君使人導之出疆
jiàn xíng **yán** tīng, gāo zé xià yú mín,
remonstrate be.realized/enacted say hear fat moist descend on people
yǒu gù ér qù, zé jūn she rén d, o zhī chū
for.some.reason and leave then ruler send man conduct OBJ:3 go.out
jiāng.
boundary
'If the **remonstrations** [of a minister] are enacted and [his] **words** are heard [by the ruler] and thus the blessings [lit.: fat and moist] have descended on the people, if then for some reason [such a minister] leaves [his country], the ruler [will] send people to conduct him beyond the boundaries.'

Even though it may look 'more natural' from the perspective of an English translator to interprete *jiàn* 'remonstrate' and *yán* 'say' nominally in (21), a conditional analysis as in 'A minister, if he remonstrates and it will be enacted, if he speaks and it will be heard by his ruler — and as a consequence blessings descend on the people, if such a minister …' is equally possible and may even be more adequate if it comes to the information structure of (21). And in fact, a few lines below, the same lexical items are embedded in the protasis of a conditional construction overtly marked by *zé* 'then' (cf. the underlined passage):

(22) The same two lexemes in a verbal position (Mencius 4B.3):
今也為臣，諫則不行，言則不聽，膏澤不下於民，有故而去，則君搏執之。
jīn yě wéi chén, **jiàn** *zé* bù xíng, **yán** zé
today TOP be minister remonstrate then NEG enact speak then
bù tīng, gāo zé bú xià yú mín, yǒu gù ér qù,
NEG hear fat moist NEG descend on people for.some.reason and leave
zé jūn bó zhí zhī.
then ruler seize capture OBJ:3
'Today, the ministers, if they **remonstrate**, it will not be enacted, if they **speak**, it will not be heard and blessings do not descend to the people — if [such ministers want to] leave for some reason, the ruler seizes them and holds them prisoners.'

The above examples show that there is a systematic asymmetry between the unambiguous analysis of object-denoting lexemes in the V-position and the ambiguous analysis of action-denoting lexemes in argument positions. In spite of this, there are instances which clearly substantiate bidirectionality. In a number of examples, the same lexeme occurs in different syntactic positions within the same sentence. In example (23), the property-denoting lexeme *bái* 'white' occurs as a modifier in 'white feather'/'white snow' and as a nominal head in 'the whiteness of a white feather'/'the whiteness of white snow':

(23) *bái* 'white' as a modifier and as a head of a possessive construction (Mencius 6A.3):
白羽之白也猶白雪之白。
bái yǔ zhī **bái** yě yóu **bái** xuě zhī **bái.**
white feather ATTR white EQ/TOP be.like white snow ATTR white
'The whitenesss of a white feather is like the whiteness of white snow.'

In the following example, the lexemes *zhǎng* 'elder, senior' and *bái* 'white' even occur in three different syntactic positions, i.e., in the V-position of the intransitive argument structure construction ('is senior' / 'is white'), in the V-position of the transitive argument structure construction ('I treat him as senior' / 'I consider him as white') and in the nominal position ('has nothing to do with seniority in me' / 'according to his whiteness'):

(24) (Mencius 6A.4)
彼長而我長之，非有長於我也，猶彼白，而我白之，從其白於外也
bǐ *zh, ng* ér wfi *zh, ng* zhī, fēi yfił *zh, ng* yú wfi
that.one elder and I elder OBJ:3 NEG.COP have elder PREP I
yě, yóu bǐ **bái** ér wfi **bái** zhī, cóng qí
EQ be.like that.one white and I white OBJ:3 according POSS:3

bái yú wài yě.
white PREP external EQ
'That that [man there] is senior to me and that I treat him as senior has nothing to do with [the presence of] seniority in me, just as that [man] is white and I consider him as white according to his whiteness, which is external [to me].' Translation by Lau (1970: 161): 'That man there is older and I treat him as older. He owes nothing of his elderliness to me, just as in treating him as white because he is white I only do so because of his whiteness which is external to me.'

Of particular interest are examples in which we find the same lexeme in a sequence, first in the V-position, then in the following N-position of the object. In example (25), the first instance of *xián* 'virtuous' takes the V-position, while the second instance takes the object position. According to the rule in (9b), this VO sequence has to be translated by 'consider virtue to be virtue'. In example (26), we find the lexeme *bìng* 'ill' in the same constellation. Finally, there are two such sequences formed by the lexemes *lǎo* 'old' and *zhǎng* 'elder, senior' in example (27):

(25) VO-construction with the same lexeme: Lunyu (1.7):
賢賢易色
xián **xián** yì sè
consider.virtuous what.is.virtuous/virtue slight colour/beauty
'consider virtue to be virtue and slight beauty'

(26) VO-construction with the same lexeme: *bìng* 'ill' (Zhuang 23.33):
然其病病者猶未病也。
rán qí **bìng bìng** zhě yóu wèi bìng yě.
be.so POSS:3S be.ill illness NML be.like still.not be.ill EQ
'The situation is such that he who considers his illness as an illness is still not quite ill.'

(27) VO-construction with the same lexemes: *lǎo* 'be old' and *zh, ng* 'elder, senior':
上老老而民興孝，上長長而民興弟。
shàng **lǎo lǎo** ér mín xīng xiào,
sovereign old old and people arise filial.piety
shàng **zhǎng zhǎng** ér mín xīng dì.
sovereign elder elder and people arise brotherly.submission
'When the sovereign behaves to his aged as the aged should be behaved to, the people become filial; when the sovereign behaves to his elders as the elders should be behaved to, the people learn brotherly submission.'

4. The lack of parts of speech sensitive morphology in preclassical Chinese

The relevance of derivational morphology for the parts of speech distinction has become textbook knowledge in linguistics. As was shown by Haspelmath (1995), even inflectional morphology can specify parts of speech. However, morphology as reconstructed for the preclassical period of Chinese does not always fall in line with textbook knowledge in linguistics, i.e., some of its individual morphemes, among them the two prominent affixes *-*s* and **s*- to be discussed here, do not link up to a specific word class. That such a constellation is possible is attested by a living language like Khmer whose individual morphemes are not associated with individual word classes either (cf. Bisang 2008b).

Before the details of morphology in Chinese can be discussed, a brief word on its division into historical periods is needed. Late Archaic Chinese (LAC; 5th — 3rd centuries BC) represents the last stage of Old Chinese (OC; 11th — 3rd centuries BC). In the preclassical period of Old Chinese between the 11th and the 6th centuries BC, Chinese had its own morphology. This morphology is still reflected in some tonal differences of the modern pronunciation of some Chinese characters like *wáng* 'king [N]' vs. *wàng* 'rule, to be king [V]' or *hǎo* 'to be good [V]' vs. *hào* 'to like, to love'.

The discussion of morphology in the preclassical period is based on Sagart's (1999) excellent book *The roots of Old Chinese*. A look at the morphemes discussed there reveals that about half of them are not specified for a particular word class, among them the suffix OC *-*s* and the prefix OC **s*-. For each example illustrating these affixes, the reconstructions of Middle Chinese (MC, reconstructions based on rhyme dictionaries between the 7th and the 12th centuries AD) and Old Chinese (OC) will be given.

The **suffix** *-*s* was first known by its tonal effects discussed above. These effects manifested themselves in the comments on the Chinese Classics from the Middle Chinese period by the fact that one and the same word (or character) was assigned to different tonal registers (for the development from *-*s* to tonality, cf. Haudricourt 1954, Wang Li 1958, Downer 1959). According to Mei (1980), the function of the suffix *-*s* is either the derivation of nouns from verbs (28) or the derivation of exodirectional verbs (*wàixiàng dòngcí*) out of endodirectional verbs (*nèixiàng dòngcí*) (29). Thus, the suffix *-*s* can be associated with the N-position as well as with the V-position.

(28) Derivation of nouns out of verbs (first 2 examples from Baxter & Sagart 1998: 54–59, next 2 examples from Sagart 1999: 133):

乘	*chéng*	MC **zying*	OC **m-ljing*	'mount, ride (V)'
乘	*shèng*	MC **zyingH*	OC **m-ljing-s*	'(*something ridden:) chariot with team of 4 horses'

傳	*chuán*	MC **drjwen*	OC **drjon*	'transmit (V)'
傳	*zhuàn*	MC **drjwenH*	OC **drjon-s*	'(*something transmitted:) a record'
入	*rù*	MC **nyip*	OC *[b]*nip*	'enter'
內	*nèi*	MC **nwojH*	OC *[b]*nip-s*	'inside'
列	*liè*	MC **ljet*	OC *[b]*ret*	'to arrange'
例	*lì*	MC **ljejH*	OC *[b]*ret-s*	'rule, usage'

(29) Exodirectional verbs out of endodirectional verbs (Baxter & Sagart 1998, Sagart 1999: 132–133):

聞	*wén*	MC **mjun*	OC *[b]*mun*	'hear'
問	*wèn*	MC **mjunH*	OC *[b]*mun-s*	'ask'
受	*shǒu*	MC **dzyuwX*	OC *[b]*duʔ*	'receive'
授	*shòu*	MC **dzyuwH*	OC *[b]*duʔ-s*	'transmit'
好	*hǎo*	MC **xawX*	OC **xuʔ*	'be good'
好	*hào*	MC **xawH*	OC **xu(ʔ)-s*	'(*consider good:) love'
雨	*yǔ*	MC **hjuX*	OC **w(r)jaʔ*	'to rain'
雨	*yù*	MC **hjuH*	OC **w(r)jaʔ-s*	'to rain something'
語	*yǔ*	MC **ngjoX*	OC **ŋ(r)jaʔ*	'speak'
語	*yù*	MC **ngjoH*	OC **ŋ(r)jaʔ-s*	'speak to, address'
假	*jiǎ*	MC **kœX*	OC **kraʔ*	'borrow'
假	*jià*	MC **kœH*	OC ** kraʔ-s*	'lend'

The **prefix** ***s-** derives verbs from object-denoting lexemes (30a) as well as nouns from action-denoting lexemes (30b). Moreover, it marks causativity (30c), directives (30d) and maybe[2] inchoatives (30e; cf. Sagart 1999: 72). Directives are defined in Mei's (1989) paper on the prefix **s-* as "acts or states directed towards external conditions or another person" (quoted from Sagart 1999: 71).

(30) a. verbs derived out of object-denoting lexemes (Sagart 1999: 71):

麗	*lì*	MC **lejH*	OC *[a]*re(ʔ)-s*	'a pair, a couple'
灑	*sǎ*	MC**sreaïX*	OC *[a]***s**-*re(ʔ)*	'to divide, bifurcate'
帚	*zhǒu*	MC **tsyuwX*	OC *[b]*tuʔ*	'a broom'
掃	*sǎo*	MC **sawX*	OC *[a]***s**-*tuʔ*	'to broom'

b. nouns derived out of verbs (Sagart 1999: 73):

射	*shè*	MC **zyæH*	OC *[b]*m-lak-s*	'to shoot with bow'
榭	*xiè*	MC* *zjæH*	OC *[b]***s**-*lak-s*	'open hall for archery exercises'

拽	*yì*	MC **yet/yejH*	OC **^{b}lat(-s)*	'to pull'
絏	*xiè*	MC **sjet*	OC **^{b}s-hlat*	'leading-string'

c. causatives (Sagart 1999: 70):

順	*shùn*	MC **zywinH*	OC **^{b}m-lun-s*	'pliant, obedient'
馴	*xún*	MC **zwin*	OC **^{b}s-lun*	'to make (a horse) obedient'
食	*shí*	MC **zyik*	OC **^{b}m-lɨk*	'to eat'
飼	*sì*	MC **ziH*	OC **^{b}s-lɨk-s*	'to feed (tr.)'

d. directives (Sagart 1999: 71):

易	*yì*	*MC *yek*	OC **^{b}lek*	'to exchange'
賜	*cì*	MC **sjeH*	OC **^{b}s-hlek-s*	'to give'

e. inchoatives (Sagart 1999: 72):

悟	*wù*	MC **nguH*	OC **^{a}ŋa-s*	'to be awake, aware'
蘇	*sū*	MC **su*	OC **^{a}s-ŋa*	'to come back to life; to wake up'

The above examples provide evidence for the lack of parts of speech sensitivity in the morphology of preclassical Chinese in the sense that individual morphemes are not associated with a particular word class. Interestingly, however, the relation betwen morphology and syntax becomes relevant at the level of individual words, i.e., at the level of the lexicon. As soon as there is some morphology added to a root, it seems that the resulting word will be associated with a particular word class relevant for that particular word. If the same morpheme occurs with another root the resulting word may be assigned to a different word class. Thus, the root OC **^{b}nɨp* 'enter' seems to be limited to the nominal function if it occurs with the suffix **-s* in OC **^{b}nɨp-s* 'inside' (cf. example (28)). If the same suffix occurs with OC **^{b}mun* 'hear' it produces the verb OC **^{b}mun-s* 'ask' (cf. example (29)).

From a more general point of view, the relevance of morphology at the level of the lexicon seems to *conventionalize* the word class of a lexeme, while the occurrence of words in a nominal or verbal position of the argument structure construction is based on *conversational implicatures* which can be flouted according to the scale of likelihood reflected by the animacy hierarchy as presented in (6). The different behaviour of lexical items at the syntactic level of morphologically unmarked words and at the level of morphology with individual morphemes affixed to these words may be due to the fact that the unrestricted application of conversational implicatures at both levels would be communicatively unfavourable because such a constellation increases the number of potential interpretations to an extent which seriously endangers the adequate on-time understanding of an utterance by the hearer.

5. Conclusion and outlook

Lexical items are precategorial in Late Archaic Chinese, i.e., they are not preclassified in the lexicon for the syntactic categories N and V. This has been shown with regard to the four prerequisites for distinguishing parts of speech as listed in (4) as well as with regard to the methodological criteria suggested by Evans & Osada (2005). It has also been shown that the linking from the lexicon to syntax is subject to stereotypical pragmatic implicatures that can be flouted for rhetoric purposes.

In this situation, the interpretation of lexical items in Late Archaic Chinese is only granted by the stable syntactic framework provided by the argument structure construction with its positions for N and V. Through the properties of this construction it is possible to state whether a given lexical item is to be understood as an object, a property or as an action and whether it is a predicate or an actor (A), an undergoer (U) or a single argument of an intransitive verb (S). The mechanism at work in the analysis of lexical items within a construction is called "coercion" in Construction Grammar (Michaelis 2004). Transferred to the situation in Late Archaic Chinese, this means that a lexical item occurring in a given position of the argument structure construction is "coerced" into a particular semantic interpretation associated with that position.

Thus, Late Archaic Chinese has a noun/verb distinction but it differs from the majority of other languages inasmuch as this distinction is limited to syntax and is mirrored neither in the lexicon nor in a considerable proportion of its morphological inventory. Without the noun/verb distinction at the syntactic level, uttterances in Late Archaic Chinese would be unanalysable.

Such a division of labour between the lexicon and syntax is typologically extremely remarkable and one may ask what might have given rise to such a system. As was pointed out in Section 4 on preclassical Chinese (11th to 6th centuries BC), morphologically marked lexical items were conventionally associated with parts of speech in the sense that their occurrence was limited either to the N-position or to the V-position. Even though the morphemes themselves were not associated with any particular word class, there existed at least a partial specification of the noun/verb distinction limited to the occurrence of morphological marking in the period that immediately preceded Late Archaic Chinese. In the course of time, however, morphology was reduced and eventually disappeared completely. Even if there might have been some morphology left at the period of Late Archaic Chinese, it was no longer prominent enough to matter for the grammatical system of that language. Thus, what basically remained was the overall syntactic structure of the argument structure construction as described in (8). This construction became the only structure which allowed the functional analysis of the lexical items occurring in it.

As soon as the argument structure construction became the only instrument for the analysis of lexical items and their function, it became more independent of the lexicon in the sense that its positions were no longer limited to a certain set of lexical items defined by their specific morphological or semantic properties. This new autonomy made the argument structure construction available for pragmatics in terms of stereotypical I-implicatures. The crucial role of this autonomy for the pragmatic use of the argument structure constructions can be described as follows: Object-denoting lexemes with a high degree of concreteness (cf. the hierarchies in (5) and (6)) only became acceptable to the V-position with its event-related meaning when their assignment to it was no longer subject to rigid cooccurrence restrictions but to floutable pragmatic implicatures that "coerced" their object-related content into a rhetorically efficient event-related meaning.

As can be seen from the above discussion, the typologically remarkable situation in Late Archaic Chinese is most likely the result of a loss of the parts of speech distinction at the morphological level. Processes of morphological change are cross-linguistically extremely common. If a language can lose parts of speech distinction in the lexicon so easily through a normal process of language change one has to conclude that classification for parts of speech at the level of the lexicon cannot be a robust property of human language.

Abbreviations

3	Third person	OBJ	Object pronoun
A	Actor	OC	Old Chinese
ATTR	Attributive marker	PF	Perfect
COP	Copula	PFV	Perfective
EQ	Equational marker/ Affirmative copula	POSS	Possessive pronoun
		PREP	Preposition
EXCL	Exclamative marker	Q	Question marker
MC	Middle Chinese	S	Argument of intransitive verb
N	Noun	TOP	Topic marker
NEG	Negation/Negative	U	Undergoer
NML	Nominalizer	V	Verb

Notes

1. There are no 3rd person pronouns for actors in Old Chinese. Sometimes, we find demonstratives in this function.

2. Sagart (1999) uses a question mark with regard to the inchoative function.

References

Baxter, William H. & Laurent Sagart. 1998. Word formation in Old Chinese. *New approaches to Chinese word formation. Morphology, phonology and the lexicon in Modern and Ancient Chinese*, Jerome L. Packard (ed.), 35–76. Berlin: Mouton de Gruyter

Bisang, Walter. 2004. Grammaticalization without coevolution of form and meaning: The case of tense-aspect-modality in East and mainland Southeast Asia. *What makes grammaticalization? A look from its fringes and its components*, Walter Bisang; Nikolaus Himmelmann & Björn Wiemer (eds.), 109–138. Berlin: Mouton de Gruyter

Bisang, Walter. 2008a. Precategoriality and argument structure in Late Archaic Chinese, *Constructional Reorganization*, Jaako Leino (ed.), 55–88. Amsterdam: John Benjamins.

Bisang, Walter. 2008b. Underspecification and the noun/verb distinction: Late Archaic Chinese and Khmer. *The discourse potential of underspecified structures: Event structures and information structures*, Anita Steube (ed.), 55–83. Berlin: Akademie-Verlag.

Bisang, Walter. 2010. Word classes. *The Oxford handbook of Language Typology*, Jae Jong Song (ed.), 280–302. Oxford: Oxford University Press.

Broschart, Jürgen. 1997. Why Tongan does it differently: Categorial distinctions in a language without nouns and verbs. *Linguistic Typology* 1(2): 123–165.

Croft, William A. 1991. *Syntactic categories and grammatical relations: The cognitive organization of information*. Chicago, IL: Chicago University Press.

Croft, William A. 2000. Parts of speech as typological universals and as language particular categories. *Approaches to the typology of word classes*, Petra M. Vogel & Bernard Comrie (eds.), 65–102. Berlin: Mouton de Gruyter.

Croft, William A. 2001. *Radical Construction Grammar. Syntactic theory in typological perspective*. Oxford: Oxford University Press.

Downer, G. B. 1959. Derivation by tone-change in Classical Chinese. *Bulletin of the School of Oriental and African Studies* 22: 258–290.

Evans, Nicholas & Osada, Toshiki. 2005. Mundari: The myth of a language without word classes. *Linguistic Typology* 9(3): 351–390.

Gabelentz, Georg von der. 1881. *Chinesische Grammatik. Mit Ausschluss des niederen Stiles und der heutigen Umgangssprache*. Leipzig: Weigel.

Goldberg, Adele E. 1995. *Constructions: A Construction Grammar approach to argument structure*. Chicago, IL: University of Chicago Press.

Goldberg, Adele E. 2005. *Constructions at work*. Oxford: Oxford University Press.

Grice, Paul H. 1975. Logic and conversation. *Speech acts*, Peter Cole & Jerry L. Morgan (eds.), 41–58. New York, NY: Academic Press.

Haspelmath, Martin. 1995. Word-class-changing inflection and morphological theory. *Yearbook of Morphology 1995*, Geert Booij & Jap Van Marle (eds.), 43–66. Dordrecht: Kluwer.

Haudricourt, André. 1954. Comment reconstruire le chinois archaïque. *Word* 10: 351–364.

Kennedy, George A. 1964. *Selected works of George A. Kennedy*. New Haven, CT: Far Eastern Publications.

Lau, D. C. 1970. *Mencius*. Middlesex: Penguin.

Levinson, Stephen C. 2000. *Presumptive meanings. The theory of generalized conversational implicature*. Cambridge, MA: The MIT Press.

Mei, Tsu-lin. 1980. Sisheng bieyi zhong de shijian cengci (Chronological strata in derivation by tone). *Zhongguo Yuwen* 6: 427–443.

Mei, Tsu-lin. 1989. The causative and denominative functions of the *s*-prefix in Old Chinese. *Proceedings of the Second International Conference on Sinology, Academia Sinica, sections on Linguistics and Paleography*, 33–51. Taipei.
Michaelis, Laura. 2004. Type shifting in construction grammar: An integrated approach to aspectual coercion. *Cognitive Linguistics* 15: 1–67.
Norman, Jerry. 1988. *Chinese*. Cambridge: Cambridge University Press.
Sagart, Laurent. 1999. *The roots of Old Chinese*. Amsterdam: John Benjamins.
Sasse, Hans-Jürgen. 1993a. Syntactic categories and subcategories. *Syntax*, Joachim Jacobs; Arnim von Stechow; Wolfgang Sternefeld & Theo Vennemann (eds.), 646–686. Berlin: Mouton de Gruyter.
Sasse, Hans-Jürgen. 1993b. Das Nomen — eine universale Kategorie? *Sprachtypologie und Universalienforschung* 46: 187–221.
Schachter, Paul. 1985. Parts of speech systems. *Language typology and syntactic description, Vol. 1: Clause structure*. Timothy Shopen (ed.), 1–61. Cambridge: Cambridge University Press.
Van Valin, Robert D. & Randy LaPolla. 1997. *Syntax. Structure, meaning and function*. Cambridge: Cambridge University Press.
Wang, Li. 1958. Hanyueyu yanjiu (Research on Sino-Vietnamese). *Hanyu Shilun Wenji*, 290–410.

Author's address

Walter Bisang
University of Mainz
Department of English and Linguistics
Jakob-Welder-Weg 18
D-55099 Mainz
Phone: ++49 6131 392–2778
Fax: ++49 6131 392–3836

wbisang@mail.uni-mainz.de

Covert word classes

Seeking your own syntax in Tukang Besi

Mark Donohue
Linguistics Program, Monash University, Australia

Examining syntactic categories in Tukang Besi, an Austronesian language of Indonesia, we find that there are additions to the traditional fixed categories. In addition to the firmly definable categories of nouns and verbs, there are many lexical items that are precategorial: they may be used, without derivation, with either nominal morphosyntax or verbal morphosyntax. Additionally, there is a class of 'adjectives' that display odd behaviour in terms of morphological markedness reversals and functional use, and which, under closer examination, turn out to have a variable categorial status, dependent on the structural position in which they are used, obligatorily appearing as part of the head of their phrase, V in a VP and N in an NP. Morphosyntactic tests for the different claims are given and discussed.

1. Recognising word classes

Word classes (syntactic categories, parts of speech) are aggregate patterns of morphosyntactic behaviours corresponding in some way to semantic prototypes (with greater or lesser amounts of overlap between categories in different languages). Implicit in our understanding of word class membership is the existence of morphosyntactically distinct patterns corresponding to (the core of) each word class.

I present data from Tukang Besi, an Austronesian language of central Indonesia, showing the existence of a covert word class, adjectives. Although the language has no distinct adjectival morphology, and although the syntactic patterns of adjectives show of a mixture of the patterns seen in other word classes, the aggregate is distinct from other major word classes.[1]

2. Recognising word classes in Tukang Besi

Tukang Besi is spoken on a chain of islands known as the *Kepulauan Tukang Besi* in Southeast Sulawesi, central Indonesia. In addition to this home location there are also

Table 1. Agreement, word order and case marking in Tukang Besi

Clause type	variant	agreement	word order	case marking		
				A	S	P
Bivalent	P indexed on V	A-V=P	V A P (~ VPA)	*te*		*na*
	P not indexed on V	A-V	V P A	*na*		*te*
Monovalent		S-V	V S		*na*	

numerous trading communities scattered across eastern Indonesia (Donohue 1999 etc.; Usmar et al 1991). Tukang Besi is a Malayo-Polynesian language in the Austronesian family, though typologically it is best characterised as a mix of northern Austronesian, (South-)Western Austronesian and Eastern Austronesian morphosyntax.

Tukang Besi is a verb-initial, subject-final Philippine-type language syntactically. Morphologically it shows obligatory agreement for the S,A by verbal prefixes, and optional (pragmatically-determined) agreement for the P by enclitic.[2] Nominal case marking follows a Philippine-style pattern (Schachter 1976, 1977 and many others both before and since), and I follow Bell (1976, 1983) and Kroeger (1993) in using the label NOM for 'nominative' to gloss the case that has variously been called the 'pivot', 'subject', 'focus' or 'topic' in these languages, and which in Tukang Besi is marked with *na*. The other nominal cases are the genitive *nu*, the non-nominative core case *te*, here glossed CORE, and the oblique *i* / *di*, the former used in future/irrealis contexts, the latter in other cases (Donohue 2008). The agreement and case marking systems interact as shown in Table 1. The choice between a bivalent verb with the P indexed and the same verb without such indexing corresponds to enough other syntactic changes, including the status of the subject, that it must be considered as a voice alternation (Donohue 2004b).

The alternation between nominative and non-nominative marking of different arguments is shown in (1) and (2), along with a monovalent clause in (3) (no alternation is possible in monovalent clauses, short of valency-affecting derivation). See Donohue (1999a, 2004b) for further discussion of the differences between forms such as (1) and (2).

(1) No-kili='e=mo te ana na lante.
3R-clean=3P=PF CORE child NOM floor
'The child (has) cleaned the floor.'

(2) No-kili=mo te lante na ana.
3R-clean=PF CORE floor NOM child
'The child cleaned (/is cleaning) (a/the/some of the) floor.'

(3) No-wila=mo na ana.
3R-go=PF CORE child
'The child left.'

In the following sections we shall see that the distinction between nouns and verbs, while clearly maintained in the morphosyntactic choices of the language, is not consistently maintained in the lexicon.

3. Word classes: Nouns, verbs and others

Words such as *kili* 'clean' are unambiguously verbs, just as *lante* 'floor' is unambiguously a noun. The following sentences illustrate the morphosyntactic differences between the two word classes in different discourse functions. In (4) we can see that a noun can be used referentially with only the (obligatory) case marker on the NP, while a verb requires infixation with the S,A infix <*um*>; these strategies are not interchangeable. In (5) the use of a noun or a verb to modify a referential expression is illustrated, and again different strategies are used, nouns modifying by appearing inside genitive NPs, while verbs obligatorily employ the same infix seen earlier. In (6) we can see that when predicative a noun appears inside a NP, just as for referential uses (there are syntactic differences, which are not relevant here), but a verb employs prefixes (as described in Table 1) that mark person, number, and status (realis or irrealis).

(4) Referential

a.	te	lante	b. *	te	kili
	CORE	floor		CORE	clean
	'the floor'			'the cleanliness / the clean one'	
c. *	te	l<um>ante	d.	te	k<um>ili
	CORE	floor<SI>		CORE	clean<SI>
	'the floor'			'the cleanliness / the clean one'	

(5) Attributive

a.	te	kau	nu	lante	b. *	te	kau	nu	kili
	CORE	wood	GEN	floor		CORE	wood	GEN	clean
	'the wood of the floor'					'the clean wood'			
c. *	te	kau	l<um>ante		d.	te	kau	k<um>ili	
	CORE	wood	floor<SI>			CORE	wood	clean<SI>	
	'the wood of the floor'					'the clean floor'			

(6) Predicative

a.	te	kau	iso	te	lante	b. *	te	kau	iso	te	kili
	CORE	wood	yon	CORE	floor		CORE	wood	yon	CORE	clean
	'That wood is a floor.'						'The wood is clean.'				
c. *	te	kau	iso	no-lante		d.	te	kau	iso	no-kili	
	CORE	wood	yon	3R-floor			CORE	wood	yon	3R-clean	
	'That wood is a floor.'						'That wood is clean.'				

Table 2. Discourse function linked to semantic type, I

	'nominal'	'verbal'
Referential	*te* X	*te* X<*um*>
Attributive	*nu* X	X<*um*>
Predicative	*te* X	*no*-X

The morphosyntax seen in examples (4) to (6) is summarised in Table 2. Here 'X' indicates the root itself, and any obligatory morphosyntax in addition to that root that is required for that type of root to function in that discourse function is shown in italics.[3]

Things so far are quite clear; nouns do not display any of the morphosyntax of verbs, and are easily distinguishable from them. Most nominals such as *lante* refer unambiguously to real-world objects, and many verbs such as *kili* refer to events.

As with many Austronesian languages, the question of word class specification raises numerous problems for many lexical items. A large number of words can be described as being precategorial roots, which may be used without (overt) derivation in a morphosyntactically identical fashion to members of several other, more easily specifiable, syntactic categories. This means that a description of the types and criteria for syntactic categories will necessarily fail to account for the variation found in about 60% of lexical roots. For instance, examine the root *tomba* in the following sentences. In (7a) the word appears as the single item in a noun phrase, functioning as the referential head of that phrase. In (7b) it serves as a modifier inside an NP, modifying the head *wuta* 'ground'.[4] In (7c) *tomba* appears with the prefixes and enclitics typical of a verbal, and not nominal, predicate.[5]

(7) a. Kambea o-koruo na tomba, o-tolaki o-mai.
reason 3R-much NOM mud 3R-late 3R-come
'Because there was a lot of mud, they arrived late.'

b. Mbeaka o-jari to-he-tade='e na wunua wo'ou=nto,
NEG 3R-become 3R-VRB-stand=3P NOM house new=1PL.GEN
te iso te wuta tomba.
CORE yon CORE ground mud
'We couldn't build our new house, it's all muddy ground there now.'

c. Dinggawi o-wande, te sala=no o-tomba=mo.
yesterday 3R-rain CORE path=3GEN 3R-mud=PF
'It rained last night, so the roads are (= have become) all muddy.'

Clearly it is not an easy matter to assign a word class such as 'noun' or 'verb' to a lexeme like *tomba*, if word class membership depends on factors of morphosyntactic distribution and semantic type.[6] When referential, it behaves exactly like a noun; when predicative, it behaves exactly like a verb. This is an expected result: verbs are the prototypical predicates, and nouns the prototypical referential expressions, so the precategorial roots are simply imitating the 'least marked' path for their realisation. They differ from

Table 3. Discourse function linked to semantic type, II

	'nominal'	'precategorial'	'verbal'
Referential	*te* X	*te* X	*te* X<*um*>
Attributive	*nu* X	X	X<*um*>
Predicative	*te* X	*no*-X	*no*-X

both of these word classes in their ability to modify other referential expressions without any morphology whatsoever.

The existence of these precategorial roots might be seen to be a challenge to the idea, and usefulness, of word classes in Tukang Besi. The concept of clear and distinct word classes is independently needed to describe the direction taken by many derivational affixes; the suffix -*'a* 'nominaliser' always derives a word that is in the syntactic category NOUN; similarly, the prefixes *he*- 'verbaliser', *hoN*- 'purposeful verbaliser', and *hoko*- 'factitive', amongst others, always unambiguously derive words that are VERBS.[7] In (8)a we can see that a nominal root, *kabali* 'machete' appears with a genitive case marker when it is attributive within an NP, a strong indicator of nominal status. This root can be derived with the *hoN*- prefix, as shown in (8b), in which case it must take verbal morphosyntax, including appearing with the typically verbal -*um*- infix when modifying a noun if it has been earlier derived as a verb with *hoN*-, as shown in (8c). It is not grammatical to use the typically nominal genitive marker, as in (8d).

(8) a. nominal root, attributive use
te mata nu kabali
CORE eye GEN machete
'the point of the machete'

b. nominal root, verbal use derived with *hoN*-
No-hong-abali te pada.
3R-VRBLZR$_1$-machete CORE kunai.grass
'They're using machetes on the kunai grass.'

c. nominal root, derived with hoN-, used attributively
te mia [m]ong-abali te pada
CORE person VRBLZR$_1$<SI>-machete CORE kunai.grass
'the people using machetes on the kunai grass'

d. * te mia nu hong-abali
CORE person GEN VRBLZR$_1$-machete
'the people using machetes'

Paradigms such as these force us to recognise that syntactic categories play a part in the organisation of the language, despite the many exceptions to their applicability as a surface descriptor. An asymmetry emerges when we consider the fact that the nominalising suffix -*'a* cannot be used on lexical items already specified as nouns, whereas, for example, *he*- may be used with items already specified as verbs. Compare (9), which shows that -*'a* may, and must, be used with specified verbal roots when nominal, and (10), where we can see that a lexical item which is already specified as a noun cannot take -*'a*.

(9) a. To-soro te kolikoli='u.
1PL.R-push CORE canoe=2SG.GEN
'We pushed your canoe.'
b. Te soro-'a=no no-ja'o ala'a.
CORE push-NMLZR=3GEN 3R-bad just
'The pushing was pretty bad.'
c. * te soro=no no-ja'o ala'a.
CORE push=3GEN 3R-bad just

(10) a. No-mobai na kau.
3R-hard NOM wood
'The wood is hard.'
b. * te kau-'a.
CORE wood-NMLZR

In contrast, the verbalising *he-* is allowed with verbs as well as nouns, with a slight meaning change, as seen in (11) and (12): while *hoN-* implies a truly 'transitive' event, with high degrees of effectiveness of the action, *he-* has no such implications, and simply implies that the action was performed, without any necessary achievement reading.

(11) a. To-hon-soro te kolikoli='u.
1PL.R-VRBLZR$_1$-push CORE canoe=2SG.GEN
'We really shoved your canoe.'
b. To-he-soro te kolikoli='u.
1PL.R-VRBLZR$_2$-push CORE canoe=2SG.GEN
'We (sort of) pushed your canoe.'

(12) a. No-hong-au='e.
3R-VRBLZR$_1$-wood=3P
'They smashed it with wood.'
b. No-he-kau='e.
3R-VRBLZR$_2$-wood=3P
'They used wood on it.'

We can conclude that not only do the derivational affixes differ in the specification of the syntactic category of their output, but also in the degree of specification of the syntactic category of the input items as well. For instance, the suffix -*'a* specifies a non-noun input, and a noun output. In contrast, *he-* and *hoN-* specify only a verb output, without reference to the syntactic category of the input item.

(13) -*'a*: X[-N] + -*'a* → X-*'a*[N]

(14) *he*-: X[±N, ±V] + *he*- → *he*-X[V]

Having established the need to recognise nouns, verbs, and precategorial roots, in the next section I shall discuss property concepts, which might correspond to adjectives in other languages, and show that while some are best described as being stative verbs, some of these lexemes are indeed adjectives, but, because of the lack of any dedicated morphosyntax, they are a covert word class.

4. Adjectives

Examining the morphosyntactic marking of different property expressions in Tukang Besi, in their different discourse functions, we find that there are three classes of such expressions, based on their morphosyntactic behaviour. In (15) and the following examples representatives of each of the three groups are shown. Predicatively all three are identical, the lexeme appearing in its usual form with a subject agreement prefix, as seen in (15).[8] It is clear that the words under consideration are not nouns; the clauses in (15) are obviously predicate-initial, unlike nominal clauses such as (6a) (see Donohue 2006 for discussion of the reality of this difference in predicate position). On the other hand, based on (15) alone we cannot decide whether *to'oge*, *moboha* and *lule* should be regarded as verbs, or as precategorial roots.

(15) Predicate

a. No-to'oge na woleke iso.
3R-big NOM rat yon
'That rat is big.'

b. No-moboha na woleke iso.
3R-big NOM rat yon
'That rat is big.'

c. No-lule na woleke iso.
3R-naked NOM rat yon
'That rat is naked/exposed.'

Attributively we see a difference firstly between the first two types of property expressions and the last, where the first two appear as bare roots, and the last requires the use of the subordinating infix -*um*-. Furthermore, the first two types do not show the patterns expected of verbs, while the last type does.

(16) Attribute in NP

a. Te woleke to'oge
CORE rat big
'the big rat'

b. Te woleke moboha
CORE rat big

c. Te woleke l<um>ule
CORE rat naked.SI
'the naked rat'

It is simple, and morphologically consistent, to hypothesise that words such as *lule* belong to the syntactic category of verb, and that *to'oge* and *moboha* are members of a syntactic category which is distinct from this. Based on what we have seen so far, we should conclude that *to'oge* and *moboha* are precategorial roots.

Continuing the exposition of the property items, we also find a difference when they are used referentially, whereas adjectives that do not begin with *mo-*, *me-* or *ma-* appear in the same form as referential heads of NPs; many verbs with the *mV-* prefix (historically productive, but synchronically fused with the root — see Donohue 2004a) LOSE this prefix. Property expressions such as *lule* again take the morphosyntax associated with verbs, and again appear with the *-um-* infix.[9]

(17) a. Te to'oge
CORE big
'the bigness / the big one'

b. Te -boha
CORE big
'the bigness / the big one'

c. Te l<um>ule
CORE naked.SI
'the naked one'

The morphological distribution for property concepts is given in Table 4.

Table 4. Morphology associated with properties: Tukang Besi

	Referential	Attributive	Predicative	
Properties	*te to'oge*	*to'oge*	*noto'oge*	: non verbal
	te baha	***mo**boha*	*no**mo**boha*	: non verbal
	*te **lum**ule*	***lum**ule*	*nolule*	: verbal pattern

Property expressions such as *moboha* cannot be regarded as precategorial, since we now have evidence of a morphosyntactic pattern (which might be described as 'subtractive', though see Donohue 2004a for detailed discussion) that is not found outside this small class of words. Yet another piece of evidence can be found when we examine the behaviour of the different word types (I do not call them 'word classes' yet, since this is still under investigation; Section 5 offers more definitive conclusions) in complex NPs involving both modification and possession by enclitic.

We have seen examples of possession being indicated by the use of a postnominal genitive phrase in an NP (see (5a)); a pronominal possessor may be shown by the use of genitive enclitics on the noun. Both of these options are shown in (18). The full paradigm of genitive enclitics is shown in (19).

(18) a. te ana nu mia
CORE child GEN person
'the person's child'
b. te ana=no
CORE child=3GEN
'her/his/their child'

(19) ana=su 'my child'
ana='u 'your (SINGULAR) child'
ana=no 'her/his/their child'
ana=mami 'our (PAUCAL) child'
ana=nto 'our (PLURAL) child'
ana=miu 'your (PLURAL) child'

When a genitive enclitic appears in an NP that is also modified by an attributive verb, the order is noun-enclitic-verb, as shown in (20). Any other orders are ungrammatical, as shown in (21).[10]

(20) te ana=su t<um>inti
CORE child=1SG.GEN run<SI>
'my running child'

(21) *te ana tuminti=su, * te tuminti ana=su, * te tuminti=su ana

Precategorial roots similarly must follow the genitive enclitic in the NP, though they do not take any overt morphology in this position.

(22) a. te ana=su akala b. * te ana akala=su
CORE child=1SG.GEN trick CORE child trick=1SG.GEN
'my tricky child'

When the modifier is a complete genitive phrase there is no unambiguous way for the genitive clitic to be added to the phase. Both possibilities are shown in (23).

(23) a. te kadera nu kau=su
CORE chair GEN wood=1SG.GEN
'my wooden chair' *or* 'the chair (that's made) of my wood'
b. te kadera=su nu kau
CORE chair=1SG.GEN GEN wood
'my wooden chair' *or* 'the wood of my chair'

Most interestingly, when the property expressions introduced in (15) are shown in complex NPs we find another pattern. The *lule*-type lexemes, predictably, behave just like the verbs in (20) and (21), following the genitive clitic and taking an overt marker of subordination. The *to'oge* and *moboha* type lexemes, however, precede the clitic.

(24) a. te ana to'oge=su
CORE child big=1SG.GEN
'my big child'

b. * te ana=su to'oge
CORE child=1SG.GEN big

(25) a. te ana moboha=su
CORE child big=1SG.GEN
'my big child'

b. * te ana=su moboha
CORE child=1SG.GEN big

(26) a. * te ana l<um>ule=su
CORE child naked<SI>=1SG.GEN
'my naked child'

b. te ana=su l<um>ule
CORE child=1SG.GEN naked<SI>

There are additional differences in attributive position. Nominal, verbal and precategorial modification allows for recursion, with multiple relative clauses or embedded possession being possible in an NP, but the *to'oge/moboha*-type lexemes only allow for a single instantiation within an NP without resorting to the use of a verbal modification strategy. In (27) and (28) we can see that multiple modifying verbs can appear with the same noun. Similarly, multiple genitive phrases can appear to allow more than one noun to modify in an NP, either recursively, as in (29), or with both modifying the one noun, as shown in (30) (subject to ambiguities that were seen in (23)), and multiple precategorial roots may modify a single nouns. For none of these complex NPs is the relative order of the modifiers important.

(27) te ana l<um>ule t<um>inti
CORE child naked<SI> run<SI>
'the naked running child'

(28) te ana t<um>inti l<um>ule

(29) te kadera [nu bela [nu iai=su]]
CORE chair GEN spouse GEN younger.sibling=1SG.GEN
'my younger sister's husband's chair'

(30) te kadera [nu kau] [nu bela=su]
CORE chair GEN wood GEN spouse=1SG.GEN
'my husband's chair' *or* 'the chair (that's made) of my husband's wood'

(31) te ana akala esempee
CORE child trick junior.high.school
'the tricky junior high school child'

(32) te ana esempee akala

When we examine the *to'oge/moboha*-type lexemes a different pattern emerges. It is grammatical for a *to'oge/moboha*-type lexeme to appear in the same NP as other modification, as seen in (33)–(38). In all cases the *to'oge/moboha*-type lexeme must precede the other modification.

(33) te ana to'oge l<um>ule
CORE child big naked<SI>
'the big naked child'

(34) *te ana lumule to'oge

(35) te ana to'oge nu tolida=su
CORE child big GEN cousin=1SG.GEN
'the big child of my cousin'

(36) *te ana nu tolidasu to'oge

(37) te ana to'oge akala
CORE child big trick
'the big tricky child'

(38) *te ana akala to'oge

When we try to construct a phrase with two *to'oge/moboha*-type lexemes, as in (39) and (40), we find that the strategies that have been used are not adequate to produce grammatical phrases, regardless of the order of the two modifiers.

(39) *te ana to'oge kabongo
CORE child big deaf
'the big deaf child'

(40) *te ana kabongo to'oge

It is possible to rescue the grammaticality of a translation of 'the big deaf child'. The morphosyntax that allows this is shown in (41), and involves treating the second *to'oge/moboha*-type lexeme as a verb. The order of these two modifiers is now quite fixed, with the (obligatorily) infixed modifier *k<um>abongo* obligatorily appearing in the second position following the noun; effectively, the second adjective is coded in a relative clause.

(41) te ana to'oge k<um>abongo
CORE child big deaf<SI>
'the big deaf child'

(42) *te ana k<um>abongo to'oge

In fact, the *<um>* infix can be used with any *to'oge/moboha*-type lexemes, but it has morphosyntactic and semantic consequences. Firstly, when a *to'oge/moboha*-type lexeme is affixed with *<um>* it can no longer appear preceding a genitive clitic, as in (43). Secondly, if the infix appears on the only *to'oge/moboha*-type lexeme in a phrase, that modifier acquires a superlative reading.

(43) te ana=su t<um>o'oge
CORE child=1SG.GEN big
'my biggest child'

(44) *te ana t<um>o'oge=su

We can summarise the behaviour of the *to'oge/moboha*-type lexemes with respect to the other word classes we have examined as shown in Table 5. Here Y indicates the head noun of an NP that is modified.

Table 5. Morphosyntactic properties examined for different word groupings

	noun	**precategorial**	**verb**	***to'oge* etc.**
Referential	*te* X	*te* X	*te* X<*um*>	*te* $X_{\text{no *ma-}}$
Attributive	*nu* X	X	X<*um*>	X
Predicative	*te* X	*no*-X	*no*-X	*no*-X
Position in NP ~ =GEN	*te* Y=GEN *nu* X *te* Y *nu* X=GEN	*te* Y=GEN X	*te* Y=GEN X<*um*>	*te* Y X=GEN
Iterative in NP?	yes	yes	yes	no

It is clear that the *to'oge/moboha*-type lexemes show as much differentiation from the other word classes as those other word classes do within themselves. Just as is the case for precategorial roots, much of the morphosyntax of these lexemes is calqued from that found with nouns or verbs, in the sense that there is no unique, dedicated morphology found with this word class, but that the morphosyntax of different word classes is 'borrowed' by the *to'oge/moboha*-type lexemes in different syntactic environments. At the same time there is enough internal semantic consistency (all of these lexemes are property concepts) to demand that they be treated as a separate word class: adjectives.[11]

Some of the criteria that we used to establish nouns and verbs do not apply to adjectives. Particularly, there are no morphological processes that derive adjectives. We have seen the use of noun-deriving and verb-deriving affixes, shown again in (45). By comparison there is no uniquely adjectival morphology.

(45)

		nominal root	precategorial root	verbal root
		lante 'floor'	*tomba* 'mud'	*pepe* 'slap'
he-	verbaliser	*he-lante* 'make / lay a floor'	*he-tomba* 'smear with mud'	**he-pepe*
-'*a*	nominaliser	**lante-'a*	*tomba-'a* 'muddiness'	*pepe-'a* 'slap (n.)'

We should mention the historical prefix *ma-, that is found on the majority of adjectives (see Donohue 2004a for a list of lexemes with and without this affix) (this is the affix that is lost when an adjective is used referentially, as seen in (17b) and Table 4). In modern Tukang Besi this historical prefix is all but fused to the root, and appears in a number of different, mostly fixed, shapes.

(46) mo-boha 'large'
me-dampa 'short'
ma-'eka 'afraid, frightened'

There is a productive modern prefix, *mo-*, the shape of which matches the most common (and most regular) reflex of **ma-*, and the meaning of which (anticausative, resulting state) is similar enough to the semantics of the adjectives to make us suspect that this might be an adjective-deriving affix. The use of this affix is shown in (47).

(47) a. No-riwa='e na karatasi=su.
3R-tear=3P NOM paper=1SG.GEN
'She tore my paper.'
b. No-mo-riwa na karatasi=su.
3R-ANTICAUS-tear NOM paper=1SG.GEN
'My paper is torn.'

Forms such as (47b) do not, however, contain an adjective, as can be seen by examining *moriwa* in an NP-internal attributive use.

(48) te karatasi=su mo-riwa
CORE paper=1SG.GEN ANTICAUS-tear
'my torn paper'

(49) te karatasi moriwa=su

Further differences between productively-derived *mo-* forms and the adjectives with a 'fused' *mo-* are listed in Donohue (2004a).

5. The position and realisation of adjectives

The data seen in the previous section support the idea that there is a special constituent, which I shall call N' for the moment, and which maximally consists of a noun and an adjective; the adjective is in effect incorporated (see also Baker 2003) into the noun. Phonological evidence for this is present in the form of stress shifting. Stress is normally penultimate, and with an adjective (but not other modifiers) this primary stress (which is easily discernible due to a marked high, flat contour) optionally shifts to the penultimate position of the N + Adj unit. In (50a) to (50c) we see that the two words, the noun and its modifier, always form separate domains for the purposes of stress assignment. In (50d), on the other hand, both a phrasing with two prosodic domains and one with a single prosodic domain are possible. That is, the noun and adjective form a single, five-syllable stress unit.

(50) a. Te 'obu [$_{DEM}$ ana] [tɛ ‘ʔoɓɯ ˈana], * [tɛ ˌʔoɓɯ ˈana]
b. Te 'obu [$_{DP}$ nu tolidasu] [tɛ ‘ʔoɓɯ nɯ ˌtoliˈɗasɯ], * [tɛ ʔoˌɓɯ nɯ ˌtoliˈɗasɯ]
c. Te 'obu [$_{RC}$ tuminti] [tɛ ‘ʔoɓɯ tɯˈmɪnti], * [tɛ ʔoˌɓɯ tuˈmɪnti]
d. Te 'obu [$_{ADJ}$ to‘oge] [tɛ ‘ʔoɓɯ toˈʔogɛ] ~ [tɛ ʔoˌɓɯ toˈʔogɛ]

These facts, the restrictions on the number of unmarked attributive adjectives, the position with respect to genitive clitic pronouns, and the pattern of stress shift, suggest an NP structure with the following relationships (ignoring the details of the rest of the NP structure):

(51)

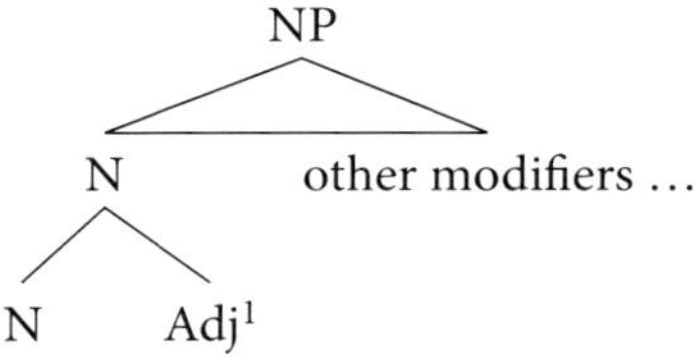

We have already seen that the basic morphosyntax associated with adjectives in predicative functions is identical to that found with verbs. In this section we shall see that other aspects of the behaviour of adjectives are identical to verbs when predicative, in contrast to nouns.

A difference between nouns and verbs in predicative positions is the ability of verbs to take the aspectual clitics *=mo =ho* and *=do*. Not all verbs may easily appear with all clitics, but all can appear with *=mo*. The clitics show the following distinctions.

(52) a. Te 'obu no-tinti=mo.
CORE dog 3R-run=PF
'The dog is running / has run.'
b. Te 'obu no-tinti=ho.
CORE dog 3R-run=still
'The dog is still running.'
c. Te 'obu no-tinti=do.
CORE dog 3R-run=EMPH
'The dog is running first.'

These clitics cannot be used to mark aspect with nominal predicates. Any aspectual information must be presented with separate particles, as in (53b), or with auxiliary verbs, (53c). Another option for inchoative readings is for the (bare) noun to incorporate into the verb *jari* 'become' (but not its synonym *membali* 'become').[12]

(53) a. Te ia te guru.
CORE 3SG CORE teacher
'He's a teacher.'

b. Te ia mondo te guru.
CORE 3SG already CORE teacher
'He's already a teacher.'

c. Te ia ane=ho te guru.
CORE 3SG exist=still CORE teacher
'He's still a teacher.'

d. Te ia no-jari guru=mo.
CORE 3SG 3R-become teacher=PF
'He's already become a teacher.'

(54) a. *Te ia te gurumo.
b. *Te ia te guruho.
c. *Te ia te gurudo.

With adjectives, the same set of clitics are used as were seen in verbs, and with the same meanings.[13]

(55) a. Te 'obu no-to'oge=mo.
CORE dog 3R-big=PF
'The dog is big / has become big already.'

b. Te 'obu no-to'oge=ho.
CORE dog 3R-big=still
'The dog is still big.'

c. Te 'obu no-to'oge=do.
CORE dog 3R-big=EMPH
'The dog is big, as it's most salient characteristic.'

Not only do adjectives take the agreement markers associated with verbs, but they also take the full range of aspectual marking, with the same set of meanings. (Neither adjectives nor verbs may appear with these clitics when they are in attributive functions inside NPs; in those cases the nominal aspect markers seen in (53) must be used.)

Another trait that predicative adjectives share with verbs, but not with nouns is the ability to take a complement.

(56) Te ana=no [$_{VP}$ no-to'oge [$_{PP}$ ngga te anu=su]].
CORE child=3GEN 3R-big than CORE whatsit=1SG.GEN
'Their child is bigger than my one.'

This information, combined with the fact that attributive adjectives are also eligible for the full range of verbal relative clause marking when forced away from the head, further suggests that adjectives, when dominated by a VP, must appear as the head of that VP, either through incorporating into an existing verb, or into an empty verbal position.

(57)

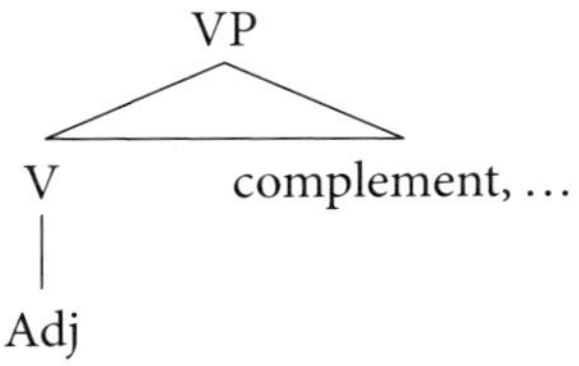

When the adjective appears in a phrase headed by an N, then it must appear as (part of) the head of that phrase; this is accomplished through incorporation with the nominal head (if present), a strategy only available for one adjective. A second (or third) adjective modifying in an NP must appear in a relative clause, where it is in a VP, and so must appear as the head of that phrase, as the item that in a main clause carries the agreement morphology and any aspect marking, and when subordinate must appear with a subordinating infix <*um*>.

We thus have a word class which is distinct from either nouns or verbs, but which only appears with the morphosyntactic characteristics of either nouns or verbs, depending on the environment in which it is found. When in an NP, the adjective must appear as (part of) the head of the NP, either through being the only referring expression ('the big [one]', where [one] is not realised in Tukang Besi) and appearing in the N^0 position, or through incorporating into a position very close to the noun. When predicative, the adjective must appear in a VP: the examples we have seen offer no evidence for incorporation, but it should be noted that inchoative meanings of properties can be expressed either with the perfective aspectual clitic, or with that clitic optionally attached to the adjective, which is incorporated into *jari* 'become', as in footnote 11. Both these options are seen in (58).

(58) a. Te ana=su iso [$_{\text{vp}}$ no-to'oge=mo].
CORE child=1SG.GEN yon 3R-big=PF
'My child has gotten big / has grown up.'

b. Te ana=su iso [$_{\text{vp}}$ no-jari-to'oge=mo].
CORE child=1SG.GEN yon 3R-become-big=PF
'My child has become big / has grown up.'

Jari is an otherwise normally inflecting verb in Tukang Besi, capable of appearing independently without an incorporated element, in (59a), or with an incorporated noun, in (59b).

(59) a. No-jari=mo na ganda ako te karia'a.
3R-become=PF NOM orchestra for CORE circumcision.festival
'The orchestra for the circumcision festival has come together.'

b. No-jari-raja=mo.
3R-become-king=PF
'He became king.'

The fact that an alternative to the adjective-as-verb treatment when predicative, namely the incorporation of the adjective into a normal verb, exists can be taken as evidence for a more abstract incorporation explaining the occurrences of adjectives when there is no overt verb: the adjective has incorporated into an 'empty' verb filling the V position.

6. Conclusions

We have seen that even in a language without dedicated adjectival morphology (such as Tukang Besi), we can find reasons to need to recognise the syntactic category of adjective. Adjectives lack any expressive morphosyntax of their own, and can only be expressed through the morphology, and structural positions, appropriate to nouns and verbs. With the treatment of adjectives in Tukang Besi we can see that there is the possibility of having an underlying syntactic category that is inexpressible at the surface, but which rides on the morphological and syntactic characteristics of other syntactic categories. In Tukang Besi the adjective can only appear under an N node if it is dominated by an NP, compounding with a pre-existent head noun if necessary, and under the V node if it is in a VP. There is no unique morphology for adjectives, and yet they are clearly shown to be a separate syntactic category.

Notes

1. Some of the data found here appeared as Donohue (1999b), though the presentation has been substantially changed to reflect further investigation. The notion of 'covert' word classes is similar to Whorf's (1945) notion of the *cryptotype*.

2. The following abbreviations have been used: 1, 2, 3 stand for first, second and third person; A, S, P stand for the most agentive and most patientive arguments of a transitive verb and the single argument of an intransitive verb, respectively. The other glosses used are: ADJ, adjective; ANTICAUS, anticausative; CORE, core case; DEM, demonstrative; EMPH, emphatic; GEN, genitive; NEG, negator; NMLZR, nominaliser; NOM, nominative; PA, paucal; PF, perfective; PL, plural; R, realis; RC, relative clause; SG, singular; SI, S,A infix; VRBLZR_1, verbaliser 1; VRBLZR_2, verbaliser 2.

3. The interested reader is referred to Croft (1991), especially pages 66, 67, for further discussion of this approach to the determination of lexical categories. Here I shall simply note that a multi-dimensional approach such as this one produces a more testable and defined answer to the question of lexical category membership than does, for instance, simply examining one morphosyntactic property in one function.

4. Since the main purpose of this article is not to discuss precategoriality, but rather the 'covert' class of adjectives, I shall not discuss them beyond the next few pages. See Enfield (2006) for a careful treatment of some of the methodological issues involved in positing precategoriality.

5. Example (7c) might be taken to imply that a predicative precategorial root has an inchoative sense: 'become X'. This is not the case, as can be judged from the two examples below. The first example is a textual extract, spoken by a woman who has been travelling disguised as a man. The second example is a typical Tukang Besi statement involving a predicative use of *wowine* 'woman'; in both cases there is no inchoative sense (and little, if any, semantic difference between the two clauses; conceivably (ii) allows for a slightly more forgrounded subject than in (i), but the difference, if any, is slight).

(i) Bara no-dahani=aku kua ku-wowine.
don't 3R-know=1SG.P COMP 1SG-woman
'Don't let them realise that I'm a woman.'

(ii) Te iaku te wowine.
CORE 1SG CORE woman
'I am a woman.'

6. Although this lexeme has a fairly real-world referential 'feel' to it, the same behaviour is found with other lexical items such as *ahaji* 'Sunday', *atiho* 'sneeze', *da'olaro* 'angry', *gau* 'desire, wish' and *gere* 'fight'. It is clear that there is no one clearly defined semantic type that matches the precategorial roots, though it is true that most real-world objects are treated precategorially in Tukang Besi, usually with either an instrumental or inchoative sense when used with verbal morphology. Some examples are given in (i)–(iv) below.

(i) a. te ba'e
CORE fruit
'fruit'

b. No-ba'e.
3R-fruit
'It's bearing fruit.' / 'It's ripened to become fruit.'

(ii) a. te ahaji
CORE Sunday
'Sunday'

b. No-ahaji.
3R-Sunday
'It's becoming Sunday.'

(iii) a. te ha'o
CORE hammer
'hammer'

b. No-ha'o.
3R-hammer
'He/She/They are hammering (something).'

(iv) a. te hoti
CORE food/drink
'meal'

b. No-hoti.
3R-donate.food/drink.or.clothes.to.the.poor
'He/She gives (food or old clothing) to the poor.'

7. Interestingly there are more affixes that derive verbs than there are nominal-deriving affixes.

8. The two verbs glossed as 'big', *to'oge* and *moboha*, have mainly the same semantic extensions, though *moboha* is more likely to be used with the meaning 'grand, spectacular'; both are in normal use when referring to size.

9. This provides an interesting counter to Croft's (1991) claim that property concepts will never appear with more morphology in attributive functions than they do in referential or predicative functions. Other examples (for instance, the behaviour of adjectives in German, which require more morphological material when attributive than when predicative) also support the view that Croft's claims are not universals, but merely tendencies across languages.

10. Any order that places the core case marker te anywhere but in initial position is not only ungrammatical, but uninterpretable for Tukang Besi speakers: *! *anasu te tuminti*, *! *anasu tuminti te*, etc.

11. Note that the converse of this statement is not true: not all property concepts are adjectives. For instance, while *meha* 'red', *biru* 'black', *ijo* 'green', *mokuri* 'yellow' and *mohute* 'white' are adjectives, *kakanda* 'yellow' is a verb. Similarly, while *kabongo* 'deaf' is an adjective, *kandala* 'blind' is a verb.

12. One clitic, =*mo*, may be used with some nominal predicates, but with a different, non-aspectual meaning. With nouns =*mo* serves to emphasise identity. In this function it probably represents a calque from Makasar Malay, in which -*mi* has both the perfective function and the emphatic identification function.

13. Adjectives, when used inchoatively, may also appear with *jari*, just as can nouns.

(i) Te 'obu no-jari-to'oge=mo.
CORE dog 3R-become-big=PF
'The dog has become big.

References

Baker, Mark C. 2003. *Lexical categories: verbs, nouns, and adjectives*. Cambridge: Cambridge University Press.

Croft, William. 1991. *Syntactic categories and grammatical relations: the cognitive organization of information*. Chicago, IL: University of Chicago Press.

Donohue, Mark. 1999a. *A grammar of Tukang Besi*. Berlin: Mouton de Gruyter.

Donohue, Mark. 1999b. Syntactic categories in Tukang Besi / À propos des catégories syntaxiques. *Revue Québécoise de Linguistique* 27 (2): 71–90.

Donohue, Mark. 2002. Voice in Tukang Besi and the Austronesian voice system. *The history and typology of western Austronesian voice systems*, Fay Wouk & Malcolm Ross (eds.), 81–99. Canberra: Pacific Linguistics 518.

Donohue, Mark. 2004a. Proto-Oceanic **ma*- and the adjectives: Oceanic as seen through possibly productive morphology in Tukang Besi. *Oceanic Linguistics* 43 (1): 149–176.

Donohue, Mark. 2004b. Voice oppositions without voice morphology. *Proceedings of AFLA 11, ZAS, Berlin 2004* (*ZAS Papers in Linguistics* 34), Paul Law (ed.), 73–88. Berlin: Zentrum für Allgemeine Sprachwissenschaft, Typologie und Universalienforschung.

Donohue, Mark. 2006. Verb-inital in non-verbal clauses? Paper presented at the *13th Annual Meeting of the Austronesian Formal Linguistics Association*. Graduate Institute of Linguistics, National Tsing Hua University and Institute of Linguistics, Academia Sinica. Hsinchu, Taiwan, March 2006.

Donohue, Mark. 2008. Case in an Austronesian language: Distinguishing case functions in Tukang Besi. *Handbook of Case*, Andrej Malchukov & Andrew Spencer (eds.). Oxford: Oxford University Press.

Enfield, Nick. 2006. Heterosemy and the grammar-lexicon trade-off. *Catching language: the standing challenge of grammar writing*, Felix Ameka, Alan Dench & Nicholas Evans (eds.), 1–24. Berlin: Mouton de Gruyter.

Usmar, Adnan, A. Kadir Manyambeang, J.F. Pattiasina & Zainuddin Hakim. 1991. *Morfologi dan sintaksis Bahasa Binongko*. Jakarta: Departemen pendidikan dan kebudayaan.

Whorf, Benjamin. 1945. Grammatical categories. *Language* 21(1): 1–11.

Author's address

Mark Donohue
Centre for Research on Language Change
The Australian National University
ACT 0200
Australia

mark@donohue.cc

Pragmatic factors in the development of a switch-adjective language

A case study of the Miyako-Hirara dialect of Ryukyuan

Yulia Koloskova and Toshio Ohori
University of Tokyo

The Miyako-Hirara dialect of Ryukyuan is a switch-adjective language, i.e. it employs both nominal and verbal strategies for its adjectival roots. The choice of the encoding option in the predicative position depends on the information structure of the sentence. If a predicative adjective is in the focus domain, the nominal strategies (adjectival root + *munu,* reduplicated forms) are used. If a predicative adjective belongs to the presupposition, the verbal strategy (*-kaɨ* forms) is employed. We argue that Miyako-Hirara employs a switch-adjective encoding in order to retain the functional distinction between the predicates in focus and those in the domain of presupposition, in the absence of other means of morphological marking for the informational status of constituents.

1. Introduction

In the typology of parts of speech systems, adjectives have played an important role due to their fluid status across languages. In this paper, we focus on the Miyako-Hirara dialect of Ryukyuan (a sister language of Japanese) and explore the various strategies which the language employs to encode adjectives in the predicative function. More specifically, Miyako-Hirara has both nominal and verbal strategies for predicative adjectives, and the aim of this paper is to reveal the factors that determine the choice of an encoding option. We argue that in Miyako-Hirara the distribution of nominal and verbal strategies is motivated by pragmatic factors, namely the informational status of the predicate. It will be shown that the switch-adjective system of Miyako-Hiarara is motivated by the need for the functional distinction between predicates in focus and those in the domain of presupposition, in the absence of other means of morphological marking.

The paper is organized as follows. Section 2 summarizes the attempts to define adjectives as a part of speech in the typological literature and introduces the phenomenon of a switch-adjective language. Section 3 deals with adjectives in Miyako-Hirara. Section 3.1 introduces basic facts about the language, Section 3.2 presents an overview of its adjectival paradigm and Section 3.3 discusses the distribution of nominal and verbal strategies mainly in the predicative position. In Section 4, we discuss the usage of predicative adjectives in other dialects of Ryukyuan and show that they do not involve a switch between nominal and verbal strategies, and that the switch-adjective phenomenon in Miyako-Hirara is a unique innovation. In Section 5, we discuss possible motivations for the nominal-verbal switch in Miyako-Hirara. Finally, some conclusions are given in Section 6.

2. Theoretical background

2.1 Adjectives in typological perspective

It has never been a simple task to provide a cross-linguistically valid definition of the lexical category "adjective". Dixon (1982) examined a number of languages that have a small closed class of adjectives and discovered a strong semantic regularity. Thus, he proposed prototypical "property concepts" such as DIMENSION, AGE, VALUE and COLOUR and less prototypical ones such as PHYSICAL PROPERTIES, HUMAN PROPENSITIES and SPEED. The inventory of cross-linguistically valid semantic classes of property concept words has been employed in typological studies on adjectival predicates (Wetzer 1996; Stassen 1997). Other typological studies on adjectives include Hengeveld (1992: 37), who proposed a syntactic definition of adjectives: "An adjectival predicate is a predicate which, without further measures being taken, can be used as a modifier of a nominal head," and Thompson (1988), who attempts to account for the cross-linguistic fluidity of adjectives by appealing to the different discourse functions adjectives may perform.

It is typologically a commonplace that adjectives are often intermediate in their grammatical characteristics between the two major categories of nouns and verbs. It has been proposed in the literature that the strategy of adjectival encoding ("verby" or "nouny") is determined by the structural characteristics of a language: the tensedness parameter[1] (Wetzer 1996; Stassen 1997) or head vs. dependent marking[2] (Dixon 2004).

2.2 Switch-adjective languages

While property concept words tend to pattern with either verbs or nouns in the predicative position, there are languages that can employ both "nouny" and "verby" morpho-syntactic strategies for their property concept words. Wetzer (1996: 80) defines such languages as a switch-adjective type. Let us consider predicative adjectives in Mundari, an Austro-Asiatic language spoken in India. The categorial status of Mundari adjectives is not fixed. They may occur as complements of the copula *menaq* 'to be' (1a) as nouns do, or be treated as intransitive verbs (1b) (Langendoen 1967: 85, adopted from Wetzer 1996: 80).

(1) a. hodo-ko marang menaq-ko-akan-a[3]
man-PL tall COP-3PL-PERF-PREDICATOR
'The men have been tall.'
b. hodo-ko marang-akan-a-ko
man-PL tall-PERF-PREDICATOR-3PL
'The men have been tall.'

Switch-adjective languages pose an interesting problem for the typological characterization of adjectives because they do not seem to validate previously proposed typological parameters for the choice of encoding strategies, such as the possibility of tense marking (Wetzer 1996; Stassen 1997) or head vs. dependent marking (Dixon 2004). Thus the question to be answered is whether the switch like the one observed above is a matter of free variation or whether there are any stronger determinants at work. Stassen (1997: 178) argues that in a switch-adjective language the choice of a morphosyntactic strategy for predicative encoding is controlled by the time stability principle formulated as follows:

(2) The universal of adjectival V-N-switching
In languages with verbal-nominal-switching for adjectives, the nominal option will always encode the more time stable reading.

On the other hand, Holton (1999) in his analysis of the switch-adjective language Tobelo, demonstrates that the crucial factor behind the switch is not a semantic one, but lies in the discourse-based notion of referentiality: nominal property words tend to modify nouns introducing new referents and verbal property words tend to modify already established referents. His results are consonant with Thompson's (1988) study which argues that the mixed categoriality of adjectives can be explained by the discourse functions of property words, since they are employed to modify established referents (as verbs do) and to introduce new referents (as nouns do).

In what follows, we present a case study of a switch-adjective language that exhibits yet another type of pragmatic motivation for the choice of encoding strategy.

3. Adjectives in the Miyako-Hirara dialect of Ryukyuan

3.1 Preliminaries

Miyako is a dialect of Ryukyuan (Luchuan), a sister language of Japanese spoken on the Okinawan archipelago that stretches between the Japanese island of Kyushu and

Taiwan in the Pacific. There is an ongoing discussion in the literature whether to regard Ryukyuan as a group of Japanese dialects or as a language in its own right (Shibatani 1990: 189–196; Matsumori 1993). However, this point will not be considered in the present paper. The Ryukyuan dialects are divided into three major groups: Amami-Okinawa dialects, Miyako-Yaeyama dialects and Yonaguni dialects. The Miyako dialect belongs to the Miyako-Yaeyama group and is spoken on Miyako island, which lies 290 km to the south-west from Okinawa island. It is an endangered language: the number of its speakers does not exceed 8,500 people by the most optimistic estimate. They are mostly over 60 years old and bilingual in their dialect and standard Japanese. The Miyako dialect belongs to the nominative-accusative type and demonstrates a SOV basic word order. The nominal morphology combines agglutinative and fusional features, while the verbal morphology is mostly fusional.

The data for the present paper were obtained during four field trips conducted by one of the authors between 2004 and 2006 in the city of Hirara and represent the Miyako-Hirara variety of the Miyako dialect. We also use the data from two other sources: Shibata (1972), which consists mainly of dialogs recorded from the speakers of Miyako-Hirara, and Namihira (1990), a collection of folktales representing the variety spoken on the southern part of Miyako island.

3.2 Morphology of adjectives

Property concept words in Miyako-Hirara form a grammatically distinct open class of lexemes that is characterized by rich variety of forms[4] (Izuyama 2002; Karimata 2002; Motonaga 2001). They match the criteria of an "adjective class" proposed by Dixon (2004: 44), i.e. they:

(3) a. are grammatically distinct from noun class and verb class;
  b. include words from some or all of the prototypical adjective semantic types — DIMENSION, AGE, VALUE, and COLOUR;
  c. (i) function either as intransitive predicates or as copula complements and/or (ii) modify a noun in a NP.

In this paper, we will mostly deal with the predicative usage of adjectives, as this is where the switch in encoding strategy is most manifest. In Miyako-Hirara, there are three major strategies for putting an adjectival root in the predicative position: (i) by the attachment of the semantically dummy noun *munu*[5] 'thing' resulting in a nominal compound, (ii) by reduplication, and (iii) by the affixation of the formative suffix *-kaɨ*. All three strategies are summarized in Table 1, which presents their morphological manifestations in three syntactic positions, namely: actant, modifier and predicate. As Stassen (1997: 30) notes "[i]n their predicative encoding, adjectives will align themselves either with verbs (and as a result have a verbal strategy), or with nominals, or with locations." This section presents an overview of the inventory of adjectival forms

Table 1. Adjectival forms in Miyako-Hirara

	Nominal compound	Reduplication	Suffixed forms (stem *-kaɨ*)
Actant	*taka-munu (vs. taka-sa)* high-thing high-ness	*taka:taka* (highly restricted usage)	*taka-kaɨ-su* high-FS-NML
Modification	*taka-jama* high-mountain	*taka:~taka- nu jama* high-REDUP-GEN mountain	*taka-kaɨ jama* high-FS mountain
Predication	***jama: taka-munu*** **mountain.TOP high-thing**	***jama: taka:~taka*** **mountain.TOP high-REDUP**	***jama-nu=du*** **mountain-NOM=FOC** ***taka-kaɨ*** **high-FS**

in Miyako-Hirara with a special emphasis on whether certain forms share their morpho-syntactic features with verbs or nouns.

3.2.1 *Nominal compound*

First, we consider the various uses of the adjectival root in compounds. Let us start with noun modification. In Miyako-Hirara, the morphological pattern "Adjectival root + Noun" (e.g., *taka-jama* 'high-mountain') is extremely productive, creating a regular strategy for noun modification. The semantics of nominal compounds is mostly compositional though there are a few exceptions, such as *miɨ-vva* 'new-child' meaning 'a new-born' or *upu-bata* 'big-belly' meaning 'a pregnant woman'. Thus, from a semantic point of view, the meaning of such combinations is rarely lexicalized. However, various phonological and morpho-syntactic tests demonstrate that the adjectival root is not an independent word modifying a noun by juxtaposition, but forms a nominal compound with it. Thus, if the first element of the modified noun is a voiceless consonant it may become voiced, e.g. *taka+ki:>taka-gi:* 'high-tree' or *ffa+tukuru> ffa-dukuru* 'dark-place'.

Furthermore, the adjectival root in compounds (i) cannot be modified by an adverb, (ii) cannot have any syntactic complement (for example cause/instrument) of its own, and (iii) cannot modify a proper noun. Examples (4) and (5) demonstrate the latter two characteristics in comparison with the behaviors of reduplicated forms which we will turn to in a moment.

(4) *sɨgutu-sji: panta-pɨtu vs. sɨgutu-sji: panta:~panta-nu pɨtu[6]
work-INS busy-person work-INS busy-REDUP-GEN person
'a person busy with work'

(5) *baka-kendzji vs. baka:~baka-nu kendzji
young-Kenji young-REDUP-GEN Kenji
'the young Kenji'

Next, an adjectival root by itself cannot occur as a syntactic actant or as a predicate. In the actant position it either employs the suffix *-sa* forming an abstract noun denoting the property itself, e.g. *taka-sa* 'high-ness', or is attached to a semantically dummy noun *munu* 'thing' with the resulting meaning referring to the bearer of the denoted property, e.g. *taka-munu* 'high thing, the high one'.

In the predicative position, the adjectival root also employs the noun *munu*. Thus, compounds with *munu* represent the nominal predicative strategy. They may require support by a copula depending on the grammatical environment. In Miyako-Hirara, nouns do not employ the copula in the present tense but require it in the past tense. Example (6) illustrates how the "adjectival root + *munu*" compound (b) follows the pattern of the predicative noun (a).

(6) a. kunu pɨto: **sjinsji: ja-taɨ**
this person.TOP teacher COP-PST
'This man was a teacher.'

b. kunu pɨto: **taka-munu ja-taɨ**
this person.TOP high-thing COP-PST
'This man was tall.'

Another condition under which a copula is required is subordination. We will return to this point in Section 3.3.3.

At the same time, there are also differences in the grammatical behavior of *munu* compounds in the predicative position which provide criteria for distinguishing them from prototypical nouns and other compounds. In particular, they (i) may be modified by an adverb[7] and (ii) do not have the same pattern of negation as nominal predication.

Finally, adjectival roots take the suffix *-fu* when they occur as a complement of the verb *naɨ* 'become', or in collocation with various particles. The root + *-fu* form is also the form used for negating the adjectival predication, and thus adjectives do not share their negating pattern either with nouns or with verbs.

3.2.2 *Reduplication*

The reduplicated form is constructed by the repetition of an adjectival root accompanied by the gemination of the final vowel of the first root, e.g. *taka* > *taka:taka* 'high'. Narrow vowels *u* and *i* are replaced with the long mid vowels *o:* and *e:*, e.g. *pisji* > *pisje:pisji* 'cold'. The reduplicated forms behave like nouns in a number of ways. First, when they are used to modify nouns, they employ genitive marker *nu* in the attributive position.

(7) taka:~taka-nu jama vs. *taka:~taka jama
high-REDUP-GEN mountain high-REDUP mountain
'high mountain'
sjinsji:-nu sjumutsɨ vs. *sjinsji: sjumutsɨ
teacher-GEN book teacher book
'teacher's book'

Second, in its predicative use, the reduplicated adjective can appear without a copula in the present tense but requires it in the past tense and in subordinate clauses (8).

(8) kunu pɨto: **taka:~taka ja-taɨ**
this person.TOP high-REDUP COP-PST
'This man was tall.'

Third, when the reduplicated forms occur as the complement of the verb *naɨ* 'become', they take the dative case marker, and not the form with the suffix *-fu*, as in (9).

(9) a. * taka:~taka-fu naɨ vs. taka-fu naɨ
high-REDUP-ADV become high-ADV become
b. taka:~taka-n naɨ vs. sjinsji:-n naɨ
high-REDUP-DAT become teacher-DAT become
'to become high (tall)' 'to become a teacher'

There are also differences between the syntactic behavior of reduplicated forms of adjectives and that of nouns in three respects. First, the usage of the reduplicated forms of adjectives as syntactic actants is highly restricted. There are very few occurrences of reduplicated adjectives in the position of a syntactic actant and all of them involve ellipsis or afterthoughts. Second, they do not have the same pattern of negation with nominal predication. Third, reduplicated forms can be used in the adverbial position without further morphological make-up, which again distinguishes them from prototypical nouns.

(10) taka:~taka tub-i
high-REDUP fly-CVB
'flying high'

3.2.3 *Suffixation (-kaɨ forms)*

The suffixed forms with *-kaɨ* appear to share many of their syntactic and morphological properties with verbs. First, both verbs and suffixed forms of adjectives can be employed as modifiers in a NP without further derivation as illustrated in (11). Likewise, adjectives with the *-kaɨ* suffix require no further derivation when they occur as predicates, as illustrated in (12).

(11) budur-i uɨ midumvva vs. taka-kaɨ jama
dance-CVB be girl high-FS mountain
'dancing girl' 'high mountain'

(12) midumvva: budur-i uɨ vs. jama-nu=du taka-kaɨ
girl.TOP dance-CVB be mountain-NOM=FOC high-FS
'a girl is dancing' 'mountain is high'

Second, in order to fill a slot of a syntactic actant, both verbs and suffixed forms of adjectives need to be nominalized with the suffix *-su*. Finally, verbs and suffixed forms of adjectives do not need a copula either in the past tense or in subordinate clauses.

(13) a. kunu pɨto: **niv:-taɨ** /*niv: ja-taɨ
this person.TOP sleep-PST sleep COP-PST
'This man slept.'

b. kunu pɨtu-nu=du **taka-ka-taɨ** /*taka-kaɨ ja-taɨ
this person-NOM=FOC high-FS-PST high-FS COP-PST
'This man was tall.'

In subordinate clauses, the *-kaɨ* suffixed adjective occurs with a variety of allomorphs that are morphologically parallel to those of the copula: *-kaɨ, -kara, -kari, -kai* etc. In addition, there is also a suffix *-kam* that can be used only in the main clause with special pragmatics which will be discussed in detail in Section 5 when we turn to the motivations that lie behind the switch-adjective pattern in Miyako-Hirara.

The *-kaɨ* suffixed forms of adjectives can be also distinguished from verbs based on several criteria. Thus, adjectives allow a more limited range for TAM elaboration and do not undergo voice derivations. As opposed to verbs, *-kaɨ* forms lack negative forms and do not co-occur with topic and focus particles, as *-fu* forms discussed in 3.2.1 perform these functions.

To summarize, there are three major strategies for putting adjectival roots into use in Miyako-Hirara: (i) nominal compounds formed by the attachment of the semantically dummy noun *munu* 'thing' to an adjectival root, (ii) reduplication, and (iii) the suffixation of *-kaɨ*. The first two forms represent nominal strategies; the last one is a

Table 2. Nominal and verbal strategies for adjectival predicates in Miyako-Hirara

	Nouns	Adjectives			Verbs
		Adjectival root + *munu*	Reduplication	Suffixed forms (*-kaɨ*)	
Genitive marker in the attributive position	+	N/A	+	–	–
Syntactic actant	+	+	Highly restricted	–	–
Nominalizer *-su*	–	–	–	+	+
Attributive and predicative forms	Different	Different	Different	Same	Same
Copula in the past tense and subordinate clauses	+	+	+	–	–
Strategy		Nominal	Nominal	Verbal	

verbal strategy of encoding. The morpho-syntactic features of these three strategies are summarized and compared with verbs and nouns in Table 2.

3.2.4 *Miyako-Hirara as a switch-adjective language*

As we observed in the preceding subsections, predicative adjectives in Miyako-Hirara use three different strategies of encoding. Two strategies, namely *munu* compounds and reduplication share their morpho-syntactic properties with nouns, while *-kaɨ* suffixation represents a verbal strategy. At this point, some justifications of our treatment of Miyako-Hirara as a switch-adjective language may be in order, as all three strategies involve some kind of elaboration on the adjectival root, which is most clearly seen in the formation of predicative adjectives. In his definition of a switch-adjective language, Wetzer excludes so-called "secondary" adjectivals from consideration. By "secondary" adjectivals he means "overtly derived adjectival forms which may be used predicatively alongside the non-derived 'primary' adjectivals from which they originate" (Wetzer 1996: 78). How does this characterization apply to the case of Miyako-Hirara?

The position we take regarding Miyako-Hirara is that all three strategies are primary, if we adequately narrow down the notion of "(overtly) derived". One striking fact about the adjectival expressions under investigation is that adjectival roots may not occur in the predicative position by themselves, and there is no way to tell whether one strategy (e.g. *-kaɨ* suffixation) is "derived" from any other (e.g. reduplication). In this sense, adjectives cannot be divided into "primary" and "secondary" forms. Since there is no "unmarked" strategy for putting adjectival roots into use, the three strategies in question are not strictly cases of overt derivation but should be better understood in more neutral terms as elaborations on the root. In this sense, there are no "secondary" forms, and hence Miyako-Hirara is duly regarded as a switch-adjective language.

Furthermore, the three derived forms demonstrate a number of features that distinguish them from verbs and nouns. We have already seen that *munu* compounds may be modified by adverbs and behave differently from nouns when they are negated (3.2.1) and that reduplicated forms are very rarely used as syntactic actants, may occur in the adverbial position, and employ a different negation pattern (3.2.2). On the other hand, *-kaɨ* suffixed forms can be distinguished from verbs in a variety of respects (3.2.3). All these facts allow us to distinguish between nominal and verbal adjectives on the one hand and prototypical verbs and nouns on the other.

3.3 Pragmatic functions of nominal and verbal strategies

Now that we have introduced the variety of predicative strategies for adjectives in Miyako-Hirara a crucial question arises: what motivates the choice among the morphological forms for expressing predicative adjectives? We claim that there are pragmatic factors at work: the choice of a predicate is primarily determined by the information structure of the sentence.

3.3.1 *Focus types*

Our approach to information structure adopted in this paper builds upon the theory of focus types developed in Lambrecht (1994).[8] Since there is a lot of disagreement and confusion regarding the terminology describing the information structure of a sentence, we will briefly introduce some basic aspects of Lambrecht's theory. Lambrecht uses three basic theoretical concepts: pragmatic presupposition, pragmatic assertion and focus.

(14) PRAGMATIC PRESUPPOSITION: The set of propositions lexicogrammatically evoked in a sentence which the speaker assumes the hearer already knows or is ready to take for granted at the time the sentence is uttered (Lambrecht 1994: 52).
PRAGMATIC ASSERTION: The proposition expressed by a sentence which the hearer is expected to know or take for granted as a result of hearing the sentence uttered (Lambrecht 1994: 52).
FOCUS: The semantic component of a pragmatically structured proposition whereby the assertion differs from the presupposition (Lambrecht 1994: 213).

Lambrecht's approach is based on the idea that "the focus articulations of sentences can be divided into a number of distinct TYPES which correspond to different kinds of pragmatically structured propositions" (Lambrecht 1994: 221). Thus, the scope of the focus domain may stretch over the whole sentence, the predicative part of the proposition, or just a single constituent. Lambrecht differentiates three distinct focus types: predicate-focus structure, argument-focus structure (also known as narrow-focus structure) and sentence-focus structure. We will concentrate on the predicate-focus vs. argument-focus distinction[9] as this is crucial to the following discussion.

The predicate-focus type corresponds to the predicative part of the proposition, which consists of two elements: a topic of discourse denoted by the subject and the comment about the topic expressed by the predicate. Lambrecht (1994: 223) illustrates this focus type with the following example.

(15) What happened to your car?
My car/it broke DOWN.

In (15), the speaker's car is pragmatically available as a topic of conversation and the predicate expresses the comment about the topic. The predicate-focus structure is universally the unmarked focus type and coincides with the traditionally recognized "topic-comment" organization of information in the sentence. It is important to note that the predicate-focus structure represents a broad type of focus that does not evoke any contrastive reading. In Miyako-Hirara the subject of the predicate-focus type clause is either marked with a topic particle or simply omitted.

The argument-focus (narrow-focus) type is a case where the focus domain covers a single constituent and the rest of the proposition is presupposed. Lambrecht (1994: 223) provides the following example.

(16) I heard your motorcycle broke down?
My CAR broke down.

The answer in (16) represents a presupposed proposition 'speaker's X broke down' with an open slot X. The communicative function of the argument-focus structure is to identify this unfilled slot. Thus, in argument-focus structure the focus domain is limited to a constituent that fills an empty slot in the presupposed proposition. This focus structure characterizes Question-Word questions and their answers as well as contrastive readings. In Miyako-Hirara the focused constituent is marked with a focus particle.

The third type, namely the sentence-focus type, represents the whole sentence within the focus domain in the absence of any presupposed elements.

3.3.2 *Predicative adjectives in main clauses*

In Miyako-Hirara, the difference between the focus types is marked not only by prosodic means but also morphologically. In the predicate-focus structure the subject is marked by a topic particle *ja* (which can be fused with the final vowel of the nominal stem in certain phonetic environments) or omitted altogether. In the argument-focus structure the focus constituent is marked by one of the focus particles *ga, nu* or *du* according to the illocutionary force of an utterance. Particle *ga* is employed to mark the focus constituent in a Question-Word question, *nu* is employed in a yes-no question and *du* in a declarative sentence.

Upon closer inspection, predicative adjectives in the main clause demonstrate a clear-cut distribution: nominal strategies (nominal compounds and reduplication) are employed in the predicate-focus constructions while the verbal strategy (suffixed forms) occurs in the argument-focus structures. Compare examples (17) and (18). (17) represents an unmarked structure where the noun phrase *kunu jama* 'this mountain' is pragmatically available as a topic of ongoing discourse and marked with a topic particle fused with the stem. On the other hand, (18) requires a contrastive reading where the focus domain is limited to the NP *kunu jama* 'this mountain' followed by a focus particle.

(17) kunu jama: **taka-munu** /**taka:~taka** /*taka-kaɨ
this mountain.TOP high-thing /high-REDUP/ high-FS
'This mountain is high.'

(18) kunu jama-nu=**du** *taka-munu /*taka:~taka /**taka-kaɨ**
this mountain-NOM=FOC high-thing / high-REDUP /high-FS
'THIS MOUNTAIN is high.'

In other words, if a predicative adjective is within the focus domain of the proposition (i.e. part of the predicate-focus structure), it selects either of the nominal strategies of encoding. If it occurs as part of the presupposition (i.e. in the argument-focus structure) it employs the verbal strategy. (19) is a further example of the predicate-focus structure where the proposition consists solely of the predicative part.

(19) **atsɨ-munu=ja:** /**atsɨ:~atsɨ=ja:** /*atsɨ-kaɨ=ja:
hot-thing=PART hot-REDUP=PART hot-FS=PART
'It is hot.'

On the other hand, (20) and (21) represent examples of an argument-focus structure. In (20) the speaker talks about traditional boat races that are popular on different islands of the Okinawan archipelago. He claims that from all of them he finds the one organized on Miyako island to be particularly interesting. Here there is a contrastive reading implied. Since in Miyako-Hirara adjectives do not have a special morphological comparative or superlative form, (20) can also acquire a comparative reading. Actually, the semantic difference between the readings "The Miyako hari-boats are interesting in contrast to other races" and "The Miyako hari-boats are more interesting than other races" is quite subtle.

(20) irunna munu-nkai butstsukar-i mi:ru-ba=du a: jappari
various thing-DAT bump-CVB see-CONJ=FOC FIL after.all
mja:ku-nu **ha:ri:-nu=du** no:tji:nja:n **umussi-kaɨ**=sa:
Miyako-GEN hari.boat-NOM=FOC somehow interesting-FS=PART
'I've seen a lot of things but after all it is the Miyako hari-boats that are (more) interesting' (Shibata 1972: 175).

Example (21) is a Question-Word question where the focus domain is limited to the Question-Word constituent and the predicate is in presupposition.

(21) atsɨka: **no:-nu=ga** nnapja: **zo:-kaɨ**=gara=ja:
so what-NOM=FOC more good-FS=PART=PART
'So, what is better?'

In either of the above examples, nominal strategies would not work.

3.3.3 *Predicative adjectives in subordinate clauses*

In a subordinate clause either the nominal or the verbal strategy can be employed, but the conditions of their use are different from those operating in the main clause. (22) and (23) come from natural discourse data providing examples of verbal (22) and nominal (23) strategies for predicative adjectives in subordinate clauses. Note that *-kai-* in (22) is an allomorph of the suffix *-kaɨ*.

(22) banta-ga **ko:-kai-ba** su:-dzja:n ti:
we-NOM hard-FS-CONJ do-MOD.NEG CIT
'[saying] we will not do it because it is hard for us.'

(23) asji gum=mai nabi=mai **upo:~upu ja:-ba** ui-nkai
thus kettle=also pot=also big-REDUPCOP-CONJ it-DAT
idzj-i-tsɨka: upa:sa=du uɨ=ju
put-CVB-if a.lot=FOC be=PART
'Thus, because the kettle and the pot are big, if [you] put [sweet potato] in it, there will be a lot.'

However, it is generally the case that the suffixed *-kaɨ* form (verbal strategy) is preferred. It appears more frequently in texts and is also evaluated as a more natural strategy by elicitation. As mentioned in Section 3.2, nominal forms (compounds and reduplicated forms) require a copula to fill the predicative slot in a subordinate clause while the suffixed form has a variety of allomorphs (*-kaɨ, -kai, -kara* etc). Thus, the reduplicated and compound forms (*taka:taka* and *takamunu*) without a copula result in an ungrammatical sentence, as in (24a). The reduplicated and compound forms with a copula are acceptable (24b), though the speaker evaluates the suffixed form (*takakaɨ*) as the most natural option (24c).

(24) a. * taka:~taka-tsɨka: /*taka-munu-tsɨka: ka:-dzja:n
expensive-REDUP-if expensive-thing-if buy-MOD.NEG
b. ?taka:~taka ja:-tsɨka: /?taka-munu ja:-tsɨka: ka:-dzja:n
expensive-REDUP COP-if expensive-thing COP-if buy-MOD.NEG
c. taka-kaɨ-tsɨka: ka:-dzja:n
expensive-FS-if buy-MOD.NEG
'If it is expensive, I do not buy it.'

Lambrecht (1994: 125) notes that "most adverbial clauses are marked for expressing pragmatically presupposed propositions." Thus, predicates of subordinate clauses rarely assert the information that is new to the hearer and therefore do not tend to appear in the focus domain. They rather provide some background information for the proposition expressed in the main clause. For this reason, subordinate clauses tend to be pragmatically presupposed via the rule of accommodation for presupposition (Lewis 1979). This might explain the tendency for predicative adjectives to opt for the verbal strategy of encoding. As in argument-focus structures, the predicate does not belong to the focus domain but forms a part of the presupposition.[10]

3.3.4 *"Actualizing utterances"*

Finally, there are other utterances that mark their predicative adjectives with the verbal strategy of encoding. Their function in discourse is not to express any new information, but rather to bring to the hearer's attention some familiar facts that are relevant in the present context, in other words, to activate some already shared information. Following Kalinina & Sumbatova (2007), we will call them "actualizing utterances".

Consider (25). The sequence comes from a tale of two families, rich and poor, which used to live in the same village. One day the rich family comes to their poor neighbors with a marriage proposal for their children. The father of the poor family refuses it saying that his daughter should get married to someone of her own social status.

(25) vva-ta:=ja unusɨku **ujaki-kaɨ**
you-PL=TOP so rich-FS
'You are so rich.'
banta=ja ko:-kai-ba vva-ta:-tu takja: ara-n-niba
we=TOP poor-FS-CONJ you-PL-COM equal.TOP be-NEG-CONJ.NEG
banta-ga midumvvo:=ba: du:-ga taki-nkai=du fu:-ttju:
we-GEN girl.ACC=TOP ourselves-GEN equal-DAT=FOC give-MOD
'Because we are poor, because we are not equals with you we are going to give our daughter to someone of our own status.' (Namihira 1990: 825)

The speaker obviously assumes the propositional content of the first sentence of (25) to be familiar to the hearer. The communicative point here is to highlight a part of the shared knowledge that is relevant to his decision not to accept the marriage proposal to his daughter. In this way, actualizing utterances depend on and must be understood with respect to the surrounding discourse. This discourse dependency often results in the speaker's providing the reason for his/her statement.

Thus, the verbal encoding of adjectives in this type of utterance once again marks that the predicate is pragmatically presupposed, i.e. expresses information that is already familiar to the addressee.

3.3.5 *Non-predicative usages*

While the present paper concentrates mainly on predicative adjectives, in this section we will briefly discuss the usage of verbal and nominal strategies in other syntactic positions.[11]

As Table 1 demonstrates, all three strategies (nominal compounds, reduplication and suffixed forms) can be employed in noun modification. However, there is a considerable difference in their functions. Nominal strategies represent a semantically unmarked option. The difference between the two nominal strategies is of pragmatic nature. When a new referent is introduced both compounds (e.g. *taka-jama* 'high-mountain') and reduplicated forms (e.g. *taka:~taka nu jama* 'high-REDUP GEN mountain') can be employed. However, nominal compounds are strongly preferred for the reference tracking of already introduced referents.

On the other hand, *-kaɨ* suffixed forms have a marked interpretation. As we demonstrated in Section 3.3.2, the verbal strategy evokes a contrastive reading. A suffixed form of an adjective filling an attributive position also bears a contrastive meaning. Thus, the NP *takakaɨ jama* does not just mean 'a high mountain' but rather 'a mountain that is high in contrast/in comparison to others'. In the absence of a specific morphological comparative or superlative form of adjectives in Miyako-Hirara this tends to give rise to a comparative interpretation. This specialization of meaning accounts for the low frequency of suffixed forms used as noun modifiers.

Occurrences of suffixed forms of adjectives as syntactic actants also involve some kind of contrast. Consider examples (26) and (27). (26) is uttered by a grocery store keeper in response to a request for a pack of milk. He asks about the size of the milk pack his customer would prefer.

(26) imi-kaɨ-su: upu-kaɨ-su:
small-FS-NMLZ.ACC big-FS-NMLZ.ACC
'[Would you like] a small one? Or a big one?' (Shibata 1972: 193)

Example (27) is a part of a sequence that discusses what to do with the fish the speaker just brought home. It is decided that the bigger ones will be eaten raw as sashimi and the rest will be given to the neighbors. Here again, the suffixed form evokes a contrastive reading and is followed by a contrastive topic particle *ba:*.

(27) unu **upu-kaɨ-su:**=ba: sasjimja: sji: [...] mata nukuɨ=ba:
this big-FS-NMLZ.ACC=TOP sashimi.TOP do.CVB again rest=TOP
tunazɨ-nkai naka:-rja=mai
neighbors-DAT give.away-CONJ=also
'We will make sashimi from the big ones, [...] and even if we will give the rest to the neighbors...' (Shibata 1972: 196)

3.4 Summary and a problem

Adjectival roots in Miyako-Hirara employ three major strategies for their predicative forms: compounds, reduplication and suffixation. The former two strategies share their grammatical and semantic features with nouns and the latter one with verbs. The distribution of encoding options marks the informational status of the predicate: if a predicative adjective is within the focus domain, i.e. if the property denoted by the adjective is new to the hearer, nominal strategies (adjectival root + *munu*, reduplicated forms) are used. If the existence of such a property is presupposed, i.e. the speaker assumes it to be familiar to or likely to be taken for granted by the hearer, the verbal strategy (-*kaɨ* forms) is employed. Thus, in main clauses nominal strategies are employed in predicate-focus structures while the verbal strategy is opted for in argument-focus structures. In subordinate clauses whose information tends to be pragmatically presupposed, both strategies are possible but the verbal strategy is preferred. Finally, the verbal strategy is also employed in pragmatically presupposed "actualizing utterances".

It is important to notice that the distributional pattern observed above is limited to predicative adjectives. Nouns and verbs in the predicative position do not follow this pattern of informational status marking: they occur as predicates regardless of the information structure of the sentence. Thus, nouns can be employed in the predicative position in argument-focus structures ((28), cf. (18)) besides predicate-focus structures, and verbs can appear in predicate-focus structures ((29), cf. (17)) in addition to argument-focus structures.

(28) kuj-ga=du sjinsji:
he-NOM=FOC teacher
'HE is the teacher.'

(29) kurja: budur-i uɨ
he.TOP dance-CVB be
'He is dancing.'

Therefore, the choice of a nominal or verbal encoding cannot be predicted from the syntactic behavior of verbs and nouns in Miyako-Hirara. The syntactic behavior of predicative adjectives cannot be accounted for by their morphological structure either. Let us consider the reduplicated form. In Miyako-Hirara nouns and verbs can also be reduplicated. For nouns the semantics of reduplicated forms roughly corresponds to that of the English suffix *-ish;* as for verbs reduplication bears aspectual meanings. However, unlike the reduplicated forms of predicative adjectives, there are no limitations for reduplicated nouns and verbs when they fill the predicative slot in argument-focus structures, i.e. they are able to mark a predicate in presupposition. So here again it is not the morphological structure that determines the choice of an encoding strategy of a predicative adjective.

(30) anga-ga=du jarabi:~jarabi
older.sister-NOM=FOC childish~ATT
"It is the older sister who is childish.'

The possible motivation for the adjectival switch proposed in the previous research does not seem to provide a reliable explanation for the situation in Miyako-Hirara. For example, the time stability parameter introduced by Stassen (1997) does not apply. Thus, (19) is an example of a temporary property denoted by the nominal strategy while (18) provides an example of a time stable reading encoded by the verbal strategy. Nor does the choice of encoding options directly reflect discourse functions of verbs and nouns described by Thompson (1988). We would expect verbal forms of predicative adjectives to share the predicating function with verbs and therefore to appear in the topic-comment structure. However, Miyako-Hirara adjectives demonstrate the opposite pattern.

To find an explanation for the adjectival switch observed in Miyako-Hirara, we will turn to other dialects of Ryukyuan.

4. Predicative adjectives in other Ryukyuan dialects: The "verby" pattern of encoding

As we observed in Section 3, the adjectival switch in Miyako-Hirara is controlled by the information structure of the sentence: nominal strategies are employed to mark a predicate within the focus domain and the verbal strategy is restricted to predicates in presupposition. However, other Ryukyuan dialects do not exhibit a switch-adjective pattern, that is they do not employ nominal strategies for their predicative adjectives. An extensive study of adjectival forms in 18 Japanese and Ryukyuan dialects by Kudo (2002) reveals that the productive reduplication of adjectival roots is found only in the dialects of Miyako group. The predicative strategy involving nominal compounds with a semantically dummy noun like *munu* is not attested in other Ryukyuan dialects either (Arakaki 2003; Izuyama 2003; Kudo 2006; Miyara 1995).[12] Thus, to the best of our knowledge, the switch-adjective strategy is limited to the dialects of the Miyako group while other dialects have only "verby" adjective pattern.

Nevertheless, other Ryukyuan dialects also distinguish between predicate-focus and argument-focus structures in adjectival predication. Examples (31) and (32) are from the Ishigaki dialect of Ryukyuan, which belongs to the Yaeyama branch of the Miyako-Yaeyama group. In (31) the finite form *taka-haN* 'high' is an instance of predicate-focus structure. On the other hand, (32) provides an example of an argument-focus structure with the focus domain limited to the NP *uri* marked by the focus particle *du*. Here, the form of an adjective is different from that in (31), namely *taka-haru,* and encodes the predicate in presupposition.

(31) taka-**haN**
high-FIN
'Is it high?' (Ishigaki dialect, Izuyama 2003: 39)

(32) uri=du taka-**haru**
this=FOC high-ATTR
'THIS is high.' (Ishigaki dialect, Izuyama 2003: 39)

From a pragmatic point of view, the difference between the two forms *taka-haN* in (31) and *taka-haru* in (32) corresponds to that between nominal strategies and verbal strategy in Miyako-Hirara, as observed in (17) and (18). The important difference between the two dialects is that the explicit morphological marking of the informational status of a predicative adjective in the Ishigaki dialect does not involve a switch of the encoding strategy but follows the "verby" pattern in encoding both types of information structure. In (31), which is an instance of the predicate-focus structure, the adjective takes a finite[13] form with a nasal consonant, which is a feature shared by verbs. On the other hand, in (32), which is an instance of the argument-focus structure, the adjective takes an attributive form. Examples (33)–(34) demonstrate the behavior of verbs in the Ishigaki dialect. The usage of the finite forms is also limited to predicates of main clauses with predicate-focus structure, as in (33): they are not employed in subordination or in the attributive position. On the other hand, in argument-focus structures where one nominal or adverbial constituent is marked with a focus particle, the main clause verbs take a non-finite (attributive) verb form as in (34).[14]

(33) aNzuKa ba: kuri kaku-**N**
then I this write-FIN
'Then I will write this.' (Ishigaki dialect, Izuyama 2003: 80)

(34) wa: no:=**du** kaku
you what=FOC write.ATTR
'What will you write?' (Ishigaki dialect, Izuyama 2003: 81)

This pattern is shared by verbs and adjectives and is attested in many Ryukyuan dialects. Given that the marking of the information structure is a complicated phenomenon and a detailed discussion of it is far beyond the scope of the present paper, we shall limit the survey of the forms of verbs and adjectives to declarative sentences in the present tense. Furthermore, we will not discuss the interaction of the information structure with other grammatical categories, such as evidentiality, aspect and modality. Table 3 summarizes predicative forms of verbs and adjectives in three Ryukyuan dialects belonging to different groups. It demonstrates that predicates occurring in the predicate-focus structure are expressed by finite forms that end with nasals. As for the predicates occurring in the argument-focus structures, Shuri (the Amami-Okinawa group) and Ishigaki dialects employ attributive forms. The Sesoko dialect, which is spoken in the northern part of the Okinawa island and also belongs to the Amami-Okinawa group, developed a new attributive form with the genitive marker *nu*, but retained the former attributive form to mark predicates in the presupposition of the argument-focus structure.

Table 3. Predicative forms in Ryukyuan dialects

	Predicate-focus type	**Argument-focus type (Declarative sentences)**	**Attributive forms**
Sesoko	*hakuN* 'write'	*haku:ru*	*haku:nu*
	takasaN 'high'	***takasaru***	*takasanu*
Shuri	*kacjuN* 'write'	*kacuru*	*kacuru*
	takasaN 'high'	***takasaru***	*takasaru*
Ishigaki	*kakuN* 'write'	*kaku*	*kaku*
	takahaN 'high'	***takaharu***	*takaharu*

Table 3 shows that the predicative adjectives in different Ryukyan dialects are all sensitive to their informational status: they distinguish morphologically between predicate-focus and argument-focus constructions. However, unlike in Miyako-Hirara, this distinction does not involve a switch between verbal and nominal strategies. The informational status of a predicative adjective is expressed by the distinction between finite and non-finite forms of "verby" adjectives. In other words, this type of marking is part of a broader syntactic pattern shared by verbs and adjectives.

The adjectival switch in Miyako-Hirara is functionally motivated by the same pragmatic needs (to mark the informational status of the predicate). However, the structural realization of this pragmatic distinction demonstrates a sharp contrast with other Ryukyuan dialects. Our next task is to explain why.

5. Why Miyako does it differently

In Section 3 we argued that the switch between nominal and verbal encoding of predicative adjectives in Miyako-Hirara is motivated by the informational status of the predicate, which is an unusual pattern from a typological point of view. This section aims to provide a functional explanation of the switch-adjective encoding strategy attested in Miyako-Hirara. There are two points that are relevant to our discussion. First, the nominal strategies of encoding predicative adjectives are an innovation observed only in the dialects of the Miyako group. As we mentioned in the previous section, they are not attested in other Ryukyuan and Japanese dialects, while the verbal strategy of encoding is characteristic of adjectives in all Ryukyuan dialects.[15] Second, nominal strategies mark predicates in the predicate-focus structure, as finite forms with nasals do in other Ryukyuan dialects.

Let us start by comparing Miyako-Hirara with the case of the Irabu dialect studied by Shimoji (forthcoming). This dialect is spoken on Irabu island, which lies just off Miyako island and belongs to the same Miyako branch of the Miyako-Yaeyama group. It is structurally very close to Miyako-Hirara. In Irabu there is a formal distinction of predicative forms between predicate-focus and argument-focus structures. Past tense forms of verbs, some auxiliary verbs and suffixed forms of adjectives have two different forms that end in *-m* and *-r*. Forms with the nasal *-m* are employed solely in the predicate-focus structure, i.e. in the sentences with a topicalized or omitted subject.

Table 4. Forms of predicates in Irabu and Miyako-Hirara dialects

	Past tense marker		Auxiliary verbs		Adjective		Vebs	
	PF	AF	PF	AF	PF	AF	PF	AF
Irabu dialect	- *tam*	- *tar*	*am, um*	*ar, ur*	*-kam*	*-kar*	*-m*	ø
Miyako-Hirara dialect	- *taɨ*	- *tai*	*aɨ, uɨ*	*aɨ, uɨ*	# *-kam*	*-kaɨ*	# *-m*	ø

The forms with *-r* occur in the argument-focus structures (as well as in the attributive position). This distribution follows the pattern attested in other Ryukyuan dialects, whereby finite forms with nasals mark predicate-focus structures and attributive forms are reserved for argument-focus structures. Furthermore, the nasal *-m* may also be attached to present tense forms of verbs though there are no corresponding *-r* forms in the argument-focus structure. Table 4 summarizes the forms discussed above and provides corresponding forms in Miyako-Hirara (PF stands for predicate-focus, AF stands for argument focus).

As Table 4 demonstrates, the distinction of predicative forms between predicate-focus and argument-focus structures is lost in the past tense markers and auxiliary verbs of Miyako-Hirara: forms *-taɨ, aɨ* and *uɨ* which correspond to Irabu *-tar, ar* and *ur* are employed in both pragmatic contexts,[16] as the following examples from the auxiliary verb demonstrate.

(35) jumunu-tu inna umu:jasɨsa: sji: **uɨ**=saj
mouse-COM dog.TOP relief.TOP do.CVB be=PART
'The mouse and the dog feel relief.' (PF structure)

(36) ba:-ga=du katsɨm-i ksji: mutj-i **uɨ**
I-NOM=FOC catch-CVB come.CVB hold-CVB be
'I have got [the mouse].' (AF structure)

Thus, forms with the nasal *-m*, which are used to mark verbs in predicate-focus structures for past tense forms and existential verbs in the Irabu dialect, are lost in Miyako-Hirara: the latter dialect does not morphologically distinguish between verbal predicates in predicate-focus and those in argument-focus structures in these contexts.

On the other hand, present tense forms of verbs and adjectives show a more complicated pattern. Table 4 demonstrates that there is an opposition between two suffixed forms of predicative adjectives in Miyako-Hirara, e.g. *taka-kam* vs. *taka-kaɨ*, as well as of two present tense verbal forms such as *kakɨ-m* vs. *kakɨ* (zero marking) 'write'.

The forms with nasals (*-kam* forms of adjectives and *-m* forms of verbs) are not compatible with argument-focus structures. Their occurrence is limited to the predicate-focus construction. However, in Miyako-Hirara the forms with nasals bear additional semantic restrictions and cannot be employed in all the sentences with the predicate-focus. Thus, verbs marked with *-m* have modal semantics of warning, threatening, speaker's discovery etc. (Izuyama 2002: 61–67). As for adjectives, the *-kam* forms are employed in the illocutionary acts of warning or threatening. Thus, (37) does not just convey the fact that something (in this case it is a cup of tea) is hot but rather represents a warning to the hearer with the possible implied meaning 'be careful', 'do not touch it', etc.

(37) atsɨ-kam=do:
hot-MOD=PART
'It is hot!'

In the same way, the communicative purpose of (38), adopted from Motonaga (2001: 357), is not just to inform the hearer about the price but to warn him against making a purchase.

(38) taka-kam ko:-na
expensive-MOD buy-IMP.NEG
'It is expensive! Do not buy it.'

As such, forms with nasals (*-m* forms of verbs and *-kam* forms of adjectives) do exist in Miyako-Hirara but their usage is restricted to certain types of modal/interactional contexts. In other words, *-m* and *-kam* are in the process of turning from a finite marker to a mood/modality marker, which is further supported by the loss of the *-m* vs. *-ɨ* contrast in past tense forms and auxiliaries, as the comparison with the Irabu dialect reveals. This creates a gap in the system that has to be filled by other morphological forms. For verbs, non-marked forms like *kakɨ* 'write' occur in all the other contexts in both argument-focus and predicate-focus structures in the present tense. The "#" in Table 4 indicates that the *-m* form is marked, a more neutral form is the unmarked one. As was shown earlier by the examples (35)–(36), the forms originally used in argument-focus structures in the past tense of verbal predicates and auxiliaries also spread into the predicate-focus structures. Thus for verbs, the gap is filled by the forms originally used in the argument-focus structure.

However, for adjectives, forms with the suffix *-kaɨ* (verbal strategy) that correspond to non-finite adjectival forms in other Ryukyuan dialects retained their original syntactic distribution: they occur in the predicative position of argument-focus structures, subordinate clauses[17] and in the attributive position. On the other hand, the suffix *-kam* is restricted in its occurrence (hence, «#» in Table 4), and the gap is filled by the innovative nominal strategy of encoding. Structurally, the choice of nominal strategies for this function is supported by the fact that they distinguish between attributive and predicative forms, i.e. they have a morphologically distinctive form for predication.

Considering all this, it seems reasonable to suggest that the usage of nominal strategies in the predicate-focus contexts in Miyako-Hirara allows the language to compensate for the lack of appropriate verbal morphology that would mark predicates in focus. Table 5 illustrates the division of labor of different forms of predicative adjectives from a functional point of view.

Table 5. The division of labor between encoding strategies of predicative adjectives in Miyako-Hirara

<table>
<tr><td>Illocutionary act of warning
Suffixed forms with -kam</td><td>Reduplication
Stem+munu
(nominal strategies)</td><td>Suffixed forms with -kaɨ
(verbal strategy)</td></tr>
<tr><td colspan="2">Predicate-focus type</td><td>Argument-focus Type</td></tr>
</table>

Thus, due to their fluidity as a category adjectives in Miyako-Hirara could also employ nominal strategies of predication besides their original verbal strategy. These innovative nominal strategies for predicative adjectives allowed the retention of the overt expression of their informational status.[18] This makes adjectives the only part of speech in Miyako-Hirara that marks its informational status in a consistent and explicit way.

6. Conclusions and theoretical considerations

In this paper, we investigated the Miyako-Hirara dialect of Ryukyuan, a language that employs both nominal and verbal strategies for its adjectival roots. We argued that although there is an overt derivation involved, Miyako-Hirara may still be considered a switch-adjective language due to the lack of distinction between "primary" and "secondary" forms. We also demonstrated that Miyako-Hirara is a counter-example to the universal of adjectival V-N-switching formulated by Stassen (1997), since its predicative adjectives are not sensitive to the time stability parameter. On the contrary, there are pragmatic, not semantic, factors behind the choice of encoding options for predicative adjectives: nominal strategies mark predicates in focus while the verbal strategy encodes predicates in presupposition. This adds typological evidence in favor of the hypothesis that discourse factors may also govern adjectival switching, as Holton (1999) demonstrated for Tobelo. Further, we have shown a special division of labor operative in Miyako-Hirara predicative adjectives.

How may the adjectival system attested in Miyako-Hirara contribute to the general theories on adjectives, and more generally, on parts of speech systems? Miyako-Hirara provides an interesting case in the light of a syntactic definition of parts of speech proposed by Hengeveld (Hengeveld 1992: 37, Hengeveld et al. 2004: 528).

(39) Verb is a lexeme, which without further measures being taken (WFM) has a predicative use only.
Noun is a lexeme, which WFM can be used as a head of a referential phrase.
Adjective is a lexeme, which WFM can be used as a modifier within a referential phrase.
Adverb is a lexeme, which WFM can be used as a modifier within a predicate phrase.

Hengeveld (1992:47) also proposes a part of speech hierarchy, claiming that "a category of predicates is more likely to occur as a separate part of speech the more to the left it is in this hierarchy".

(40) Verb > Noun > Adjective > Adverb

Miyako-Hirara virtually does not employ its roots referring to property concepts in any syntactic position without further derivational processes. Thus, we turn to the derived lexemes (suffixed *-kaɨ* forms and reduplicated forms). As we demonstrated in Section 3.2, suffixed forms can be used as modifiers within a referential phrase without further measures being taken. Furthermore, suffixed forms can also be used in the predicative position without a copula (cf. (13)), i.e. they combine the functions of unmarked predicates and unmarked modifiers of a nominal head. Let us note that verbs in Miyako-Hirara demonstrate the same distribution (cf. (11). Thus, according to Hengeveld (1992), Miyako-Hirara belongs to the flexible type, conflating the categories of verbs and adjectives. Beck (2002: 101) describes a similar situation in Salishan languages. On the other hand, reduplicated forms, such as *taka:taka* 'high', require the genitive marker *nu* in the attributive position (cf. (7)) but can be employed as modifiers within the predicate phrase without any markers (cf. (10)) and thus should be treated as adverbs under Hengeveld's classification. This creates a problem for the hierarchy represented in (40), since Miyako-Hirara conflates the categories of verbs and adjectives but has a separate class of adverbs (although virtually all these adverbs are derived).

As for the theories claiming that the strategy of adjectival encoding is determined by the structural characteristics of a language: the tensedness parameter (Wetzer 1996; Stassen 1997) or head vs. dependent marking (Dixon 2004), Miyako-Hirara does not represent a counter-example but does not provide any supporting evidence either. Since it is a tensed and dependent marking language the innovative nominal strategies seem to provide arguments in favor of both theories. However, it should be noticed that the development of nominal strategies of adjectival encoding was not accompanied or preceded by the changes of these structural properties.

Finally, the case of Miyako-Hirara might demonstrate a possible mechanism for the development of a switch-adjective language. In the absence of separate morphology for the predicate-focus and argument-focus structures, only the switch pattern of predicative adjectives allowed Miyako-Hirara to retain the explicit marking of this functionally important distinction that tends to be encoded in other dialects of Ryukyuan.

Acknowledgements

First and foremost, we would like to thank our language consultants, in particular Yonezo Higa, Kiyo Higa, Kenji Taira and Hiroshi Sunakawa. We are also grateful to Atsuko Izuyama for her help and guidance, as well as to Michinori Shimoji for sharing his Irabu materials and providing valuable comments on an earlier version of this paper. We also thank two anonymous reviewers for their valuable comments and suggestions.

Notes

1. The tensedness universals of adjective encoding are formulated as follows (Stassen 1997: 357):

   If a language is tensed it will have nouny adjectives.
   If a language has nouny adjectives it will be tensed.
   If a language is non-tensed it will have verby adjectives.
   If a language has verby adjectives it will be non-tensed.

2. Adjectives of type II (non-verb-like) tend to be found in languages of type D (dependency-marking at clause level). Adjectives of type I (verb-like) tend to be found in languages of type H (head-marking), and in languages with neither H nor D marking. (Dixon 2004: 33).

3. We use the following abbreviations in the glosses: ACC – accusative; ADV – adverbial, ATT – attenuative; ATTR – attributive; CIT – citation; COM – comitative; CONJ – conjunctive; COP – copula; CVB – converb; DAT – dative; FIL – filler; FIN – finite; FOC – focus; FS – formative suffix; GEN – genetive; IMP – imperative; INS – instrumental; MOD – modality; NEG – negation; NMLZ – nominalizer; NOM – nominative; PART – particle; PST – past tense; PERF – perfect; PL – plural; REDUP – reduplication; TOP – topic.

4. Unlike Standard Japanese (Backhouse 2004), the Miyako-Hirara dialect of Ryukyuan does not divide its property concept words into two classes in the lexicon. There is no special lexical class corresponding to the Japanese uninflected adjectives (*na*-adjectives). The lexical borrowings of Japanese *na*-adjectives are either categorized on a par with other adjectives or treated as nouns.

5. The word *munu* is a Miyako-Hirara cognate of Japanese *mono* 'stuff, thing'.

6. The phoneme /ɨ/ can be accompanied by a degree of friction in certain phonetic environments and is phonetically realized as [ɿ], [ɿ^{s}] or [ɿ^{z}].

7. Shimoji (2006) first provided this criteria in his study of adjectives in the Irabu dialect. He argues that it is the sign of grammaticalization of *munu* from a noun to a formative element.

8. As shown in 3.3.2, Miyako-Hirara uses morphological marking to encode different focus type structures. Thus, we do not classify Miyako-Hirara sentences into argument-focus and predicate-focus structures on the basis of our intuition, but use a formal criterion to distinguish between two types of structures (usage of a focus particle). We use Lambrecht's terminology, as a language-neutral reference widely employed in the literature on the topic. However, as was pointed out by one of the reviewers, further usage-based research is necessary to elaborate on pragmatic functions of adjectives in Miyako-Hirara.

9. The sentence-focus type is not considered in the present paper for two reasons. First, since sentence-focus structures bear the communicative functions of introducing a new discourse referent or reporting an event, they are hardly compatible with predicative adjectives. Second, in Miyako-Hirara sentence-focus structures are formally marked in the same way as argument-focus ones.

10. However, we should point out that the behavior of predicative adjectives in subordinated clauses is less straightforward than the distribution they demonstrate in main clauses.

11. We mainly limit ourselves to the predicative usage. This is because the switch of the encoding strategy is most clearly manifest in this position. Further discussion on non-predicative usages would lead us away from our main argument.

12. The line delimiting nominal compounds occasionally used in the predicative position and a nominal strategy for predicative adjectives that involves a dummy noun is very fine. Thus, a more careful analysis of the morpho-syntactic properties as well as the text frequencies may be necessary.

13. They are also called predicative forms, since they can occur only in the predicative position in contrast with non-finite forms that can also fill the attributive slot.

14. Thus, the information structure is marked twice: a focus particle marks a constituent in focus and the presupposed status of a predicate is expressed by the fact that it takes a non-finite form. The syntactic phenomenon of non-finite predicates in argument-focus structures is widely known in traditional Japanese linguistics as the *kakari-musubi* construction (Miyara 1995; Schaffar 2001; Schaffar 2003; Shinzato 1999). Besides Ryukyuan dialects, it is also attested in Classical Japanese.

(i) waN-nee tigami kacu-N
I-TOP letter write-FIN
'I write a letter.' (Shuri dialect, Arakaki 2003: 181)

(ii) 'uree waN-ga-ru kacu-ru
it I-NOM-FOC write-ATTR
'I will write it.' (Shuri dialect, Arakaki 2003: 190)

15. The "verby" adjectives in Ryukyuan dialects were historically formed by the compounding of the existential verb to the adverbial or nominalized forms of adjectival stems.

16. Actually, the data from Namihira (1990) reflecting varieties spoken in the southern part of Miyako island also provide some examples of verbal forms with nasals (*-tam, am, um*). However, they are not always used consistently in the predicate-focus structure, demonstrating that the process of their loss is underway. However, the data provided by our informants as well as the data collected by Shibata (1972) demonstrate the occurrences of *-tai, ui* and *ai* forms in predicate-focus in main clause. Therefore, in Miyako-Hirara verbs do not use the formal marking of their informational status in the predicative position.

17. However, they also appear in the pragmatically presupposed contexts of «actualizing utterances».

18. Iwasaki (1993) discusses another case of functional transfer in the history of Japanese, where nominalized predicates in Modern Japanese acquired functions of attributive sentences that were lost in the history of Japanese.

References

Arakaki, Tomoko. 2003. A grammatical study in Luchuan. *Studies on Luchuan grammar.* Atsuko Izuyama (ed.), 163–216. Kyoto [ELPR Publication Series A4–024].

Backhouse, Anthony E. 2004. Inflected and uninflected adjectives in Japanese. *Adjective classes. A cross-linguistic typology,* R.M.W. Dixon & Alexandra Y. Aikhenvald (eds.), 50–73. Oxford: Oxford University Press.

Beck, David. 2002. *The typology of parts of speech systems. The markedness of adjectives.* London: Routledge.

Dixon, R.M.W. 1982. Where have all the adjectives gone? *Where have all the adjectives gone? and other essays in semantics and syntax,* R.M.W. Dixon, 1–62. Berlin: Mouton.

Hengeveld, Kees. 1992. Parts of speech. *Layered structure and reference in a functional perspective,* Michael Fortescue, Peter Harder & Lars Kristofferson (eds.), 29–56. Amsterdam: John Benjamins.

Hengeveld, Kees; Jan Rijkhoff & Anna Siewierska. 2004. Parts-of-speech systems and word order. *Journal of Linguistics* 40(3): 527–570.

Holton, Gary. 1999. Categoriality of property words in a switch-adjective language. *Linguistic Typology* 3: 341–360.

Iwasaki, Shoichi. 1993. Functional transfer in the history of Japanese language. *Japanese/Korean linguistics,* Patricia M. Clancy (ed.), vol.2: 20–32. Stanford, CA: CSLI.

Izuyama, Atsuko. 2002. A study on the grammar of Miyako-Hirara dialect in Luchuan. *Grammatical aspects of endangered dialects in Japan (2),* Shinji Sanada (ed.), 35–97. Kyoto [ELPR Publication Series A4–012].

Izuyama, Atsuko. 2003. The grammar of Ishigaki Miyara dialect in Luchuan. *Studies on Luchuan grammar,* Atsuko Izuyama (ed.), 1–162. Kyoto [ELPR Publication Series A4–024].

Kalinina, Elena & Nina Sumbatova. 2007. Clause structure and verbal forms in Nakh-Daghestanian languages. *Finiteness: theoretical and empirical foundations,* Irina Nikolaeva (ed.), 183–249. Oxford: Oxford University Press.

Karimata, Shigehisa. 2002. Notes on adjectives in Miyako dialects of the Ryukyuan language. *Preliminary research on endangered Ryukyuan language,* Shigehisa Karimata, Toshiko Tsuhako, Shin-ich Kajiku & Toshizo Takahashi (eds.), 44–70. Kyoto [ELPR Publication Series A4–019].

Kazenin, Konstantin I. 2002. Focus in Daghestanian languages and word order typology. *Linguistic Typology* 6: 289–316.

Kudo, Mayumi. 2002. *Hoogen-ni-okeru dooshi-no bunpooteki kategorii-no ruikeironteki kenkyuu (Grammatical categories in verbs in Japanese dialects: a typological study).* Osaka University.

Kudo, Mayumi. 2006. *Hoogen-ni-okeru jutsugo koozoo-no ruikeironteki kenkyuu II (Structures of predicates in Japanese dialects: a typological study II).* Osaka University.

Lambrecht, Knud. 1994. *Information structure and sentence form.* Cambridge: Cambridge University Press.

Langendoen, D. Terrence. 1967. The Copula in Mundari. *The Verb 'Be' and its synonyms 1,* John W.M. Verhaar (ed.), 75–100. Dordrecht: Reidel.

Lewis, David. 1979. Scorekeeping in a language game. *Semantics from different points of view,* R. Baeuerle, U. Egli & A. von Stechow (eds.), 172–187. Heidelberg: Springer.

Matsumori, Akiko. 1993. Ryukyuan: past, present and future. *Multilingual Japan,* John C. Mahler & Kyoko Yashiro (eds.) 19–45. Clevedon: Multilingual Matters.

Miyara, Shinsho. 1995. *Minami Ryuukyuu Yaeyama Ishigaki hoogen-no bunpoo. (Grammar of the southern Ryukyuan dialect Yaeyama Ishigaki).* Tokyo: Kuroshio.

Motonaga, Moriyasu. 2001. Miyako Hirara hoogen-no keiyooshi (Adjectives in Miyako-Hirara dialect). *Ryuukyuu hoogen koo* (Reflections on Ryukyuan dialects), Inoue Fumio (ed.), 388–396. Tokyo: Yumani shooboo.

Namihira, Isao (ed.). 1990. *Gusuketyoo-shi. Daigokan minwahen* (History of Gusuke-city.Vol. 5: Folktales). Gusuke-tyoo.

Nevskij, Nikolai. 2005. *Miyako hoogen nooto* (Notes on the Miyako dialect). Hirara-shi: Insatsu sentaa Yonamine.

Schaffar, Wolfram. 2001. Kakari musubi, *noda*-constructions, and how grammaticalization theory meets formal grammar. *Japanese / Korean linguistics*, Noriko Akatsuka (ed.), vol. 10, 320–333. Stanford, CA: CSLI.

Schaffar, Wolfram. 2003. *Die Informationsstruktur der japanischen Sprache.* Muenster: Lit Verlag.

Shibata, Takeshi. 1972. *Zenkoku hoogen shiryoo vol 11. Ryuukyuuhen II.* (Materials on Japanese dialects, vol. 11. Ryukyuan dialects II). Tokyo: NHK Publisher.

Shibatani, Masayoshi. 1990. *The languages of Japan.* Cambridge: Cambridge University Press.

Shimoji, Michinori. 2006. Adjectives in Irabu Ryukyuan. A paper presented at Japan centre seminar, Australian National University.

Shimoji, Michinori. (Forthcoming). Minami Ryuukyuugo Miyako Irabu hoogen (Grammar of the southern Ryukyuan dialect Miyako Irabu). *Kizyutsu gengogaku komyuniti bunpoo sukecchishuu* (Collection of grammatical sketches of the descriptive linguistics community).

Shinzato, Rumiko. 1999. Kakari-musubi revisited: its functions and development. *Japanese/Korean linguistics,* David J. Silva (ed.), vol. 8, 203–216. Stanford, CA: CSLI.

Stassen, Leon. 1997. *Intransitive predication.* Oxford: Clarendon Press.

Thompson, Sandra A. 1988. A discourse approach to the cross-linguistic category "adjective". *Explaining language universals,* J. A. Hawkins (ed.), 167–185. Oxford: Blackwell.

Uchima, Naohito. 1992. Sesoko (Okinawahokubu) hoogen (Sesoko dialect of northern Okinawa). *Gendai nihongo hoogen daijiten* (Dictionary of dialects of modern Japanese), Teruo Hirayama (ed.), 297–301. Tokyo: Meijishoin.

Wetzer, Henry. 1992. «Nouny» and «verby» adjectivals: a typology of predicative adjectival constructions. *Meaning and grammar: crosslinguistic perspectives,* Michael Kefer & Johan van der Auwera (eds.), 223–62. Berlin: Mouton de Gruyter.

Wetzer, Henry. 1996. *The typology of adjectival predication.* Berlin: Mouton de Gruyter.

Authors' address

Yulia Koloskova
Department of Language and Information Sciences
University of Tokyo
3-8-1 Komaba, Meguro-ku
Tokyo, 153–8902, Japan

ikolosk@gmail.com, tohori@boz.c.u-tokyo.ac.jp

The acquisition of syntactic categories in Jakarta Indonesian

David Gil
Max Planck Institute for Evolutionary Anthropology

This paper presents empirical evidence for a theory of syntactic categories in the tradition of categorial grammar, in which more complex categories are derived from simpler ones by means of category formation operators. In Jakarta Indonesian, almost all words and larger expressions belong to a single open syntactic category, S(entence), while a small residue of semantically heterogeneous items belong to a single closed syntactic category S/S. The theory predicts that in first-language acquisition, simpler categories are acquired before more complex ones. Thus, for Jakarta Indonesian, it predicts that the category S is be acquired before the category S/S. Examination of a naturalistic corpus of almost one million utterances provides support for this prediction, deriving from errors of over-generalization, in which members of S/S exhibit the distributional properties of members of S.

1. Introduction

There are so many different theories of syntactic categories out there competing with each other in the linguistic literature: how does one go about evaluating them, and choosing the one that is best? A sensible strategy is to identify fundamental design features distinguishing between different theories, formulate some testable empirical consequences entailed by these alternative design features, and then look at the facts to see which way they point.

One central design feature distinguishing between different theories of syntactic categories pertains to the internal organization of their syntactic category inventories. The most basic distinction is between theories whose inventories are mere unordered sets, and theories that posit inventories endowed with additional internal structure. An example of the former kind is provided by the Classical Greek system, which — in at least some of its versions — posited an unstructured set of eight parts of speech: noun, verb, participle, article, pronoun, preposition, adverb and conjunction. In contrast, in most contemporary theories, syntactic category inventories are not just unordered sets but are endowed with additional internal structure involving various kinds of relationships obtaining between the individual syntactic categories.

Theories in which syntactic category inventories are associated with additional internal structure may in turn be of either of two types: *equitory* or *dominatory*. Equitory theories are those in which different syntactic categories are of equal rank, and do not stand in any inherent relationship of domination. An example of an equitory theory is provided by the lexical categories in a framework such as that of Chomsky (1970), in which the four categories of N(oun), V(erb), A(djective) and P(reposition) are defined in terms of two binary features +/-NOUN and +/-VERB. These binary features impose structure on the lexical categories; for example, N and A share the value +NOUN, while V and P share the opposite value -NOUN. However, these binary features do not impose any intrinsic ranking relationship between individual categories: there is no sense in which, say, the category N is prior to, comes before, or dominates, the category A.

In contrast, dominatory theories are those in which an inherent relationship of domination obtains between at least some syntactic categories. The most elementary kind of domination is that associated with the relationship of set inclusion. Any theory of syntactic categories that involves the notions of super-category and sub-category may be characterized as dominatory. Within such a theory, a syntactic category inventory may be likened to a classificatory tree whose nodes are the individual categories themselves. For example, nouns and adjectives may group together to constitute the super-category of substantives; similarly, nouns may be divided into subcategories of inalienably possessed and non-inalienably possessed nouns. Accordingly, substantives dominate nouns, and nouns in turn dominate inalienably possessed nouns. Moreover, since domination is a transitive relationship; substantives also dominate inalienably possessed nouns. However, the relationship of domination effects a partial rather than a total ordering; thus, for example, nouns and adjectives do not stand in a relationship of domination with one another.

Set inclusion is not the only relationship, giving rise to dominatory theories of syntactic categories. One example of a dominatory theory not based on set inclusion is provided by the X-bar theory proposed by Chomsky (1970), Jackendoff (1977) and others. Within X-bar theory, the bars impose an intrinsic relationship of domination between syntactic categories, in which XPs dominate X"s, X"s dominate X's and X's dominate Xs. Another example of a dominatory theory not based on set inclusion is provided by the architecture of categorial grammar, such as Ajdukiewicz (1935), Montague (1970a,b), which begins with a set of primitive syntactic categories, and then builds up derived syntactic categories by means of category formation operators such as the 'slash' operator denoted '/'. For example, if A and B are syntactic categories, one may then form the derived category A/B, or 'A slash B'. Since A/B is formed from A and B, A and B may both be said to dominate A/B. Thus, within categorial grammar, the process of deriving syntactic categories from other syntactic categories imposes an inherent relationship of domination, in which derived categories are dominated by the categories from which they are derived. Thus, both X-bar theory and categorial grammar involve a relationship of domination not based on set inclusion.

This paper is concerned with a particular theory of syntactic categories of the latter kind, that is to say, one involving a relationship of domination not based on set inclusion. In fact, the theory invoked herein constitutes a synthesis of X-bar theory and categorial grammar. Section 2 below sketches the formal outlines of the theory. Section 3 then formulates some testable empirical predictions of the theory in the domain of first-language acquisition, suggesting that the acquisition of syntactic categories follows the dominatory relationship, with dominating categories being acquired before the categories that they dominate. Section 4 puts these predictions to the test. Drawing on a large naturalistic corpus of early child language in the Jakarta dialect of Indonesian, evidence from errors of overgeneralization is shown to support the claim that children go through a stage of acquisition in which they possess but a single syntactic category, that which dominates all other possible categories allowed for by the theory. Thus, the way in which children acquire the syntactic categories of Jakarta Indonesian provides support for a particular theory of syntactic categories of a dominatory but non-set-inclusory nature.

2. A theory of syntactic categories

The theory of syntactic categories examined in this paper was first presented in Gil (2000); this section presents a summary of its main features, largely recapitulating the material in pp. 183–190 therein.

The theory is expressly syntactic, in the sense that syntactic categories are defined in terms of syntactic properties, such as distributional privileges, not morphological properties or semantic ones. For example, the set of words that may be inflected for plurality and definiteness in a particular language constitutes a morphological category, not a syntactic one. Similarly, the set of words that refer to concrete objects constitutes a semantic category, not a syntactic one. Accordingly, the theory has no place for familiar categories such as nouns, verbs, adjectives and prepositions, which are typically defined in terms of clusterings of morphological, syntactic and semantic properties.

In terms of its architecture, the theory falls within the tradition of Categorial Grammar. In Categorial Grammar, one begins with a set of Initial (or Primitive) Categories, and a set of Category-Formation Operators. These Category-Formation Operators apply to simpler categories to derive more complex categories, and so on recursively. Each category name spells out the history of that category's derivation, and how it is obtained by application of the Category-Formation Operators to the Initial Categories. In addition, each category name also provides a characterization of the distributional privileges of members of that category.

The theory presented in this paper posits one Initial Category and two Category-Formation Operators; these are spelt out in (1) below. After that, in (2), the ways in which categories group together to form syntactic structures are indicated:[1]

(1) *Category Formation (Paradigmatic)*
  a. Initial Category: S^0
  b. Category-Formation Operators:
    i. Slash Operator:
    For any two categories X and Y, X/Y is a category, called 'X slash Y'.
    ii. Kernel Operator:
    For any category X^n, X^{n+1} is a category, called 'the kernel category of X^n'.

(2) *Category Combination (Syntagmatic)*
  a. Identity Combination: $X \leftrightarrow [X, X, X \ldots]$
  b. Slash Combination: $X \leftrightarrow [Y, X/Y, X/Y \ldots]$

As specified in (1a), the theory makes use of a single Initial Category, S^0. The letter 'S' may be construed as a rough mnemonic for 'Sentence', while the superscript '0' reflects the basic nature of the category in question. Indeed, the category S^0 may be thought of as corresponding approximately to the traditional category of sentence.

The theory accordingly assigns privileged status to the sentence, characterizing it as the most basic or fundamental syntactic category. In this respect it follows in the footsteps of a long tradition, encompassing, among others, American Structuralism and Generative Grammar. Thus, for example, Boas (1911:23) writes: "Since all speech is intended to serve for the communication of ideas, the natural unit of expression is the sentence; that is to say, a group of articulate sounds which convey a complete idea." Echoing this insight, phrase structure grammars such as that of Chomsky (1965) typically begin with a formula such as '$S \rightarrow \ldots$'. However, in this regard, the present theory differs from previous versions of Categorial Grammar, which generally posit more than one Initial Category. Thus, Ajdukiewicz (1935) posits two Initial Categories, corresponding to S and NP; Montague (1970a,b) and many others opt for three, corresponding to S, NP and N; while some, for example Morrill (1994), even postulate four, corresponding to S, NP, N and PP.

We are now in a position to examine the first of the two Category Combination rules, namely Identity Combination, as specified in (2a). What this rule says is that an expression of category X may consist of any number of daughter expressions also of category X, in what amounts to a conjunction, apposition or juxtaposition of coordinate elements. For example, an S^0 may consist of two, three, four, or any number of daughter S^0's, in a construction of the form $S^0 \leftrightarrow [S^0, S^0, S^0 \ldots]$.

In order to enrich the inventory of syntactic categories, recourse is required to the two Category-Formation Operators, as specified in (1b). The first of these, in (1b/i), is the familiar binary Slash Operator, which is at the heart of all previous theories of Categorial Grammar. What it says, quite simply, is that if X and Y are both syntactic categories, then so is X/Y. For example, from S^0 we can form the category S^0/S^0; from these two categories we can form the categories S^0 / (S^0/S^0), (S^0/S^0) / S^0, and (S^0/S^0) / (S^0/S^0); and so forth.

In its appearance, the Slash Operator is reminiscent of the division sign in elementary algebra, and for good reason. To see why, let us turn our attention to the second Category Combination rule, namely Slash Combination, in (2b). What this says is that an expression of category X may consist of an expression of category Y in construction with one or more expressions of category X/Y. For simplicity, assume for the moment that the number of X/Y expressions is just one. Then what Slash Combination is saying is that a Y expression in construction with an X/Y expression results in an expression of category X: X ↔ [Y, X/Y]. Which looks just like the elementary algebraic equation $X = Y \cdot X/Y$. To take a real example now, an expression of category S^0 may consist of an expression of category S^0 in construction with, say, three expressions of category S^0/S^0: $S^0 \leftrightarrow [S^0, S^0/S^0, S^0/S^0, S^0/S^0]$.

As noted above, the Slash Operator is common to most or all versions of Categorial Grammar. However, whereas most versions, such as Montague (1970a,b) and Keenan and Faltz (1985), allow only for binary branchings, the present version permits multiple branchings, thereby reflecting a body of evidence that has accumulated to the effect that at least some constructions, in some languages, are endowed with flat rather than hierarchical syntactic structure; see, for example, Hale (1982,1983), Gil (1983), Austin and Bresnan (1996). Also, whereas some versions, such as Bar-Hillel (1953) and Lambek (1958), build linear order into the theory, typically by introducing distinct slash symbols, the present framework follows Ajdukiewicz (1935), Keenan and Faltz (1985) and others in positing syntactic structures and syntactic rules that are unspecified for linear order. This is motivated by the observation that a large proportion of the generalizations governing the syntactic structures of languages and the ways in which these structures are interpreted do not require recourse to linear order; see, for example, Šaumjan (1965), Sanders (1975) and Keenan (1978).

The second Category-Formation Operator, in (1b/ii), is the unary Kernel Operator. The effect of this operator is, quite simply, to add 1 to the value of the superscript of the category to which it applies. For example, it applies to S^0 to yield S^1, to S^1 to yield S^2, and so forth. In addition, it can apply to categories resulting from the application of the Slash Operator, in which case the category produced by the Slash Operator is understood to bear the default superscript 0. For example, the Slash Operator may produce the category S^0/S^0, actually $(S^0/S^0)^0$; the Kernel Operator then may apply to $(S^0/S^0)^0$ to yield the category $(S^0/S^0)^1$.

The Kernel Operator is an innovation within the tradition of Categorial Grammar, but elsewhere it is almost familiar. Almost, but not quite: in fact, it is an upside-down version of the bar operator of X-bar theory, as proposed by Chomsky (1970),

Jackendoff (1977) and others. Within X-bar theory, words are associated with lexical categories, which are taken to be basic, and are accordingly assigned the superscript 0. These categories, or X-zeroes then project upwards, resulting in phrasal categories with ascending indices, X-bar, X-double-bar, etc., until an arbitrary limit, usually taken to equal three, is reached, at which point the resulting category is renamed as an XP (and also referred to as the 'maximal projection' of X). X-bar theory thus characterizes the word, rather than the sentence, as the most fundamental linguistic unit. However, as is suggested below, there are good reasons to believe that it is the sentence that is the more basic of the two. Or, more generally, that for any X, it is XP that is more basic than X. Accordingly, the Kernel Operator turns the tables on X-bar theory, starting at the top, with what corresponds, very roughly, to the XPs, assigning these the superscript 0, and then working its way down, as far as may be necessary. A corollary of the above definitions is that within the present theory there is no distinction between lexical and non-lexical, or phrasal categories. Specifically, all categories can contain both words and longer, multi-word expressions.

In addition to the Initial Category and the two Category-Formation Operators, it is necessary to introduce one more primitive into the theory, namely headedness. Given an expression X consisting of daughter expressions X_1 … X_n, the head of X is that expression X_i which is characteristically associated with a range of properties which include some or all of the following: (a) obligatoriness: the head cannot be omitted; (b) hyponymy: the construction as a whole is a hyponym of its head; (c) percolation of features: the construction as a whole acquires grammatical features from its head; (d) agreement: the head controls agreement of the other elements in the construction; and (e) government: the head determines the morphological form of other words in the construction. The notion of head is well supported within linguistic theory; see for example Tesnière (1959), Zwicky (1985) and Hudson (1990). In particular, the notion of head plays a central role within X-bar theory, where, for any X, X is taken to be the head of the X', X" and XP containing it. Nevertheless, the notion of head is logically independent of the mechanisms of X-bar theory, and is of greater generality. Thus, for example, the notion of head has been argued to be relevant in a variety of cognitive domains where the notions of X-bar structure are not applicable, such as the theory of tonal music proposed by Lerdahl and Jackendoff (1983).

In the present theory, headedness correlates with the rules of Category Combination in the following ways:

(3) *Headedness (Syntagmatic)*
   a. Identity Combination:
      In a construction of the form X ↔ [X, X, X …], one of the daughter X's may be head.
   b. Slash Combination:
      In a construction of the form X ↔ [Y, X/Y, X/Y …], Y is head.

Rule (3a) says that in a construction of the kind formed by Identity Combination, one of the daughter expressions may be head, but this is not a necessity: the construction may remain headless. Such freedom, however, is not the case for constructions formed by Slash Combination: here rule (3b) specifies that in a construction of the form [Y, X/Y, X/Y ...], it is invariably Y that is the head.

Among the syntactic categories generated by the Category Formation rules in (1), two particular kinds stand out as worthy of mention:

(4) *Syntactic Categories: Two Kinds*
   a. *Modifier Categories*
      A Modifier Category is a category of the form X/X, for some category X.
   b. *Argument Categories*
      An Argument Category is a category of the form X/Y, for some categories X and Y, where Y is the Kernel Category of X.

Modifier Categories are referred to as such because, in accordance with the rule of Slash Combination in (2b), one or more X/X expressions combine with an X expression to yield another superordinate X expression: X ↔ [X, X/X, X/X, X/X ...]. In such cases, the X/X expression(s) may be characterized as the modifier(s) of its/their sister X expression, which, in accordance with (3b), is the head of the construction. Some examples of Modifier Categories are S^0/S^0, S^1/S^1, (S^0/S^0) / (S^0/S^0), (S^0/S^1) / (S^0/S^1), and so forth. Argument Categories are given this name because, also in accordance with the rule of Slash Combination in (2b), one or more X/Y expressions combine with an X expression to yield a superordinate Y expression: Y ↔ [X, X/Y, X/Y, X/Y ...]. In such instances, the X/Y expression(s) may be characterized as the argument(s) of its/their sister X expression, which, again in accordance with (3b), is the head of the construction. Some examples of Argument Categories are S^0/S^1, S^1/S^2, (S^0/S^0) / $(S^0/S^0)^1$, (S^0/S^1) / $(S^0/S^1)^1$ and so forth.[2]

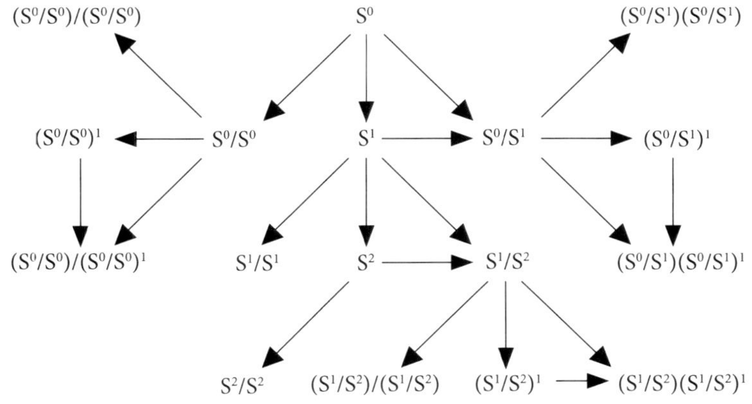

Figure 1. The Syntactic Category Tree (Partial)

The rules of Category Formation in (1) generate an infinite number of syntactic categories from the Initial Category S^0. This set may be visualized in terms of a tree structure. Since the actual tree is boundless, it is unrepresentable; however, a very small subset of it is shown in Figure 1.

In Figure 1, the root node of the tree, at top centre, is the Initial Category S^0. Arrows lead from nodes representing syntactic categories to other nodes representing other syntactic categories that are derived from them by application of a Category-Formation Operator.

The above tree provides an overt and explicit representation of the dominatory nature of the theory. These dominatory relationships are captured in the following definitions:

(5) *Parent and Ancestor Syntactic Categories*
  a. For any syntactic category X, the parents of X are the categories from which X is formed by a single application of a Category-Formation Operator.
    i. If X is the kernel category of Y, for some Y, then Y is the parent of X.
    ii. If X is of form Y/Z, for some Y and Z, then Y and Z are the parents of X.
  b. For any syntactic category X, the ancestors of X are the categories from which X is formed by one or more applications of Category-Formation Operators.

In terms of the Syntactic Category Tree in Figure 3, the parents of a category X are the nodes immediately dominating it, while the ancestors of X are the nodes simply dominating it. For example, in accordance with (5a/i), S^0 is the single parent of S^1; S^1 is the single parent of S^2; S^0/S^1 is the single parent of $(S^0/S^1)^1$; and so forth. Similarly, in accordance with (5a/ii), S^0 and S^1 are the two parents of S^0/S^1; S^1 and S^2 are the two parents of S^1/S^2; S^0/S^1 and $(S^0/S^1)^1$ are the two parents of (S^0/S^1) / $(S^0/S^1)^1$; and so on.

Since the set of syntactic categories generated by the Category Formation rules in (1) is infinite, only a very small proportion of these categories will be of relevance to linguistic theory. In particular, the actual syntactic category inventory of any given language will be finite, and in fact very small. Accordingly, constraints on syntactic category inventories need to be imposed.

The most important constraint on syntactic category inventories across languages makes reference to the definition of Ancestor Category in (5) above; this constraint is given in (6) below:

(6) *The Ancestral Constraint on Syntactic Category Inventories*
For any language L:
If X is a syntactic category in L, then all X's ancestors are syntactic categories in L, of equal or greater productivity.

The Ancestral Constraint says that each individual language constructs its inventory of syntactic categories in accordance with (1), beginning with the Initial Category S^0, and then forming additional syntactic categories by means of the Slash and Kernel operators. That is to say, a language selects its inventory by starting at the top of the Syntactic Category Tree and working its way down to a certain point, and then stopping. Or, to be more precise, tapering off. This is because once the inventory of open categories is established, the Category Formation rules may continue to apply, to produce closed categories of lesser and lesser degrees of productivity.

Some examples of syntactic inventories permitted by the Ancestral Constraint are given in (7) below:

(7) *Some Category Inventories Permitted by the Ancestral Constraint*
  a. $\{ S^0 \}$
  b. $\{ S^0, S^0/S^0 \}$
  c. $\{ S^0, S^1 \}$
  d. $\{ S^0, S^1, S^0/S^1 \}$
  e. $\{ S^0, S^0/S^0, S^1 \}$
  f. $\{ S^0, S^0/S^0, S^1, S^0/S^1 \}$

However, many other inventories are excluded by the Ancestral Constraint. For example, $\{ S^0, S^0/S^1 \}$ is not a possible inventory, since it does not include S^1, which is an ancestor to S^0/S^1. Similarly, $\{ S^0/S^0 \}$, $\{ S^1, S^0/S^1 \}$, and $\{ S^0/S^0, S^1, S^0/S^1 \}$ are not possible inventories, since they do not include S^0, which is an ancestor to each of the categories in each of these inventories. In fact, since S^0 is the Initial Category, it is an ancestor to all syntactic categories, which leads to the following corollary of the Ancestral Constraint:

(8) *Corollary of the Ancestral Constraint*
  The Initial Category S^0 is contained in the syntactic category inventory of every language.

However, S^0 is the only syntactic category that is universal in this sense.[3]

The Ancestral Constraint establishes a correlation between the complexity of a syntactic category and its cross-linguistic distribution. The complexity of a syntactic category can be measured by the length of its derivational history, as reflected in the number of symbols in its name, and the height of the numerical indices. Equivalently, the complexity of a syntactic category can be gauged by its distance from the root node S^0 in the Syntactic Category Tree. Thus, the Ancestral Constraint makes an intuitively appealing statement about the relationship between complexity and cross-linguistic distribution, namely: simpler categories will be more widespread, while more complex categories will occur less frequently in the languages of the world.

However, the Ancestral Constraint alone is insufficiently restrictive; further constraints are required to restrict the class of possible syntactic category inventories.

Imagine a language with the inventory in (7c), namely { S^0, S^1 }. In such a language, no construction could contain expressions belonging to both of these categories: given the rules of Category Combination in (2), there is no way that expressions from these two classes could come together in a single construction. This clearly does not make sense. A similar problem arises with the inventory in (7e), { S^0, S^0/S^0, S^1 }, as well as many other inventories permitted by the Ancestral Constraint. Hence the following additional constraint:

(9) *The Syntagmatic Constraint on Syntactic Category Inventories*
For any language L:
If X and Y are syntactic categories in L, then L must have constructions containing expressions belonging to both X and Y.

The Syntagmatic Constraint thus rules out syntactic category inventories that are disjoint, that is to say, contain categories which can never enter into any kind of construction together.[4]

An additional constraint on syntactic category inventories makes reference to the two kinds of categories defined in (4), and to the distinction between open and closed categories:

(10) *The Open-Category Constraint on Syntactic Category Inventories*
For any language L:
If X/Y is an open category in L, then X/Y is either a Modifier Category (ie. Y equals X) or an Argument Category (ie. Y is the Kernel Category of X).

The Open-Category Constraint says that Modifier Categories and Argument Categories are the two most important types of categories, in the sense that they alone can be open categories in any given language. All other categories can only be closed categories. So far, all of the examples of categories that have been discussed, or portrayed in Figure 1, have been either Modifier or Argument Categories. Some examples of categories belonging to neither of these two types are S^1/S^0, S^0 / (S^0/S^0), (S^0/S^0) / S^0, and many others; such categories, if present in a language, can only be closed.

Together, the Ancestral, Syntagmatic, and Open-Category Constraints define a set of permissible syntactic category inventories which different languages may choose from. The four simplest inventories permitted by these three constraints are listed in (11) below:

(11) *The Four Simplest Syntactic Category Inventories*
a. { S^0 }
b. { S^0, S^0/S^0 }
c. { S^0, S^1, S^0/S^1 }
d. { S^0, S^0/S^0, S^1, S^0/S^1 }

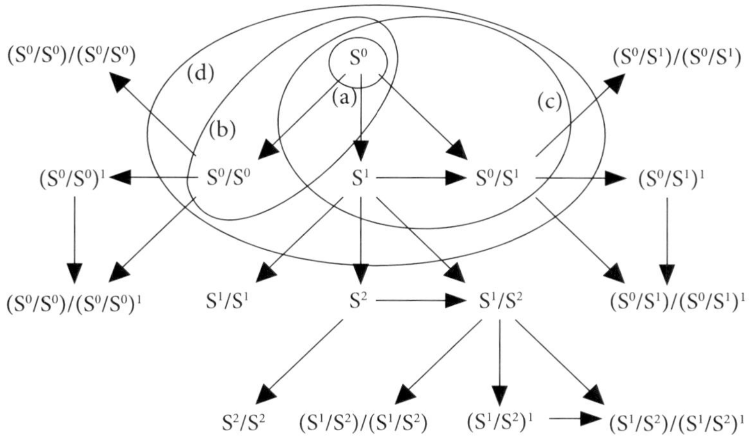

Figure 2. The Four Simplest Syntactic Category Inventories

And these same four inventories are plotted onto the Syntactic Category Tree, by means of ovals, in Figure 2.

Of the syntactic category inventories in (11), that in (11a), consisting of the single category S^0, is the simplest; languages with this syntactic category may be characterized as *monocategorial*. However, in subsequent sections of this paper, we shall be more concerned with the second simplest of the syntactic category inventories, that in (11b), consisting of the two categories S^0 and S^0/S^0.

3. Testable empirical predictions

The presentation, above, of the theory of syntactic categories already foreshadowed some possible testable empirical predictions. These and other predictions will now be made more explicit.

The fundamental insight is that syntactic categories that are simpler, or higher up in the Syntactic Category Tree, are existentially prior to syntactic categories that are more complex, or lower down on the Syntactic Category Tree. Such existential priority is manifest in three ontologically distinct domains, *typology*, *phylogeny* and *ontogeny*, resulting in the following empirical predictions:

(12) *Three empirical predictions of the Syntactic Category Tree:*

a. *Typological:*
   If a language has a certain syntactic category, it has all of its ancestor categories.
   (Categories higher on the tree are more cross-linguistically widespread.)

b. *Phylogenetic:*
If a stage in the evolution of language has a certain syntactic category, it has all of its ancestor categories.
(Categories higher on the tree evolved earlier.)

c. *Ontogenetic:*
If a stage in first-language acquisition has a certain syntactic category, it has all of its ancestor categories.
(Categories higher on the tree are acquired earlier.)

The first domain, typology, was already mentioned in the previous section: (12a) above is a recapitulation of the Ancestral Constraint in (6). However, by generalizing the notion of 'language' from the typological to the phylogenetic and ontogenetic domains, the Ancestral Constraint may also be construed as making the empirical predictions shown in (12b) and (12c).

Some possible evidence for the phylogenetic prediction in (12b) is provided in Gil (2005a, 2006a). Consideration of the linguistic abilities of captive apes such as the bonobo Kanzi and the orangutan Chantek suggests that they have acquired mastery of a grammatical system in which previously learned signs may be combined to form novel utterances. However, their linguistic behaviour provides no evidence for the existence of distinct syntactic categories: their syntactic inventory is the simplest one possible, consisting of the single syntactic category S^0 — their grammatical competence may thus be characterized as monocategorial. On the basis of such facts, monocategoriality may be reconstructed back to the common ancestor of humans and great apes, some ten million or more years in the past. Accordingly, it may be concluded that the category S^0 evolved before other syntactic categories, in accordance with the prediction in (12b).

This paper, however, focuses on the third, ontogenetic prediction, that in (12c). Broadly speaking, there are three main kinds of approaches to the first-language acquisition of syntactic categories. Innatist approaches, generally associated with generative grammar, assert that the knowledge is either there from the outset or else comes into being, or 'matures', at a certain stage of development, as a result of biological development more than actual input of real-language data from the surrounding community (see, for example, Wexler and Culicover 1980; Wexler 1999). In contrast, constructivist approaches, such as those associated with construction grammar and cognitive grammar, hold that children begin with low-level generalizations pertaining to individual words and smaller constructions, and only gradually, with continual exposure to the language, expand the scope of the generalizations, setting the stage for the formation of larger and larger syntactic categories (see, for example, Tomasello 1992, 2003).

However, the prediction in (12c) is inconsistent with both innatist and constructivist approaches, pointing instead to a third kind of approach, which might be labelled deconstructivist. The deconstructivist approach differs from innatist ones, resembling instead constructivist approaches, in that it recognizes that the child's linguistic abilities develop over time, as a result of exposure to the language of the environment, and inferences made on the basis of such exposure. However, it differs with regard to the main direction of such development, in the domain of syntactic categories at least. Whereas constructivist approaches generally assert that the development is from the particular to the general, and hence from large inventories of small categories to small inventories of large categories, the deconstructivist approach posits an opposite development, from the general to the particular, and hence from small inventories of large categories to large inventories of small categories.

Thus, the prediction in (12c) states that in the process of first-language acquisition, children start at the top of the Syntactic Category Tree and work their way downwards until they reach the syntactic category inventory of the target adult language. At the outset, they have but the single category S^0, and they persist with monocategoriality until exposure to the facts of the language forces them to posit the existence of additional syntactic categories, which they form by means of the two Category Formation Operators in (1b). Again and again, as they learn more of their language, they apply these two operators to enrich their syntactic category inventories, until they reach the final, adult grammar.

In this paper, we shall be concerned specifically with the first stage of the developmental process predicted in (12c), that in which the child's inventory of syntactic categories consists of the single category S^0. However, in order to do so, it is first necessary to take cognizance of the logical relationship that obtains between the child's inventory of syntactic categories and his or her syntagmatic competence, the ability to string words together to form longer utterances. As is well known, children begin with a one-word stage, lacking the ability to combine words into longer utterances. But at the one-word stage, all words have the same syntactic distribution, and hence they belong to the same syntactic category, namely S^0. Thus, the fact that children start out monocategorially is a logical consequence of the one-word stage, and hence cannot be taken as providing support for the prediction in (12c). In order to conduct a substantive test of the prediction in (12c), it is necessary to examine the syntactic category inventory at a stage in which the child is capable of dealing with multi-word utterances, which provide the potential for distinguishing between syntactic categories on distributional grounds.

In this paper, we shall examine the following more specific prediction, stemming from that in (12c):

(13) *Testable Prediction: The Multi-Word Monocategorial Stage:*
First-language acquisition passes through a multi-word monocategorial stage, in which children have already acquired mastery of multi-word utterances, but still possess only the single syntactic category S^0.

The above prediction is put to the test in the next section of this paper.

4. The multi-word monocategorial stage in Jakarta Indonesian

We shall now provide evidence for the existence of a multi-word monocategorial stage in the first-language acquisition of Jakarta Indonesian. Section 4.1 provides a brief introduction to Jakarta Indonesian. Section 4.2 presents an analysis of the syntactic category inventory of adult Jakarta Indonesian, arguing that it consists of a single open category S^0 plus a single closed category S^0/S^0. Section 4.3 introduces the naturalistic child-language corpus on which the present study is conducted. And Section 4.4 presents examples of overgeneralization errors from the corpus involving S^0/S^0 words that are treated instead as S^0 words, and argues that they support the prediction, made in (13), of a multi-word monocategorial stage, in the acquisition of Jakarta Indonesian.

4.1 Jakarta Indonesian

Jakarta Indonesian is the general colloquial language used in Jakarta, the capital and largest city of Indonesia, in most everyday contexts, for inter-ethnic and increasingly also intra-ethnic communication; in addition, it is gaining in currency as an informal lingua franca throughout Indonesia. Until quite recently, Jakarta Indonesian had not been subject to serious scientific investigation; however, this has begun to change, with recent studies by, among others, Wouk (1989, 1999), Sneddon (2003), Cole and Hermon (2005), Cole, Hermon and Tjung (2005), and Tjung (2006).

Jakarta Indonesian is distinct from Betawi Malay, the native dialect of the indigenous ethnic community of Jakarta, now a small minority of the total population of the city, described by Kähler (1966), Abdul Chaer (1976), Ikranagara (1980), Muhadjir (1981), Grijns (1991) and others. Jakarta Indonesian is also distinct from Standard Indonesian, used in more formal contexts in Jakarta and throughout Indonesia, and familiar to many general linguists from an extensive literature. However, as is often the case in situations of diglossia, there exists a continuum of language varieties between Jakarta Indonesian and Betawi Malay, and between Jakarta Indonesian and Standard Indonesian.

Jakarta Indonesian also differs from related language varieties with respect to the manner in which it is acquired. Jakarta Indonesian is acquired naturally, automatically and completely, at a young age, by most or all children growing up in Jakarta. In contrast, Betawi Malay is acquired by at most a small minority of Jakarta children, alongside Jakarta Indonesian. And Standard Indonesian is acquired by children at a generally later age, largely from the media and via conscious schooling; its acquisition is inherently imperfect, inasmuch as nobody may be considered to be a true native speaker of the standard language.

Jakarta Indonesian is one of a number of colloquial varieties of Indonesian associated with particular regions throughout the country. In this respect, it resembles Riau Indonesian, which has already featured in much recent discussion of syntactic categories. Although they are quite distinct dialects, Jakarta and Riau Indonesian share a common typological profile, and most of the general grammatical claims made about Riau Indonesian carry over straightforwardly also to Jakarta Indonesian.

4.2 Syntactic categories in Jakarta Indonesian

Compared to many other languages, the syntactic category inventory of Jakarta Indonesian is very impoverished, bearing, instead, a close resemblance to that of Riau Indonesian, as described in Gil (1994, 2000, 2001a,b, 2005a,c, to appear). The syntactic category inventory of Jakarta Indonesian consists of the two syntactic categories S^0 and S^0/S^0, as represented in (11b), and plotted on the Syntactic Category Tree in Figure 3 below:

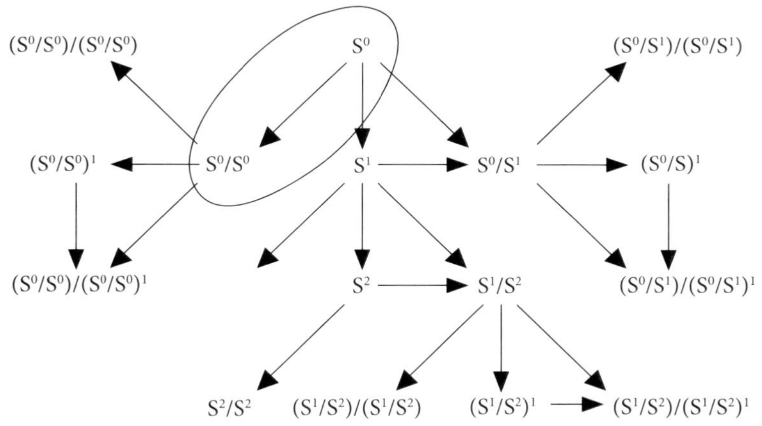

Figure 3. The Syntactic Category Inventory of Jakarta Indonesian

The two syntactic categories of Jakarta Indonesian are of quite different status. Whereas S^0 is an open category, containing all multi-word expressions and almost all single-word expressions in the language, S^0/S^0 is a closed category, consisting of just a few dozen single-word expressions.

A partial lexicon of Jakarta Indonesian, showing the breakdown into two syntactic categories, is provided in (14) and (15) below:[5]

(14) *A Partial Lexicon of Jakarta Indonesian: S^0 words*

a. ayam chicken	b. buku book	c. rumah house
d. ijo green	e. gede big	f. laper hungry
g. lari run	h. makan eat	i. kasi give

j.	Pian [name of person]	k.	Olimo [name of place]	l.	Lebaran [name of holiday]
m.	abang elder.brother	n.	gue 1:SG	o.	ini DEM:PROX
p.	gini like-DEM:PROX	q.	sini LOC-DEM:PROX	r.	tadi PST:PROX
s.	tiga three	t.	semua all	u.	lain other
v.	apa what	w.	mana where / which	x.	kapan when
y.	ada exist	z.	punya have	aa.	bisa can
bb.	udah PFCT	cc.	paling SUPERL	dd.	nggak NEG
ee.	lagi more / again	ff.	sendiri alone / REFL	gg.	sama same / with

(15) *A Partial Lexicon of Jakarta Indonesian: S^0/S^0 words*

Preceding

a.	kayak like	b.	untuk for	c.	buat for
d.	di LOC	e.	ke to	f.	dari from
g.	dengan with	h.	tentang about	i.	gara-gara because:ADVRS
j.	tiap every	k.	pada PL	l.	ato or
m.	yang REL	n.	si PERS	o.	kalo TOP

Following

p.	doang only	q.	aja just	r	juga also
s.	kek UNCRT	t.	diri REFL	u.	dong EMPH

Almost all words in Jakarta Indonesian belong to S^0; (14) presents just a very small sample thereof. As evident from the above, S^0 words in Jakarta Indonesian may denote things, as in (30a)–(30c); properties, as in (30d)–(30f); or activities, as in (30g)–(30i). In addition, S^0 words may be names of people, places or times, as in (30j)–(30l); deictic, as in (30m)–(30r); quantificational, as in (30s)–(30u); or interrogative, as in (30v)–(30x). Finally, S^0 words may have a variety of meanings which, in most other languages, are typically expressed by means of various grammatical markers; these include existence, as in (30y); possession, as in (30z); ability, as in (30aa); aspect, as in (30bb); superlativity, as in (30cc); negation, as in (30dd); and various macrofunctional words, as in (30ee), (30ff) and (30gg).

As S^0's, almost all words in Jakarta Indonesian exhibit identical syntactic behaviour. In particular, there are no syntactic differences between words referring to things and words referring to activities. As S^0's, almost all words can occur readily as complete non-elliptical sentences in a wide range of contexts; moreover, any S^0 word can combine with any other S^0 words, in accordance with the rule of Identity Combination in (2a), to yield a multi-word S^0 expression, and so on recursively. Thus, any string of S^0 words, with any associated constituent structure, is syntactically well-formed, though it may turn out to be semantically anomalous.

Whereas a monocategorial language would stop here, Jakarta Indonesian goes just one small step further, introducing a closed modifier category of S^0/S^0 expressions. While the list in (14) represents a tiny proportion of the S^0 words in the language, the list in (15) actually includes a large proportion of the existing S^0/S^0 words, which probably does not exceed a few dozen. As evident from the list in (15), S^0/S^0 expressions are a very mixed bag semantically: if any generalization can be made, it is that their meanings are all of an abstract nature. Interestingly, many S^0/S^0 expressions in (15) correspond closely in their meanings to other S^0 expressions in (14). For example, the universal quantifier *tiap* in (15j) is the distributive counterpart of the non-distributive universal quantifier *semua* in (14t), while the reflexive *diri* in (15u) is a hyponym of the macrofunctional *sendiri* in (14ff). The only motivation for the S^0/S^0 category is thus syntactic. As suggested by their category name, members of S^0/S^0 cannot stand by themselves as complete sentences; rather, they combine with S^0 expressions to form S^0 expressions, in accordance with the rule of Slash Combination in (2b). Moreover, as suggested in (15), S^0/S^0 expressions may be further classified with regard to their linear order in relationship to their heads. Whereas the forms in (15a)–(15o) obligatorily precede their head S^0's, those in (15p)–(15u) invariably follow their heads.

The inventory of syntactic categories exemplified in (14) and (15) above allows for the following three basic constructions characteristic of the syntax of Jakarta Indonesian indicated and exemplified in (16) below:

(16) *The Three Basic Syntactic Constructions of Jakarta Indonesian:*

a. *Construction A*

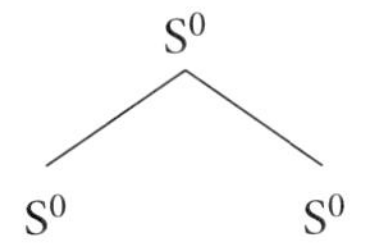

eg. Ayam makan
chicken eat

b. *Construction B*

S^0

S^0/S^0 S^0

eg. Yang makan

REL eat

c. *Construction C*

S^0

S^0 S^0/S^0

eg. Ayam aja

chicken just

In any text in Jakarta Indonesian, most of the syntax makes use of the first construction, that represented in (16a), in which two open-class S^0 expressions are put together by means of the rule of Identity Combination in (2a). However, when items belonging to the closed syntactic category S^0/S^0 are present, they enter into one of the remaining two constructions represented in (16b) and (16c), combining with S^0 expressions in accordance with the rule of Slash Combination in (2b).

Table 1. The Max Planck Institute Jakarta Child Language Corpus: A Numerical Profile

Target Child		*Age at First Coded Utterance*	*Age at Last Coded Utterance*	*Number of Coded Utterances*
Timo	(M)	1;6	5;0	34,325
Hizkia	(M)	1;8	5;11	35,111
Rizka	(F)	1;9	6;1	63,960
Michael	(M)	2;0	3;10	28,668
Priska	(F)	2;7	6;0	47,224
Larissa	(F)	2;10	6;4	33,657
Ido	(M)	3;4	6;5	35,497
Pipit	(F)	4;5	8;9	36,025
TOTAL: Target children				314,467
Other children				127,696
TOTAL: all children (under 12)				442,163
TOTAL: all adults				470,416
GRAND TOTAL				912,579

4.3 The Max Planck Institute Jakarta Child Language Corpus

In order to investigate the acquisition of Jakarta Indonesian, eight largely monolingual children residing in Jakarta were studied longitudinally for periods ranging from roughly two to four years. Their speech, and that of other children and adults in their immediate environment, was transcribed, coded, and entered into a database, which constitutes the MPI Jakarta Child Language Corpus. A numerical profile of the MPI Jakarta Child Language Corpus is provided in Table 1.

The MPI Jakarta Child Language Corpus has formed the basis for a number of previous studies of various aspects of the acquisition of Jakarta Indonesian, in Cole, Gil, Hermon and Tadmor (2001, 2008), Gil (2006b), Tjung (2006), and Tadmor (to appear). The MPI Jakarta Child Language Corpus was recently made available for public access through the Child Language Data Exchange System CHILDES.

4.4 Errors of overgeneralization in the Corpus

With just S^0 and S^0/S^0, there is limited scope for developmental patterns in the acquisition of syntactic categories in Jakarta Indonesian. Nevertheless, the prediction in (12c) entails that S^0 will be acquired before S^0/S^0, while its more specific variant in (13) posits the existence of a stage in the acquisition of Jakarta Indonesian with multi-word utterances but still only the single category S^0.

Evidence for the existence of a multi-word monocategorial stage in the acquisition of Jakarta Indonesian may be derived from errors of overgeneralization in which S^0/S^0 words are used as though they were S^0 words. Such errors may be of the following two kinds:[6]

(17) Types of Overgeneralization:
  a. *Type 1 overgeneralizations:*
     S^0/S^0 words occurring on their own as complete non-elliptical sentences.
  b. *Type 2 overgeneralizations:*
     S^0/S^0 words occurring in construction with their S^0 heads, but in the wrong order.

Type 1 overgeneralizations make reference to the most salient characteristic of S^0 expressions, their ability to stand on their own as complete non-elliptical sentences. In Type 1 overgeneralizations, S^0/S^0 words occur as complete non-elliptical sentences: in such cases, it is reasonable to infer that the child is treating them as S^0 words, presumably because he or she has not yet figured out the existence of an additional S^0/S^0 category. Type 2 overgeneralizations make reference to another important characteristic of S^0 expressions, their flexibility with respect to linear order. In Type 2 overgeneralizations S^0/S^0 words occur on the wrong side of their S^0 heads, that is to say, in violation of the linear order prescribed in (15). In such cases too, one may plausibly conclude that the child is treating the words in question as S^0 words, presumably because he or she has not yet acquired the additional category S^0/S^0.

Examples from the MPI Jakarta Child Language Corpus of overgeneralizations of types 1 and 2 are presented and discussed below. Example (18) provides an illustration of a type 1 overgeneralization involving the S^0/S^0 word *kayak* 'like':[7]

(18) **Michael (2;08)** and experimenter playing with a doll.

(-5) Heh, kamu ape? — *Michael*
EXCL 2 what
'Hey, what's with you?'

(-4) Hmm... — *Michael*
EXCL
'Here.'

(-3) 'Eh, jangan taro di kepalaku, dong.' — *experimenter*
EXCL NEG:IMP put LOC head-1:SG EMPH
"Hey, don't put that on my head."

(-2) 'Kepalaku 'kan botak.' — *experimenter*
head-1:SG Q bald
"My head's bald."

(-1) 'Kayak kepala kamu, nggak?' — *experimenter*
like head 2 NEG
"Like your head, right?"

(0) ***Kayak.*** — ***Michael***
like
'Right.'

In example (18) above, Michael and the experimenter are playing with a doll with a shiny bald head. In (18/-5) and (18/-4) Michael addresses the doll, and tries to stick something on its head. In (18/-3), (18/-2) and (18/-1) the experimenter assumes the role of the doll, chiding Michael, and then teasing him for also having a bald head, like that of the doll. Utterance (18/-1) ends with the yes-no tag *nggak*, to which Michael, in (18/0) responds in the affirmative, with the S^0/S^0 expression *kayak*.

Michael's response, *kayak*, provides an example of type 1 overgeneralization, with an S^0/S^0 expression standing alone as a complete non-elliptical utterance. In adult Jakarta Indonesian, utterance (18/0) is ungrammatical; *kayak* must be followed by its head S^0 expression. However, Michael's utterance in (18/0) suggests that he is not yet aware of the existence of a class of words, *kayak* among them, that cannot stand on their own as complete non-elliptical utterances. Although, at the age of 2;08, he is well into the multi-word stage, his grammar is thus still monocategorial; he has not yet acquired the category of S^0/S^0. These observations are summarized below, with analyses of Michael's utterance in (18/0) from the dual perspectives of the adult grammar, in (19a), and Michael's monocategorial grammar at the time of utterance, in (19b):

(19) *Analysis of (18/0):*

a. *Adult Grammar*

S^0

S^0/S^0 S^0

Kayak

like ↑

missing

b. *Child Grammar*

S^0

Kayak

like

It is worthy of note that the non-adultlike aspect of Michael's linguistic behaviour revealed in example (18) is purely syntactic, not semantic or pragmatic. Michael has a perfectly good understanding of the meaning of *kayak*, and in the above discourse he reacts in appropriate manner to the good-natured teasing by the experimenter. All that he is lacking is the syntactic knowledge that *kayak* behaves differently from most other words in the language. To appreciate the purely syntactic nature of Michael's deficit, we may construct a paraphrase of the final exchange in (18/-1) and (18/0) by replacing the S^0/S^0 word *kayak* 'like' with a nearly synonymous S^0 word *mirip* 'resemble': *Mirip kepala kamu, nggak? Mirip.* Such a paraphrase would be grammatical and completely natural in adult Jakarta Indonesian, in which, as in many other languages, the most common way of answering a yes-no question in the affirmative is not with a word meaning 'yes', but rather by repeating the main word in the preceding utterance. Moreover, in the given context, it would have been every bit as appropriate as the original exchange in (18). Michael's actual response in (18), with *kayak*, shows that he has already mastered this discourse pattern; all that he doesn't know is that *kayak* is one of a small set of words which, for purely syntactic reasons, cannot be used in this way.

A second example of type 1 overgeneralization, involving the S^0/S^0 word *juga*, is given in (20) below:

(20) **Larissa (4;10)**, older sister and experimenter sitting in front of the computer.

(-2) Awas! *elder sister*
watch.out
'Move over!'

(-1) Kak(ak) mo minum dulu, ah. *elder sister*
elder.sibling want drink first EXCL
'I want to get something to drink.'

(0) ***Juga.*** ***Larissa***
also
'Too.'

(1) Juga. *experimenter*
also
'Too.'

(2) He-em. *Larissa*
EXCL
'Uh-huh.'

(3) Om juga. *experimenter*
uncle also
'Me too.'

In (20), the speakers are sitting in front of the computer; in (20/-2) and (20/-1) Larissa's elder sister gets up to get something to drink. In (20/0) Larissa attempts to say 'me too', and produces the utterance exemplifying a type 1 overgeneralization. In (20/1) the experimenter echoes her ungrammatical construction; in (20/2) Larissa responds with an affirmation of her wish for a drink, and then, in (20/3), the experimenter says that he wants one too, this time using a grammatical construction.

Larissa's utterance in (20/0) provides another example of a type 1 overgeneralization, with an S^0/S^0 expression standing alone as a complete non-elliptical utterance. Whereas *kayak* is an S^0/S^0 expression that must be followed by its head, *juga* is an S^0/S^0 expression that must be preceded by its head, as indeed it is in the grammatical (20/3). However, Larissa, though already at the age of 4;10, appears to be unaware of this fact, as suggested by her utterance in (20/0). Rather, she seems to be treating *juga* as an S^0 expression, which is consistent with her not yet having acquired the category S^0/S^0. This is summarized in the following analysis of (20/0), from the perspectives of the adult and child grammars respectively:

(21) *Analysis of (20/0):*

a. *Adult Grammar*

S^0
S^0 S^0/S^0
Juga
↑ also
missing

b. *Child Grammar*

S^0
Juga
also

Thus, (18) and (20) provide examples of type 1 overgeneralizations, in which S^0/S^0 words stand on their own as complete non-elliptical utterances, thereby suggesting that the children uttering them are still at a multi-word monocategorial stage of language acquisition, and have not yet acquired the category S^0/S^0.

We now turn to consider cases of type 2 overgeneralization. Example (22) below provides an illustration of a type 2 overgeneralization involving the S^0/S^0 word *untuk* 'for':

(22) **Michael (2;10)** examining a toy first aid kit.

(-9) Apa ini? *Michael*
what DEM:PROX
'What's this?'

(-8) Ini apa ini? *Michael*
DEM:PROX what DEM:PROX
'What's this?'

(-7) Ini apa ini? *Michael*
DEM:PROX what DEM:PROX
'What's this?'

(-6) Ini namanya… *experimenter*
DEM:PROX name-ASSOC
'This is called …'

(-5) Ini yang me(rah)-merah apa? *Michael*
DEM:PROX REL DISTR-red what
'What's this red thing?'

(-4) Palang merah. *experimenter*
cross red
'A red cross.'

(-3) Yang merah-me(rah). *Michael*
REL DISTR-red
'The red thing.'

(-2) Palang merah apa? *Michael*
cross red what
'What's a red cross?'

(-1) Hmm? *experimenter*
EXCL
'Huh?'

(0) Palang merah *apa* ***untuk***? ***Michael***
cross red what for
'What's the red cross for?'

(1) Palang merah ini. *experimenter*
cross red DEM:PROX
'This is a red cross.'

(2) Bantuan untuk orang sakit. *experimenter*
help-AUG for person sick
'It's for helping sick people.'

In example (22) above, Michael is asking about a toy first aid kit on which a red cross is prominently displayed, in the repetitive and persistent fashion characteristic of inquisitive children: 'What's this?' 'A red cross.' 'What's a red cross?' When his question in (22/-2) receives no satisfactory response in (22/-1), he amplifies it by adding the S^0/S^0 word *untuk* 'for' in (20/0).

The resulting construction, *apa untuk*, looks just like its English translation 'what for'; however, it is completely ungrammatical in Jakarta Indonesian. The expression *untuk* 'for' is a S^0/S^0 word of the kind that must be followed by its S^0 head, as in fact it is in (22/2) *untuk orang sakit*. However, in (22/0), *untuk* is instead preceded by its S^0 head *apa* 'what'. Thus, the construction *apa untuk* exhibits incorrect word order: it should have been *untuk apa*. The construction *apa untuk* accordingly displays the flexibility of word order characteristic of the way in which S^0 expressions are combined. Michael's production of this construction therefore suggests that he considers not just *apa* but also *untuk* to be a member of the category S^0; it thus points towards the conclusion that, at the time of utterance, he had not yet acquired the category S^0/S^0. These observations are summarized below, with analyses of Michael's utterance of *untuk apa* in (22/0) from the perspectives of the adult grammar, in (23a), and Michael's own grammar at the time of utterance, in (23b):[8]

(23) *Analysis of (22/0):*

a. *Adult Grammar*

S^0

S^0	S^0/S^0
apa	untuk
what	for

← *wrong order* →

b. *Child Grammar*

S^0

S^0	S^0
apa	untuk
what	for

A second example of type 2 overgeneralization, involving the S^0/S^0 relative marker *yang*, is given in (24) below:[9]

(24) **Michael (2;09)** pretending to be a cook.

(-4) Maunya mi goreng? *Michael*
want-ASSOC noodles fry
'Do you want fried noodles?'

(-3) Sapi aja. *mother*
cow just
'I want beef.'
(-2) Mau mi goreng. *Michael*
want noodles fry
'Fried noodles.'
(-1) Oh, iya, mi goreng, deh. *mother*
EXCL yes noodles fry EXCL
'Oh alright, fried noodles then.'
(0) *Mi gorengnya* ***yang*** berapa? ***Michael***
noodles fry-ASSOC REL how.much
'How many fried noodles?'
(1) Tiga. *mother*
three
'Three.'
(2) Tiga. *Michael*
three
'Three.'
(3) He-em. *mother*
EXCL
'Uh-huh.'

In example (24) above, Michael is pretending to be a food-stall operator, and his mother assumes the role of customer. Michael offers fried noodles in (24/-4); his mother prefers beef (24/-3), but fried noodles is all there is (24/-2), so fried noodles it is (24/-1). At which point Michael asks how many portions he should prepare (24/0).

Utterance (24/0), *Mi gorengnya yang berapa,* takes a bit of explaining. To begin with, in the context of a food-stall, *berapa* can mean either 'how many' (portions) or 'how much' (money). And the relative marker *yang* is an S^0/S^0 expression that, in the adult language, must occur before its S^0 head. Accordingly, in the adult language, utterance (24/0) can only be parsed in such a way that *yang* occurs in construction with *berapa*: *[Mi gorengnya] [yang berapa?]*. As it turns out, in the context of a food-stall, such a parsing yields a plausible interpretation, albeit one that is hard to express in idiomatic English: 'The fried noodles that are how much?' For example, if there is a 5000 Rupiah fried noodles dish and a 7000 Rupiah fried noodles dish, *Mi gorengnya yang berapa* might be used to ask which of the two dishes, the 5000 one or the 7000 one, the customer wants. Nevertheless, although the grammatical parsing of the utterance yields a plausible interpretation, the continuation of the discourse makes it clear that this was *not* the interpretation that was intended. Rather, what Michael meant, and what Michael's mother understood, was 'How many portions of fried noodles.' To appreciate this, it is necessary to take into account the fact that in Indonesian food-stalls, people typically eat in groups and order the same item. Thus, when Michael's mother says 'three', and Michael repeats her response, it is clear that she is referring to the number of portions that she is ordering, perhaps for herself and two imaginary companions. However, in the adult language, the way to ask 'How many portions of fried noodles' is not as in (24/0) but rather *Yang mi gorengnya berapa*, in which the S^0/S^0 relative marker *yang* occurs in front of its head S^0 expression *mi gorengnya*, and the resulting constituent, *Yang mi gorengnya* means something like 'the ones that are fried noodles' or 'the ones that want fried noodles'. Accordingly, it would seem as though the most appropriate analysis of Michael's utterance in (24/0) is one in which he 'should have' said (and was understood as saying) *Yang mi gorengnya berapa*, but actually said *Mi gorengnya yang berapa*.

Thus, utterance (24/0) provides another example of a type 2 overgeneralization, in which an S^0/S^0 expression occurs on the wrong side of its S^0 head. What makes it possible for Michael to utter (24/0) is the fact that he has not yet acquired the category S^0/S^0, and is therefore treating the relative marker *yang* as any other S^0 expression, which can occur either before or after its sister constituent. The analysis of (24/0) from adult and child perspectives is summarized in (25a) and (25b) respectively:[10]

(25) *Analysis of (24/0):*

a. *Adult Grammar*

S^0

S^0 S^0/S^0

mi gorengnya yang

noodles fried-ASSOC REL

← *wrong order* →

b. *Child Grammar*

S^0

S^0 S^0

mi gorengnya yang

noodles fried-ASSOC REL

Thus, (22) and (24) provide examples of type 2 overgeneralizations, in which S^0/S^0 words occur on the wrong sides of their S^0 heads, thereby suggesting that the children uttering them are still at a multi-word monocategorial stage of language acquisition, and have not yet acquired the category S^0/S^0.

5. Conclusions and further questions

In Section 4.4 above, a detailed examination was presented of four naturalistic passages from the MPI Jakarta Child Language Corpus exemplifying overgeneralizations of the two types predicted in (17): S^0/S^0 words occurring on their own as complete non-elliptical sentences, and S^0/S^0 words occurring in construction with their S^0 heads but in the wrong order. These and other examples of overgeneralization provide support for the analysis of Jakarta Indonesian as possessing just two syntactic categories, S^0 and S^0/S^0, presented in Section 4.2, and for the existence of a multi-word monocategorial stage in the acquisition of Jakarta Indonesian, as predicted in (13). In turn, the demonstrated existence of such a multi-word but monocategorial stage of acquisition constitutes empirical support for a theory of syntactic categories of a dominatory nature, such as that sketched in Section 2, in which more complex syntactic categories are derived from simpler ones. In summary, then, what the errors of overgeneralization show is that children acquiring syntactic categories follow the Syntactic Category Tree in Figure 1, generated by the Slash and Kernel Operators defined in (1a). Or in other words, children acquire simpler syntactic categories before more complex ones.

The present study raises a number of further questions, which can only be touched upon briefly here. One question is whether the child acquiring a new category immediately identifies all of its members, transferring them from the old category to the new one in one fell swoop, or whether individual items are reassigned in piecemeal fashion as the evidence accrues. In the preceding discussion, it was tacitly assumed that the former scenario is the case: if the child treats an S^0/S^0 word as an S^0 word, this is because he or she has not yet acquired the category S^0/S^0. However, it could potentially be the case that the child has already acquired the category S^0/S^0, but still thinks that the word in question is an S^0 word. In order to adjudicate between these two scenarios, it is necessary to examine the linguistic behaviour of individual children in much greater detail. For example, the reader may have noticed that three out of the four errors of overgeneralization came from a single child, Michael. Closer inspection of Michael's linguistic behaviour may possibly reveal that, of the eight children studied, he is the one for whom the evidence for a multi-word monocategorial stage is the most robust. Conversely, the reader may also have been struck by the relatively advanced age of Larissa, 4;10, in example (20), where she treats the S^0/S^0 word *juga* 'also' as an S^0 word. Examination of Larissa's behaviour may thus reveal — contrary to the discussion in the preceding section — that at age 4;10 she had already acquired the category S^0/S^0 and populated it with several of the appropriate items, but had simply not yet realized that *juga* was also an S^0/S^0 word.

As evident from the partial lexicon in (15), the category S^0/S^0 is semantically heterogeneous: knowing that one word is in S^0/S^0 provides no clues as to whether some other word is also in S^0/S^0. In fact, one might wonder how the child acquiring Jakarta Indonesian makes the initial leap and realizes that the category S^0/S^0 exists, that is to say, that not all words enjoy the unconstrained distributional privileges of the category S^0. One possible answer is that children make use of negative indirect evidence, as proposed by Pinker (1981, 1984) and Goldberg (1995): if the child observes that in certain contexts an otherwise preferred construction is repeatedly avoided, he or she may accordingly infer that, in the contexts in question, this construction is disallowed. For example, the child observes that in particular contexts members of S^0 occur by themselves as complete non-elliptical utterances; however, when, in similar contexts, a certain word occurs over and over again in construction with another expression, he or she may conclude that the word in question cannot occur on its own and therefore must belong to a new syntactic category S^0/S^0. Similarly, the child observes that in particular contexts members of S^0 occur on either side of their sister expressions; however, when, in similar contexts, a certain word invariably occurs on the same side of its sister expressions, he or she may conclude, again, that the word in question cannot occur on the other side of its sister expressions, and must therefore also belong to the new syntactic category S^0/S^0.

Finally, one may ask the obvious question to what extent the account presented in this paper generalizes from Jakarta Indonesian to other languages. Prima facie, it is not unreasonable to suspect that all languages, at the beginning of the multi-word stage of acquisition, pass through a period of monocategoriality, before the differentiation of syntactic categories sets in. However, a more substantive test of the theory proposed in this paper would involve applying it to a language with a more elaborate syntactic category inventory than that of Jakarta Indonesian, to see whether indeed the acquisition of syntactic categories progresses, step by step, down a richer subset of the Syntactic Category Tree. In order to conduct such a test, though, it is first necessary to provide an adequate analysis of the syntactic category inventory of the target language within the present theoretical framework, so as to obtain a clear picture of where the process of acquisition is headed.

Acknowledgements

This paper would not have been possible without the gracious and enthusiastic cooperation of the eight children who were willing to have camcorders pointed at them regularly over a period of years, Hizkia, Ido, Larissa, Michael, Pipit, Priska, Rizka, and Timo, and well as their many friends and family members who also played a role in the project. The MPI Jakarta Child language Corpus would not have come into being without the tireless efforts of the MPI Jakarta Field Station staff in the period between 1999 and 2005: Sarah Chakrawati, Dini Andarini, Erni Farida Sri Ulina Ginting, Liana Husain, Ferdinand Okki Kurniawan, Lanny Hidayat, Like Raskova Octaberlina, Betty Litamahuputty, Dalan Mehuli, Guy Sharett, Antonia Soriente, Uri Tadmor, Brad Taylor, Yassir Nasanius Tjung, Widya Setiabudi, Yanti, and Yokebed Triwigati. The MPI Jakarta Field Station itself would not be in existence if not for the support and assistance of our host institution Universitas Katolik Indonesia Atma Jaya and the staff at the Pusat Kajian Bahasa dan Budaya, and in particular Bambang Kaswanti Purwo and Soenjono Dardjowidjojo. Versions of this paper were presented at the International Symposium of Linguistics and Speech-Hearing Sciences, Universiti Kebangsaan Malaysia, Kuala Lumpur, Malaysia, 22 October 2002; the Department of Linguistics, University of Delaware, Newark, DE, USA, 25 October 2002; the Konferensi Linguistik Tahunan Atma Jaya 1 (Kolita 1), Pusat Kajian Bahasa dan Budaya (PKBB), Unika Atma Jaya, Jakarta, Indonesia, 18 February 2003; and the Working Group on Language Acquisition, at the Twenty-Fifth Annual Meeting of the Deutsche Gesellschaft für Sprachwissenschaft, Munich, Federal Republic of Germany, 26 February 2003; I am grateful to participants at all of these events for many helpful comments and suggestions.

Notes

1. In (1) and subsequently, square brackets denote unordered sets; that is to say, syntactic constituents whose internal parts are unspecified for linear order.

2. Thus, in constructions such as Y ↔ [X, X/Y, X/Y, X/Y ...], the head of the Y expression is a member of the Kernel Category of Y. This underscores the affinity between the Kernel Category-Formation Operator and the mirror-image bar operator of X-bar theory.

3. The Ancestral Constraint thus provides the primary motivation for turning X-bar theory upside down, as is done with the Kernel Operator. Assume X and Y are categories such that X is the kernel category of Y. What the Ancestral Constraint says is that there can be languages with Y but not X, but not languages with X but not Y. Or, translated into X-bar theory: there can be languages with X^{n+1}'s but not X^{n}'s, but not languages with X^{n}'s but not X^{n+1}'s. And as a corollary: there can be languages with XPs but not Xs, but not languages with Xs but not XPs. Thus, beginning at the top, as the Kernel Operator does, rather than at the bottom, as per X-bar theory, reflects the cross-linguistic distributional facts, with more widespread syntactic categories associated with lower indices than less commonly occurring categories.

4. The Syntagmatic Constraint also rules out may other inventories that are, independently, ruled out also by the Ancestral Constraint, such as { S^0, S^0/S^1 } and { S^0/S^0, S^1, S^0/S^1 }. However, other inventories, such as { S^0/S^0 } and { S^1, S^0/S^1 }, satisfy the Syntagmatic Constraint but are ruled out by the Ancestral Constraint, thereby showing that these two constraints are logically independent.

5. For the interlinear glosses presented in this paper, the following abbreviations are used: ADVRS adversative; ASSOC associative; AUG augmentative; DEM demonstrative; DISTR distributive; EMPH emphatic; EXCL exclamation; IMP imperative; LOC locative; NEG negative; PERS personal; PFCT perfect; PROX proximate; PST past; Q question; REFL reflexive; SG singular; SUPERL superlative; TOP topic; UNCRT uncertainty; 1 1st person; 2 2nd person.

6. The two types of overgeneralization shown in (17) do not exhaust the logical possibilities; two additional types of overgeneralization are discussed in Gil (2003).

7. In (18) and subsequent examples of overgeneralization, the utterance exemplifying overgeneralization is presented in its discourse context, involving a few preceding and in some cases also following utterances. The utterance exemplifying overgeneralization is indicated in boldface

italics, and is assigned the number 0, while preceding and following utterances are assigned the appropriate serial numbers in relation to it. The speaker of each utterance is identified on the right. Each example is preceded by a brief description of the situation in which the discourse occurred, typically involving the target child, with name and age at time of utterance indicated in boldface, the experimenter, and members of the child's family.

8. It is interesting to speculate what meaning Michael might have associated with the word *untuk* 'for' and the construction *apa untuk*. In Southeast Asian languages, it is common to find patterns of macrofunctionality in which the word 'for' also denotes a semantically general activity such as 'give' or 'do'. In fact, a similar pattern is also in evidence in Jakarta Indonesian, albeit panglossically, in conjunction with the standard language. In Jakarta Indonesian, *untuk* is actually not the most common word for 'for'; more common is the word *buat*. (In fact, the combination *buat apa* is a very frequent way of asking 'why'.) However, in Standard Indonesian, *buat* means 'do'. And since most speakers of Jakarta Indonesian know at least some Standard Indonesian, they are accordingly aware of the connection between 'for' and 'do'. This, then, raises the possibility that Michael, at 2;10, thinks *untuk* means 'do'. But then why did he choose to place the interrogative *apa* 'what' before *untuk*, seeing as how the analysis in (23b) allows for either order? In general, content interrogative expressions occur in situ, that it to say, in the same positions as the corresponding non-interrogative expressions. If Michael had meant to say 'what does it do', then he would have placed *apa* after *untuk*, since this is the typical position for patients. Instead, it seems that what Michael had in mind was an identificational construction, something along the lines of 'what is the doing', or, to use another English word with similar meaning, 'what is the function'. In general, in identificational constructions, word order is flexible, and this is true also when one of the two terms of the construction is interrogative. Indeed, both ordering options can even be observed in Michael's speech in (22): whereas in (22/-9) *apa* occurs before *ini*, in (22/-2) *apa* occurs after *palang merah*. Thus, it would seem as though *apa untuk* in (22/0) mirrors the similar but in this case perfectly grammatical *apa ini* in (22/-9).

9. The term 'relative marker' is used in a loose sense, to capture the fact that *yang* frequently occurs in constructions whose English translations involve relative clauses. Indeed, Jakarta Indonesian *yang* is often referred to in the literature as a relative marker; see for example Cole and Hermon (2005) and Tjung (2006). However, work in progress suggests that this characterization may be inappropriate, and that Jakarta Indonesian may not have relative clauses; see Gil (2005b) for analogous arguments for the Riau dialect of Indonesian. Still, for the purposes of the present paper, none of this matters; the only important fact about *yang* is one that nobody disputes, namely that it must always occur before some other constituent, be it a relative clause, as in some analyses, or a head S^0 expression, as per the analysis presented herein.

10. Taking note of the fact that Michael is of Chinese ethnicity, it may be suggested that his utterance *mi gorengnya yang* in (24/0) exhibits interference from some variety of Chinese to which Michael may have been exposed, in which the relative marker follows its sister constituent rather than preceding it. However, this is very unlikely. To begin with, Michael's linguistic environment is almost exclusively Indonesian, with very little exposure to any Chinese languages. Moreover, in Chinese-influenced varieties of Malay/Indonesian, such as the so-called 'bazaar Malay', in which the internal syntax of the NP is largely patterned after that of Southern Min dialects, the relative marker, e.g. Hokkien e^{24}, is invariably replaced not by *yang* but rather by a form based on the Malay/Indonesian *punya* 'have'.

References

Abdul, Chaer. 1976. *Kamus Dialek Jakarta*. Ende: Nusa Indah.

Ajdukiewicz, Kazimierz. 1935. Die syntaktische Konnexitat. *Studia Philosophica* 1: 1–27.

Austin, Peter & Joan Bresnan. 1996. Nonconfigurationality in Australian Aboriginal Languages. *Natural Language and Linguistic Theory* 14: 215–268.

Bar-Hillel, Yehoshua. 1953. A quasi-arithmetical notation for syntactic description. *Language* 29: 47–58.

Boas, Franz (ed.). 1911. *Handbook of American Indian languages*, Smithsonian Institution, Bureau of American Ethnology, Washington.

Chomsky, Noam A. 1965. *Aspects of the theory of syntax*. Cambridge, MA: The MIT Press.

Chomsky, Noam A. 1970. Remarks on nominalization. *Readings in English transformational grammar*, R.A. Jacobs & P.S. Rosenbaum (eds.), 184–221, Washington, DC: Georgetown University Press.

Cole, Peter; David Gil; Gabriella Hermon & Uri Tadmor. 2001. The acquisition of in-situ WH-questions and WH-indefinites in Jakarta Indonesian. *Proceedings of the 25th Annual Boston University Conference on Language Development, Volume 1*, A. H.-J. Do; L. Domínguez & A. Johansen (eds.), 169–179. Somerville MA: Cascadilla.

Cole, Peter; David Gil; Gabriella Hermon & Uri Tadmor. 2008. The acquisition of WH forms in Jakarta Indonesian, A preliminary study. *Studies in the acquisition of Malay / Indonesian,* U. Tadmor (ed.), NUSA Linguistic Studies in Indonesian and Languages in Indonesia. Jakarta: Universitas Atma Jaya.

Cole, Peter & Gaby Hermon. 2005. Subject and Non-Subject Relativization in Indonesian. *Journal of East Asian Linguistics* 14: 59–88.

Cole, Peter; Gaby Hermon & Yassir Nasanius Tjung. 2005. How irregular is WH in situ in Indonesian? *Studies in Language* 29: 553–581.

Gil, David. 1983. Stacked adjectives and configurationality. *Linguistic Analysis* 12: 141–158.

Gil, David. 1994. The structure of Riau Indonesian. *Nordic Journal of Linguistics* 17:179–200.

Gil, David. 2000. Syntactic categories, cross-linguistic variation and universal grammar. *Approaches to the Typology of Word Classes.* Petra M. Vogel & Bernard Comrie (eds.), 173–216. Berlin: Mouton [Empirical Approaches to Language Typology].

Gil, David. 2001a. Creoles, complexity and Riau Indonesian. *Linguistic Typology* 5: 325–371.

Gil, David. 2001b. Escaping Eurocentrism: Fieldwork as a process of unlearning. *Linguistic Fieldwork*, P. Newman & M. Ratliff (eds.), 102–132. Cambridge: Cambridge University Press.

Gil, David. 2003. How children acquire syntactic categories in Jakarta Indonesian. *Kolita 1, Konferensi Linguistik Tahunan Atma Jaya,* Katharina Endriati Sukatmo (ed.) Pusat Kajian 265–269. Bahasa dan Budaya, Jakarta: Unika Atma Jaya.

Gil, David. 2005a. Isolating-monocategorial-associational language. *Handbook of categorization in cognitive science*. H. Cohen & C. Lefebvre (eds.), 347–379. Oxford: Elsevier.

Gil, David. 2005b. Getting by without relative clauses: How Riau Indonesian does it. Paper presented at Workshop on the Typology, Acquisition and Processing of Relative Clauses, Max Planck Institute for Evolutionary Anthropology, Leipzig, Germany, 12 June 2005.

Gil, David. 2005c. Word order without syntactic categories: How Riau Indonesian does it. *Verb first: On the syntax of verb-initial languages*, Andrew Carnie; Heidi Harley & Sheila A. Dooley (eds.), 243–263. Amsterdam: John Benjamins.

Gil, David. 2006a. Early human language was isolating-monocategorial-associational. *The evolution of language, proceedings of the 6th international conference (EVOLANG6)*, A. Cangelosi, A.D.M Smith & K. Smith (eds.), 91–98. Singapore: World Scientific.

Gil, David. 2006b. The acquisition of voice morphology in Jakarta Indonesian, *The Acquisition of verbs and their grammar: The effect of particular languages*, N. Gagarina & I Gülzow (eds.), 201–227. Dordrecht: Springer.

Gi, David. To appear. Riau Indonesion: A language without nouns and verbs. *Flexible word classes*, Jan Rijkhoff & Eva van Lier (eds.). Oxford: Oxford University Press.

Goldberg, Adele E. 1995. *Constructions, A construction grammar approach to argument structure*. Chicago, IL: University of Chicago Press.

Grijns, C.D. 1991. *Jakarta Malay: A multidimensional approach to spatial variation*. Leiden: KITLV Press.

Hale, Ken. 1982. Preliminary remarks on configurationality. *Proceedings of the Twelfth Annual Meeting of the North Eastern Linguistic Society*, James Pustejovsky & Peter Sells (eds.), 86–96. Amherst, MA.

Hale, Ken. 1983. Warlpiri and the grammar of non-configurational languages. *Natural Language and Linguistic Theory* 1: 5–47.

Hudson, Richard A. 1990. *English word grammar*. Basil Blackwell: Oxford.

Ikranagara, Kay. 1980. *Melayu Betawi grammar*. Jakarta: Universitas Atma Jaya. [NUSA Linguistic Studies in Indonesian and Languages in Indonesia, Vol. 9]

Jackendoff, Ray. 1977. *X' syntax: A study of phrase structure*. Cambridge, MA: The MIT Press.

Kähler, Hans. 1966. *Wörterverzeichnis des Omong Djakarta*. Berlin: Dietrich Reimer.

Keenan, Edward L. 1978. On surface form and logical form. *Linguistics in the seventies: Directions and prospects*, B.B. Kachru (ed.), 163–203. Champaign-Urbana, IL: University of Illinois.

Keenan, Edward L. & Leonard M. Faltz. 1985. *Boolean semantics for natural language.*, Dordrecht: Reidel.

Lambek, Joachim. 1958. The mathematics of sentence structure. *American Mathematical Monthly* 65: 154–170.

Lerdahl, Fred & Ray S. Jackendoff. 1983. *A generative theory of tonal music*. Cambridge, MA: The MIT Press.

Montague, Richard. 1970a. English as a formal language. *Linguaggi Nella Società e Nella Tecnica,* Bruno Visentini et al (eds.), 189–224. Milan: Edizioni di Comunità.

Montague, Richard. 1970b. Universal grammar. *Theoria* 36: 373–398.

Morrill, Glyn V. 1994. *Type logical grammar, categorial logic of signs*. Dordrecht: Kluwer.

Muhadjir. 1981. *Morphology of Jakarta dialect, affixation and reduplication*, Jakarta: Universitas Atma Jaya. [NUSA Linguistic Studies in Indonesian and Languages in Indonesia, Vol. 11].

Pinker, Steven. 1981. Comments on the Paper by Wexler. *The logical problem of language acquisition*, C.L. Baker & J.J. McCarthy (eds.), 53–78. Cambridge, MA: The MIT Press.

Pinker, Steven. 1984. *Language learnability and language development*. Cambridge, MA: Harvard University Press.

Sanders, Gerald A. 1975. *Invariant ordering*. The Hague: Mouton.

Šaumjan, Sebastian. 1965. *Strukturnaja Lingvistika*. Moscow: Izdatel'stvo Nauka.

Sneddon, James Neil. 2003. Diglossia in Indonesian. *Bijdragen tot de Taal-, Land- en Volkenkunde* 159: 519–549.

Tadmor, Uri. To appear. The acquisition of pronouns in Jakarta Indonesian. *Studies in the acquisition of Malay / Indonesian,* U. Tadmor (ed.), Jakarta: Universitas Atma Jaya [NUSA Linguistic Studies in Indonesian and Languages in Indonesia].

Tesnière, Lucien. 1959. *Élements de syntaxe structurale*. Paris: Librairie Klincksieck.
Tomasello, Michael. 1992. *First verbs: A case study of early grammatical development*. Cambridge: Cambridge University Press.
Tomasello, Michael. 2003. *Constructing a language: A usage-based theory of language acquisition*. Cambridge, MA: Harvard University Press.
Tjung, Yassir Nasanius. 2006. The formation of relative clauses in Jakarta Indonesian. A subject-object asymmetry, PhD Dissertation, University of Delaware, Newark.
Wexler, Kenneth. 1999. Maturation and growth of grammar, *Handbook of child language acquisition* W.C. Ritchie & T.K. Bhatia (eds.), 55–105. San Diego CA: Academic Press.
Wexler, Kenneth & Peter Culicover. 1980. *Formal Principles of Language Acquisition*. Cambridge: MIT Press.
Wouk, Fay. 1989. *The Impact of Discourse on Grammar: Verb Morphology in Spoken Jakarta Indonesia*. PhD Dissertation, UCLA, Los Angeles.
Wouk, Fay. 1999. Dialect Contact and Koineization in Jakarta, Indonesia. *Language Sciences* 21: 61–86.
Zwicky, Arnold M. 1985. Heads. *Journal of Linguistics* 21: 1–29.

Author's address

David Gil
Department of Linguistics
Max Planck Institute for Evolutionary Anthropology
Deutscher Platz 6
Leipzig, 04103
Germany

gil@eva.mpg.de

Possible phonological cues in categorial acquisition

Evidence from adult categorization*

Jan Don and Marian Erkelens
ACLC, University of Amsterdam

This paper reports an experiment in which adult native speakers of Dutch were asked to categorize nonce stems. These were presented without any morphological or other information about their potential class-membership. We expected that subjects would be able to categorize these words solely on the basis of phonological information. Nouns in Dutch have a richer possible syllable-structure than verbs (Trommelen 1989) and therefore, we expected that stimuli with a 'nominal' syllable make-up could be identified by the subjects as nouns where the other stimuli were ambiguous between nouns and verbs. The results show that this is indeed the case, adding to the evidence that native speakers of a language are able to use phonological information to categorize the words of their language.

1. Introduction

In this paper we report an experiment on the abilities of native Dutch speakers to determine the category of nonce words solely on the basis of phonological information. Research in the domain of language acquisition has proven that both the semantic and syntactic properties of words play an important role in the acquisition of word categories. In these studies it is proposed that certain correlations exist between syntactic properties of a word and its semantic properties, and it is demonstrated that children make use of these correlations in order to arrive at the correct meaning of a word, or to acquire certain syntactic properties (such as argument structure, category).

In a famous study on language learnability, Pinker (1987) elaborates on a 'bootstrapping' mechanism of this type, claiming that children use the semantic properties of a word as a bootstrap to the syntactic structure. A bootstrapping mechanism such as Pinker's would enable the child to infer the syntactic category of a word from a rough semantic categorization like 'thing', 'causal agent', and 'true in the past'. Although this proposal has received a lot of criticism over the years, the basic idea that the semantic and syntactic properties have correspondences that the child may use to start its syntactic categorization has survived.

Our ultimate goal is to investigate whether language-learning children also make use of phonological information to arrive at the proper categorization of the words of the ambient language. Before embarking upon such a methodologically complicated and potentially impossible undertaking, we wanted to establish that adult speakers are able to categorize words solely on the basis of their phonology. Although Cassidy and Kelly (1991) already provide experimental evidence that 3–4 year old English-learning children make use of phonological information to distinguish nouns from verbs, the idea of phonological bootstrapping has so far received only little attention in the literature. Recently, some investigations into the relationship between phonology and syntax have revealed that phonology indeed may play a role as a tell-tale of categorial information. Kelly (1996) draws attention to the fact that phonological cues have more predictive power in relation to lexical category than often has been thought.

More specifically, recent work by Shi, Morgan and Allopenna (1998) and Durieux and Gillis (2001) shows that learning algorithms are able to quite successfully distinguish function words from content words and verbs from nouns on the basis of phonological information only. Shi, Morgan and Allopenna (1998) conclude on the basis of research on Mandarin Chinese and Turkish that phonological information has predictive power for determining whether a certain word belongs to the class of function words or to the class of lexical words. Thus, lexical categories can be distinguished from functional categories in these languages on the basis of their phonological properties only. In mother-child dyads, it was found that a combination of different phonological cues, such as duration, vowel height and consonant quality (taken from Kelly 1996) could predict the super-ordinate category (i.e. lexical or functional) of words. To test the predictive power of these cues Shi, Morgan and Allopenna (1998) trained a self-organizing neural network and tested the performance on category prediction of novel items. The network succeeded in correctly predicting whether a given item was lexical or functional in more than 80% of the test cases. These results indicate that, even across typologically distinct languages, children's input contains sets of phonological cues sufficient to support the categorization of words.

Similarly, Durieux and Gillis (2001) studied the discrimination of three different lexical categories: verb, noun and adjective. They used an artificial learning system (constructed on Instance-Based Learning) that had to predict the lexical category of a word, on the basis of phonological and prosodic information. Several experiments were conducted, varying in target language and cue-combination. The overall results show that both in English and Dutch, the learning system predicted the lexical categories most successfully if learning was done on the basis of a combination of raw segmental data. This means that the most useful bootstrapping information is given not so much by phonological cues like those presented by Kelly (1996), but rather by simple segmental encoding in onset, nucleus, coda and stress pattern. Durieux and Gillis (2001) conclude that the link between phonology and lexical category is suitable for use in acquisition. The fact that learning mechanisms of this type were able to make correct predictions for the vast majority of new words does not tell us, however, whether humans are also able to make use of such phonological cues. To establish such a conclusion, we need experimental data with human subjects.

On the basis of a corpus analysis, Monaghan et al. (2005) show that phonological cues may be especially useful in categorizing low frequency items. This corpus-based prediction was corroborated in an artificial language learning experiment, showing that learners indeed may use this kind of information to categorize items.

Furthermore in a series of experiments Farmer et al. (2006) show that subjects are sensitive to the word-class typicality of a phonological form in processing (English) words: a noun which has the typical phonological form of nouns is more easily processed than a noun which does not have a typical noun-like phonology. Typicality was expressed as the 'phonological distance' to other members of the same category. Their results show that humans are indeed sensitive to such phonological typicality. The experiment reported here confirms these results but method and language (Dutch) differ. Moreover, we do not reason on the basis of typicalities but on the basis of linguistic impossibilities, which were first brought to light by Trommelen (1989).

In this study Trommelen observes that there are several generalizations in Dutch that relate the phonological form of a (content) word to its lexical category. The studies mentioned above indicate that it is not coincidental that Trommelen found such relations. We therefore conducted an experiment in which we tested if adult native speakers of Dutch are able to use the phonological cues that we can deduce from Trommelen's generalizations in assigning lexical categories to (nonce) words.

The organization of the paper is as follows. First, in Section 2 we will go into the generalizations found by Trommelen (1989) and formulate several cues that we can use in our experiment. In Section 3 we will sketch the experiment. Section 4 discusses the results, from which we conclude that adults are indeed able to make use of phonological information in deciding on the category of nonce-words. In Section 5 we draw some conclusions and sketch a perspective on further research on phonological bootstrapping in language learning children.

2. Form and Category: Generalizations

Trommelen (1989) states that in Dutch the interaction of phonological, morphological and syntactic behavior of a word can give cues to the category of that word. She describes the way in which a word class is connected to, or derivable from, certain phonological properties of the word in Dutch. By analyzing all possible clusters in verbs and nouns she shows that the complexity of final rhymes in underived words can be an indication for word class. With respect to verbs, Trommelen observed that, generally speaking, they conform to a set of phonological restrictions: many phonological forms which would make perfect nouns in Dutch, are simply not possible as verbs. Based on her observations Trommelen formulated the following generalizations about Dutch underived verbs:

- verbs are monosyllabic;
- verbs do not end in a monophthongal vowel (including schwa).[1] We do find *brei* [brei͡] 'to knit', *brouw* [brau͡] 'to brew', etc. but not #kra [kra], #bro [bro], or #made [madə];
- rhymes larger than three elements do not occur in verbs, apart from *peins* 'to consider', and *veins* 'to pretend' both with the diphthongue [ei͡];
- verbs ending in schwa, followed by [n] or [r] and [l] do occur, but verbs ending in schwa, followed by [m] do not occur.

Some exceptions to these phonological restrictions exist, but those words are either denominal, foreign, or extremely rare. The possible phonological form of an underived verb thus forms a proper subset of the possible phonological form of Dutch (underived) words. Only nouns can make use of the full range of possible phonological forms.

For ease of exposition, we will henceforth refer to the set of possible phonological forms of an underived verb, as the phonological **frame** of a verb.

The first of Trommelen's generalizations requires some explanation. With respect to their phonological make-up, typical Dutch verbs come in two types: monosyllabic, or bisyllabic with schwa as the kernel vowel of the final syllable. Kager & Zonneveld (1986) argue at length that phonologically speaking 'bisyllabic with schwa' in fact means 'monosyllabic'. Adopting this analysis, we can confirm the monosyllabicity generalization above, albeit that a small number of counterexamples exist.[2]

It is important to note, as Trommelen did, that there are in fact many verbs that apparently do not obey the above-mentioned generalizations. These verbs come in two types. First, there are verbs ending in the affix *-eer* (*argument-eer* 'argue'; *public-eer* 'publish'). These verbs are clearly derived, while the phonological generalizations only hold for *underived* verbs. Second, there are seeming counter-examples like *olie* [oli] 'to oil' and *ruzie* [ryzi] 'to quarrel', but these verbs all have phonologically identical and semantically related nominal or adjectival counterparts. Therefore, these verbs can be safely assumed to be conversions of these 'underlying' adjectives, or nouns. For example, the verb *olie* is evidently derived from the phonological identical noun *olie* [oli] 'oil', and we can safely assume that the same holds for *ruzie*. Moreover, there are other types of independent evidence which show that the seeming counter-examples can safely be regarded as 'conversions' (cf. Don 1993).

Turning now to nouns, the first observation is that they allow for all the possibilities that verbs have in Dutch, and many more. Hence, the phonological frame of verbs is a proper subset of the phonological frame of nouns in Dutch. To illustrate, let us give several examples. 'True' polysyllabic nouns, that is nouns with more than a single full vowel, freely exist (*gordijn* [xɔrdɛ͡ɪn] 'curtain', *banaan* [banan] 'banana', *antenne* [antɛnə] 'antenna', *cement* [səmɛnt] 'cement' etc.), as well as nouns ending in monophthongal vowels (*zee* [ze] 'sea', ra [ra] 'yard', *dominee* [domine] 'vicar', *knie* [kni] 'knee', *po* [po] 'potty', etc.), and nouns that have rhymes with more than three elements (*angst* [aŋst] 'fear', *herfst* [hɛrfst] 'autumn', *oogst* [oxst] 'harvest'). Furthermore, there are several nouns ending in schwa (*kade* [kadə] 'quay', *commune* [kɔmynə] 'commune') or in schwa followed by a labial nasal (*bezem* [bezəm] 'broom'). Therefore, words having one (or more) of the following phonological characteristics can be classified as a noun:

- true polysyllabic words (with more than one full vowel)
- words ending in a long vowel
- words with 'more than super-heavy' rhymes (VVCC, or VCCC)
- words with a final schwa
- words with a final syllable consisting of schwa, followed by a labial nasal.

Summarizing, one could say that in Dutch only three types of phonological forms do not give any clue about the category of a word: monosyllabic words ending in a single consonant, monosyllabic words ending in a consonant cluster with an obstruent as the second consonant and monosyllabic words that end in a diphthong.[3] All other rhymes can be categorized as nominal.

The fact, that certain phonological patterns are possible in one and not in the other lexical category, obviously is a necessary but not a sufficient condition to argue that phonology plays a role in the discrimination of nouns and verbs. We need to establish that language users, whether consciously aware of this knowledge or not, are actually able to make use of this knowledge once they are asked to.

3. Method

We designed a decision task to test if adult Dutch speakers are able to use phonological information in the categorization of content words: participants had to decide whether certain nonce stems are nominal or verbal. Using nonce stems in isolation is a good way to test phonological awareness only. The participants' semantic, morphological and syntactic knowledge is ruled out because nonce stems have no meaning, morphological structure or sentential context. Of course, we cannot exclude the possibility that subjects interpret some nonce forms as being morphologically complex. However, the phonological form of the nonce forms was chosen in such a way that no existing affix could be recognized in these words. We further assumed that, although many nouns in Dutch can be 'converted' to verbs without any overt phonological affix, subjects would still be inclined to immediately recognize such words as nominal rather than verbal.

The stimuli used in the experiment are based on the generalizations made by Trommelen (1989). Since the relation between the nominal and the verbal frame in

Dutch is a superset (nouns)–subset (verbs) relation, we could only design stimuli as either *nominal* or as *ambiguous* between nominal and verbal. The specific properties that define a particular stimulus as 'nominal', as discussed in the previous section, are the following:

- nouns can have more than one syllable
- nouns can end in a monophthongal long vowel
- nouns can have more than super-heavy rhymes
- nouns can end in a schwa
- nouns can end in a schwa followed by a labial nasal

We created a set of 20 nonce stems, which are all phonologically possible stems in Dutch. Of these 20, 11 were designed as nouns, according to the generalizations made by Trommelen. The other 9 stems were designed as being ambiguous between nouns and verbs. In Appendix 1 the stimuli are listed together with the design principles.

The participants of the experiment were 28 adults whose native language was Dutch. The stimuli were presented on paper with a brief introduction. The participants were asked to choose for each of the presented words, whether they were stems of nouns or stems of verbs. In order to make sure that our subjects understood the notion of a 'stem', we gave an example of both a nominal and a verbal stem in Dutch. Moreover, the terms 'nominal' and 'verbal' were briefly introduced and the task was explained. The task itself was presented as a three-column sheet. In the first column all stimuli were listed. The second and the third column were headed by 'nominal' and 'verbal' respectively. The participants were asked to tick a mark for only one of the columns for each stimulus; the nominal column if they thought the stimulus was a nominal stem, and the verbal column if they thought it was a verbal stem. All participants understood the task.

Our expectations were that subjects would answer 'nominal' more often on the stimuli that were designed as 'nouns', and that they would perform at chance level for the ambiguous stimuli.

4. Results

Now that the background and the method of the experiment have been set out, we can turn to the results. First, we will sketch the general picture of the outcomes of the decision task. Then, we will analyze the results in some more detail to see which phonological generalization is the most reliable predictor of word class in Dutch.

A first look at the data shows that there are some general patterns observable across the participants. In Figure 1 we depicted for each stimulus the number of participants judging the stimulus as either being nominal or verbal.

We ordered the stimuli in such a way that, read from left to right, we can observe a decreasing percentage of subjects that regarded the stimulus as a potential noun. For

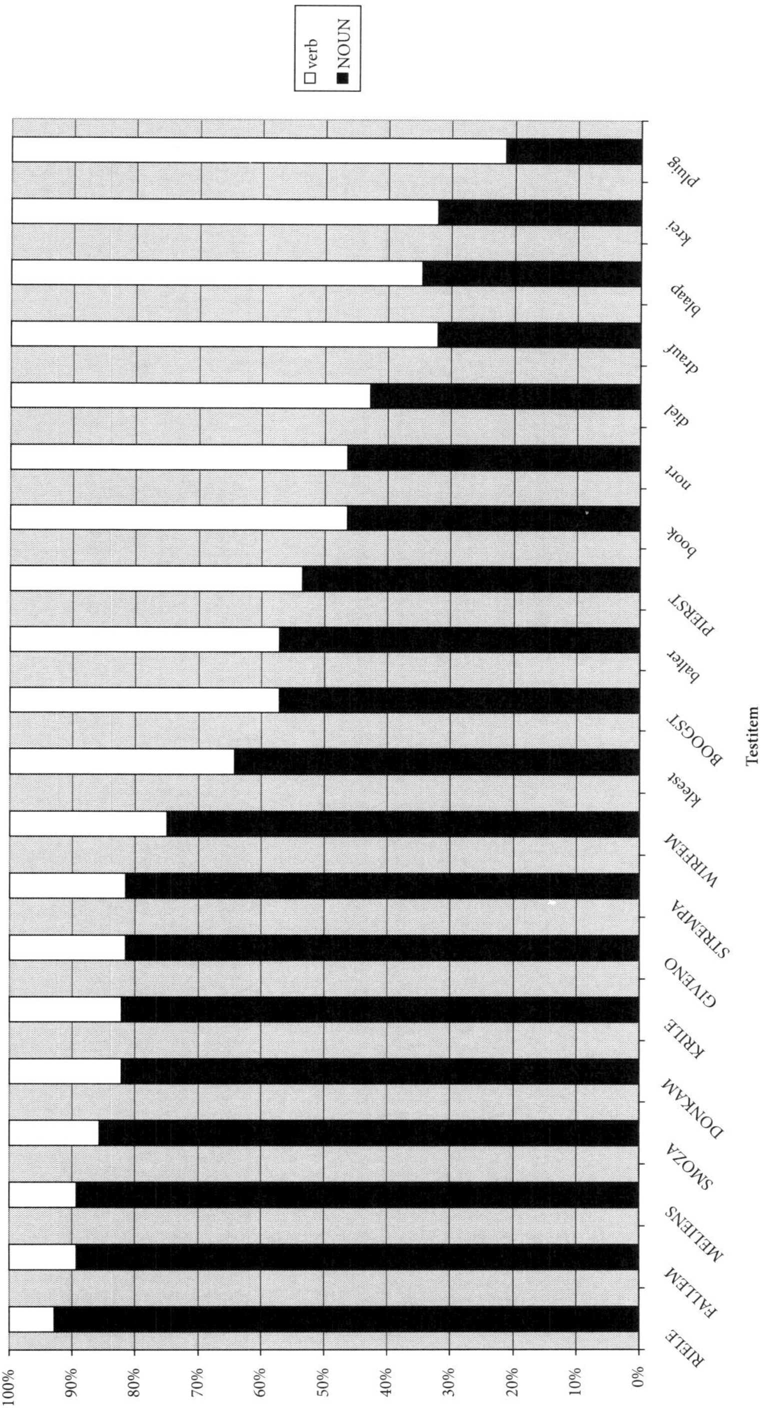

Figure 1. Responses per stimulus

Table 1. Responses of all subjects per stimulus design

Design / Category	Noun	Verb
Ambiguous	105 (42%)	145 (58%)
Nominal	242 (79%)	65 (21%)

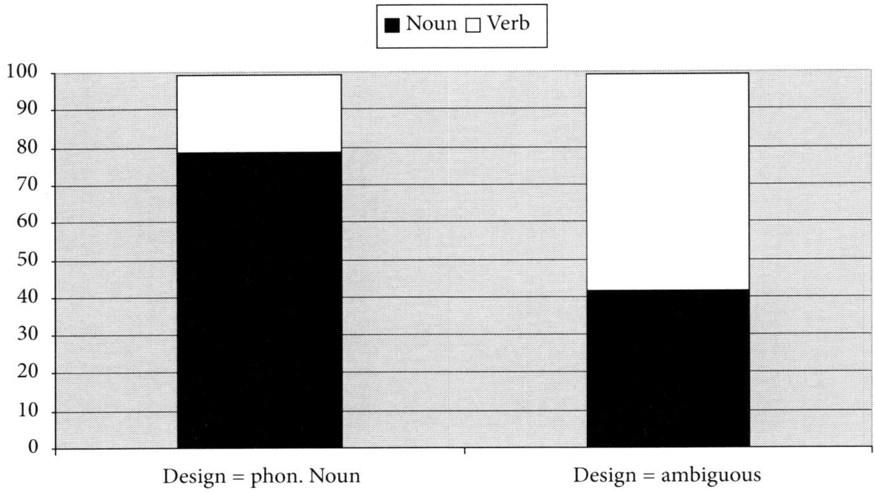

Figure 2. Percentages of responses per stimulus design

example, at the left half of the figure, we see that a large majority of the participants categorized the stimuli 'riele', 'giveno', 'strempa', and 'donkam' as nominal, but on the right hand, the stimuli 'pluig', 'drauf', and 'krei' were considered verbal by a majority of the subjects. This first look at the data indicates that participants judge the stimuli as being different with respect to word class. This proves to be true (χ^2 (19) = 117.1; $p < .01$).

However, the fact that this observation is true does not yet tell us anything about its nature. Therefore, the more interesting question is where this significant difference comes from. In other words: did the participants indeed respond 'nominal' more often to the stimuli that we designed as nominal? And did they respond at chance level to the stimuli we designed as ambiguous? Table 1 shows the relationship between the design of the stimuli and the responses. In Figure 2 we visualized these data.

The scores in Table 1 show that, for the stimuli designed as ambiguous, the participants slightly preferred a verbal response. The pattern for the stimuli designed as nominal clearly shows the expected asymmetric pattern: the subjects categorize almost 80% of the nominally designed stimuli as nominal stems. Subjects used the response 'noun' significantly more often for stimuli which were designed as nouns (χ^2 (1) = 102.0 ; $p < .001$), but for the stimuli designed as ambiguous, the difference was not significant (χ^2 (1) = 6.4 ; $p = .025$).

Since 11 items were designed as 'nominal', subjects could give the answer 'noun' 11 times for the items of that design. On average, subjects gave the answer 'noun' 8.64

Table 2. Responses of all subjects per design principle

Principle	Noun	Verb
bisyllabic	48 (85 %)	8 (15 %)
final long vowel	68 (83 %)	14 (17 %)
more than superheavy rhyme	31 (55 %)	25 (45 %)
final schwa	49 (88 %)	7 (12 %)
final schwa + nasal	46 (82 %)	10 (18 %)

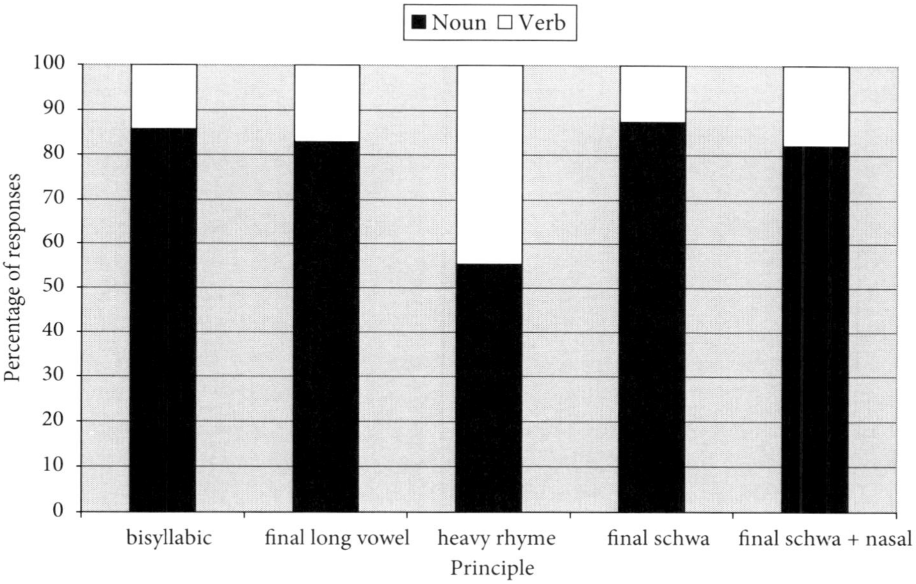

Figure 3. Percentage of responses per design principle

times (range 5–11, SD = 1.97) and the answer 'verb' 2.32 times (range 0–7, SD = 2.02). There was some individual variation across subjects: 3 subjects gave the answer 'noun' only 5 times, 3 subjects 6 times, and 1 subject 7 times; the other 21 subjects answered 'noun' 8 times or more.

We have now established that, taken together, the principles that we used to design stimuli as nominal in general indeed lead participants to categorize stimuli as nominal stems. However, we also would like to know whether all principles have contributed equally to these results. The remaining question then is whether the different principles determining the noun-hood of the stimuli have different predicting values. There are five different types of nominal stimuli: bisyllabic ones, stimuli ending in a long vowel, stimuli with superheavy rhymes, stimuli ending in a schwa, and stimuli ending in a schwa followed by a labial nasal (see Appendix 1 for an overview of the stimuli). In Table 2 and Figure 3 the scores for the stimuli falling into one of these five types are listed and visualized.

Every design principle, each corresponding to one of the generalizations found by Trommelen, triggered the participants to judge the corresponding stimuli as nominal in more than 80% of the cases, except for the principle of 'more than superheavy' rhymes. The stimuli designed according to this principle were categorized as nominal in only 55% of the cases. Overall we found a statistically significant difference in response patterns for all stimuli designed as phonological nouns. These 11 stimuli can be subdivided according to the five principles (bisyllabic, final long vowel, heavy rhyme, final schwa, final schwa + [m]). A one-way ANOVA of response*design principle shows a significant effect of design principle on the responses ($F_{(5,19)} = 13.3, p < .001$). Post hoc comparisons show that the response pattern for the stimuli based on four of the five principles differs significantly from the response pattern on stimuli designed as ambiguous (Tukey's HSD procedure). Only the principle of heavy rhyme does not cause a significant difference and hence does not contribute to the overall significant effect.

We may conclude from these results that, of the five phonological principles presented by Trommelen, four principles do indeed give enough cues for adult Dutch speakers to categorize stems as nominal. Three questions remain at this point, however. First, it is not exactly clear why one of the Trommelen generalizations did not trigger the expected responses. The conclusion would have to be that this generalization does not belong to the speakers' competence and that the observations on which Trommelen based this generalization are coincidental. Second, we may wonder if and to what extent lexical information available to the native speakers somehow plays a role in the determination of category. It cannot be excluded that some of the stimuli remind the subjects of existing words in their lexicon and that the decision for noun or verb is influenced by this resemblance. It could be that precisely in the case of the 'more than superheavy rhymes' this potential lexical effect plays a role. Note that more than superheavy rhymes have a quite specific form segmentally since the phonology of Dutch does not allow just any range of final consonants. The possibilities are quite limited and therefore reminiscence to existing lexical forms might be more obvious in these cases than in those forms where the lexical space is much larger. A follow-up study in which such lexical effects are better controlled for could possibly shed light on this issue. Third, our assumption that 'conversion' would not disturb the behavior of our subjects turned out to be true. Remember that almost all nouns in Dutch have the ability to become verbs through a morphological process of conversion that does not change the phonological form of the stems. Still, the stimuli designed as 'nominal' were indeed recognized as such by most subjects. Therefore, the subjects respond as if the stimuli are not cases of conversions but truly underived stems.

The results of this experimental study allow us to conclude that adult speakers of Dutch are able to make use of phonological cues in the discrimination of nouns and verbs. This result strengthens the idea of phonological bootstrapping as a plausible strategy to follow for children acquiring words. Of course, whether this is indeed the case can only be established once we have some experimental results on children.

5. Conclusion

Trommelen's cues except for one ('more than superheavy rhymes') are reliable predictors of the nominal word class in Dutch. Adults can use their phonological knowledge to classify stimuli that are designed according to these cues, correctly.

What do these results say about the generalizability of Trommelen's cues to other languages? If we recall the results of the study conducted by Durieux and Gillis (2001), we see that the bare segmental information of words was at least as good a predictor of word class as the cues presented by Kelly (1996; duration, vowel height, nasality of consonants, number of phonemes) for English. They concluded that Kelly's cues might be too narrow. Probably the universality of the relationship between phonology and word class is not in the kind of phonological cues, but in the fact that structural relations exist between the possible phonological make-up of a noun versus the possible phonological make-up of a verb. The same suggestion is made by Farmer et al. (2006:12207), who state that "Analyses of languages, such as Dutch, French, Japanese, Mandarin and Turkish [...] suggest that phonological cues to lexical categories are not unique to English but may be a universal property of language".

To conclude, although the phonological cues presented by Trommelen are probably specific for Dutch (modulo 'genetic' correspondences to other languages), the fact that phonological information is available for adults in classification is a very interesting finding. If adults can actively use the link between phonology and category membership, the idea that language-learning children may use this information to get at the proper categorization becomes more promising.

Notes

*. We would like to thank two anonymous reviewers for helpful suggestions and valuable comments, and the audience of the TIN-dag 2005 for valuable comments on an earlier version of this paper.

1. Trommelen's second generalization is also confronted with the following counter-examples: *ga* [xa] 'go', *doe* [du] 'do', *sta* [sta] 'stand' and *zie* [zi] 'see'.

2. So far we have found the following counterexamples to the generalization that Dutch underived verbs exist only in a single syllable: bakkelei [bɑkəlɛ͡ɪ] 'fight', plavei [plɑvɛ͡ɪ] 'pave', ravot [ravɔt] 'romp about', krioel [kriul] 'teem', kidnap [kɪtnɛp] 'kidnap', soebat [subɑt] 'pester', poleist [polɛ͡ɪst] 'polish'.

3. As an anonymous reviewer points out, it might be the case that even within this group there are tendencies such that certain combinations of phonemes are more or less reliable indicators of category-membership. Testing this remains a task for future research.

References

Cassidy, Kimberley W. & Michael H. Kelly. 1991. Phonological information for grammatical category assignments. *Journal of Memory and Language 30*(3): 348–369.

Don, Jan 1993. *Morphological conversion*. Utrecht: LEd, OTS.

Durieux, Gert, & Steven Gillis. 2001. Predicting grammatical classes from phonological cues: An empirical test. *Approaches to bootstrapping*, Jürgen Weissenborn & Barbara Höhle (eds.), 189–229. Amsterdam: John Benjamins.

Farmer, Thomas, A.; Morten H. Christiansen & Padraic Monaghan. 2006. Phonological typicality influences on-line sentence comprehension. *Proceedings of National Academy of Sciences* 103(32): 12203–12208.

Gleitman, Lila. 1990. The structural sources of verb meanings. *Language Acquisition* 1(1): 3–55.

Kager, René & Wim Zonneveld. 1986. Schwa, syllables, and extrametricality in Dutch. *The Linguistic Review* 5(3): 197–221.

Kelly, Michael H. 1996. The role of phonology in grammatical category assignments. *Signal to syntax. Bootstrapping from speech to grammar in early acquisition*, J. L. Morgan & Karen Demuth (eds.), 249–262. Mahwah, NJ: Lawrence Erlbaum.

Monaghan, Padraic; Nick Chater & Morten H. Christiansen. 2005. The differential role of phonological and distributional cues in grammatical categorisation. *Cognition* 96 (2): 143–182.

Pinker, Steven. 1987. *The bootstrapping problem in language acquisition*. Hillsdale, NJ: Lawrence Erlbaum.

Shi, Rushen; James L. Morgan & Paul Allopenna. 1998. Phonological and acoustic bases for earliest grammatical category assignment: A cross-linguistic perspective. *Journal of Child Language*, 25(1): 169–202.

Trommelen, Mieke. 1989. Lettergreepstruktuur en woordkategorie. *De Nieuwe Taalgids* 82(1): 64–77.

Authors' address

Jan Don / Marian Erkelens
Amsterdam Center for Language and Communication
University of Amsterdam
Spuistraat 134
1012 VB Amsterdam
The Netherlands

j.don@uva.nl, m.a.erkelens@uva.nl

Appendix 1. Stimuli

Stimulus		Designed as	Principle
donkam	dɔnkam	Noun	Bisyllabic
meliens	melins	Noun	Bisyllabic
giveno	xiveno	Noun	final long vowel

strempa	strɛmpa	Noun	final long vowel
smoza	smoza	Noun	final long vowel
boogst	boxst	Noun	heavy rhyme
pierst	pirst	Noun	heavy rhyme
riele	rilə	Noun	final schwa
krile	krilə	Noun	final schwa
fallem	fɑləm	Noun	final schwa + m
wirfem	wɪrfəm	Noun	final schwa + m
book	bok	Ambiguous	
pluig	plœ͡ɪx	Ambiguous	
diel	dil	Ambiguous	
drauf	drɑ͡uf	Ambiguous	
blaap	blap	Ambiguous	
nort	nort	Ambiguous	
krei	krɛ͡ɪ	Ambiguous	
balter	bɑltər	Ambiguous	
kleest	klest	Ambiguous	

Appendix 2. Responses of all subjects per stimulus

Stimulus	Nominal	Verbal
Kleest	18	10
Book	13	15
boogst	16	12
giveno	22	5
strempa	22	5
donkam	23	5
pluig	6	22
riele	26	2
fallem	25	3
balter	16	12
wirfem	21	7
smoza	24	4
meliens	25	3
diel	12	16
pierst	15	13
drauf	9	19
krile	23	5
blaap	9	17
nort	13	15
krei	9	19

Lexical semantic constraints on noun roots and noun borrowability*

Lynn Nichols
University of California, Berkeley, USA

While nouns are thought to be more easily borrowed than verbs, this investigation demonstrates that there may be limitations on noun borrowing into certain languages. The case of Zuni is examined, in which conditions of contact similar to that of neighboring languages nevertheless result in a different treatment of the noun lexicon. The possibility of borrowing natural kind nouns into Zuni exists alongside a tendency against borrowing nouns of the artifact type. It is argued that the source of this tendency against artifact noun borrowing in Zuni is the grammatical complexity of the lexical semantic representation for these nouns: grammatical complexity in Zuni noun roots appears to be dispreferred. These findings belie the claim of Thomason and Kaufman (1988) that "any linguistic feature can be transferred to any other language" given an appropriate degree of contact.

1. Introduction

Work on the borrowability of verbs has yielded a complex picture of the nature of verb borrowing and variation in the limitations on verb borrowability crosslinguistically. Cordero-D'Aubuisson and Wohlgemuth (2006) in particular detail several different behaviors with respect to verb borrowability depending on the morphosyntactic strategies available and the grammatical complexity of verb lexical semantics involved. The understanding of noun borrowing appears to be somewhat less nuanced, with a picture of only a more general, and one sided, nature. Several studies of borrowing agree that while verbs are often hard to borrow, nouns are easily borrowed (Haugen 1965; Moravcsik 1978; van Hout and Muysken 1994; Myers-Scotton 2002; Wichmann 2004). The privileged status of nouns is usually ascribed to their semantic and lexical properties. In a study of English borrowing in Canadian French, Poplack, Sankoff and Miller (1988) find that nouns are borrowed more frequently than any other category at a rate more than 5:1, and in part ascribe this to nouns having more lexical content. Similarly, van Hout and Muysken (1994: 42; cited in Brown 1999) argue that "one of the primary motivations for lexical borrowing ...is...to extend the referential potential of a language. Since reference is established primarily through nouns, these are the elements borrowed most easily."

The goal of the current study is to show that noun borrowability crosslinguistically is likely a much more nuanced phenomenon, and that conclusions concerning noun borrowing in one language context cannot necessarily predict the behavior of noun borrowing in another. The investigation focuses on the case of Zuni (isolate, New Mexico) and shows on the basis of Zuni lexical evidence that noun borrowing in certain languages may indeed be limited. Moreover, there is a pattern to this differential rate of noun borrowing in Zuni, suggesting that grammatical constraints, rather than simply socio-historical factors, are involved. In particular, it is shown that there is grammatical complexity to the lexical semantics of some nouns and that languages vary in their ability to encode the full range of this complexity in their noun roots. As a result, noun borrowing is limited into languages — like Zuni — in which particular constraints exist concerning the lexical semantic content of noun roots. These findings contradict arguments by Thomason and Kaufman (1988: 14) that "any linguistic feature can be transferred from any language to any other language" given an appropriate degree of contact. Moreover, their suggestion that lexical borrowing (possible with less contact) and structural borrowing (possible with greater degree of contact) occur at different ends of the scale of contact implies that structural/grammatical factors and lexical factors operate independently with respect to the issue of borrowing. Not only does the Zuni evidence indicate that structural factors do not necessarily operate independently of the lexicon in the case of borrowing, this research make the novel claim that lexeme-internal structural factors (as contrasted with lexeme-external structure such as morphosyntax) may present constraints on borrowing.

This study of noun borrowing in Zuni not only reveals that it is possible for there to be limitations on noun borrowability but in addition allows for greater precision in characterizing the lexical semantic properties of Zuni noun roots as well as grammatical divisions within the root lexicon more generally. As a result, what emerges are the beginnings of a new kind of typological classification of languages according to noun root lexical properties. Moreover, the classification of noun roots may serve as a typological nexus of sorts in cases where other structural aspects of the grammar may depend on the nature of noun roots. Such is the case for Zuni; it is argued in the appendix that an alternative strategy for relative clauses must be sought in Zuni due to the manner in which certain kinds of meaning are formally represented in nouns. Thus it may be possible to trace certain morphosyntactic properties found in a language back to semantic properties of the part-of-speech lexicon. This case for the lexical semantic-syntax connection remains tenuous when made on the basis of a single example but is suggestive of consequences of enough significance to highlight the importance of further crosslinguistic research into noun root lexical semantics.

This study is concerned with the lexical semantic properties of monomorphemic noun roots as well as noun loans that are treated in the borrowing language as noun roots. The behavior of noun roots is distinguished from nouns more generally, which may include nouns derived from other lexical sources. In the following section the case is made on the basis of data from the Americas that languages do vary in the rate at which they borrow nouns, and it is argued that this variation can be due to grammatical factors. Lexical semantic restrictions on native Zuni noun roots are discussed that contribute to the low noun borrowing rate in that language. In Section 3 two kinds of noun meaning are discussed, and in Section 4 it is shown that Zuni noun roots may only encode one of these, while the other may only be expressed via complex (deverbal) nominal derivation. The discussion in the appendix considers the effect of the derivational requirement on this portion of the noun lexicon on the form of Zuni relative clauses. In Section 5, implications for this division within the noun root lexicon for genetic comparison and language typology are considered.

2. Noun borrowability

A detailed investigation of lexical borrowing in languages of the Americas is offered by Brown (1999), in which patterns of lexical borrowing for items of acculturation, i.e. nouns resulting from contact with European languages, are examined.[1] This study reveals that there is in fact widespread variation in the amount of noun borrowing possible for individual languages.

2.1 Differential borrowing rates

Focusing on the languages of the New Mexico Pueblos, Table 1 illustrates Brown's findings that three geographically proximal languages from different families display different rates of noun borrowing. While Acoma and Tewa show rates of 65% or above, Zuni displays a borrowing rate less than half of that of the others. Putting these values in perspective, other languages of the Americas show an even higher rate of borrowing than Acoma and Tewa for nouns referring to items of acculturation; examples of such languages are give in Table 2. This suggests that the rates for Acoma and Tewa fall in the mid range and that the noun borrowing rate for Zuni is comparatively low both in the southwest region as well as among languages of North and Meso America.

Brown (1999) suggests that possible reasons for lower rates of noun borrowing may include on the one hand a lesser degree of contact compared to other languages and on the other hand conscious social resistance to borrowing; Mixco (1977) documents at least one case of social resistance to borrowing among the Americas. Geographical proximity (Acoma and Zuni Pueblo are approximately 75 miles from one another) as well as the historical record indicate a similar degree of contact with both Spanish and English speakers, hence Zuni's particular contact situation does not provide for an explanation of its low noun borrowing rate. As for the second factor, if a

Table 1. Rates of borrowing among languages of the Pueblo Southwest

Language	Rate of borrowing for items of acculturation
Acoma (Keresan)	68%
Tewa (Tanoan)	65%
Zuni (Isolate)	27%

Data from Brown 1999

Table 2. Languages of the Americas with high rates of borrowing

Language	Rate of borrowing for items of acculturation
Cupeño (Uto-Aztecan)	97%
Mocho (Mayan)	91%
Totonac (Xicotepec de Juarez)	83%
Aymara (Quechumaran)	82%

Data from Brown 1999

language (successfully) resists lexical borrowing for social/ideological reasons, it might reasonably expected to have a very low rate of borrowing. Contrary to such expectations, in Zuni the lexical borrowing rate does not approach zero. Instead, Zuni's 27% rate indicates the presence of some degree of noun borrowing. In the end, the impact of such social/ideological constraints against borrowing prove difficult to assess and a closer look at individual grammars themselves suggest alternative explanations.

Thus when the actual lexical items that make up the small set of loans for Zuni are examined, it can be seen that the low rate of noun borrowing in Zuni represents borrowing of a skewed nature that is not predicted by either of the factors (degree of contact, ideological influence) suggested above. Example (1) shows loan noun data collected independently of Brown's study, drawn from Newman (1958), Bunzel (1933) and the author's work with native speakers. As this data indicates, noun lexical items acquired via borrowing in Zuni with few exceptions fall into only certain categories: animals, other naturally occurring items, food, people. This pattern of borrowing is repeated with noun loans from other indigenous languages, also included in (1), not just loans from European source languages as in Brown's study. Conspicuously missing from the list are large numbers of lexical items for tools, items made by hand, or manufactured items which might be expected to occur as a commonplace result of cultural contact.[2]

(1) Loan nouns into Zuni from various source languages[3]
(drawn from Newman 1958; Bunzel 1933; author's fieldwork)

Category		Source Language
Animals		
čiwa:tu	'goat'	Spanish
mu:la	'mule'	Spanish
kyane:lu	'sheep'	Spanish

si:wolo	'buffalo'	Spanish
wa:kaši	'cow'	Spanish
ye:wa	'mare'	Spanish
pula:kya	'butterfly'	Keresan
k'yaššita	'fish'	Keresan
suski	'coyote'	Keresan
pitsu:ti	'pig'	Uto-Aztecan
Naturally occurring (elements, body parts)		
la:ta	'silver'	Spanish
*senta:wanne	'5 cent piece'	Spanish
*liya:li	'real'	Spanish
masonne	'muscle'	English
Food/Produce		
keso	'cheese'	Spanish
mansan	'apple'	Spanish
'uwa	'grape'	Spanish
melu:na	'melon'	Spanish
kapiči	'cabbage'	English
kewats	'carrots'	English
tome:ta	'tomato'	English
People		
wake:la	'cowboy'	Spanish
tehha:na:k^{w}e	'outlaw, cattle rustler'	Spanish
li:kunne	'rich person'	Spanish
mu:ma	'Mormon	English
melikya	'Anglo'	English
'uwakya	'great grandson'	Keresan
šiwa:ni	'rain priest'	Keresan
***Other (non-exceptional)**		
mił	'thousand'	Spanish
tuminku	'week'	Spanish
***Other (sacred)**		
santu	'doll, saint'	Spanish
timu:ši	'arrowhead'	Uto-Aztecan
Other (exceptional)		
lansa	'spear'	Spanish
ma:kinanne	'tractor'	Spanish
kołta	'court of law'	English

Note: Items marked with (*), see note 3.

A few exceptions such as *ma:kinanne* 'tractor' appear among the data. Given the idiosyncratic nature of the lexicon and the borrowing process, however, no lexical constraint is a perfect filter and such cases are to be expected; their scarcity confirms their exceptionality.[4] Overwhelmingly it is the case that loan nouns into Zuni fall into only certain categories. Contrast items that might have presented an opportunity for borrowing but in fact are represented by native Zuni derived formations, (2).

(2)	**Zuni Noun**	**Gloss**	
	k'yak^{w}e-n lata-pa	house-SG wing-PL	'airplane'
	šiwaya-nne	steam-SG	'automobile'

The few categories of possible Zuni borrowings are characterizable as a semantically coherent class of natural kinds, suggesting that grammatical factors are at work in constraining the borrowing behavior of Zuni. This possibility is underscored by the fact that in contrast to Zuni, Hopi and Santa Ana Keresan, two other languages spoken in the southwest region (and with similar history of contact) do not display this restriction. As (3) shows, artifact nouns are represented among loanwords from Spanish in both languages (both lists below are non-exhaustive).

(3) a. Loans from Spanish in Hopi (Hill et al. 1998)

kareeta	'wagon'	karaváato	'hook'
simtsa	'cinch, buckle'	liima	'file, rasp'
kotsaala	'spoon'	siyara	'saw (tool)'
kolaasa (Sp. coraza 'armor')	'leather, leather strap'		

b. Loans from Spanish in Santa Ana Keresan (Davis 1964)

'ará:ru	'plow'	lelû:SA	'watch, clock'
'isdû:pA	'stove'	madí:ya	'hammer'
Bá:ra	'bullet'	naBá:hU	'pocket knife'
guyá:ri	'yoke, horse collar'		

While Brown (1999) and Thomason and Kaufman (1988) both suggest that grammatical structure does not play a role of any significance in lexical borrowing, actual patterns of noun borrowing behavior in various contexts indicate otherwise. In particular, cases from three different regions of the America attest to the fact that properties of individual languages must be a factor in determining the borrowing behavior of the language. First, Table 3 indicates the rate of borrowing words for items of acculturation (nouns) among languages with a significant degree of contact with English or French historically; compared to other languages in similar high contact situations in the Americas (cf. Table 2) these languages all show extremely low rates of noun borrowing, much lower even than Zuni.

Table 3. Mean European loanword percentages for genetic groupings of languages primarily influenced by English and/or French (data from Brown 1999)

Mean loanword percentage	language grouping
28	Salishan
17	Eskimo
15	Others[5]
14	Muskogean
12	Athapascan
12	Algonquian
9	Iroquoian
3	Siouan

Such low rates paired with the significant degree of contact experienced by these particular language groups suggests that grammatical factors in the individual languages likely play a role in whether noun lexical items may be borrowed.

Another such case can be illustrated by borrowing behavior in the Otomanguean family. Brown (1999) cites the mean rate of noun borrowing for Otomanguean languages as a group as 38%, while all other Mexican language from Middle America together show a mean noun borrowing rate of 56%. Moreover, the mean noun borrowing rate for non-Otomanguean languages in the same region is 62%. The contrast in borrowing behavior between Otomanguean and non-Otomanguean languages suggests again that properties of individual grammars play a role in the lower lexical borrowing rates found here. Finally, in the Gran Chaco region of South America, languages with a loan noun rate of 22%≤ belong to a single genetic grouping, Guayacuruan, while languages with a loan noun rate of 21%> belong to the Matacoan family (with the exception of one language belonging to Maskoian). Assuming Spanish cultural influence on these groups has been similar, the difference in borrowing rates for items of acculturation is suggestive of differences attributable to histories in which grammar plays a crucial role.

2.2 Grammatical factors and borrowability in Zuni

Thus there is good independent motivation for attributing the low rate of noun borrowing in the case of Zuni to properties of the grammar that prevent indiscriminant borrowing by placing constraints on what a possible noun loan may be. When a noun is borrowed into Zuni, it effectively enters the language as a root, i.e. as a single unanalyzable morphosemantic unit. An examination of the native Zuni noun root lexicon provides insight as to what constraints on borrowing, and thereby coining, new "roots" might be. Interestingly, the native Zuni root lexicon is itself small, restricted to a few semantic categories more or less able to be classified as natural kinds: animals, plants, other naturally occurring elements, body parts, people, etc. Some representative examples of the possible noun roots in Zuni are listed in (4). While Brown (1999) detected in Amerindian languages a greater tendency for use of European loans for natural kinds than for artifacts, this tendency alone cannot explain Zuni noun borrowing patterns as it does not account for the asymmetry between natural kinds and artifacts in the native Zuni lexicon.

(4) Examples of categories for native Zuni nouns roots (from Newman 1958)

Animals		**Plants**	
'eto:wa	'turtle'	'ayyik'o	'juniper'
łanak'o	'fox'	'a:ku	'purple sage'
Body parts		**People**	
sak^wi-nne	'leg'	wiha	baby'
tsu-'le'	'stomach'	tačču	'father'
Naturally occurring			
ma-'le'	'piece of rock salt'	(-'le' SG)	
sa-'le'	'bone'	(-'le' SG)	
k'ya-we'	'water'	(-we' PL)	

If the character of the native noun root lexicon is indicative of what is a semantically possible noun root in Zuni, then restrictions on the native noun root lexicon provide an explanation for the low borrowing rate into Zuni, in particular why only certain semantic categories of nouns may be borrowed. Borrowed nouns must fall into the categories permitted by constraints on the native root lexicon that limit noun roots to natural kinds. In other words, the low rate of borrowing nouns in Zuni is tied more generally to the fact that in Zuni the noun root lexicon is limited in a particular way.[6]

The Zuni borrowability evidence has implications well beyond its own particular context, however. The conclusions drawn on the basis of Zuni suggest that we can expect not to be able to make any universal statements about noun borrowing behavior based simply on the categorial notion 'noun' that will hold crosslinguistically. Instead, the character of noun borrowability instead depends on lexical semantic properties of — and potentially constraints on — the native noun root lexicon. Thus noun borrowability appears to be much like verb borrowability crosslinguistically, namely dependent on language-particular properties and limitations.

3. Noun meanings and semantic restrictions on noun roots

The semantic limitations on the Zuni noun root lexicon are not idiosyncratic but rather derive from the fact that members of the syntactic-categorial class of what are called 'noun' (both derived and underived) in fact belong to different classes of meaning type. Consider the study of Labov (1973), the putative intention of which was the examination of fuzzy category boundaries in word meaning. The investigation attempted to determine whether English words such as *cup, mug, bowl* were discretely and exhaustively definable or whether some variation in semantic properties was nonetheless compatible with inclusion in a particular category. The starting point of the study was a componential analysis definition of the objects of the sort illustrated in (5), defining the objects almost exclusively in terms of their physical properties.

(5) Componential analysis definition of <u>cup</u> (Labov 1973):
The term cup is used for an object which is (a) concrete and (b) inanimate and (c) upwardly concave and (d) a container (e) with a handle (f) made of earthenware or other vitreous material and (g) set on a saucer and (h) used for the consumption of food (i) which is liquid …

It is not the category boundary issue but rather the ancillary result of that study that is of relevance to the Zuni case. In the Labov study, English speakers were asked to categorize various cup-, mug-, and bowl-like objects while imagining they contained substances such as coffee, soup, potatoes, or rice. Interestingly, variation in categorization depending on foodstuff contents indicated that speakers behaved as if words like *cup, mug, bowl* were not defined in terms of the physical properties of the object but rather in terms of their function.

From this the conclusion can be drawn that there are at least two classes of meaning type for nouns in English (and more generally), (a) nouns whose meaning is based on physical properties of the object denoted, and (b) nouns whose meaning includes function as part of its denotation. Those belonging to type (a) include words for natural kinds such as *birch, granite, deer,* while those belonging to type (b) include words for artifacts such *cup, bowl, mug.* A simple test and confirmation for the difference comes from the ability of nouns of the second type to shift their reference while those of the first type may not, a point also made by Bloom (1996). Thus any number of objects — a watch, a tree branch, a pebble, a plastic bottle — can be referred to as *toy* regardless of physical characteristics since *toy* is a noun whose meaning lies in its function. In contrast, only objects with certain physical properties may be referred to as *birch* or *granite.* A recent study of artifact naming by children likewise suggests that the meaning of an artifact term includes a description of function. Nelson, Herron and Holt (2003) found that children based novel names for artifacts on physical characteristics unless information about the objects' use was introduced; in that case children suggested names based on function.

This distinction between types of noun meaning may explain why there are differences in borrowing behavior for different subsets of the Zuni noun lexicon. In particular, it characterizes an important boundary of the Zuni noun root lexicon. Monomorphemic Zuni noun roots are semantically constrained in that they can only have the natural kind type of meaning and are not permitted to encode as meanings the function of a class of referents. Contrast English (cf. *birch* vs. *toy*) for which it is possible to encode both types of meaning in noun roots. The dynamics of the Zuni lexicon in circumstances of borrowing reveal that languages may in fact differ with respect to the packaging of the different types of noun meaning into noun roots. The question remains, however, as to why this difference in meaning type is reflected in a different susceptibility to borrowing. In the following section we address this issue, namely what is special about the functional information included in the meaning of artifact terms.

4. Zuni derived nouns and canonically associated event meaning

A central issue in lexical semantic investigation is the organization of the semantic information making up word meaning (cf. Goddard and Wierzbicka 1994; Pustejovsky 1995; Jackendoff 2003; Levin and Rappaport Hovav 1995, 2005 for a range of different approaches). Much work in lexical semantics proceeds from the notion that lexical meaning is decomposable, the task being to determine the nature of the semantic components and the most precise formalization that will capture the intended generalizations. Thus, Pustejovsky (1995) argues that noun meanings have internal grammatical complexity, in part in order to account for what he recognizes as adjectival polysemy in case like *good cake, good athlete, good crop, good knife*. Some of the meaning components (qualia) he ascribes to nouns, in particular the telic and agentive components of noun meaning, reflect this view that noun meaning is not reducible simple to denotation or a detailing of physical properties.

The question remains, however, whether word meaning may be broken down into smaller components of meaning at all (Fodor and Lepore 1998, 2000; Pustejovsky 1995, 1998; Pulman 2005). One of the arguments made by Pustejovsky that word meanings may be grammatically complex rests on the purported difference between the meanings for nouns denoting natural kinds vs. those denoting artifacts. The meanings of artifact nouns are claimed by Pustejovsky to include, in part, a lexical representation of the purpose or function of the item denoted; this representation of function is part of a grammatical complex of information that interacts with the meaning of other items in the phrase, for example in the case of verbs to produce polysemous verb meaning. In contrast, natural kind nouns are thought to be simplex and contain no such structured information. Fodor and Lepore (1998, 2000) argue that the evidence put forth for this type of claim does not bear scrutiny and that instead all meaning, that of both natural kind nouns as well as artifact nouns, consists simply of denotation. That is, artifact meaning is atomistic with no more internal grammatical complexity to the lexical representation than any other type of noun.

The asymmetrical noun borrowing patterns observed in Zuni in the current investigation provide a different type of evidence to support the idea that artifact meaning may have some internal grammatical complexity and that, consequently, lexical meanings may consist of something more than denotations. It is noteworthy, for example, that while Zuni noun roots may be semantically restricted in not being able to encode meanings such as 'function' as a root meaning, such meanings are not entirely absent from the Zuni noun lexicon. The complexity of lexical form that artifact nouns assume in Zuni may arguably be taken as support of Pustejovsky's view that the meaning of artifact terms is reflected in a grammatical complexity.

Artifact terms, with their associated functional meaning, are represented in Zuni almost exclusively as derived deverbal nominalizations. Example (6) indicates the typical morphological sources that such nominalizations draw from.

(6) Zuni derived nominal composition:
(N) – V of position/result state/change of state – (ASP)–(CAUS)–(ASP)–(STAT)

Examples of the nominalized forms for 'toy', 'strap', 'saw', 'screw' and 'flour' are illustrated in (7a–e). At first glance the derivational composition of these nouns appears to corresponds to what, following, Labov (1973) might be called the functional definition of the object, e.g. a 'toy' is 'that which is played with.'

(7) Zuni deverbal nominalizations

a. *toy*
'ik'oš-na-nne — cf. 'ik'oš-na-'kya
play-STATIVE-SG — play-STATIVE-PAST
lit. 'that which is played with' — 'It was played with.'

b. *strap*
'ana-š-na-nne — cf. 'ana-š-e-kkya
run.away-NEG.CAUS-STATIVE-SG — run.away-NEG.CAUS.-CONT.-PAST
lit. 'that which causes something to not run away' — 'He made her stay.'

c. *saw*
łiti-ti-na-nne — cf. łitłi-ti-k'ya-kya
make.scratch-SEMELF.REDUP-STATIVE-SG — scratch-REPET-INCH-CAUS-PAST
lit. 'that which scratches' — 'He scratched it off.'

d. *screw*
y-allup-na-nne
REFL-turn.x.around.facing.self-STATIVE-SG
lit. 'that which turns around'

e. *flour*
'o-we'
be pulverized-SG
lit. 'that which is ground'

A closer look at these Zuni nominal formations indicate, however, that a refinement is necessary, for 'function' does not accurately represent the meaning of these nouns when their names were coined. Consider a few of the Zuni derived nouns and their glosses based on their derivational composition:

(8)	Zuni noun gloss	Gloss based on derivational composition
	'toy'	that which is played with
	'saw'	that which scratches repeatedly
	'screw'	that which is turned around facing self
	'flour'	that which is ground

If morphemic composition can be taken as an indication of meaning — that is, the meaning assigned to a term (at least) when the term is originally coined — then the meaning of these nouns cannot be characterized as designating the function of the item labeled by the noun. Rather this meaning is better characterized as designating properties of the canonical event associated with the item. In contrast, Zuni natural kind terms such as *'eto:wa* 'turtle', *ky'awe'* 'water', *sa'le'* 'bone', etc. do not have what will be called here a Canonically Associated Event (CAE).[7]

Capturing but refining the insights of both Labov (1973) and Pustejovsky (1995) it can be concluded that there are at least two types of noun meaning, (a) nouns whose meaning is based on physical properties of the referent, and (b) nouns whose meaning is represented by the canonical event associated with the referent. Furthermore, languages may vary in the ability of their root lexicon to encode these different meaning types. A more complete characterization of the Zuni noun root lexicon therefore is that Zuni monomorphemic noun roots have (as yet ill-understood) grammatical properties that make them unable to express the complex grammatical meaning of a Canonically Associated Event. And Zuni resists borrowing CAE type nouns (the artifacts, tools etc. missing from the list in (1)) because borrowed nouns are treated as noun roots, monomorphemic forms that are unanalyzable in terms of their native (source language) constituent morphology.[8]

There are therefore two types of nouns in Zuni, (i) a small set of nouns consisting of just roots (along with their inflectional morphology) limited to meanings of the natural kind sort, and (ii) a class of nouns derived from predicate formations intended to represent the associated event meaning of an item. Only nouns with the natural kind semantics of type (i) may be borrowed into Zuni, while novel cultural items construed with an associated event, type (ii), must be constructed derivationally from native morphology.

5. Further implications

Zuni noun roots are grammatically special in their limitation to natural kind type meanings and their inability to encode Canonically Associated Event meanings, a type of meaning that is found encoded in the noun roots of, for example, English. In the grammar of Zuni, two repercussions of the restricted lexical semantic character of noun roots were identified: [1] a restriction against borrowing CAE nouns from other languages into Zuni, and [2] the formation of CAE nouns via morphologically complex deverbal nominalization. The issue of noun root semantics is therefore not merely a minor issue concerning the size of the noun root lexicon. A small cluster of grammatical properties may be attributable to the semantic constraints imposed by Zuni grammar on its noun roots.

At least three further implications arise from these findings. First, the existence of a constraint on the semantic content of noun roots in a language carries with it important consequences for genetic comparison and classification. Individual languages may appear to show faster rates of vocabulary replacement due to grammatical factors such as the development of constraints on root lexical semantics that mask the effect of more canonical historical change of the phonological type due simply to time depth of separation. A related issue concerns the genetic provenance of Zuni itself. Zuni is considered to be a linguistic isolate; perhaps this is coincidence, though it may be that due to restrictions on the lexicon we do not have enough root lexical material to establish a relatedness that may exist at only a great temporal distance. Research on the lexical semantic properties of a language therefore has the potential for far greater impact than simply characterization of properties of individual lexical items themselves.

Second, the discovery of lexical semantic constraints of the sort found in Zuni suggests the importance of crosslinguistic lexical semantic investigation and lexical semantic typology toward understanding of the nature of the lexicon more generally. In the current instance, the existence of semantic constraints on noun roots (and the aspects of meaning that roots cannot encode) reveals a grammatical complexity to noun root lexical semantics and provides a new type of evidence to add to the debate (cf. Fodor and Lepore 1998; Pustejovsky 1995, 1998) over whether noun lexical semantic meaning is simple or grammatically complex.

Finally, the rich vs. restricted lexical semantic character of the noun root may serve as a determinant of other grammatical properties. It may therefore be possible to identify a cluster of grammatical properties as systematically and typologically related rather than arbitrary facts of the grammar.

Notes

* I am grateful to two anonymous reviewers for their incisive comments on this work. I also thank Johanna Nichols and Alexandra Aikhenvald for discussion and comments on these ideas; errors remain my own. Unless otherwise indicated, Zuni examples come from the author's field notes.

1. Transfers of non-native terms as well as native translations of non-native terms are classified as borrowings by Brown (1999). Loan bends, constructions based on both borrowed and native terms, are considered native.

2. Brown (1999: 21) notes the following nouns which turn up in other contact situations in the Americas: *soap, bottle, ribbon, box, scissors, match, nail, candle, spoon, shovel, board, cup, pistol, window, clock, book, needle, paper, thread, fork.*

3. An attempt has been made to control for codeswitching in this data and only include words that are considered true loans, though in the case of English loans it is sometimes difficult to distinguish between the two. In addition, in some cases exceptional words enter the lexicon initially and are subsequently remade following native semantic and morphological criteria for possible words.

Nouns like *la:ta* 'silver' and *liya:li* 'real' represent unexceptional borrowings; 'silver' falls into the category of naturally occurring items, while 'real' is treated like *he'le'* 'coin' (cf. *he-* 'round metal' -*'le'* 'sg.'), i.e., salient in Zuni for its metallic composition rather than any other properties it might have. The nouns *miɫ* 'thousand' and *tuminku* 'week' fall outside the naturally occurring types of categories that are borrowed into Zuni, but more importantly neither do these belong to the category of words excluded from borrowing, i.e. artifacts. *santu* 'doll, saint' and *timu:ši* 'arrowhead' appear to be unexceptional borrowings; for the first because Zuni already possesses noun roots for native religious icons (e.g. *kokko* 'katchina') and for the second because arrowheads are likewise sacred items in Zuni culture and their semantic class affiliation is more nuanced than simply 'artifact'.

4. For example, Zuni noun root *te-* 'pot' would seem to fall into the artifact/tool class. However, the forms *te-* 'ground, terrestrial (derivational prefix)' and *te-'-peha-nne* 'pottery drum; lit. *te*-be. wrapped-SG' indicate the origin of the root *te-* 'pot' in a natural kind term referring to the pot material, e.g. 'clay' or 'earth'. Similarly *sa-* 'cup, dish' and *sa-* 'horn, antler'. Thus sometimes perhaps the linguist's understanding is at fault, where an item that may seem to an English speaker to be an artifact may be in origin based on a natural kind in Zuni.

5. Including Arikara, Atakapa, Comanche, Gitksan, Haida, Haisla, Heiltsuk, Kiowa, Klamath, Natchex, Nex Perce, Quileute, Tonkawa, Tunica and Yakima (Brown 1999).

6. Two potential morphological factors that might also be imagined to affect borrowability can be dismissed. An inability to inflect borrowed nouns does not play a role in Zuni as on the one hand there already exists an uninflected class of native nouns in Zuni and on the other hand there exist borrowed nouns that are observed to take prefixal (*'a:-kyane:lu* 'PL-sheep') or suffixal (*maso-nne* 'muscle-SG') noun inflection. In addition, it is not the case that loanwords that bear inflection in the source language are resisted (*šiwa:ni* 'rain priest' < Keresan, with Keresan noun suffix *-ni*).

7. A specific claim is made here for Zuni based on observable behavior of the Zuni noun lexicon. This is not to claim that natural kinds such as animals or natural phenomena may not have Canonically Associated Events (CAE) in other languages; it is clear that the idiosyncratic nature of lexical semantic encoding make such CAE associations possible determinants of the lexical form of nouns in some languages, cf. the occurrence of animal names as noun roots in Yurok vs. the use of complex morphological derivations for animal names in Hupa (Bright 2004), and the morphological expression of associated events (via relational classifiers; Lichtenberk 1983) for plants in some Oceanic languages.

8. These Canonically Associated Event noun meanings should be distinguished from event nominalizations of the sort discussed in Grimshaw (1990), (i), which are the nominalization of a predicate plus argument structure whose denotation is the event (rather than a type of artifact).

(i) a. John's winning the race impressed all of us.
b. Feeding children is always difficult.
(ii) c'ana 'ito-k'ya-na-kya teni
child eat-CAUS-STATIVE-NOM hard
'Feeding children is hard.'

The Zuni example in (ii) illustrates that Zuni event nominalizations are not only semantically but formally (morphologically and syntactically) distinguishable from Zuni derived CAE nouns. The derived event nominal contains both a syntactic NP argument (*c'ana* 'child') as well as a *-kya* nominalizing suffix not found in CAE noun formations.

9. In the Iroquoian languages, complex derived nouns take the form of relative clauses (although in contrast to Zuni these appear to be verbal and lack nominalization morphology). In addition, and in contrast to Zuni, these languages also have open-variable syntactic relative clauses (Mark Baker, p.c.). The Iroquoian case appears to differ from that of Zuni, however, in that while an open variable is understood in the interpretation of the Zuni deverbal nouns, in place of an open variable the Iroquoian derived noun forms possess agreement morphology that is itself referential, e.g. Tuscarora *katéskrahs* 'goat', lit. 'it stinks' (Williams 1974: 30). Thus the predictive correlation between the presence of open-variable lexical forms and the absence of open-variable syntactic relative clauses still holds: the Iroquoian derived nouns are not open-variable property derivations.

References

Bunzel, Ruth L. 1933. *Zuni texts.*. New York, NY: G.E. Stechert & Co. [Volume XV, Publications of the American Ethnological Society].

Bloom, Paul. 1996. Intention, history, and artifact concepts. *Cognition* 60: 1–29.

Bright, William. 2004. 'Analyzability' of nouns in Northwestern California. Paper presented at *Conference on the Ecology of Language*, University of California, Berkeley.

Brown, Cecil H. 1999. *Lexical acculturation in Native American languages.* Oxford: Oxford University Press.

Cordero-d'Aubuisson, Caroline & Jan Wohlgemuth. 2006. Typological aspects of loan verbs. Poster presented at Workshop on Universality and Particularity in Parts-of-Speech Systems, University of Amsterdam.

Davis, Irvine. 1964. The language of Santa Ana pueblo. *Anthropological Papers* 69: 53–190. Bureau of American Ethnology Bulletin, 191. Washington, DC: Smithsonian Institution.

Fodor, Jerry & Ernie Lepore. 1998. The emptiness of the lexicon: Critical reflection on J. Pustejovsky's The Generative Lexicon. *Linguistic Inquiry* 25: 269–288.

Fodor, Jerry & Ernie Lepore. 2000. Morphemes matter. The continuing case against lexical decomposition. Ms, Rutgers University.

Goddard, Cliff & Anna Wierzbicka. 1994. Introducing lexical primitives. *Semantic and lexical universals: Theory and empirical findings,* Cliff Goddard & Anna Wierzbicka (eds.), 31–54. Amsterdam: John Benjamins.

Grimshaw, Jane. 1990. *Argument structure.* Cambridge, MA: The MIT Press.

Hill, Kenneth C. (editor in Chief) and the Hopi Dictionary Project. 1998. *Hopi dictionary: Hoìiikwa Lavàytutuveni: A Hopi-English dictionary of the Third Mesa Dialect.* Tucson, AZ: University of Arizona Press.

Haugen, Einar. 1956. *Bilingualism in the Americas: A bibliography and research guide*. Tuscaloosa, AL: University of Alabama Press.
Hout, Roeland van & Pieter Muysken. 1994. Modeling lexical borrowability. *Language Variation and Change* 6: 39–62.
Jackendoff, Ray. 2003. *Foundations of language*. Oxford: Oxford University Press.
Kemler Nelson, Deborah G.; Lindsay Herron & Morghan B. Holt. 2003. The sources of young children's name innovations for novel artifacts. *Journal of Child Language* 30: 823–843.
Labov, William. 1973. The boundaries of words and their meanings. *New ways of analyzing variation in English*, C. Bailey & R. Shuy (eds.), 340–373. Washington, DC: Georgetown University Press.
Levin, Beth & Malka Rappaport Hovav. 1995. *Unaccusativity*. Cambridge, MA: The MIT Press.
Levin, Beth & Malka Rappaport Hovav. 2005. *Argument realization*. Cambridge: Cambridge University Press.
Lichtenberk, Frantisek. 1983. Relational classifiers. *Lingua* 60: 147–176.
Moravcsik, Edith A. 1978. Universals of language contact. *Universals of human language, Vol. 1: Method and theory*, Joseph H. Greenberg et al. (eds.), 93–122. Stanford, CA: Stanford University Press.
Myers-Scotton, Carol. 2002. *Language contact: Bilingual encounters and grammatical outcomes*. Oxford: Oxford University Press.
Mixco, Mauricio J. 1977. The Kiliwa response to Hispanic culture. *Proceedings of the Annual Meeting of the Berkeley Linguistics Society* 3: 12–23.
Newman, Stanley. 1958. *Zuni dictionary*. Publication 6, Indiana University Research Center in Anthropology, Folklore, and Linguistics.
Poplack, Shana; David Sankoff & Christopher Miller. 1988. The social correlates and linguistic processes of lexical borrowing and assimilation. *Linguistics* 26: 47–104.
Pulman, Stephen G. 2005. Lexical decomposition: For and against. *Charting a new course: Natural language processing and information retrieval: Essays in honor of Karen Spärck Jones*, John I. Tai (ed.), 155–174. Dordrecht: Kluwer.
Pustejovsky, James. 1995. *The generative lexicon*. Cambridge, MA: The MIT Press.
Pustejovsky, James. 1998. Generativity and explanation in semantics: A reply to Fodor and Lepore. *Linguistic Inquiry* 29: 289–310.
Thomason, Sarah & Terrence Kaufman. 1988. *Language contact, creolization, and genetic linguistics*. Berkeley, CA: University of California Press.
Wichmann, Søren. 2004. Loan verbs in typological perspective. Linguistic Circle of Copenhagen.
Williams, Marianne Mithun. 1974. *A grammar of Tuscarora*. New York, NY: Garland.

Author's address

Lynn Nichols
Department of Linguistics
1203 Dwinelle Hall #2650
University of California
Berkeley, CA 94720

nich@berkeley.edu

Appendix: Deriving CAE nouns and the form of relative clauses

While the investigation of noun borrowability in Zuni uncovers an important lexical semantic distinction in the Zuni noun root lexicon, the sensitivity of the grammar to this semantic distinction within the lexicon may have implications beyond merely the issue of borrowability. In particular, the manner in which CAE nouns must be derived in Zuni suggests a potentially far-reaching effect on other parts of Zuni grammar, particularly the syntactic structure. If certain of the syntactic properties of Zuni are indeed ultimately linked to properties of the noun root lexicon, then a conclusion of some crosslinguistic significance follows: the semantic properties of a language's part-of-speech root lexicon play an important role in determining the typological character of a language beyond the lexicon itself. A case may be made, for example, for the connection between derived CAE nouns in Zuni and the syntactic form of Zuni relative clauses. While this connection must remain speculative at this stage and not crucial to the particular lexical semantic claims of this study the suggestive possibility of a lexical source for the properties of a syntactic phenomenon indicates the greater potential import of the findings of the investigation.

The relationship between relative clause form and noun lexical form arises from the circumstance that Zuni Canonically Associated Event meanings must be conveyed in Zuni via derived forms. Example (9) describes in greater detail the relationship between meaning and the structure of these forms. Given the basic verb meaning in (9a), for example, a transitive predicate may be formed by filling in the variable x with an argument, (9b). In the Zuni CAE complex nominal forms, however, the denotatum takes the place of the value for the variable x. The CAE nominalized form is therefore a verb complex expressed as a property of one of its arguments. This is represented in (9c) (corresponding to Zuni example (7d) above) with the interpretation *some [denotatum] x has the property such that [some agent] turns x around facing self.*

(9) a. turn x around facing self
b. Transitive predicate: turn [metal object] around facing self
c. Derived nominal: λx : turn x around facing self

In other words, to derive a CAE noun in Zuni the event type expressed by the predicate with participant x is converted to a description used to denote x. The result is that all the morphosemantic information appearing in the Zuni predicate to describe the event will then appear in the derived deverbal nominalization.

Related to the fact that Zuni derived CAE nouns rely on open-variable property derivation is the fact that open-variable syntactic relative clauses do not occur in Zuni. Generally speaking, open-variable syntactic relative clauses take the form illustrated in (10) for English, in which a head noun is coindexed with a variable in an argument position of the associated subordinate clause. The NP and subordinate clause are syntactically linked via a type of predication relation.

(10) [the pig$_i$ [that you fed x_i]]

Instead of an open-variable structure, for its relativization strategy Zuni uses nominalized subordinate clauses. The nominalized subordinate clause and the main clause containing it are not linked by coindexation of an open position. One consequence of this absence of dependence is that, as shown in (11), any argument of the Zuni nominalized subordinate clause may be interpreted as the relativized argument of the main clause (an instance of the so-called internally-headed relative clause type).

(11) 'akcek'i picu:ti 'ito-k'e-kkowa' Pablo yato-kya
boy pig eat-CAUS-PAST.NOM Pablo strike-PAST

Interpretation 1: 'Pablo struck the boy that fed the pig.'
Interpretation 2: 'Pablo struck the pig that the boy fed.'

This state of affairs, namely the absence in Zuni of an open-variable strategy for syntactic relativization may ultimately have a lexical source. Specifically, the open-variable derivation in Zuni at the lexical level to produce derived CAE nouns as described in (9c) may preclude open-variable derivation of relative clauses at the syntactic (clausal) level. Consider again how such CAE nouns are derived in Zuni. In the course of the lexical derivation, the content of the variable position contained in the property description is assigned to the denotatum that the property characterizes. To form a syntactic relative clause using the same strategy, however, the open variable in the predicate must remain available for coindexation with an NP in the main clause. In the case of Zuni the latter type of coindexation is not possible as the value of the variable has already been assigned by lexical rule to some denotatum.[9]

Pending further supporting evidence, the connection between the inability of Zuni noun roots to encode CAE meaning and the structure of Zuni relative clauses may be considered circumstantial. However circumstantial, it is suggestive enough to warrant serious consideration, in Zuni as well as crosslinguistically, of the effects of root lexical semantics beyond the lexicon. The correlation between root semantics and syntactic structure has the potential to be an important classificatory tool in typological linguistics as well as a valuable predictive tool in the detailed morphosyntactic analysis of a language.

Degree words, intensification, and word class distinctions in Romance languages*

Ventura Salazar-García
University of Jaén

This paper emphasises the explanatory possibilities of a parts of speech theory in which the notions of **differentiation**, **flexibility**, and **rigidity** are not perceived as mutually exclusive typological paths, but as potentially compatible grammatical strategies. The type of analysis such a theory makes possible is first applied to Spanish quantifiers and subsequently extended to **degree words** expressing intensification in modern Romance languages. The paper also pays attention to the formal mechanisms associated with the expression of degree words. One of the most significant conclusions is that degree words classified as **differentiated adverbs** tend to function as modifiers of modifiers. The modification of predicates and that of terms (especially, mass nouns) are roles usually played by **flexible modifiers**.

1. Introduction

The present study analyses the grammatical behaviour of degree words expressing intensification in Romance languages, in accordance with a functional theory of parts of speech systems. The starting point will be the model proposed by Hengeveld (1992a; 1992b: 47–72), the most recent formulation of which is presented in Hengeveld *et al.* (2004). In accordance with Anward (2000: 4f), I will refer to this proposal as **the Amsterdam model**. This model is highly attractive because it combines a wide predictive capacity with a relatively simple formulation. Besides, it has resulted in important empirical findings, such as the **parts of speech hierarchy** (henceforth: PoSH). However, in its current state the Amsterdam model contains some problematic aspects, two of which I will discuss here.

First of all, within the domain of adverbs the model limits itself to **manner adverbs**, while other types of adverb are not taken into consideration. This article will partly make up for this by investigating the behaviour of **degree adverbs**, with the aim of showing to what extent the Amsterdam model may be applied to this realm. Contrary to earlier claims (e.g. Samuelsdorf 1998; Mackenzie 2001), I will argue in

Section 3 that degree adverbs are lexical items, rather than functional (morphosyntactic) elements. This argument is necessary to show that this category can indeed be analysed in the light of a general theory of parts of speech systems.

The second problematic aspect of the Amsterdam model is the lack of attention to intralinguistic variation. The Amsterdam model has been conceived as a taxonomy for the typological classification of the different languages of the world. For this reason, it has been assumed that every language can be assigned to a unique parts of speech system. This assumption is confronted with a large number of counter-examples, because, in actual practice, languages tend to participate, to some extent, in two or more parts of speech systems. Besides, the typological classification of a language in terms of its parts of speech system may change diachronically, which necessarily implies the existence of variation in synchrony. The attempts made till now to solve this question (for instance, by means of intermediate types) are clearly unsatisfactory. At least implicitly, they respond to the assumption that variation constitutes an irregular and paradoxical fact, contrary to the initial expectancies of the model. In contrast with this position, I consider that variation must be incorporated as a central element of any general theory of parts of speech systems. As contemporary sociolinguistic research has shown, variation constitutes an inherent feature of the synchrony of any living language as a manifestation of its historical, social, and geographic dynamism (Hudson 1980: 34; García Marcos 1999: 32). The inadequacy of the current version of the Amsterdam model, in this respect, may be solved by adopting a new approach: a **constituent-based** interpretation of parts of speech systems that I set out as alternative to the **language-based** interpretation developed by Hengeveld *et al.* (2004). Throughout this article, I will attempt to show that this new approach improves the descriptive and explanatory capacity of the model considerably, and opens up promising new perspectives for typological research.

My proposal thus introduces an important modification with respect to the current formulation of the Amsterdam model. However, I do not want to transmit the impression that it constitutes a radical change. It simply extends the fundamental basis of the theory to another domain of application. I continue to use a number of core points of the Amsterdam model: the role of the PoSH, the definition of word classes in terms of syntactic slots, the classification of parts of speech systems by means of the basic notions of **differentiation**, **rigidity**, and **flexibility**, etc.

With respect to flexibility, understood as categorial plurality, it is worth highlighting the novelty that the semantic perspective adopted by the Amsterdam model supposes. While other authors have identified categorial plurality as a semantic relationship like homonymy (cf. Jespersen 1942: 84) or polysemy (cf. Evans 2000: 729), Hengeveld *et al.* (2004: 539ff) state that the semantic characterization of flexibility lies within the general concept of **ambiguity**. According to such a statement, a flexible lexeme represents a unique monosemic entry in the lexicon, with a semantically vague meaning. I adopt the latter approach here, because it allows one to explain some correlations between the PoSH and other grammatical phenomena, apparently very distant. Hengeveld *et al.* (2004) have convincingly proved the existence of such correlations with respect to word order. In the present article, I would like to highlight the existence of a correspondence between the flexibility of degree words and their formal expression in such aspects as morphological inflection or their integration within partitive structures. In a functional conception of language, such correlations are explainable on the basis of the idea that the formal articulation of flexible lexemes acts as a compensatory mechanism guaranteeing the communicative efficiency of these lexemes, which are compromised by semantic vagueness and categorial ambiguity.

The article will be developed as follows. In Section 2, there is a critical presentation of the parts of speech typology proposed by Hengeveld (1992a) and Hengeveld *et al.* (2004), paying special attention to those aspects that, I believe, need to be revised seriously. Section 3 discusses the grammatical status of degree words, and presents some arguments that justify the treatment of these units as lexical items. Section 4 studies fifteen Spanish quantifiers, in keeping with the theoretical framework presented in Section 2 (i.e., a constituent-based interpretation of parts of speech systems) and using an analytical procedure inspired by Anward (2000). Section 5 extends this analysis to the expression of intensification in the modern Romance languages. This section will highlight the cross-linguistic relevance of the generalizations initially observed in Spanish. The article finishes with a number of conclusions.

2. The Amsterdam model of Parts of Speech systems: A critical approach

2.1 The Amsterdam model was initially developed in the early 90's, when Hengeveld (1992a; 1992b: 47–72) formulated a proposal to explain the different parts of speech systems that may be recorded in the languages of the world. This model has been refined over the last few years until evolving into its current version, represented by Hengeveld *et al.* (2004). The core of the Amsterdam model is the aforementioned PoSH, which can be formulated as follows:

(1) **Parts of Speech Hierarchy (PoSH)** (Hengeveld 1992a: 47):
Verb > Noun > Adjective > Manner Adverb

This hierarchy does not involve all parts of speech recognised in traditional grammar, but focuses on major **lexical categories**. In the theoretical framework of Dik's (1997) Functional Grammar, within which Hengeveld's research falls, these lexical categories are present in the **fund** of the grammar as (basic or derived) predicates (Dik 1989: 54). This point is important, since a correct interpretation of the PoSH must take into consideration its limitation to lexical units. As a result, several word classes are unaffected by the PoSH. These words may be classified in two groups. The first group is constituted by **basic terms** (in Dik's terminology); essentially, they are pronouns and proper nouns. Basic terms, which are universal[1] (Moreno Cabrera 1997: 207), lack lexical meaning, but they have a referential value that justifies their presence in the lexicon of a language. The second group includes other traditional parts of speech with a grammatical meaning: adpositions, determiners, etc. They are analysed in Dik's Functional Grammar as grammatical operators, which means they are not part of the lexicon (cf. Dik 1989: 61ff). This premise remains problematic, because languages show a relative lack of determination within this realm that questions a classification of categories in totally discrete terms (cf. Hopper & Traugott 2003: 2). However, and from a practical point of view, I think that the lexicographical criterion is operative enough when differentiating between lexical categories (linked to the PoSH) and other parts of speech. In keeping with this criterion, lexical words are susceptible to being defined by paraphrases of their content. However, words that do not belong to the lexical categories do not have this possibility; they can be **explained**, but not **defined** (Seco 1978: 225; Salazar 2004: 248).

The PoSH specifies that the least marked lexical category is the verb, followed by the noun and the adjective. As for the (manner) adverb, it has the most marked position, and is thus the category that can be missing most easily in a language. The existence of a category necessarily implies the existence of all the categories placed to its left, but not necessarily of those placed to its right. Thus, if a language has adjectives, it will also have nouns and verbs, but not necessarily manner adverbs.

Languages that have the four lexical categories are referred to by Hengeveld *et al.* (2004) as **differentiated languages**.[2] In languages lacking at least one of these categories, two grammatical codification possibilities can be discerned: **flexible** and **rigid**. The flexible option is characterised by the fact that the absence of a category is compensated for by a functional fusion with the preceding category. For example, a language that reduces the components of the PoSH to three lexical categories by means of a flexible procedure retains nouns and verbs. However, adjectives and adverbs form a single category that I will here refer to as **flexible modifier**.[3] The lexical units linked to this new category assume both the adjectival function and the adverbial function in

Table 1.

PoS Systems		**Head of predicate phrase**	**Head of referential phrase**	**Modifier of referential phrase**	**Modifier of predicate phrase**
Flexible	1	contentive			
	2	verb	non-verb		
	3	verb	noun	flexible modifier	
Differentiated	4	verb	noun	adjective	adverb
Rigid	5	verb	noun	adjective	–
	6	verb	noun	–	–
	7	verb	–	–	–

(cf Hengeveld *et al.* 2004: 537)

an integrated way. Thus, in such a language, strictly speaking there are neither adverbs nor adjectives. Rigid languages, on the other hand, are characterised by a mere absence of the lexical category concerned (in this case, the manner adverb), without any kind of categorial fusion. The adverbial function is codified by means of alternative procedures (for example, adpositional phrases). A *continuum* between flexibility and rigidity offers seven typological possibilities with differentiation in the middle. This can be synthesised as in Table 1.

2.2 While not denying the positive aspects of the Amsterdam model, there are, in its present formulation, some points that are open to serious debate. Until now, the classification of the parts of speech systems included in Table 1 has been conceived as a taxonomy of languages, in which each parts of speech system appears as a typological option excluding the others. This makes it a rather static model, forcing the linguist to assign languages to one specific type in this classification. Such an approach does not match the dynamism of languages in this aspect of grammatical encoding. In fact, Hengeveld (1992a: 47f) himself points out that the typology derived from Table 1 responds more to preferential tendencies than to single solutions within each language and "that parts of speech systems are constantly changing." In the current version of the Amsterdam model, some attempts have been made to reduce these problems by contemplating the possible existence of intermediate types (Hengeveld *et al.* 2004: 538f). Thus, a lot of Indo-European languages, including Spanish, can be considered as differentiated languages, but with a tendency towards flexibility. Subsequently, these languages should be represented between types 3 and 4. This does not solve the problem entirely, however, since it only predicts the compatibility within a single language of two contiguous types, while there are data that support the idea that within a single language there may be elements representative of three or more PoS systems. I will illustrate this situation with some examples from European Spanish:[4]

(2) Spanish:

a. María camin-a rápid-o (flexible: type 3)
   María walk-3SG.PR fast-M.SG

b. María camin-a rápid-a-mente (differentiated: type 4)
   María walk-3SG.PR fast-F.SG-AR

c. María camin-a con rapid-ez (rigid: type 5)
   Mary walk-3SG.PR PRP FAST-NR
   'María is walking fast'

The above three sentences share the same truth conditions and can be considered as essentially synonymous. They are simply different in the codification procedure of their verb modifiers. Example (2a) represents a flexible grammatical strategy with a lexical modifier (in its unmarked morphological form, singular masculine), which in this case plays the role of an adverb, but which is still capable of assuming adjectival functions as well. Example (2b) represents the differentiating strategy with an adverb in the strict sense of the word. Finally, (2c) represents the rigid strategy in which a syntactically construed unit, in this case, a prepositional phrase with a nominal head, fulfills the adverbial function. All these sentences are perfectly correct in current Spanish, which means that this language is not only situated between types 3 and 4, but that it also participates in type 5, at least partially.

The examples 3a–d are even further away from the predictions derived from the Amsterdam model. Next to the three types above, a fourth type is also recorded in Spanish, at least sporadically: type 2 (opposition **verb/non-verb**). With a very limited group of verbs, the modifiers that simultaneously show intensification and valuation can be codified by several lexical items like *jamón* 'ham', *bomba* 'bomb', *pipa* 'pipe', etc. (cf Kovacci 1999: 714). These items, despite the fact that they would normally be recognised as nouns, function in these contexts as verb modifiers. This procedure may be understood as a case of **second-degree flexibility**, i.e. type 2 (cf 3a). This option is compatible with the three already given: first-degree flexibility, with a flexible modifier (3b), a differentiating option (3c), with a real adverb, and a rigid option (3d), with a prepositional phrase:

(3) Spanish:
a. Lo pas-aban jamón (flexible: type 2)
   CLT.3SG pass-3PL.PST ham
b. Lo pas-aban divin-o (flexible: type 3)
   CLT.3SG pass-3PL.PST divine-M.SG
c. Lo pas-aban estupend-a-mente (differentiated: type 4)
   CLT.3SG pass-3PL.PST marvellous-F.SG-AR
d. Lo pas-aban de película (rigid: type 5)
   CLT.3SG pass-3PL.PST PRP movie
   'They had a whale of a time'; 'They had a terrific time'

The differences between examples (3a–d) are less of a semantic than a sociolinguistic, dialectal, and stylistic nature. Sentence (3a) is a highly colloquial expression. To a lesser degree, (3b) and (3d) are also colloquial expressions in European Spanish, but (3b) is a neutral option in many dialects of American Spanish.[5] Sentence (3d) is marked according to the sociolinguistic variable of **age**, and is a characteristic of youth talk. Finally, (3c) is the least marked sentence in sociolinguistic terms, and it is probably the preferred option in formal style.

2.3 As a consequence of what has been shown here, I think that the Amsterdam model should be modified. The best alternative seems to be that of considering the concepts of flexibility, differentiation, and rigidity not to be mutually exclusive typological characteristics, but (potentially) compatible grammatical strategies. Languages can make a combined use of all of them in a variable proportion. This variation along the synchronic axis is what provides the basis for change along the diachronic axis.

The three grammatical strategies under consideration may be defined as follows:

Differentiation: a grammatical strategy that applies when a function is performed by a lexical item which may be classified within one of the word classes composing the PoSH: verb, noun, adjective, or adverb.

Flexibility: grammatical strategy that applies when a function is performed by a lexical item which may be classified within one of the word classes resulting from the categorial fusion of two or more members of the PoSH: flexible modifier, non-verb, or contentive (cf Table 1).

Rigidity: grammatical strategy that applies when a function is performed by a non-lexical item. This item may be a morphological marker or a syntactically construed constituent. The rigid strategy admits a wide range of codification procedures: affixation, incorporation, reduplication, noun phrases, adpositional phrases, relative constructions, serial verbs, etc.

The recognition of the existence of three compatible grammatical strategies forces us to a change of perspective when interpreting the parts of speech systems presented in Table 1. Broadly speaking, my hypothesis adds a constituent-based interpretation, opposed to the language-based interpretation of the current version of the Amsterdam model; i.e., what must be classified as flexible, differentiated, or rigid, are **linguistic units**, taken individually, rather than **languages** in themselves. Contrary to what happens when the lexicon of a language as a whole is classified, there are no impediments, from this new perspective, to identify flexible, differentiated, and rigid strategies in one and the same language.

In practice, the standard version of the Amsterdam model admits compatibility between different parts of speech systems. So, the inclusion of the intermediate type 3–4 admits the compatibility between flexible and differentiated strategies, while type 4–5 does so with respect to differentiated and rigid strategies. Thus, the only significant difference that my hypothesis adds is the compatibility between flexible and rigid strategies. Probably Hengeveld *et al.* (2004) do not consider this last possibility due to the discontiguity of flexible and rigid types in the visual presentation in Table 1. Such a visual presentation is useful because it clearly shows the connection between the parts of speech systems and the PoSH, but it is merely conventional and should not preclude the compatibility among other types. Examples 2 and 3 show empirically that flexibility and rigidity may coexist in the same language as alternative options, at least with respect to the function of **modifier of a predicate phrase**.

To conclude this section, I should add that there is an asymmetry between the rigid strategy, on the one hand, and the flexible and differentiated strategies, on the other. This is implicitly perceived in the current version of the Amsterdam model, where flexible and differentiated languages are defined positively, while rigid languages are defined negatively. Thus, if a language has all the parts of speech of the PoSH, it is automatically classified as differentiated; meanwhile, if any type of systematic categorial fusion is recorded (for instance, by the presence of flexible modifiers) the language is automatically classified as flexible. On the other hand, the feature which defines rigid languages is not the presence, but the lack of one or more word classes. In the alternative version I propose in these pages, such asymmetry is explained from the fact that the rigid strategy is not manifested by means of lexical items.

3. Grammatical status of degree words: Some remarks

3.1 Within the framework of the Amsterdam model, the references to adverbs are specifically applied to manner adverbs (cf Hengeveld 1992a: 42). Certainly manner adverbs can be more readily recognised as a kind of lexical word. Nevertheless, this does not imply that other kinds of adverbs should be excluded from the typology of parts of speech. Rather, their status in relation to this model is in need of more detailed research. One of the purposes of this article is precisely to define the theoretical framework with respect to degree adverbs. Before I can do so, two problems should be dealt with.

In the first place, many authors prefer to analyse degree adverbs as grammatical operators rather than as lexical items. In such circumstances the use of the term **adverb** is a problem in itself. In fact, authors like Bolinger (1972) prefer to use the expression **degree words**. It is a neutral denomination that does not prejudge whether these words are operators or lexical items, and in this later case, whether they are adverbs or not. The term **degree** only makes reference to the fact that its meaning operates on a one-dimensional quantificational scale. I have no problem making use of this neutral denomination, as a merely practical option. It avoids a terminological debate that would entail digressing away from the purposes of the present article.

The second problem is motivated by the fact that, traditionally, degree adverbs have been identified with one very marked syntactic function only: the modification of adjectives and of other adverbs, i.e. the modification of modifiers. This seem to confer on adverbs of this kind a different grammatical status to that of other kinds of adverbs, whose function would be the modification of the verb, or the modification of complex syntactic units (predication, proposition, utterance) which prototypically have a verb as their head.

3.2 Regarding the first question, and confining myself to Dik's Functional Grammar, which is the theoretical framework within which the Amsterdam model has been developed, Hengeveld (1997: 126) assumes the lexical character of degree adverbs without any reservation. Contrary to this position, authors like Samuelsdorff (1998: 274ff) and Mackenzie (2001: 125f) state that they are grammatical operators, which are not part of the lexicon of a language, but are generated by expression rules.

It is true that degree words express very general and abstract content. The generality of their meaning, as well as some distributional restrictions, make them potential candidates for being considered as morphosyntactic operators. But other factors that notably qualify this first impression should be taken into account. For example, in a language like English, degree words with the value of intensification or reduction are free forms the prosodic behaviour of which is analogous to that of lexical words in general. Likewise, along with basic units (*quite, very,* etc.), there are derived units that operate along a quantificational scale: *hardly, barely, moderately, reasonably, remarkably, extremely*, etc. These units are obtained by a productive derivational process aimed at creating new vocabulary rather than new grammatical forms.[6] Furthermore, some of these adverbs impose selection restrictions on the words they modify, which is a strong argument in favour of their analysis as lexical units. The examples that follow show the different behaviour of *very* (which does not impose selection restrictions) and *seriously* (which only modifies adjectives with a negative axiology):

(4) a. A guest is very ill.
b. A guest is very optimistic.
c. A guest is seriously ill.
d. * A guest is seriously optimistic.

The conclusion to be reached is that there is no reason to consider degree words to be necessarily grammatical operators. The lexical behaviour shown for English equally applies to degree words in the Romance languages, for which reason we will treat them as such in what follows.

3.3 Moving on to the second question, traditional grammar has long defended the idea that the category of degree is a genuine property of adjectives and adverbs (cf Martínez Amador 1953: 689),[7] which does not affect nouns or verbs. But in many languages, the same elements used for the expression of degree are also used as modifiers in nominal and/or verbal phrases. This has led authors like Jacobson (1978: 80) and Egea (1979: 176) to remark that there is no semantic incompatibility between degree words and verbal heads, and that the category of degree is also applicable to verbs. Baker (2003: 213) extends this possibility to nouns. However, there are a number of arguments which show that degree words, when they modify nouns or verbs, do not really express degree. When they modify nominal heads, they express **referential quantification**[8] (5c); when they modify verbal heads, they express **quantificational aspect** (Dik 1989: 204), with the value of intensification (5b) or frequency (6b):[9]

(5) French:

a. Il a conduit assez bien
he AUX.3SG.PST drive.PRT QNT well
'He drove quite well'

b. Il a assez étudi-é
he AUX.3SG.PST QNT study.PRT
'He studied quite [a lot]'

c. Assez d'-enfant-s sont arriv-és au musée
QNT PRP-child-PL AUX.3PL.PST arrive-PRT.PL PREP.ART.M.SG museum
'Quite a lot of children arrived to the museum'

(6) Spanish:
a. Es bastante valiente
COP.3SG.PR QNT brave
'S/He is quite brave'
b. Visit-a bastante el museo
visit-3SG.PR QNT ART.SG museum
'S/He visits the museum frequently'

In accordance with these facts, it seems that referential quantification, quantificational aspect and degree can all ultimately be included within the more general category of **quantification**. It is this common content that allows a single unit to participate in several syntactic types of modification. In fact, it has been noted in many languages that quantifiers have an intercategorial relationship with the traditional parts of speech classification (López Palma 1999: 48). Thus, one quantifier may belong to several word classes: pronoun, adjective, adverb, etc. Its identification with each one of these parts of speech will depend on the role it plays in each context. From my point of view, these facts can find a satisfactory explanation in the framework of a constituent-based interpretation of the Amsterdam model of parts of speech systems, if considered in the light of the notion of flexibility. The evaluation of this hypothesis will be the subject of the next pages.

4. Degree words and categorial flexibility: The case of Spanish

4.1 In order to evaluate whether the intercategorial nature of quantifiers can be explained in the light of the notion of flexibility, I will take the main Spanish degree words as my point of departure, and use an analytical procedure based on Anward (2000). It basically consists in establishing the correspondence between the different words considered and the prototypical functions used in a syntactic approach to the parts of speech. Such functions derive from the **syntactic slots** that the words occupy within the sentence (Hengeveld 1997: 121f). I will exclude the function of **head of a predicate phrase** (prototype of the verbs) here, since no Spanish degree word can perform this function **directly**. Thus, my analysis is limited to four fundamental functions:

(7) Function 1. Term (T), i.e. a referential constituent.
Function 2. Term Modifier (TM).
Function 3. Predicate Modifier (PM).
Function 4. Modifier of Modifier (MM).

We have to add a further subdistinction within the TM function. There is ample evidence to show that, in the case of quantification of entities, the opposition **count/non-count** is grammatically relevant. This leads to a differentiation between two subtypes within the TM function. The features <+count> and <−count> are understood as selection restrictions that are imposed on the terms modified.

Table 2.

	T	TM <+count>	TM <−count>	PM	MM
1) *alguien* 'someone'	+<+hum>	–	–	–	–
2) *algo* 'something'; 'anything'; 'a little'; 'some'; 'somewhat'	+<−hum>	–	+[part]	+	+
3) *alguno* 'some'; 'any'	ANAPH	+[n;g/tr]	–	–	–
4) *uno* Sg: 'a'; 'one'. Pl: 'some'; 'any'	ANAPH	+[n;g/tr]	–	–	–
5) *varios* 'several'	ANAPH	+[pl;g]	–	–	–
6) *poco* 'few'; 'little'; 'not much'; 'not many'	ANAPH	+[pl;g]	+[sg;g]	+	+
7) *un poco* 'a little'/pl: 'a few'	ANAPH	+[pl;g]	+[sg;part]	+	+
8) *bastante* 'quite'; 'rather'; 'enough'	ANAPH	+[pl]	+[sg]	+	+
9) *mucho* 'much'; 'many'	ANAPH	+[pl;g]	+[sg;g]	+	–
10) *demasiado* 'too much'; 'too many'; 'too'	ANAPH	+[pl;g]	+[sg;g]	+	+
11) *más* 'more'	ANAPH	+	+	+	+
12) *menos* 'less'	ANAPH	+	+	+	+
13) *tanto* 'so much'	ANAPH	+[pl;g]	+[sg;g]	+	–
14) *muy* 'very'	–	–	–	–	+
15) *tan* 'as'; 'so'; 'such a'	–	–	–	–	+

ANAPH: anaphoric; g: inflection in gender; +hum: human referent; −hum: non-human referent; n: inflection in number; part: partitive structure; pl: plural; sg: singular; tr: truncation in the masculine singular form.

Within the framework of the Amsterdam model, TM is a prototypically adjectival function. On the other hand, PM and MM are prototypically adverbial functions. Hengeveld (1992a: 40; 1997: 126f) only considers the function PM in his work, probably because he understands that the lexical category of the head (verb, adjective, or adverb) does not essentially alter the role of the modifier. I think, however, that the distinction between PM and MM, introduced by Anward (2000: 24), is fully necessary. As we have seen in 3.3, it is the MM function, and not the PM function, that traditional grammar has considered to be prototypical for degree adverbs. Besides, there is a semantic difference between degree (applied to adjectives and adverbs) and quantificational aspect (applied to verbs) so that it is reasonable to postulate that the syntactic slot occupied by the head affects the functional characterization of the quantificational modifier. Finally, T is a function shared by both pronouns and nominal phrases. In the case at hand the degree words that fulfil this function should be classified as pronouns, because their referential value is not attached to the conceptual meaning of nouns.

Given these premises, the results of the analysis can be synthesised as in Table 2, which contains a total of fifteen quantifiers.

4.2 The synthesised data in Table 2 lead to some interesting conclusions. In the first place, it becomes evident that there is a high degree of flexibility among the quantifiers, since most of them can occupy more than one syntactic slot. Nevertheless, we do find some forms that, because they are specialised in one function only, can be understood as instances of a differentiating strategy. This is what happens with *alguien* 'someone', an indefinite term with human reference, *varios* 'several' (feminine: *varias*), a modifier of plural and countable nouns, *muy* 'very', a modifier of adjectives and adverbs with an intensifying value, and *tan* 'such' 'as', a modifier of adjectives and adverbs, with a comparative or an emphatic value, depending on the construction it is involved in. These words do not offer any kind of ambiguity in relation to the parts of speech recognised by the Amsterdam model: *alguien* is a pronoun, *varios* is an adjective, *muy* and *tan* are adverbs.[10] It can also be seen that not all the words that perform the T function do so in the same way. Only two of them directly and prototypically occupy this syntactic slot: *alguien* 'someone' and *algo* 'something'. Both are characterised by the lack of morphological inflection. Nevertheless, all degree words that can modify terms (or, at least, countable terms), can likewise be used as anaphoric pronouns, as long as the entity referred to is easily identifiable in the communicative context. This viability of anaphoric usage is not an exclusive property of the quantifiers concerned, but is a general property of nearly all Spanish adjectives and determiners. In their anaphoric use, degree words keep their morphological inflection, and should agree with the term to which they make reference.[11] Notice how in (8a) the quantifier *varias* 'several' appears in its feminine plural form, agreeing in gender and number with the noun *postales* 'postcards'. The same inflectional form appears in (8b), where the noun is not explicitly present, but is inferable from the context:

(8) Spanish:

a. Pedro ha compr-ado vari-as postal-es
Pedro AUX.3.SG buy-PRT QNT-F.PL postcard-PL
'Pedro has bought several postcards'

b. Yo también he compr-ado vari-as
I also AUX.1.SG buy-PRT QNT-F.PL
'I have also bought several' (**postcards**, inferable from the context)

Thus, we may conclude that the anaphoric use of degree words[12] does not constitute a sign of categorial flexibility. Rather, the possibility of acquiring a referential value is a property common to a large number of term modifiers.

4.3 A second important fact that can be inferred from Table 2 is that flexibility between adjectives and adverbs does not show up in the same way for all the functions implied. The application of a constituent-based interpretation of the Amsterdam model, together with the distinction between two adjectival functions (TM<+count> and TM<−count>) and two adverbial ones (PM and MM), shows that indeed the degree of flexibility in degree words varies from one to the other. This intralinguistic variation is not at random, but can be captured in terms of a number of implicational relations. More specifically, we find four implications that restrict the potential range of functions of flexible modifiers. These are listed in (9):

(9) **Implicational relations of degree words in Spanish:**

a. If a degree word has the functions TM <+count> and PM, then it also has the function TM <−count>.
b. If a degree word has the functions TM <−count> and MM, then it also has the function PM.
c. If a degree word behaves like a differentiated adjective, then it will have the function TM <+count> exclusively.
d. If a degree word behaves like a differentiated adverb, then it will have the function MM exclusively.

The implicational relations listed in 9 allow us to deduce that quantitative modification is organised in Spanish around three main word classes: differentiated adjectives specialised in the function TM<+count>, differentiated adverbs specialised in the function MM, and flexible modifiers having at least the functions TM<−count> and PM.

It seems that this characterization may correspond to a more general tendency in Spanish. In several cases, the modification of a predicate may be carried out by either a flexible modifier or an adverb (cf 10a–b); however, only a differentiated adverb may modify a term modifier (cf 10c–d):

(10) Spanish:

a. Miguel anud-ó fuerte la cuerda
Miguel knot-3.SG.PST strong.SG ART.F.SG rope

b. Miguel anud-ó fuerte-mente la cuerda
Miguel knot-3.SG.PST strong.SG-AR ART.F.SG rope
'Miguel knotted the rope strongly'

c. *La cuerda, fuerte anud-ad-a,
ART.F.SG rope strong.SG knot-PRT-F.SG
nos permit-ió pas-ar el río
1.PL.ACC allow-3.SG.PST cross-IF ART.M.SG river

d. La cuerda, fuerte-mente anud-ad-a,
ART.F.SG rope, strong.SG-AR knot-PRT-F.SG,
nos permit-ió pasar el río
1.PL.ACC allow-3.SG.PST cross-IF ART.M.SG river
'The rope, strongly knotted, allowed us to cross the river.'

Taking into account these facts, it may be affirmed that a constituent-based interpretation of parts of speech systems does not reduce the typological adequacy of the Amsterdam model. On the contrary, it leads to new insights concerning the intra-linguistic distribution of lexical categories across functions. The implicational relations gathered in 9a–d, which point to a possible **modifier hierarchy**, are the first testimony of this.

4.4 In accordance with the Amsterdam model, categorial flexibility between adjective and adverb implies that flexible modifiers are ambiguous in their lexical meaning. The resolution of such ambiguities within speech acts requires the intervention of grammatical strategies, ultimately, the context. Amongst the grammatical procedures relevant for disambiguation, Hengeveld *et al.* (2004) show the important role that word order plays. In the case of Spanish degree words, word order has some importance, but is not a decisive element. There are other factors that are much more relevant. I have already mentioned the existence of truncated forms for some specific functions (cf 4.2, note 11). Other strategies concern morphological inflection and the use of partitive structures.

As for word order, TM and MM degree words always precede their heads. PM degree words predominantly follow their heads, while the pre-head position is a marked option. Within the class of flexible modifiers word order thus in most cases uniquely identifies PM words, while not distinguishing between TM and MM words.

The morphological inflection in gender and number is probably the most effective procedure for the disambiguation of degree words. The adverbial functions PM and MM are fulfilled by invariable items, the form of which coincides with the unmarked form of adjectives: singular masculine. Thus, a degree word with a feminine form is identified immediately as having an adjectival function. Obviously, number is not relevant in TM<–count>, which is necessarily singular. The TM<+count> function also admits the use of singular in some cases, but it is more frequent for it to take the plural form, which eliminates all possible ambiguity. Thus inflection disambiguates the readings of degree words that are not disambiguated by word order.

As for the partitive structure, it appears when the quantifier and the element quantified are linked by a preposition. In Spanish, this preposition is *de*, which in these contexts equals the English preposition *of*. In Table 2, the partitive structure appears in two cases: *algo de* and *un poco de*. Both are invariable from the morphological point of view and used in the TM<−count> function. These morphosyntactic characteristics find their origin in the fact that, etymologically, both quantifiers are terms (*algo* as a pronoun; *un poco* as a nominal phrase) that maintain their primitive codification procedure. Thus, although semantically these degree words behave as modifiers of a term, syntactically the relation is the opposite: it is the quantified term which acts as a prepositional modifier of a quantificational head.[13] This situation is analogous to that of the English quantifiers *a bit of*, *a lot of*, etc.:

(11) Spanish:
Quier-e [[un] poc-o [de leche]]
want-3.SG.PR IND QNT-M.SG PRP milk
'S/He wants a little milk'; 'S/He wants a bit of milk'

The combination of the aforementioned procedures (truncation, word order, morphological inflection, and partitive structures) lessens the ambiguity derived from the dominant flexibility in Spanish degree words. The cases without complete differentiation are rare and relatively marginal. For example, *más* 'more' and *menos* 'less' are items with high flexibility and lack of inflection. But we have to take into account that they are degree words with comparative meaning, so their use is restricted to very specific grammatical constructions. This means that, in practice, their flexibility does not create any kind of problem when interpreting the statements in which they appear. For this reason, I believe that the only important case of ambiguity is that which affects *algo* (item 2 in Table 2) when it appears with an adjective. Under such circumstances, this degree word can be used both as a pronoun (T function), modified by the adjective, or as an adverb (MM function) that modifies an adjective mentioned earlier. Sometimes, disambiguation is possible thanks to other elements present in the linguistic context: verbal valence, the presence of a nominal head for the adjective (cf. 12a), etc. But when these clues do not exist, then the ambiguity is grammatically irresolvable. In 12b–c, we can see how the same speech sequence admits of two interpretations, conditioned by the relation between adjective and quantifier. Only the communicative context will allow the listener to decide in which cases he/she should choose one or the other:

(12) Spanish:
a. Compr-ó [[un] regalo [[algo] caro]]
buy-3.SG.PST IND present QNT expensive
'S/He bought a somewhat expensive present'
b. Est-o es [algo [caro]]
DEM-SG.NT COP QNT expensive
'This is something expensive'

c. Est-o es [[algo] caro]
DEM-SG.NT COP QNT expensive
'This is somewhat expensive'

5. Flexibility and intensification in Romance languages

5.1 The analysis presented in the previous section has made it possible to establish some significant features concerning the distribution of Spanish quantifiers across functions. There are reasons to think that this distribution is not an idiosyncratic fact of Spanish but has a wider cross-linguistic scope. Obviously, checking such a claim requires wide-ranging typological research that is still pending. However, and taking a first step in this direction, I will here compare the main degree words dedicated to the expression of intensification (i.e. superlative degree) in the modern Romance languages. This sample of languages is not at all representative, but it offers the possibility of a first systematic approach to this question using a contrastive method.

In accordance with the analytical procedure developed for Spanish degree words, the data of the Romance languages under study can be synthesised in Table 3, where the function T has been excluded since it is not relevant here. For each function, only the degree word that, with the data available, can be considered to be the most neutral one in sociolinguistic terms as well as the most widely used, has been taken into

Table 3.

Language	TM <+count>	TM <–count>	PM	MM
Catalan (Badia 1994)	*molts* [pl;m] *moltes* [pl;f]	*molt de* [sg;m] *molta* [sg;f]	*molt*	*molt*
French (Chevalier *et al.* 1964; Wagner & Pinchon 1991)	*beaucoup de* <+pl>	*beaucoup de* <+sg>	*beaucoup*	*très*
Galician (Carballo 1966)	*moitos* [pl;m] *moitas* [pl;f]	*moito* [sg;m] *moita* [sg;f]	*moito*	*moi*
Italian (Battaglia & Pernicone 1960)	*molti* [pl;m] *molte* [pl;f]	*molto* [sg;m] *molta* [sg;f]	*molto*	*molto*
Portuguese (Vázquez & Da Luz 1971; Figueiredo & Ferreira 1974)	*muitos* [pl;m] *muitas* [pl;f]	*muito* [sg;m] *muita* [sg;f]	*muito*	*muito*
Rumanian (Rauta 1947)	*mulți* [pl;m] *multe* [pl;f]	*mult* [sg;m] *multă* [sg;f]	*mult*	*foarte*
Spanish	*muchos* [pl;m] *muchas* [pl;f]	*mucho* [sg;m] *mucha* [sg;f]	*mucho*	*muy*

f: feminine; m: masculine; pl: plural; sg: singular.

consideration. As in the analysis of the Spanish data, I indicate the morphological inflection for gender and number, as well as the presence of the preposition *de* that is characteristic of partitive structures.[14]

5.2 Table 3 shows that, within this area, the tendency towards flexibility detected above for Spanish is a common feature of all Romance languages. In all of them, at least three of the four syntactic slots taken into consideration are filled by flexible modifiers. This can be partially explained by the etymological affinities of these quantifiers. Most of them are cognates, derived from the Latin item *multum* (with inflection in gender and number). The only exceptions are found in French and, partially, in Rumanian. Rumanian maintains the derivates from *multum* in all functions except for that corresponding to MM, where it has a specialised degree word that comes from the grammaticalization of an adjective: Latin *fortem* 'strong' (Lausberg 1962: II, 136). As for French, this is the only language that lacks modifiers stemming from *multum*, *beaucoup* being the result of the grammaticalization of a nominal phrase (*beau coup* 'beautiful knock' 'beautiful blow'), and *très* derives from a preposition with spatial value (Latin *trans* 'beyond'). However, until the 16th century, this language had the quantifier *moult*, which coexisted with the present forms for several centuries (Dauzat *et al* 1971: 79). Likewise, until at least the 17th century, the word *beaucoup* competed with *très* in the MM function (Wagner & Pinchon 1991: 438). In any case, the etymological particularities of French and Rumanian do not alter the fact that they offer a functional behaviour that is completely analogous to that of other Romance languages, such as Spanish or Galician. On the other hand, this situation of competition between forms is not exclusive to French. In medieval Portuguese, for example, the flexible modifier *muito* existed along with the truncated *mui* that specialised in the MM function (Vázquez & Da Luz 1971: I, 205). In the present synchrony, this situation is recorded at least in Asturian, a Romance dialect in the north of Spain. For the MM function, this language has a full degree word (*muncho*), which can occupy several syntactic slots, and a truncated one (*muy*), which is exclusively used for the modification of modifiers:

(13) Asturian (ALA 1999: 329):

a. Yeren muncho viey-o-s
   COP.3PL.PST QNT old-M-PL

b. Yeren muy viey-o-s
   COP.3PL.PST QNT old-M-PL
   'They were very old'

These examples stress the fact that, in a given language, the same semantic content (in this case, the superlative degree applied to adjectives and adverbs) can be expressed at least by means of two compatible grammatical strategies: flexible strategy (13a) and differentiating strategy (13b). This situation of cohabitation between both strategies can be maintained for an indefinite time, or it can be diachronically solved in favour of one or the other. As shown above, this is what we see in French and Portuguese, with opposite results. In French, the differentiating strategy, represented by the degree word *très*, finally took over the MM function to the detriment of the flexible strategy represented by the quantifiers *moult* (which disappeared completely) and *beaucoup* (which still exists as a flexible modifier in the other functions, but not in the MM function). In Portuguese, on the contrary, the competition between the full *muito* and its truncated correlate *mui* ended with the generalization of the flexible strategy.[15]

One of the most important conclusions that can be drawn on the basis of Table 3 is that the implicational relations found in Spanish (cf 9) are fully valid for the expression of intensification in all Romance languages. There are certainly no new arguments in favour of (9c), because no differentiated adjective showed up in our analysis, but it is also true that there are no arguments against it. The implications in (9a–b) are supported by the Romance data, and (9d) is also confirmed in all the Romance languages under study: four of them have forms that, in accordance with the parts of speech theory stated in Section 2, have a syntactic behaviour that can be identified as a differentiating strategy. This means that these four degree words can be recognised as adverbs. But such adverbs only act as MM, never as PM. The cognates *moi* (Galician) and *muy* (Spanish) are originally truncated forms, derived from their flexible correlates. The French *très* and the Rumanian *foarte*, as we have seen, do not have any etymological relation with the other quantifiers. In any case, the differences in the historical origin of these adverbs do not alter their similarities in typological terms. In this respect, the case of Rumanian seems to be especially significant. This language is different from the rest of the Romance family in that it lacks native manner adverbs. Instead, it makes generalised use of what is normally known as **conversion** of the adjective into an adverb[16] (Hummel 2002: 19f), which corresponds in the Amsterdam model to the concept of **flexible modifier**. In the standard version of this model, Rumanian should accordingly be classified as a type 3 language. Despite this fact, here we see that it has at least one degree word (*foarte*) that acts as a differentiated adverb. For me, this is an important testimony in favour of the hypothesis I have been defending in this article, in accordance with which the notions of rigidity, differentiation, and flexibility are not static typological options, but compatible grammatical strategies.

Table 3 also confirms the role played by morphological inflection and partitive structures when reducing the ambiguity associated with the use of flexible modifiers. While adverbial functions (PM and MM) are associated with uninflected forms, the adjectival function (TM) is characterised by having gender and number inflection. For the latter, there is further specialization: plural forms are necessarily associated with countable nouns; singular forms only modify non-countable nouns. The exception to such tendencies is once again French. Due to the fact that in origin *beaucoup* was a syntactically construed constituent, it has been established as an invariable form, and does not tolerate morphological inflection in any of its functions. However, the disambiguation between adverbial and adjectival functions is possible thanks to the fact that, in the latter, the use of a partitive structure has been generalised by means of the preposition *de*. The modified term is necessarily codified as a bare nominal (Chevalier *et al*: 1964: 225). In writing, countable nouns appear in the plural, and non-countable ones in the singular, even if we have to take into account that normally both forms are now neutralised in spoken language.[17]

The partitive structure does not only appear in French. It also exists in Catalan, but in a special way. Badia (1994: 527) points out that many Catalan quantifiers allow either the presence or the absence of the preposition as alternative options. Nevertheless, this optionality is sociolinguistically conditioned. In standard Catalan, the preposition *de* appears compulsorily when the modified term is singular masculine and it is omitted in all other cases. Other options are classified as colloquial forms. Besides, they are practically unknown in some dialects, e.g. the Southern dialect (Valencian) (Lacreu 1996: 114). In particular, the absence of the preposition *de* in the singular masculine (14a) and its presence in the plural feminine (16a) are strongly rejected in sociolinguistic terms:

(14) Catalan:
a. ??Joan va arrib-ar amb molt retard
Joan 3SG.PST arriv-IF PRP INTS delay
b. Joan va arribar amb molt de retard
Joan 3SG.PST arriv-IF PRP INTS PRP delay
'John arrived very late'

(15) Catalan:
a. ?El pastís necessit-a molt-a de farina
ART.M.SG cake need-3SG.PR INTS-F.SG PRP flour
b. El pastís necessit-a molt-a farina
ART.M.SG cake need-3SG.PR INTS-F.SG flour
'The cake needs a lot of flour'

(16) Catalan:
a. ??El pastís necessit-a molt-es de maduix-es
ART.M.SG cake need-3SG.PR INTS-F.PL PRP strawberry-F.PL
b. El pastís necessit-a molt-es maduix-es
ART.M.SG cake need-3SG.PR INTS-F.PL strawberry-F.PL
'The cake needs a lot of strawberries'

The reason for such a complex situation resides in the fact that the singular masculine is the morphologically unmarked item in the function TM, and its form coincides with that of the quantifier used as PM and MM: *molt*. The partitive structure appears then as an explicit device disambiguating between adjectival and adverbial functions. In other cases, especially in the plural feminine, this structure is redundant, due to the presence of morphological inflection for gender and number. So, the use of the preposition in such cases can be explained by an analogical extension which, at least for the moment, has not penetrated the standard language. For this reason, we find a conflict between two general linguistic principles: the principle of economy, which applies a formal distinction only to the strictly necessary cases, and the principle of analogy, which tends to maintain a homogeneous morphological paradigm. The sociolinguistic variation in Catalan shows different attempts to solve this conflict.

In general, it can be said that the combination of both formal procedures (morphological inflection and partitive structures) lessens the cases in which a single item can have more than one function. In Table 3 we only find two quantifiers flexible enough to fill three different functions (TM<–count>, PM, and MM) without any formal mechanism to identify them: the Portuguese *muito* and the Italian *molto*.

Word order seems to have a relatively minor effect. The only case in which it seems to perform an important function is in that of the disambiguation of the adverbial functions, PM and MM, in the languages in which the latter function is performed by a flexible modifier rather than a differentiated adverb. Such is the case in the following Catalan examples. The non-marked order for the PM function (17a) places the quantifier (*molt*) after the head, whereas MM function (17b) necessarily requires the quantifier to be placed in a pre-head position:

(17) Catalan:

a.	El	teu	vestit	[m'-agrad-a	[molt]]	
	ART.M.SG	POSS.2SG	dress	CLT1-like-3SG.PR	INTS.M.SG	
	'I like your dress a lot'					
b.	El	teu	amic	es	[[molt]	agradós]
	ART.M.SG	POSS.2SG	friend	COP.3SG.PR	INTS.M.SG	pleasant
	'Your friend is very pleasant'					

6. Conclusions

I have shown in previous sections how in most cases a quantifier is capable of carrying out more than one function, as a consequence of categorial flexibility which is present in varying degrees from one quantifier to the other. These facts respond to two fundamental features that must be taken into account in any functional analysis of languages: a) there is no isomorphism between expression and content; b) all living languages vary in synchrony. Till now, the standard version of the Amsterdam model of parts of speech systems did not take into account the second feature appropriately. I have proposed some changes in the model, in order to explain linguistic variation in parts of speech systems in a more satisfactory way. My proposal aims at a constituent-based interpretation of parts of speech systems, within which differentiation, flexibility, and rigidity are (potentially) compatible strategies. I have shown that this offers an improvement in the descriptive and explanatory capacities of the Amsterdam model. Moreover, my proposal does not reduce its typological adequacy. Quite on the contrary, my analysis has revealed that intralinguistic variation in degrees of flexibility is not random, but can be captured, for Spanish, in terms of several implicational relations, repeated in (18), which point at the existence of an implicational hierarchy:

(18) **Implicational relations of degree words:**
  a. If a degree word has the functions TM <+count> and PM, then it also has the function TM <−count>.
  b. If a degree word has the functions TM <−count> and MM, then it also has the function PM.
  c. If a degree word behaves like a differentiated adjective, then it will have the function TM <+count> exclusively.
  d. If a degree word behaves like a differentiated adverb, then it will have the function MM exclusively.

The validity of such implications has been fully demonstrated in Spanish quantifiers, and its cross-linguistic reach is confirmed at least in the degree words expressing intensification in Romance languages in general. This fact corroborates that the analysis of degree words in the framework of the Amsterdam model is viable. It is furthermore an important argument in favour of the hypothesis (defended in Section 3) that degree words are lexical units rather than morphosyntactic operators.

It is worth noting that, in the field of adverbial functions in Romance languages, the differentiating strategy appears exclusively in the syntactic slot characteristic of the modification of modifiers; that is, only those degree words that modify adjectives or other adverbs can be identified as real adverbs. However, those degree words that play the role of predicate modifiers (prototypically, verbal predicates) do not act as adverbs, but as flexible modifiers, because they also play other roles, including at least the modification of non-count nouns. In fact, flexibility is the dominant strategy — although it is not exclusive — in the field of the main degree words of Romance languages. The functional ambiguity associated with this strategy (Hengeveld *et al.* 2004) is efficiently mitigated by means of other formal procedures, amongst which one should underline morphological inflection and partitive structures. Thanks to this, the real cases of irresolvable ambiguity are exceptional and of little importance.

This research has a limited scope, as I have concentrated on a specific type of items (degree words) in a small number of related languages. It cannot be but a first step of a more wide-ranging research project that necessarily requires the increase of the number and representativeness of languages under study, as well as the extension to other kinds of lexical units. Notwithstanding these limitations, the results offered here are promising, and constitute a first confirmation of the appropriateness of this line of research.

Notes

* The present study is part of the research project HUM2004-04296/FILO, financed by the Ministry of Education and Science (Spain). I thank Paula García Ramírez and Mary Joan Dunmall for checking the English version of the text. I also thank Salvador Valera for his useful comments, and two anonymous reviewers for their insightful remarks. Last but not least, I express my gratitude to Kees Hengeveld, for his teaching and continuous support. Abbreviations used in glosses: 1 = first person, 3 = third person, ACC = accusative, AR = adverbialiser, ART = definite article, AUX = auxiliary, CLT = clitic, COP = copula, DEM = demonstrative, F = feminine, IF = infinitive, IND = indefinite article, INTS = intensifier, M = masculine, NR = nominaliser, NT = neuter, PL = plural, PR = present, PRP = preposition, PRT = participle, PST = past, QNT = quantifier, SG = singular.

1. Such universality is a sign that basic terms are not conditioned by typological implications derived from PoSH.

2. This term replaces that of **specialised languages**, initially used by Hengeveld (1992a, 1992b).

3. This category was named **modifier** by Hengeveld *et al.* (2004). However, as this term can refer to other types of constituents (for example, adpositional phrases or other rigid constructions), I find it more precise to introduce the qualification **flexible**.

4. With the examples included in 2 and 3, I will indicate in parentheses the linguistic type within which they should be included in accordance with the present version of the Amsterdam model.

5. As Bosque (1989: 131) and Kovacci (1999: 715), amongst others, have warned, American Spanish makes a higher use of the categorial flexibility adjective-adverb than European Spanish. This has been empirically proved by sociolinguistic research (cf De Mello 1992). Some diachronic factors are also relevant here, because in American Spanish there are still remnants of European Spanish of the 16th and 17th centuries, when the flexible strategy had a wider presence than that recorded in the present synchrony.

6. Nilsen (1972: 184f) found thirty-nine *–ly* degree modifiers in his research on English adverbials. He considers that this class of adverbs (like manner adverbs) "could be extended almost indefinitely."

7. This statement only applies to gradable adjectives and adverbs. Adjectives and adverbs that codify their content in terms of a radical counter-position (presence or absence of the property, to the exclusion of other possibilities) do not admit gradation, e.g. *alphabetical* (adjective) and its derived adverb *alphabetically*.

8. In accordance with Brown (1985), quantification by degree words is relative in nature, which opposes it to the absolute quantification expressed by numerals.

9. Moreno Cabrera (1991, 1992) considers that the quantification of predicates (which I have called **quantificational aspect**) corresponds to two basic semantic types that he considers to be universal. On the one hand, there is iterative quantification (frequency), which makes reference to time intervals; on the other, there is multiplicative quantification (intensification), which makes reference to events. More evidence in this respect is provided by, for example, Hengeveld (1992c).

10. It is interesting to note that the latter two degree words have arisen from a derivative process, as they are truncated forms of *mucho* and *tanto*, respectively. This means that, although they are recorded from the very origin of the language, in the latter instance they are an evolutionary innovation in relation to their flexible correlates.

11. The only important formal difference happens in the singular masculine of some quantifiers; in these cases, they have truncated forms when they work as TM (cf Table 2, as *tr*), while they use full forms when they work as anaphoric pronouns: *algún/alguno*; *un/uno*.

12. In the peripheral Romance languages, amongst which we find Spanish and Rumanian, term modifiers can be used directly as terms. In central Romance languages, this possibility is only feasible if they perform the role of subject; in other cases, they need the support of a real anaphoric pronoun: Italian: *ne*; French and Catalan: *en*.

13. Within the framework of Brown's formulation (1985), the degree words that directly modify the term offer a non-proportional quantification. On the other hand, the partitive structure included here would codify the quantification in proportional terms; it is a quantification that defines the subgroup within a **domain ensemble**. In these cases, the domain ensemble is not specified, because, in the latter instance, it coincides with the **universal ensemble** that groups all the parts (or measures, in case of non-countable terms) of the entity. For Brucart (1994), authentic partitive structures are those in which the domain ensemble is clearly determined (e.g.: *three of **the seven** books*). On the contrary, structures that do not specify the domain ensemble (which are those we are considering here; cf 11) are catalogued as **pseudopartitives**.

14. The Spanish data are mine. For the rest of the languages, I have used the grammar books quoted in the first column; besides, I have asked some expert informants, who have given me some of the examples. I want to mention their names as a proof of my gratitude to them: Mila Espinosa Irles (Catalan), Manuela Merino (French), Javier Díaz Pérez (Galician and Portuguese), Chiara Manfredini (Italian), and Catalina Iliescu (Rumanian).

15. Nowadays, *mui* is still used, but as an archaic, non-standard form.

16. Undoubtedly, flexibility and conversion bear a close relationship, which deserves to be studied in depth. However, there are important differences. Here I want to focus my attention on one of them. Conversion is normally understood as a derivational process oriented to the creation of new vocabulary (Bauer & Huddleston 2002: 1640). This implies the existence of a **directionality** from a primary word to a derivative one; e.g.: $milk_N$ > $milk_V$. Štekauer (1996: 127–133) showed that such a directionality may only be established by means of diachronic data. For its part, flexibility is conceived in strictly synchronic terms, and it does not presuppose any type of directionality. Diachronically, it admits a polygenetic origin, as much derivative as non-derivative. In fact, many apparent cases of conversion are not so, because the derivative process is etymologically excluded; e.g.: $love_N$ < *[Old English] lufu*; $love_V$ < *[Old English] lufian* (Štekauer 1996: 60).

17. The distinction just remains for nouns that have irregular plural forms: *cheval* 'horse' (plural *chevaux* 'horses'), *oeil* 'eye' (plural *yeux* 'eyes'), etc.

References

Academia de la Llingua Asturiana (ALA). 1999. *Gramática de la llingua asturiana*. Oviedo: ALA, 2001.

Anward, Jan. 2000. A dynamic model of part-of-speech differentiation. *Approaches to the typology of word classes*, Petra M. Vogel & Bernard Comrie (eds.), 3–45. Berlin: Mouton de Gruyter.

Badia i Margarit, Antoni M. 1994. *Gramàtica de la llengua catalana*. Barcelona: Proa, 1995.

Baker, Mark C. 2003. *Lexical categories*. Cambridge: Cambridge University Press.

Battaglia, Salvatore & Pernicone, Vincenzo. 1960. *Grammatica Italiana*. Torino: Loescher.

Bauer, Laurie & Huddleston, Rodney. 2002. Lexical word-formation. *The Cambridge grammar of the English language*. Rodney Huddleston & Geoffrey Pullum (in collaboration with other authors) (eds.), 1621–1721. Cambridge: Cambridge University Press.

Bolinger, Dwight. 1972. *Degree words*. The Hague: Mouton.

Bosque, Ignacio. 1989. *Las categorías gramaticales. Relaciones y diferencias*. Madrid: Síntesis.

Brown, D. Richard. 1985. Term operators. *Predicates and terms in Functional Grammar*. A. Machtelt Bolkestein; Casper de Groot & J. Lachlan Mackenzie (eds.), 127–145. Dordrecht: Foris.

Brucart, José María. 1994. Concordancia *ad sensum* y partitividad en español. *Contribuciones al estudio de la lingüística hispánica. Homenaje al profesor Ramón Trujillo*. M. Almeida & J. Dorta (eds.), 157–184. Santa Cruz de Tenerife: Montesinos. (Vol. I).

Carballo Calero, Ricardo. 1966. *Gramática elemental del gallego común*. Vigo: Galaxia.

Chevalier, Jean-Claude ; Claire Blanche-Benveniste, Michel Arrivé & Jean Peytard. 1964. *Grammaire Larousse du français contemporain*. Paris: Larousse, 1987.

Dauzat, Albert ; Jean Dubois & Henri Mitterand. 1971. *Nouveau dictionnaire étymologique et Historique*. Paris: Larousse.

De Mello, George. 1992. Adjetivos adverbializados en el español culto hablado de diez ciudades. *Lingüística Española Actual* 14(2): 225–242.

Dik, Simon C. 1989. *The theory of Functional Grammar. Part I: The structure of the clause*. Dordrecht: Foris.

Dik, Simon C. 1997. *The theory of Functional Grammar.* 2 vols. Kees Hengeveld (ed.). Berlin: Mouton de Gruyter.

Egea, Esteban Rafael. 1979. *Los adverbios terminados en '-mente' en el español contemporáneo*. Bogotá: Instituto Caro y Cuervo.

Evans, Nicholas. 2000. Word classes in the world's languages. *Morphology: A handbook on inflection and word formation*, Geert Booij; Christian Lehmann & Joachim Mugdan (eds.), 708–732. Berlin: Walter de Gruyter [vol. I].

Figueiredo, J. M. Nunes de and Ferreira, A. Gomes. 1974. *Compêndio de gramática portuguesa*. Oporto: Porto.

García Marcos, Francisco J. 1999. *Fundamentos críticos de sociolingüística*. Almería: Universidad de Almería.

Hengeveld, Kees. 1992a. Parts of Speech. *Layered Structure and Reference in a Functional Perspective*, Michael Fortescue, Peter Harder and Lars Kristoffersen (eds.), 29–55. Amsterdam: John Benjamins.

Hengeveld, Kees. 1992b. *Non-Verbal Predication*. Berlin: Mouton de Gruyter.

Hengeveld, Kees. 1992c. Adverbial quantification in British Romani, Dutch, and Turkish. *Adverbial Quantification and Other Adverbalia*, Juan Carlos Moreno Cabrera (ed.), 19–29. *Eurotyp Working Papers* 4.

Hengeveld, Kees. 1997. Adverbs in Functional Grammar. *Toward a Functional Lexicology*, Gerd Wotjak (ed), 121–136. Frankfurt am Main: Peter Lang.

Hengeveld, Kees, Rijkhoff, Jan and Siewierska, Anna. 2004. Parts-of-speech systems and word order. *Journal of Linguistics* 40(3): 527–570.

Hopper, Paul J. and Traugott, Elizabeth Closs. 2003. *Grammaticalization* (2nd ed.). Cambridge: Cambridge University Press.

Hudson, Richard A. 1980. *La sociolingüística*. Barcelona: Anagrama, 1981.

Hummel, Martin. 2002. Sincronía y diacronía del sistema atributivo de las lenguas románicas. *Lengua* 13: 9–48.

Jacobson, Sven. 1978. *On the Use, Meaning, and Syntax of English Preverbal Adverbs*. Stockholm: Almqvist & Wiksel International.

Jespersen, Otto. 1942. *A Modern English Grammar on Historical Principles. Vol. VI: Morphology*. London: George Allen & Unwin, 1974.

Kovacci, Ofelia. 1999. "El adverbio". *Gramática descriptiva de la lengua española*, Ignacio Bosque and Violeta Demonte (eds.), Madrid: Gredos, vol. I, 705–786.

Lacreu, Josep. 1996. *Gramàtica valenciana*. (5th ed.) Valencia: Bromera, 2002.

Lausberg, Heinrich. 1962. *Lingüística románica*. 2 vols. Madrid: Gredos, 1965–1966.

López Palma, Helena. 1999. *La interpretación de los cuantificadores*. Madrid: Visor.

Mackenzie, J. Lachlan. 2001. Adverbs and adpositions: the cinderella categories of Functional Grammar. *Revista Canaria de Estudios Ingleses* 42: 119–135 .

Martínez Amador, Emilio M. 1953. *Diccionario gramatical*. Barcelona: Sopena.

Moreno Cabrera, Juan Carlos. 1991. Once upon a time: two tentative universals of adverbial quantification and their typological consequences. *Adverbalia*, Johan Van der Auwera (ed.), 53–65. *Eurotyp Working Papers* 1.

Moreno Cabrera, Juan Carlos. 1992. Adverbial quantification in the languages of Europe. A typological survey. *Adverbial Quantification and Other Adverbalia*, Juan Carlos Moreno Cabrera (ed.), 7–18. *Eurotyp Working Papers* 4.

Moreno Cabrera, Juan Carlos. 1997. *Introducción a la lingüística. Enfoque tipológico y universalista*. Madrid: Síntesis.

Nilsen, Don Lee Fred. 1972. *English Adverbials*. The Hague: Mouton.

Rauta, Aurelio. 1947. *Gramática rumana*. Salamanca: CSIC and Universidad de Salamanca.

Salazar García, Ventura. 2004. Acercamiento crítico a la selección objetiva de contenidos léxicos en la enseñanza de E/LE. *Estudios de Lingüística* 18: 243–273.

Samuelsdorff, Paul O. 1998. Pronouns, adpositions, 'adverbs' and the lexicon. *The Structure of the Lexicon in Functional Grammar*, Hella Olbertz, Kees Hengeveld and Jesús Sánchez García (eds.), 267–278. Amsterdam: John Benjamins.

Seco, Manuel. 1978. Problemas formales de la definición lexicográfica. *Estudios ofrecidos a Emilio Alarcos Llorach*, vol. 2. Oviedo: Universidad de Oviedo, 217–239.

Štekauer, Pavol. 1996. *A Theory of Conversion in English*. Frankfurt am Main: Peter Lang.

Vázquez Cuesta, Pilar and Da Luz, Maria Albertina Mendes. 1971. *Gramática portuguesa*. 2 vols. Madrid: Gredos.

Wagner, Robert Léon and Pinchon, Jacqueline. 1991. *Grammaire du français classique et moderne*. Paris: Hachette.

Author's address

Ventura Salazar García
Departamento de Filología Española
Facultad de Humanidades
Universidad de Jaén. Edif. D-2
E-23071. Jaén (Spain)

vsalazar@ujaen.es

On flexible and rigid nouns

Jan Rijkhoff
Department of Linguistics, University of Aarhus, Denmark

This article argues that in addition to the major flexible lexical categories in Hengeveld's classification of parts of speech systems (Contentive, Non-Verb, Modifier), there are also flexible word classes within the rigid lexical category Noun (Set Noun, Sort Noun, General Noun). Members of flexible word classes are characterized by their vague semantics, which in the case of nouns means that values for the semantic features Shape and Homogeneity are either left undetermined or they are specified in such a way that they do not quite match the properties of the kind of entity denoted by the flexible item in the external world. I will then argue that flexible word classes constitute a proper category (i.e. they are not the result of a merger of some rigid word classes) in that members of flexible word categories display the same properties regarding category membership as members of rigid word classes. Finally this article wants to claim that the distinction between rigid and flexible noun categories (a) adds a new dimension to current classifications of parts of speech systems, (b) correlates with certain grammatical phenomena (e.g. so-called number discord), and (c) helps to explain the parts of speech hierarchy.

1. Introduction

The central claim of this paper is that nouns that are used cross-linguistically to refer to a single, concrete object can be divided into flexible and rigid subtypes. A rigid noun has a narrow content, which means that the values for certain semantic features (Shape, Homogeneity) match the properties of a concrete object in the physical world. A flexible noun, on the other hand, is semantically vague: values for these features are either left unspecified or they are specified in such a way that they do not quite correspond with the properties of a single, concrete object in the external world. Thus, in addition to major flexible word categories such as Contentive or Non-verb (Hengeveld 1992; Hengeveld et al. 2004; Hengeveld and Rijkhoff 2005), we also find flexible nominal (sub)categories within the category Noun (Section 4).

It is then claimed that a flexible word class is not a merger of some rigid word classes, but constitutes a proper category in its own right in that category membership can be described in terms of subsective and intersective gradience (Section 5). This article generally demonstrates the importance of the rigid/flexible distinction in classifications of parts of speech systems. Apart from the fact that the distinction between rigid and flexible noun categories refines current classifications of parts of speech systems, it is shown that flexible categories correlate with certain grammatical phenomena (such as so-called number discord) and that the features that are used to define flexible and rigid noun categories also play an important role in the parts of speech hierarchy (Verb > Noun > Adjective > Adverb; Section 6).

2. Parts of Speech systems

Whereas words in many languages can be categorized in terms of the traditional word classes (Verb, Noun etc.), there are also quite a few languages which are deemed to have a major lexical word class whose members do not seem to belong to any of the traditional (rigid) word classes like Verb, Noun or Adjective. This is captured in Hengeveld's classification of parts of speech (PoS) systems, which has a major division between languages with a flexible PoS system and languages with a rigid PoS system (Figure 1). A simplified version of this classification is given in Figure 1. In languages with a flexible PoS system, some or all of the functions of a lexeme in an actual linguistic expression (i.e. verbal, nominal, adjectival, adverbial function) are performed by the same group of lexemes (Types 1–3). In languages with a rigid PoS system (Types 4–7) these functions are distributed over distinct, non-overlapping groups of lexemes. One could also say that a flexible lexeme (a contentive, a non-verb or a modifier) is semantically vague in the sense of Cruse (1986: 51) in that it has a general meaning, which covers two or more of the specific possibilities.

Figure 2 shows how the seven PoS systems in Hengeveld's classification are distributed in a representative sample of the world's languages (n=52). Since I will largely ignore adverbs, the number of PoS systems considered here can be reduced to five. Notice that I have included intermediate types 3/4 and 4/5 which have a minor class of adjectives and nouns, respectively (see also Hengeveld et al. 2004 and Smit 2001 for a more detailed presentation of languages with an intermediate PoS system).

<table>
<tr><td rowspan="3">FLEXIBLE PoS</td><td>1</td><td colspan="6">Contentive</td></tr>
<tr><td>2</td><td colspan="3">Verb</td><td colspan="3">Non-verb</td></tr>
<tr><td>3</td><td colspan="2">Verb</td><td colspan="2">Noun</td><td colspan="2">Modifier</td></tr>
<tr><td rowspan="4">Rigid PoS</td><td>4</td><td>Verb</td><td colspan="2">Noun</td><td colspan="2">Adjective</td><td>(manner) Adverb</td></tr>
<tr><td>5</td><td colspan="2">Verb</td><td colspan="2">Noun</td><td colspan="2">Adjective</td></tr>
<tr><td>6</td><td colspan="3">Verb</td><td colspan="3">Noun</td></tr>
<tr><td>7</td><td colspan="6">Verb</td></tr>
</table>

Figure 1. Hengeveld's classification of parts of speech systems (slightly modified).

Type 1: ***flexible***	***'Contentive'***	**Samoan**
Type 2: ***flexible***	**V – *'Non-verb'***	**†Hurrian, Imbabura Quechua, Turkish**
Types 3:	V – N – A	Abkhaz, Alamblak, Basque, Berbice Dutch Creole, Bukiyip (=Mountain Arapesh), Burushaski, Dutch, Georgian, Guaraní, †Hittite, Hmong Njua, Hungarian, Ika, Kayardild, Ket, Nama Hottentot, Nasioi, Ngalakan, Ngiti, †Sumerian, Wambon
Type 3/4	V – N(– A)	Babungo, Bambara, Chukchi, Gude, Kisi, Oromo, Pipil, Sarcee, Tamil
Type 4	V – N	Burmese, Galela, Hixkaryana, Koasati, Korean, Krongo, Lango, Mandarin Chinese, Nivkh (=Gilyak), Nung, Nunggubuyu, Tsou, Vietnamese, West Greenlandic
Type 4/5	V(– N)	Cayuga
Type 5	V	
Type unknown		*†Etruscan, †Meroitic, Nahali*

Figure 2. The distribution of Parts of Speech systems [without manner adverbs] in a representative sample of the world's languages (Rijkhoff 2004: 18).

Samoan is the only language in the sample with an extremely flexible PoS system (see Hengeveld & Rijkhoff 2005 and Broschart & Dawuda 2000 on other languages without a rigid verb/noun distinction). It has a single word class, whose members can be used as

- head of the clause (verbal function), as in (1a),
- head of the 'noun phrase' (nominal function; notice that 'noun phrase' is actually a misnomer here), as in (1b), or
- modifier of these heads (adverbial or adjectival function).

Type 1:
Samoan (Austronesian; Mosel and Hovdhaugen 1992: 80, 73, 74)

(1) a. 'Ua lā le aso
PERF sun ART day
'The sun is shining today.'
(lit. 'The day suns')

b. 'Ua mālosi le lā
PERF strong ART sun
'The sun is strong.'
(lit. 'The sun strongs.')

Galela and Hausa are both examples of languages with two rigid classes: verbs and nouns. To express adjectival notions Galela uses participial forms of stative verbs, whereas Hausa employs an attributive NP headed by an abstract noun.

Type 4:
Galela (Papuan; van Baarda 1908: 35)
(2) awi ḍohu **i lalamo**
his foot it be_big:PRT
'his big foot'

Hausa (Afro-Asiatic; Schachter 1985: 15)
(3) mutum **mai alheri / arzaki / hankali**
person with kindness / prosperity / intelligence
'a kind/prosperous/intelligent person'

Experts disagree whether there are languages with a single lexical word class that consists of just verbs (cf. Hengeveld and Rijkhoff 2005: 408), but Cayuga and Tuscarora seem to come rather close to a Type 5 language:

Type 4/5:
Cayuga (Iroquoian; Sasse 1993: 657)
(4) a-hó-htǫ:' ho-tkwę't-a' nę:kyé hǫ-kweh
PAST-it:to_him-become_lost it:him-wallet-be this he:it-man
'This man lost his wallet.'
(the literal meaning, however, would be something like (Sasse: ibid.): "it became lost to him, it is his wallet, he is this man" or "it LOSTed him, it WALLETs him, the one who MANs")

Tuscarora ((Iroqiouan: Mithun Williams 1976: 32)
(5) rakwá:tihs wahratkáhthoʔ katéskrahs
ra-kwatihs wa-hr-at-kahtho-ʔ ka-teskr-ahs
M-young AOR-M-look_at-PNCT NONH-stink-SER
he_is_young he_looked_at_it it_stinks
'The boy looked at the goat'

It appears that flexibility in the PoS system correlates with a variety of grammatical phenomena, such as: fixed word order, suppletion, absence of gender and number (transnumerality), no copula support with bare predicates, and absence of transitive lexemes (Rijkhoff 2003, 2004; Hengeveld et al. 2004; Hengeveld and Rijkhoff 2005).

3. The vague semantics of flexible lexemes

Hengeveld's classification of PoS systems (Figure 1) contains three major word classes whose members are semantically vague: *Contentive*, *Non-verb* and *Modifier*. In the sample, Samoan is an example of a language with contentives. Apparently "there are no lexical or grammatical constraints on why a particular word cannot be used in the one or the other function" (Mosel and Hovdhaugen 1992: 73–4, 77):

> "... the categorization of full words is not given a priori in the lexicon. [...] It is only their actual occurrence in a particular environment which gives them the status of a verb or a noun. [...] What is given in the lexicon, is not a particular word class assignment, but the potential to be used in certain syntactic environments as a noun or a verb.[1]
> [...] all full words which function as noun and verb phrase nucleus can also be used as attributive modifiers."

In other words, it is the use of a vague lexeme in a certain context (the actual linguistic expression) that brings out certain parts of its meaning, giving the category neutral item a verbal, nominal, etc. flavour (see below on *coercion*). Inspired by Wilkins's account of noun semantics in Arrernte (Wilkins 2000), an outline of what may happen when a member of a flexible word class is used in an actual linguistic expression was presented in Hengeveld et al. (2004) and Hengeveld and Rijkhoff (2005). In this approach the vague meaning of a flexible lexeme consists of meaning components A B C D E etc. (where A B C etc. can be, for example, features, definitions, descriptions, knowledge structures). By placing the contentive in a particular syntactic slot the speaker *highlights* those meaning components that are relevant for a certain lexical (verbal, nominal, etc.) function, *downplaying* other meaning components. A very simplified representation of this process may look as follows:

(6) Meaning components of Samoan *lā* (A B C D E)

	A	B	C	D	E ...	Highlighted properties of *lā*:	
Slot: head of clause	+		+		+	A C E =>	verbal meaning (*lā* 'be_sunny')
Slot: head of 'NP'		+		+	+	B D E =>	nominal meaning (*lā* 'sun')
Slot: modifier of 'noun'		+	+	+		B C D =>	adjectival meaning (*lā* 'sunny')

Notice that no meaning is added, i.e. there is no semantic increment. Rather, the context highlights certain meaning components that are already present in the meaning of the lexeme, giving the flexible item its verbal, nominal or adjectival flavour. It will be argued below that the same approach ('coercion') can be used to account for the meaning of a flexible noun in an actual utterance.

4. Flexible and rigid nouns

The distinction between flexible and rigid PoS systems in *Figure* 1 is also relevant within the rigid word classes verb and noun. In some languages verbs are semantically specified for the familiar event-type (*Aktionsart* 'mode of action') features such as Telicity; in other languages verbs are vague (underdetermined or underspecified) with

<table>
<tr><td rowspan="2">Flexible PoS</td><td>1</td><td colspan="3">Contentive</td></tr>
<tr><td>2</td><td>Verb</td><td colspan="2">Non-verb</td></tr>
<tr><td rowspan="5">Rigid PoS</td><td>3a</td><td>Verb</td><td>Noun^{N} ('narrow content')</td><td>Adjective</td></tr>
<tr><td>3b</td><td>Verb</td><td>Noun^{W} ('wide content')</td><td>Adjective</td></tr>
<tr><td>4a</td><td>Verb</td><td colspan="2">Noun^{N} ('narrow content')</td></tr>
<tr><td>4b</td><td>Verb</td><td colspan="2">Noun^{W} ('wide content')</td></tr>
<tr><td>5</td><td colspan="3">Verb</td></tr>
</table>

Figure 3. Parts of speech systems with rigid ('narrow content') and flexible ('wide content') nouns (cf. Figure 6).

respect to such features (Ikegami 1985; see also e.g. Bisang 1996: 520; Bohnemeyer 2002). Here, however, we will only be concerned with nouns (i.e. languages of type 3–4 in Figure 2). I will argue below that nouns that are used to refer to a single concrete object have a *narrow semantic content* (Noun^{N}) if the values for the semantic features Shape and Homogeneity match the properties of a single object in the physical world. This is not so in the case of nouns with a *wide semantic content* (Noun^{W}), which are semantically vague. In the case of a flexible noun we find that the values for certain features are either left unspecified (Homogeneity) or are specified in such a way that they do not quite match the properties of a concrete object in the real world (Shape). For example, a language such as Thai, which, unlike e.g. Dutch, uses transnumeral nouns for concrete objects such as 'table', 'car', or 'knife', can be said to have nouns with a wide semantic content (Hundius and Kölver 1983: 181f):

> "[...], Thai nouns do not in themselves contain any numerical or referential indications. [...] they are purely conceptual labels which, in order to be appropriately related to objects of the non-linguistic world, always and in principle stand in need of interpretation which has to be inferred from both linguistic and non-linguistic context."

Thus, in addition to languages with flexible word classes such as Contentive or Non-verb, whose members can be characterized as semantically vague, we also find that there are languages with flexible nouns that are characterized by vague semantics (Figure 3).

4.1 Noun classification: *Seinsarten*

A cross-linguistic classification of nouns requires that languages are studied against each other in terms of the same property (Song 2001: 11). So even if we have established that certain languages have a true class of nouns according to the criteria employed in Hengeveld's classification of PoS systems (Hengeveld 1992; Hengeveld and Rijkhoff 2005), we still have to make sure that we make a valid comparison between nouns in different languages. To achieve this, I have assumed that there are concrete objects in the external physical world ('common sense metaphysics') and that they can be used as reference points (*tertium comparationis*). In other words, I have investigated properties of nouns in a representative sample of the world's languages that are used to refer to a single concrete object in the external, physical world. Obviously this excludes languages with a PoS system that does not include the category Noun, i.e. languages of type 1, 2 and 5 in *Figure* 3. I have also ignored special or exceptional cases such as (1) derived nouns (e.g. *sainthood*), (ii) *pluralia tantum* (e.g. *scissors, measles*), or (iii) *singularia tantum* (e.g. *dust*). Singularia tantum are often actually mass nouns (*snow*), verbal nouns/infinitives (Dutch *het verkopen van* ... lit. 'the selling of ...'), abstract nouns (*thirst, hate*), proper names (*Max, Lisa*) and names for chemical elements (*helium*).

Since a concrete object is typically characterized by a definite spatial outline (i.e. it has a shape) and an internal structure containing parts or components (i.e. it is not a homogeneous entity), this investigation mainly focused on the two semantic features Shape and Homogeneity (likepartedness). As only entities with a definite outline can be counted, it was assumed that nouns that can be quantified directly have a positive value for the feature Shape. Conversely, nouns that require the presence of some kind of classifier (or 'individualizer'; Lyons 1977: 462) were deemed to have a negative value for the feature Shape (but see note 14). Thus, both Dutch and Oromo use +Shape nouns, even though in Oromo nouns are transnumeral whereas in Dutch they aren't (Andrzejewski 1960: 71):

> "The vast majority of [Oromo nouns] are associated with neither plurality nor singularity, i.e. the forms themselves give us no information as to whether what is denoted by them is one or more than one. When such forms are used, only the context can provide us with information about the number of what is denoted."

Oromo (Stroomer 1987: 59): SET NOUN

(7) gaala lamaani [noun+numeral; no plural]
camel(s) two
'two camels'

I have called nouns of the kind attested in Oromo 'set nouns' since they seem to denote a set, which can have any cardinality (including 'one').[2] Basically there are two kinds of sets: singleton sets with only one member and multiple sets with more than one member. By contrast, in Dutch the unmarked noun denotes a singular object and plural marking is obligatory with and without a numeral higher than 'one'.

Dutch: SINGULAR OBJECT NOUN

(8) twee boek-en [numeral+noun+plural]
two book-PL
'two books'

Thus, it seems that in Dutch the numeral specifies the number of individual objects, whereas in Oromo the numeral specifies the size of a set (for a more detailed comparison between singular object nouns and set nouns, see Rijkhoff 2003: 219–220; Rijkhoff 2004: Chapter 2).

Thai is one of the languages with nouns that cannot be quantified directly. According to Hundius and Kölver (1983: 166, 181–182) this is because Thai nouns: "[…] purely denote *concepts* and, for this reason, are incompatible with direct quantification".

Thai (Hundius and Kölver 1983: 172): SORT NOUN
(9) rôm sǎam khan [noun+numeral+sortal_classifier]
umbrella(s) three CLF:long, handled object
'three umbrellas'

The appearance of a classifier is required because the meaning of a sort noun does not seem to include the notion of spatial boundedness or discreteness. They are labeled sort nouns because they occur with so-called sortal or numeral classifiers (perhaps a better name would be 'concept nouns'). Sort nouns must not be confused with mass nouns like 'water' or 'sugar', which occur with a MEASURE WORD or MENSURAL CLASSIFIER ('a litre/bucket/bottle/cup(ful) of water'; on the difference between sortal and mensural classifiers see e.g. Hundius and Kölver 1983; Cheng and Sybesma 1999; Rijkhoff 2004: 48; Huang and Ahrens 2003).

Thai (Hundius and Kölver 1983: 170): MASS NOUN
(10) náamtaan sǎam thûaj [noun+numeral+mensural_classifier]
sugar three cup
'three cups of sugar'

Yucatec also uses classifiers, but in this language there does not seem to be a fundamental distinction between sortal and mensural classifiers (Lucy 1992: 43, 74, 83):[3]

> "Interpretatively, in Yucatec all nouns […] are neutral with respect to logical unit or shape."
>
> "Outside of the restriction on compatibility with other classifiers, little in the grammar of Yucatec appears to hinge on, or correlate with, this 'sortal' […] versus 'mensural' distinction, and it is difficult to know what status it should be given."

Yucatec (Lucy 1992: 74): GENERAL NOUN

		a/one-CLF	banana(s)	[numeral+general_classifier+noun]
(11)	a.	'un-tz'íit	há'as	'one/a 1-dimensional banana (i.e. the fruit)'
	b.	'un-wáal	há'as	'one/a 2-dimensional banana (i.e. the leaf)'
	c.	'un-kúul	há'as	'one/a planted banana (i.e. the plant/tree)'
	d.	'un-kúuch	há'as	'one/a load banana (i.e. the bunch)'
	e.	'um-p'íit	há'as	'one bit banana (i.e. a bit of the fruit)'

Homogeneity is best illustrated by masses (e.g. 'water') or collective entities (e.g. 'family'). What masses and collectives have in common is that they both consist of parts, called *portions* and *members* respectively, which can be referred to by same name. The portions of a mass such as 'water' can also be referred to as 'water' and, conversely, when water is added to water the final product is also referred to as 'water' (i.e. masses are divisible and agglomerative entities). Similarly, any number of members of a collective entity such as 'family' higher than one are also 'family' and when a new member is added to the collective, we can still refer to it as 'family' (i.e. collectives are also divisible and agglomerative entities; see Kuhn 1982 for a detailed treatment of the notion 'collective').

Singular object nouns and sort nouns, on the other hand, only apply to the whole object. For example, the Dutch noun *fiets* 'bicycle' cannot be used to refer to any of its parts or components (e.g. the wheel, the chain, the handle bar). Set nouns and general nouns seem to be neutral with respect to the feature Homogeneity. A set noun can refer to a single concrete object or to a multiplicity of concrete objects. Similarly a general noun can be used to refer to, for example, a single concrete object or to a mass entity (see Yucatec example above). This classification of nouns is captured in Figure 4, in which each noun category specifies a different *Seinsart* ('mode of being'; comparable to *Aktionsart* 'mode of action' in verb semantics; see Rijkhoff 2004 (Chapter 2) for details).[4]

	–HOMOGENEITY	+HOMOGENEITY
–SHAPE	*General Noun*	
	Sort Noun	Mass Noun
+SHAPE	*Set Noun*	
	Singular Object Noun	Collective Noun

Figure 4. Noun categories: *Seinsarten* (Rijkhoff 2004: 54)

In sum, across languages four noun categories are used to refer to a single concrete object in the physical world (printed in italics in Figure 4):[5]

Singular object noun (+Shape, –Homogeneity): the noun designates a property that is characterized as having a definite outline and as being **non**-agglomerative;

Set noun (+Shape): the noun designates a spatial property that is only characterized as having a definite outline;

Sort noun (–Shape, –Homogeneity): the noun designates a spatial property that is characterized as **not** having a definite outline and as being **non**-agglomerative;

General noun (–Shape): the noun designates a spatial property that is only characterized as **not** having a definite outline.

Apparently no language uses mass nouns or collective nouns, i.e. nouns with a positive value for the feature Homogeneity, to refer to a single, concrete object:[6]

Mass noun (–Shape, +Homogeneity): the noun designates a spatial property that is characterized as **not** having a definite outline and as being agglomerative (parts: portions);

Collective noun (+Shape, +Homogeneity): the noun designates a spatial property that is characterized as having a definite outline and as being agglomerative (parts: members).

Table 1 shows the distribution of singular object nouns, set nouns, and sort nouns in the languages listed in *Figure* 2. The fourth nominal category that is used to refer to a single concrete object (General Noun) is attested in Yucatec, which is outside the original sample.[7] Notice that a language may employ members from more than one noun category to refer to a single concrete object (e.g. singular object nouns to refer to human or animate entities and set nouns to refer to non-human or inanimate entities; see note 7). Notice furthermore that the sample contains a number of languages that defy straightforward classification (for details see Rijkhoff 2004: 28–56). There are basically four problems. The first problem relates to the fact that in some languages number is not marked on the noun but on the noun phrase (as in Alamblak, Bambara, Guaraní and Nama Hottentot; hence these languages have no value in *Table* 1). Then there are languages in which the numeral is not a noun modifier, but a sentence adverb (e.g. Hixkaryana), the head of a non-noun modifying clause (e.g. Koasati) or some other kind of non-attributive expression (such as the body-part counting systems of the Papuan languages, where counting involves touching the relevant body-part). Finally, nouns may be in transition so that they display properties of 'old' noun category X and at the same time exhibit features of 'new' noun category Y (e.g. Nivkh; see also note 5).

The information contained in Table 1 shows, among other things, that flexible noun categories (involving nouns with a 'wide semantic content' such as set nouns or sort nouns) are attested in more languages than the rigid category of Singular Object Noun (whose members are characterized by a 'narrow semantic content') and that sort nouns seem to be restricted to languages with two rigid word classes: verbs and nouns (Type 4; the values of these Type 4 languages are highlighted by the box in *Table* 1). We will return to the second point in Section 6.

4.2 The semantics of rigid and flexible nouns: 'Narrow' versus 'wide' semantic content

It was mentioned above that a singular object noun (which belongs to a rigid noun category) can be said to have a narrow semantic content in that the values for the features Shape and Homogeneity are set in such a way that they match the properties of a concrete object in the physical world (+Shape, –Homogeneity). For example, a chair has a spatial outline and consists of certain components. The values for the features Shape and Homogeneity of the English noun 'chair' (+Shape, –Homogeneity) seem to correspond with these properties in that the noun can be in a direct construction with any cardinal numeral ('two chairs' — only bounded entities can be counted) and is only used to refer to the whole object (and not to any of its parts).

Table 1. The distribution of three noun categories (whose members are used to refer to a single, concrete object) in a representative sample of the world's languages: SINGULAR OBJECT NOUN, SET NOUN, AND SORT NOUN (Rijkhoff 2004: 30–31).

	SINGULAR OBJECT N^N	SET N^W	SORT N^W
TYPE 3: V-N-A			
Abkhaz	+	+?[−Human/+Animate]	
Alamblak			
Basque		+	
Berbice Dutch		+	
Bukiyip	+		
Burushaski	+	+	
Chukchi		+[NUM=bound, except if case=ABS]	
Dutch	+		
Georgian		+	
Guaraní			
Hittite	+[Masc/Fem. gender]	+[Neuter gender]	
Hungarian		+	
Ika		+	
Kayardild		+	
Ket	+	+	
Hmong Njua		+	[see Rijkhoff 2000]
Nama Hottentot			
Nasioi	+[+Human]	+[−Human]	
Ngalakan		+	
Ngiti	+[+Human]	+[−Human]	
Sumerian		+	
Wambon		+	
TYPE 3/4: V-N(-A)			
Babungo	+		
Bambara			
Gude		+	
Kisi	+		
Oromo		+	
Pipil	+?	+?	
Sarcee	+?[+Human]	+[−Human]	
Tamil	+[+Human]	+[−Human]	
TYPE 4: V-N			
Burmese			+
Galela		+	
Hixkaryana		+	
Koasati			
Korean			+
Krongo	+	+	
Lango		+	
Mandarin Chinese			+
Nivkh		+[NUM=bound]	+
Nung			+
Nunggubuyu	+[+Human]	+	
Tsou		+	
Vietnamese			+
West Greenlandic	+		
Type unknown:			
Nahali		+	

Set nouns, sort nouns and general nouns (all members of flexible or 'underspecified' noun categories) can be said to be semantically vague, with a wide semantic content: values for the features Shape and Homogeneity are either left unspecified (*Homogeneity*) or they are specified in such a way that they do not quite match the properties of a real world concrete object. Furthermore set nouns, sort nouns and general nouns are transnumeral and in the case of general nouns the meaning is so vague it can even be used to refer to, for example, a mass or a collective (see (11) above).

In spite of these semantic differences, singular object nouns, set nouns, sort nouns and general nouns are all equally good exemplars of the lexical category Noun from a cross-linguistic perspective. There are no good reasons to assume that, for example, singular object nouns in English are on the whole better or worse than sort nouns in Thai. The narrow meaning of a singular object noun may seem attractive for those who prefer a close correspondence between the intension and the extension of a noun, but it makes the singular object noun rather inflexible for referential purposes. Conversely, the ambiguous or vague semantics of nouns with a wide meaning (set nouns, sort nouns and general nouns) may be difficult to handle for grammatical theories that do not take linguistic or extra-linguistic contextual factors into account, but it makes them rather versatile ('flexible') for referential purposes (on the role of various kinds of contexts in Functional Discourse Grammar, see Rijkhoff 2008).

4.3 Coercion of flexible lexemes

We have argued in Section 3 (referring to Hengeveld and Rijkhoff 2005) that a vague lexeme like a contentive or a non-verb gets its categorical flavour by placing it in a certain syntactic slot (*syntactic coercion*) or by providing it with a special morphological marker (*morphological coercion*). In the case of nouns that are characterized by vague semantics (set nouns, sort nouns, general nouns), syntactic coercion cannot produce the intended meaning, since (at least in current theories of grammar) the syntactic slot does not distinguish between members of different noun categories.[8] From a morphosyntactic perspective then, the only alternative is coercion by morphological markers, and this is exactly what we find for each of the three noun categories whose members are characterized by vague semantics. Thus we see that singulative or collective markers (dubbed 'nominal aspect markers' in Rijkhoff 2004: Chapter 4) are employed with set nouns, and classifiers (or individualizers) in the case of nouns belonging to the −Shape categories:

(12)

Nominal category	Specific sense coerced by
set noun:	singulative or collective marker
sort noun:	sortal classifier[9]
general noun:	general classifier

In Oromo, which has set nouns, the singulative and collective marker specify *what kind of set* is being referred to by the speaker: a singleton set or a collective set (the *kind* distinction is a qualitative rather than a quantitative distinction; Rijkhoff 2004; see Rijkhoff 2008, 2010 for a somewhat different and more recent account in terms of the layered representation of linguistic structures):

Oromo (Stroomer 1987: 76–77, 84–85)

(13) Unmarked set: *nama* 'man/men' vs. Singleton set: *namica* 'a/the man'

(14) Unmarked set: *saree* 'dog/dogs' vs. Collective set: *sareellee* 'dogs'

In the following examples from Mandarin Chinese, "the classifier *duo* refers to 'bud' of a plant or flower, while *zhu* refers to the plant itself" (Huang and Ahrens 2003: 360). In either case, the classifier coerces the noun to have a certain reading depending on the information 'entailed' in the classifier:

Mandarin Chinese (Huang and Ahrens 2003: 361 — no tones indicated in original)[10]

(15) a. yi duo hua
one CL flower/plant
'one flower'

b. yi zhu hua
one CL flower/plant
'one plant'

Thus, classifiers allow the speaker to emphasize different aspects of an entity (Adams 1989: 3). As in the case of contentives and other flexible word classes in Figure 3, certain meaning components of nouns belonging to the flexible category N^W are highlighted whereas others are downplayed. This is illustrated in (16) with the Yucatec examples given in (11).

(16) *Highlighting/Downplaying* of meaning components of a general noun (A B C etc. are the meaning components of Yucatec *há'as*):

a/one-CLF	banana	A	B	C	D	E …	Highlighted properties of *há'as*	
'un-tz'íit	há'as	+		+		+	A C E … =>	a banana
'un-wáal	há'as	+	+	+			A B C … =>	a leaf (of a banana tree)
'un-kúuch	há'as		+		+	+	B D E … =>	a bunch of bananas
'um-p'íit	há'as	+		+	+		A C D … =>	a portion (of a banana mass)

In sum, both in the case of (a) contentives and non-verbs and (b) certain noun categories (set nouns, sort nouns, general nouns) we are dealing with lexemes with a wide semantic content. The actual meaning of contentives and non-verbs in an utterance can be coerced by syntactic or morphological means (Hengeveld et al. 2004), whereas in the case of flexible noun categories a more specific sense is coerced by morphological elements (nominal aspect marker, classifier).

5. Flexible word classes as true categories

A flexible word class is sometimes regarded as merger of two or more rigid classes (see e.g. Evans and Osada 2005: 366), but this is not correct.[11] A flexible word class like *Contentive* is not some kind of union of the rigid categories Verb, Noun, and Adjective, but a distinct category in itself, just like a rigid word class. Perhaps the main semantic difference between rigid and flexible word classes has to do with the value for certain meaning components. We will see below, for example, that contentives are not characterized by a positive value for the feature Transitive. Thus, the fact that *contentives* can be used in verbal, nominal and adjectival function does not imply that they combine typical properties of verb, nouns and adjectives. Rather, a contentive is neither a verb nor a noun nor an adjective, precisely because it does NOT have certain values for important features (more on this in Section 6 below).

If a flexible word class it is not the result of some kind of merger of rigid word classes but constitutes a proper lexical category in its own right, then we may expect to find, for instance, that problems regarding category membership of rigid word classes are also relevant for flexible word classes. Such problems are discussed in a recent article by Aarts (2004a), who proposes that varying degrees of category membership and overlaps between categories can be modeled in terms of gradience. He distinguishes between two types of gradience (Aarts 2004a: 1).[12]

> "One type I will call *Subsective Gradience* (SG). It is intra-categorial in nature, and allows for members of a class to display the properties of that class to varying degrees. The other type is called *Intersective Gradience* (IG). This is an inter-categorial phenomenon which is characterized by two form classes 'converging' on each other."

Subsective gradience can be investigated in terms of prototype theory (which says that some members of a category are better examples of the category than others in they resemble the prototype more closely; Rosch 1973), whereas intersective gradience involves cases of categorial overlap, as when a member displays features of more than one category. The difference between subsective and intersective gradience (involving members of the rigid categories Noun and Verb in English) is shown in examples (17) and (18):

	<u>Subsective Gradience</u>: e.g. degree of nouniness (PROTOTYPE THEORY)		
(17)	*chair, spoon, …*	vs.	*sheep, water, linguistics, …*
	more typical	vs.	less typical

In English the prototypical noun is generally assumed to denote a concrete entity (e.g. 'chair') and to inflect for plural number ('chair-s'). In this view, a noun such as 'sheep' is rather atypical (for English, that is) in that it does not inflect for number. In other words, in English 'chair_N' is a better examplar of the category Noun than 'sheep_N'.

Subsective gradience is also found among members of flexible word classes. Prototypical properties are known to correlate strongly with certain important aspects of human behaviour and together these correlations are referred to as 'prototype effects' (Cruse 2004: 130–1). One of the prototype effects concerns frequency. What we see in a language such as Samoan is that members of the flexible word class Contentive can be ranked according to frequency of occurrence in certain functions. For example, the more typical exemplars of the category Contentive occur with the same frequency in verbal and nominal function, whereas the less typical exemplars are attested more often in one of these functions (Mosel and Hovdhaugen 1992: 77; see also the quotation in note 1).

In the case of intersective gradience we are dealing with vagueness across category boundaries.

Intersective Gradience: e.g. nominal and verbal properties of gerunds (OVERLAP)

(18) a. Brown's PAINTING of his daughter vs.
more nominal: 'verbal noun'
b. Brown's PAINTING his daughter
more verbal: 'nominal verb'

Thus 'painting' in both (18a) and (18b) has properties of verbs as well as nouns (albeit in different degrees; for details see Aarts 2004a). This kind of gradience, which involves category overlap, is also attested among members of flexible word classes. For example, it has been established for a wide variety of languages that collective markers are a common source for plural markers. This diachronic development from collective to plural marker has been observed in, for example, the Kartvelian, the Mesoamerican and the Semitic languages (Rijkhoff 2004: 117). Since collective markers appear with set nouns and plural marking is a property of singular object nouns, we may hypothesize that, along with the change from collective to plural marker, set nouns have become singular object nouns in the languages in question. Since such a change does not happen overnight, we may assume that for some time the old category of set nouns must have overlapped partially with the new, emerging category of singular object nouns in the languages where this change has occurred.

6. Flexible and rigid nouns and grammar

The distinction between flexible and rigid nouns is important for various reasons. First of all, it improves our general understanding of PoS systems in that it adds a new dimension to current classifications of lexical word categories (Figure 3). Secondly, the features Shape and Homogeneity, which have been used to distinguish between the various noun categories (Figure 4), seem to correlate with important grammatical phenomena such as number agreement, more specifically with so-called number discord. Consider the following examples:

Georgian (Harris 1981: 22)
(19) sami ḳnuṭi goravs
three kitten roll:3SG
'Three kittens are rolling.'

Lango (Noonan 1992: 168)
(20) gúlú àdêk ɔ̀tɔ̀ɔ̀
pot three 3SG:die:PERF
'Three pots broke.'

Oromo (Stroomer 1987: 107)
(21) gaala lamaani sookoo d'ak'-e
camel two market go-3SG.M.PAST
'Two camels went to the market.'

In each example we see that a plural subject triggers singular agreement with the person/number marker on the verb. In my sample (Figure 2) this phenomenon is only attested in languages with set nouns, a flexible noun category whose members denote spatially bounded properties but are neutral with respect to the feature Homogeneity (Rijkhoff 2004: 105). Apparently, agreement in these languages is with the set, which — irrespective of the number of individuals it contains — is always a singular entity (Rijkhoff 1993).[13] In other words, it seems we can only make sense of so-called number discord (but notice that the term appears to be a misnomer) if we take into account the fact that different languages use different noun categories (some of them flexible) to refer to concrete objects in the physical world.

The features that we used to specify the difference between rigid and flexible noun categories also play a role in a recent attempt to account for the PoS hierarchy (Rijkhoff 2003).

Parts of Speech hierarchy (Hengeveld 1992)
(22) Verb > Noun > Adjective > (manner) Adverb

This hierarchy says that, if a languages employs members of a certain rigid category 'down' the hierarchy (e.g. Adjective), it also employ members of the rigid categories 'up' the hierarchy (Verb, Noun). One question that could be asked regarding this hierarchy is: what are the necessary conditions to allow for appearance of the next rigid word class in the hierarchy? For example, some languages with the category Noun also have the category Adjective (languages of Type 3 in Figure 3), but other languages do not (languages of Type 4 in Figure 3). It appears to be the case that adjectives are only attested in languages with +Shape noun categories (Singular Object Noun, Set Noun; see *Table* 1 above).[14] This is also seen in Figure 5, which shows that there are no languages

✓ *If a language has adjectives, it has +Shape nouns*

WHEN CAN A LANGUAGE HAVE ADJECTIVES?	LANGUAGES WITH A MAJOR, DISTINCT CLASS OF ADJECTIVES (TYPE 3 IN FIGURE 3)	LANGUAGES WITHOUT A MAJOR, DISTINCT CLASS OF ADJECTIVES
LANGUAGES WITH +SHAPE NOUNS	<u>Type 3</u>. Abkhaz, Alamblak, Basque, Berbice Dutch Creole, Bukiyip (=Mountain Arapesh), Burushaski, Dutch, Georgian, Guaraní, †Hittite, **Hmong Njua (see Rijkhoff 2000)**, Hungarian, Ika, Kayardild, Ket, Nama Hottentot, Nasioi, Ngalakan, Ngiti, Oromo, †Sumerian, Wambon	<u>Type 3/4</u>: Babungo, Bambara, Chukchi, Gude, Kisi, Oromo, Pipil, Sarcee, Tamil <u>Type 4</u>: Galela, Hixkaryana, Koasati, Krongo, Lango, Nunggubuyu, Tsou, West Greenlandic <u>Type 4/5</u>. Cayuga
LANGUAGES WITH −SHAPE NOUNS	**(no languages)**	<u>Type 4</u>. Burmese, Korean, Mandarin Chinese, Nivkh, Nung, Vietnamese
?	†Etruscan, †Meroitic, Nahali	
FLEXIBLE		*Samoan, †Hurrian, Imbabura Quechua, Turkish*

Figure 5. Languages with and without a major, distinct class of adjectives.

with adjectives that employ −Shape nouns to refer to a single, concrete object (Rijkhoff 2000). Apparently having +Shape nouns is a necessary (though not a sufficient) condition for a language to have a distinct class of adjectives. In other words, if a language has adjectives, then it uses +Shape nouns (i.e. individual object nouns or set nouns) to refer to a single concrete object (Figure 6). From this we may conclude that nouns in a language must be defined 'narrowly' with respect to the feature Shape before it can have a distinct class of adjectives.

Further research suggests that there are also certain conditions that must be met before a language can have the categories Verb or Noun in its PoS system (Rijkhoff 2003). Figure 7 shows that languages with the category Contentive (Type 1 in Figure 3) are the only languages without transitive lexemes in the basic lexicon.[15]

Transitive lexemes designate a dynamic relationship between two obligatory participants: an agent/subject and a patient/object. Whereas all languages with a major,

<table>
<tr><td rowspan="2">Flexible</td><td>1</td><td colspan="6">Contentive</td></tr>
<tr><td>2</td><td colspan="3">Verb</td><td colspan="3">Non-verb</td></tr>
<tr><td rowspan="3">Rigid</td><td>3</td><td colspan="2">Verb</td><td colspan="2">Noun [+Shape]</td><td colspan="2">Adjective</td></tr>
<tr><td>4</td><td colspan="3">Verb</td><td colspan="3">Noun [±Shape]</td></tr>
<tr><td>5</td><td colspan="6">Verb</td></tr>
</table>

Figure 6. Modified classification of PoS systems: a language only has the category Adjective, if it uses members of a +Shape noun category to refer to a single, concrete object.

✓ *If a language has nouns, it has transitive lexeme (i.e. verbs) — but not the other way around.*

WHEN CAN A LANGUAGE HAVE NOUNS?	LANGUAGES WITH A MAJOR, DISTINCT CLASS OF NOUNS (TYPES 3, 3/4, 4 IN FIGURE 3)	LANGUAGES WITHOUT A MAJOR, DISTINCT CLASS OF NOUNS
LANGUAGES WITH TRANSITIVE LEXEMES	Type 3: Abkhaz, Alamblak, Basque, Berbice Dutch Creole, Bukiyip (=Mountain Arapesh), Burushaski, Dutch, Georgian, Guaraní, †Hittite, Hmong Njua, Hungarian, Ika, Kayardild, Ket, Nama Hottentot, Nasioi, Ngalakan, Ngiti, †Sumerian, Wambon Type 3/4: Babungo, Bambara, Chukchi, Gude, Kisi, Oromo, Pipil, Sarcee, Tamil Type 4: Burmese, Galela, Hixkaryana, Koasati, Korean, Krongo, Lango, Mandarin Chinese, Nivkh, Nung, Nunggubuyu, Tsou, Vietnamese, West Greenlandic	Type 2 [non-verbs]: †Hurrian, Imbabura Quechua, Turkish Type 4/5[minor N]: Cayuga
LANGUAGES WITHOUT TRANSITIVE LEXEMES	**(no languages)**	Type 1: Samoan *(outside this sample e.g. Halkomelem, Squamish, and other Salish lgs.)*
?	†Etruscan, †Meroitic, Nahali	

Figure 7. Languages with and without a major, distinct class of nouns.

distinct class of verbs have a set of basic transitive lexemes in the lexicon, such lexemes are absent in Samoan (Rijkhoff 2003):

> "With the exception of a very small class of locative verbs [...], Samoan verbs do not require more than one argument, i.e. S or O. If we define obligatory transitive verbs as bivalent verbs which express transitive actions and which require two arguments referring to the agent and the patient, then Samoan does not have obligatory transitive verbs." (Mosel 1991: 188)

> "If we compare Samoan verbs with transitive and intransitive verbs in other languages where these two categories are distinguished in terms of the number of obligatory arguments, then there are no cardinal transitive verbs in Samoan, i.e. bivalent verbs expressing transitive actions. Except for a very small class [...], all Samoan verbs (including ergative verbs) maximally require one argument, namely S or O, both of which are expressed by absolutive noun phrases in basic verbal clauses." (Mosel & Hovdhaugen 1992: 724)

✓ *If a language has verbs, it has transitive lexemes (and vice versa).*

WHEN CAN A LANGUAGE HAVE VEBRS?	LANGUAGES WITH VERBS (TYPES 2, 3, 3/4, 4, 4/5)	LANGUAGES WITHOUT A MAJOR, DISTINCT CLASS OF VERBS (TYPE 1)
LANGUAGES WITH TRANSITIVE LEXEMES	Type 2: †Hurrian, Imbabura Quechua, Turkish Type 3: Abkhaz, Alamblak, Basque, Berbice Dutch Creole, Bukiyip (=Mountain Arapesh), Burushaski, Dutch, Georgian, Guaraní, †Hittite, Hmong Njua, Hungarian, Ika, Kayardild, Ket, Nama Hottentot, Nasioi, Ngalakan, Ngiti, Oromo, †Sumerian, Wambon Type 3/4: Babungo, Bambara, Chukchi, Gude, Kisi, Oromo, Pipil, Sarcee, Tamil Type 4: Burmese, Galela, Hixkaryana, Koasati, Korean, Krongo, Lango, Mandarin Chinese, Nivkh, Nung, Nunggubuyu, Tsou, Vietnamese, West Greenlandic Type 4/5: Cayuga	**(no languages)**
LANGUAGES WITHOUT TRANSITIVE LEXEMES	**(no languages)**	Type 1 [Contentive]: Samoan (*outside this sample e.g. Halkomelem, Squamish, and other Salish languages*)
?	†Etruscan, †Meroitic, Nahali	

Figure 8. Languages with and without a major, distinct class of verbs (see note 15).

Having a set of transitive lexemes is only a necessary condition for a language to have a category Noun as there are also languages with transitive lexemes but without nouns (e.g. languages of Type 2 in Figure 3), but having transitive lexemes is both a necessary and a sufficient condition for a language to have the category Verb (Figure 8).

These data from a representative sample of the world's languages indicate that the number of distinct word classes in a language (and the order in which they appear) is determined by the value for certain lexical features (TRANSITIVE, SHAPE). Only when the relevant feature has a positive value (+TRANSITIVE, +SHAPE) does the PoS system allow for the occurrence of the next word class in the hierarchy.

(23) Features: **necessary** conditions in the PoS hierarchy (Rijkhoff 2003):
VERB → NOUN → ADJECTIVE → MANNER ADVERBS
[+**TRANSITIVE**] [+**SHAPE**] [+***GRADABLE***?]

Recall that the presence of a set of transitive items in the basic lexicon is a necessary and sufficient condition for a language to have a distinct class of verbs, but only a necessary condition for the occurrence of a distinct class of nouns in the PoS of a language. The adjectival feature Gradable has a question mark, because it still has to be established whether it is a positive value for this particular feature that makes it possible for manner adverbs to occur in the PoS system of a language.

At a more abstract level these data seem to suggest that a language can only have distinct classes of verbs, nouns, and adjectives if the basic meaning of lexical items somehow encodes the prototypical properties of temporal and spatial entities (events and things). The prototypical event is an activity that involves an agent and a patient (+Transitive); the prototypical thing is a concrete object (+Shape). Thus, a language can only have major, distinct classes of verbs, nouns and adjectives if the lexicon contains (a) items that designate a dynamic relationship between an agent and a patient, and (b) items that designate a property that is specified as having a boundary in the spatial dimension.

7. Conclusion

In this article I have tried to show that, across languages, the rigid category Noun itself includes rigid and flexible noun types. It appears that members of four noun categories are used by speakers of different languages when they talk about a single, concrete object in the external world: Singular Object Noun, Set Noun, Sort Noun and General Noun. Singular object nouns (+Shape, −Homogeneity) can be called rigid: they are characterized by a narrow semantic content in that the values for the features Shape and Homogeneity match properties of the kind of entity they denote (a single, concrete object). As in the case of the flexible parts of speech Contentive and Non-verb, members of the flexible noun categories Set Noun, Sort Noun and General Noun have vague semantics (i.e. they have a wide semantic content). Flexible nouns have a neutral value for the feature Homogeneity and/or a negative value for the lexical feature Shape, which does not correspond with the fact that a concrete object in the external word is typically a non-homogeneous entity with a definite spatial contour. Individualizing strategies are required to make the property denoting members of the −Shape noun categories Sort Noun and General noun countable (Section 4).

I then argued that a flexible word category is not a merger of some rigid word classes, as has sometimes been suggested. A flexible word class is a true category, whose members can be ranked in terms of category membership, just like the members of a rigid word class. Finally I showed how the distinction between flexible and rigid noun categories provides new insights into PoS systems of languages spoken across the globe and how these systems interact with other parts of the grammar. Last but not least, I have claimed that the features that are relevant for the distinction between flexible and rigid categories (Transitive, Shape) also play a central role in an account of the parts of speech hierarchy.

Notes

1. The text continues as follows (Mosel and Hovdhaugen 1992: 77): "Not all roots occur with the same frequency as verbs and nouns. Some roots predominantly function as verbs, whereas others are more likely to be found in the function of nouns. Until now we have not, for instance, found *alu* "go" in a nominal function [but, as was noted in Hengeveld and Rijkhoff (2005: 412), the authors actually provided an example of *alu* in nominal function themselves some pages earlier — JR] or *mea* "thing" in a verbal function [...]. But we hesitate to say that *alu* is inherently a verb and mea inherently a noun for two reasons. Firstly, we cannot find any functional explanation why *alu* should not be used as a noun and mea as a verb, whereas, for instance, *gaoi* "thief, to steal" and *tagata* "person, to be a person" are bifunctional. And, secondly, previous experience taught us to be careful with classifications. The more texts we analyzed, and included in our corpus, the more items were unexpectedly found in nominal or verbal function."

2. When a cardinal numeral modifies a set noun, it specifies the size of the set (i.e. the number of individuals contained in the set) rather than the number of sets (Rijkhoff 2004: 147).

3. Sort nouns and general nouns are both vague in the sense that their meaning definition does not seem to contain any information about the spatial contour of the entity. This does not necessarily mean that the speakers of e.g. Thai or Yucatec do not *know* that a table in the physical world is a discrete object, but rather that this particular piece of knowledge is simply not part of the meaning of the noun (instead it would be part of e.g. the 'encyclopedic knowledge' about the referent of the NP; for a similar point see e.g. Unterbeck 1993). However, the idea that the employment of members of different nominal categories (*Seinsarten*) for the same thing may reflect "differences in the ontological beliefs the speakers of these languages hold about the referents of nouns" is discussed in e.g. Foley (1997: 231). On the subject of *ontological relativity* see also Quine (1960, 1969), Lucy (1992), Imai and Gentner (1993).

4. Since this is not an ontological but a linguistic classification, there is in principle no direct relationship between noun category (*Seinsart*) and real-world entity (*Sein*-correlate). Hence the same object can be referred to by using nouns from four different categories.

5. I am not aware of other classifications of nouns based on facts from a wide range of typologically different languages. Consequently this classification differs in some important respects from other, non-typological discussions of noun categories (for example, it contains some novel categories: set nouns, general nouns). Furthermore this classification does not assign any special status to plural nouns (cf. Jackendoff 1991), simply because plural nouns do not represent a different noun category (categorization is about types not tokens). Notice, incidentally, that boundaries between noun categories are not always clear cut. For example, simple tools can be more or less homogeneous objects (if you break a stick you have two sticks), i.e. certain concrete objects

are +Shape and +Homogenous but they are not collectives. Categorization is also a matter of (inadequate) perception (Russell 1923; cf. Aarts 2004a: 27; Langacker 2006: 116). Thus 'hair' is a mass noun in 'much hair' but an individual object noun in 'many hairs'. Finally, category membership may not always be clear due to the gradual nature of language change (on the change from one noun category to another, see Rijkhoff 2004: 117).

6. It is not clear why the feature Shape is relevant for all *Seinsarten*, whereas the feature Homogeneity helps to define only four nominal subcategories. Yet this classification confirms Friedrich's observation that "the category of shape appears to be a typological universal in grammar [..], and of not inconsiderable significance for a theory of semantics in grammar" (Friedrich 1970: 380; see also Wierzbicka 2006). The fact that in this classification the feature Shape is more important than the feature Homogeneity (Figure 4) may also have to do with the idea that spatial orientation is primary in human cognition and links up nicely with observations in other grammatical domains ('Localism').

7. Speakers of a language may use more than one of these noun types to refer to concrete objects. In Ngiti, for example, singular object nouns are used for human entities and set nouns for nonhuman entities (Kutsch Lojenga 1994: 340, 355).

8. But one can easily imagine a theory employing NP structures with syntactic slots that can only be filled by members of certain noun categories (Singular Object Noun, Mass noun, etc.).

9. For a recent treatment of classifiers in Mandarin Chinese see Huang and Ahrens (2003: 360), who argue that "contextual information will 'coerce' a sense by eliminating other possible interpretations in a richly encoded but under-specified lexicon". Interestingly, they add that semantic coercion can be predicted through a well encoded qualia structure as proposed in Pustejovsky (1995).

10. The situation may be more complex than what is shown here. At least some Mandarin nouns seem to be able to combine with the three different types of classifiers distinguished by Huang and Ahrens (2003), each type coercing another sense of the same noun. INDIVIDUAL CLASSIFIERS (CLF_IND) are attested most often and are used to refer to a concrete object; KIND CLASSIFIERS (CLF_KD) are used to refer to a particular kind of entity, and EVENT CLASSIFIERS (CLF_EV) coerce an event reading (Huang and Ahrens 2003: 371)

Individual	Kind	Event
a. yi jia feiji	b. yi zhong feiji	c. yi ban feiji
one CLF_IND airplane	one CLF_KD airplane	one CLF_EV airplane
'one airplane'	'one kind of airplane'	'one scheduled flight'

These data suggest that at least some Mandarin nouns are perhaps even more vague and consequently even more versatile or flexible than previously assumed (Huang and Ahrens 2003: 355).

11. Allowing for vagueness is not an attractive option for some linguists, perhaps because of the strong human propensity to see the world as being structured in terms of discrete entities (cf. Aarts 2004a: 4; see also Aarts 2004b, Aarts 2006).

12. Ultimately Aarts (2004a) defends a position that allows for gradience, while keeping sharp boundaries between categories. See also Sorace and Keller (2005) on gradience in grammar.

13. Note that in the case of collectives one can also have agreement with the collective (singular) or with the individuals in the collective (plural); see e.g. Bock et al. 2006.

14. Notice that this does not mean that adjectives cannot occur in a classifier language, which typically but not necessarily has Sort Nouns or General Nouns (both of which have a negative value for the feature Shape). In many languages numeral classifiers have developed into markers of other grammatical categories such as definiteness, specificity or topicality (Rijkhoff 2004: 51). In such cases the erstwhile classifiers no longer serve as 'individualizers' in the sense of Lyons (see Section 4.1). For example, nouns in Hmong (in bold print in *Figure* 5) have all the properties of Set Nouns (+Shape) and the element that used to be a classifier now serves as a collective aspect marker (Rijkhoff 2000). Another reason why adjectives and classifiers are not mutually exclusive is that some languages use Singular Object Nouns or Set Nouns (both +Shape) as well as Sort Nouns or General Nouns (both −Shape) to refer to concrete objects. This seems to be the case in Yucatec, which has a group of General Nouns (Section 4.1) but also a group of animate nouns that are probably best categorized as Set Nouns: they may occur with an optional so-called "plural marker" which is absent when the NP contains a numeral (Lucy 1992: 46–49).

15. I use the neutral label 'transitive lexeme' to avoid being forced to discuss lexemes in terms of the traditional word classes (Verb, Noun, etc.), but since having a set of transitive lexemes is both a necessary AND a sufficient condition for a language to have a class of verbs, 'transitive lexeme' is of course synonymous with 'verb' (Figure 8).

References

Aarts, Bas. 2004a. Modelling linguistic gradience. *Studies in Language* 28(1): 1–49.

Aarts, Bas. 2004b. Conceptions of gradience in the history of linguistics. *Language Sciences* 26(4): 343–389.

Aarts, Bas. 2006. Conceptions of categorization in the history of linguistics. *Language Sciences* 28(4): 361–385.

Aarts, Bas; David Denison; Evelien Keizer & Gergana Popova (eds.). 2004. *Fuzzy grammar: A reader*. Oxford: Oxford University Press.

Adams, Karen Lee. 1989. *Systems of numeral classification in the Mon-Khmer, Nicobarese, and Aslian subfamilies of Austroasiatic*. Canberra: Australian National University (Pacific Linguistics B-101).

Andrzejewski, Bogumił W. 1960. The categories of number in noun forms in the Borana dialect of Galla. *Africa* 30: 62–75.

Bisang, Walter. 1996. Areal typology and grammaticalization: processes of grammaticalization based on nouns and verbs in East and mainland South East Asian languages. *Studies in Language* 20(3): 519–597.

Bock, Kathryn; S. Butterfield; Anne Cutler; J. Cooper Cutting; Kathleen M. Eberhard & Karen R. Humphreys. 2006. Number agreement in British and American English: disagreeing to agree collectively. *Language* 82: 64–113.

Bohnemeyer, Jürgen. 2002. *The grammar of time reference in Yucatec Maya*. Munich: LINCOM Europa [LINCOM Studies in Native American Linguistics 44].

Broschart, Jürgen & Carmen Dawuda. 2000. Beyond nouns and verbs: typological studies in lexical categorisation. Working Paper no. 113 of *Arbeiten des Sonderforschungsbereichs 282* (Düsseldorf — Wuppertal — Köln), Institut für Sprache und Information, Heinrich-Heine-Universität, Düsseldorf.

Cheng, Lisa Lai-Shen & Rint Sybesma. 1999. Bare and not-so-bare nouns and the structure of NP. *Linguistic Inquiry* 30: 509–542.

Czaykowska-Higgins, Ewa & M. Dale Kinkade. 1998. Salish languages and linguistics. *Salish Languages and Linguistics: theoretical and descriptive perspectives*, Ewa Czaykowska-Higgins & M. Dale Kinkade (eds.), 1–68. Berlin: Mouton de Gruyter (Trends in Linguistics: Studies and Monographs 107).

Cruse, D. Alan. 1986. *Lexical semantics*. Cambridge: Cambridge University Press.

Cruse, D. Alan. 2004. *Meaning in language: an introduction to semantics and pragmatics* (2nd edition). Oxford: Oxford University Press.

Evans, Nicholas & Toshiki Osada. 2005. Mundari: the myth of a language without word classes. *Linguistic Typology* 9(3): 351–390.

Foley, William A. 1997. *Anthropological linguistics: an introduction*. Oxford: Blackwell.

Friedrich, Paul. 1970. Shape in grammar. *Language* 46(2): 379–407 [Reprinted in Paul Friedrich, 1979, *Language, context, and the imagination*, 340–359. Stanford, CA: Stanford University Press].

Harris, Alice Carmichael. 1981. *Georgian syntax: a study in relational grammar*. Cambridge: Cambridge University Press (Cambridge Studies in Linguistics 33).

Hengeveld, Kees. 1992. *Non-verbal Predication: theory, typology, diachrony*. Berlin: Mouton de Gruyter.

Hengeveld, Kees; Jan Rijkhoff & Anna Siewierska. 2004. Parts-of-speech systems and word order. *Journal of Linguistics* 40(3): 527–570.

Hengeveld, Kees & Jan Rijkhoff. 2005. Mundari as a flexible language. *Linguistic Typology* 9(3): 406–431.

Huang, Chu-Ren & Kathleen Ahrens. 2003. Individuals, kinds and events: classifier coercion of nouns. *Language Sciences* 25: 353–373.

Hundius, Harald & Ulrike Kölver. 1983. Syntax and semantics of numeral classifiers in Thai. *Studies in Language* 7(2): 164–214.

Ikegami, Y. 1985. 'Activity'-'Accomplishment'-'Achievement': a language that can't say 'I burned it but it didn't burn' and one that can. *Linguistics and philosophy: essays in honor of Rulon S. Wells*, A. Makkai & A. K. Melby (eds.), 265–304. Amsterdam: Benjamins.

Imai, M. & D. Gentner. 1993. Linguistic relativity vs. universal ontology: cross-linguistic studies of the object/substance distinction. *What we think, what we mean and how we say it: papers from the parasession on the correspondence of conceptual, semantic and grammatical representations*, K. Beals; G. Cooke; D. Kathman; S. Kita; K. McCullough & D. Teston (eds.), 171–186. Chicago: Chicago Linguistic Society.

Jackendoff, Ray. 1991. Parts and boundaries. *Cognition* 41: 9–45.

Kuhn, Wilfried. 1982. Kollektiva und die Technik KOLLEKTION am Beispiel des Deutschen. *Apprehension. Das sprachliche Erfassen von Gegenständen. Teil I: Bereich und Ordnung der Phänomene*. Hansjakob Seiler & Christian Lehmann (eds.), 84–97. Tübingen: Gunter Narr (LUS, 1/I).

Langacker, Ronald W. 2006. On the continuous debate about discreteness. *Cognitive Linguistics* 17(1): 107–151.

Lucy, John A. 1992. *Grammatical categories and cognition: a case study of the linguistic relativity hypothesis*. Cambridge: Cambridge University Press [Studies in the Social and Cultural Foundations of Language 13].

Lyons, John. 1977. *Semantics* (2 volumes). Cambridge: Cambridge University Press.

Mithun Williams, Marianne. 1976. *A grammar of Tuscarora*. New York: Garland.
Mosel, Ulrike. 1991. Transitivity and reflexivity in Samoan. *Australian Journal of Linguistics* 11: 175–194.
Mosel, Ulrike and & Even Hovdhaugen. 1992. *Samoan reference grammar*. Oslo: Universitetsforlaget AS.
Noonan, Michael P. 1992. *A grammar of Lango*. Berlin: Mouton de Gruyter (Mouton Grammar Library 7).
Pustejovsky, James. 1995. *The generative lexicon*. Cambridge, MA: MIT Press.
Quine, Willard Van Orman. 1960. *Word and object*. Cambridge, MA: MIT Press.
Quine, Willard Van Orman. 1969. *Ontological relativity and other essays*. New York: Columbia University Press.
Rijkhoff, Jan. 1993. 'Number' disagreement. *Proceedings of the XVth International Congress of Linguists*, André Crochetière; Jean-Claude Boulanger & Conrad Ouellon (eds.), 274–276. Sainte-Foy, Québec: Presses de l'Université Laval.
Rijkhoff, Jan. 2000. When can a language have adjectives? An implicational universal. *Approaches to the typology of word classes*, Petra M. Vogel & Bernard Comrie (eds.), 217–257. Berlin/New York: Mouton de Gruyter.
Rijkhoff, Jan. 2003. When can a language have nouns and verbs? *Acta Linguistica Hafniensia* 35: 7–38.
Rijkhoff, Jan. 2004. *The noun phrase*. Oxford: Oxford University Press [expanded paperback edition of 2002 hardback publication].
Rijkhoff, Jan. 2008. Layers, levels and contexts in Functional Discourse Grammar. *The noun phrase in Functional Discourse Grammar*, Daniel García Velasco & Jan Rijkhoff (eds.), 63–115. Berlin/New York: Mouton de Gruyter.
Rijkhoff, Kan. 2010. Functional categories in the noun phrase: on jacks-of-all-trades and one-trick-ponies in Danish, Dutch, and German. To appear in *Deutsche Sprache* 2, 2010.
Rosch, Eleanor. 1973. Natural categories. *Cognitive Psychology* 4: 328–350.
Russell, Bertrand. 1923/1996. Vagueness. *Australian Journal of Philosophy and Psychology* 1, 84–92 [Reprinted in Rosanna Keefe & Peter Smith (eds.), 1996, *Vagueness: A reader*, 61–68. Cambridge, MA: MIT Press; also reprinted in Aarts *et al.* 2004.]
Sasse, Hans-Jürgen. 1993. Syntactic categories and subcategories. *Syntax: an international handbook of contemporary research* (2 vols.), Joachim Jacobs; Arnim vom Stechow; Wolfgang Sternefeld & Theo Vennemann (eds.), 646–686. Berlin: Walter de Gruyter.
Schachter, Paul. 1985. Parts-of-speech systems. *Language typology and syntactic description. Volume I: Clause structure*, Timothy Shopen (ed.), 3–61. Cambridge: Cambridge University Press.
Smit, Niels. 2001. *De rol van derivatie bij lexicale specialisatie*. MA thesis, Department of Linguistics, University of Amsterdam.
Song, Jae Jung. 2001. *Linguistic typology: morphology and syntax*. Harlow: Pearson [Longmans Linguistics Library].
Sorace, Antonella & Frank Keller. 2005. Gradience in linguistic data. *Lingua* 115: 1497–1524.
Stroomer, Harry. 1987. *A comparative study of three southern Oromo dialects in Kenya: phonology, morphology and vocabulary*. Hamburg: Buske [Cushitic Language Studies 6].
Unterbeck, Barbara. 1993. *Kollektion, Numeralklassifikation und Transnumerus*. Frankfurt am Main: Peter Lang.

van Baarda, M.J. 1908. *Leiddraad bij het bestuderen van 't Galela'sch dialekt, op het eiland Halmaheira* [Manual for the study of the Galela dialect, on the island of Halmahera]. The Hague: Nijhoff.

Wierzbicka, Anna. 2006. Shape in grammar revisited. *Studies in Language* 30(1): 115–177.

Wilkins, David P. 2000. Ants, ancestors and medicine: a semantic and pragmatic account of classifier constructions in Arrernte (Central Australia). *Systems of nominal classification*, Gunter Senft (ed.), 147–216. Cambridge: Cambridge University Press [Language, Culture and Cognition 4].

Author's address

Jan Rijkhoff
Institut for Lingvistik, Aarhus Universitet
Nordre Ringgade 1, Building 1410, Office 338
8000 Aarhus C
Denmark

linjr@hum.au.dk

Parts of speech and dependent clauses in Functional Discourse Grammar*

Kees Hengeveld and Eva van Lier
University of Amsterdam

In this paper we use the Theory of Functional Discourse Grammar to show that parts of speech (PoS) and dependent clauses (DCs) can both be defined in terms of the functions they may express. On the basis of this parallel treatment, we predict that the functional possibilities of PoS and DCs in languages are comparable. This hypothesis is tested using a sample of 23 languages. The results do show similarities between the functional patterns of the two types of constructions.

1. Introduction

In this paper we investigate the relationship between the functional distribution of lexical elements on the one hand and complex constructions in the form of dependent clauses on the other hand, in a sample of 23 languages. We use the theory of Functional Discourse Grammar (FDG) to show that parts of speech (PoS) classes and dependent clause (DC) constructions can be defined in a way that makes them comparable in terms of their functional possibilities. We start, in Section 2, by introducing our language sample. Section 3 provides a general outline of FDG, and specifically introduces those parts of the theory that are directly relevant to our study. In Section 4 we show how PoS classes are defined in FDG (4.1), and we classify the languages in our sample with respect to their PoS systems (4.2). Section 5 does the same for DC constructions: 5.1 shows how they are defined in FDG, while 5.2 gives the DC systems of our sample languages. In Section 6, we address the question whether, in a specific language, the distribution of PoS classes is similar to the distribution of DC constructions. In Section 6.1 we explain why such distributional similarities are expected to occur; in Section 6.2 we formulate specific hypotheses, and in Section 6.3 we test these predictions against the data presented in Sections 4 and 5. Finally, in Section 7 we round off with our conclusions.

2. The sample

We make use of a sample of 23 languages, given in Table 1. It must be stressed that the sample is not completely balanced. For the purpose of the present study, we have included languages with a wide range of different PoS systems. This allows for explorative research into the relationship between distributional patterns of PoS classes and DC constructions, which will be followed up on a larger scale (Van Lier 2009).

3. Functional Discourse Grammar

3.1 General lay-out[1]

Functional Discourse Grammar (FDG), as presented in Hengeveld (2005) and Hengeveld & Mackenzie (2006, 2008), is the grammatical component of a wider theory of verbal interaction (see Dik 1997), in which it interacts with non-linguistic components of the process of human communication. In the FDG model four interacting levels of organization are distinguished: the interpersonal level, the representational level, the morphosyntactic level, and the phonological level, in that hierarchical order. The general architecture of the model is represented in Figure 1.[2]

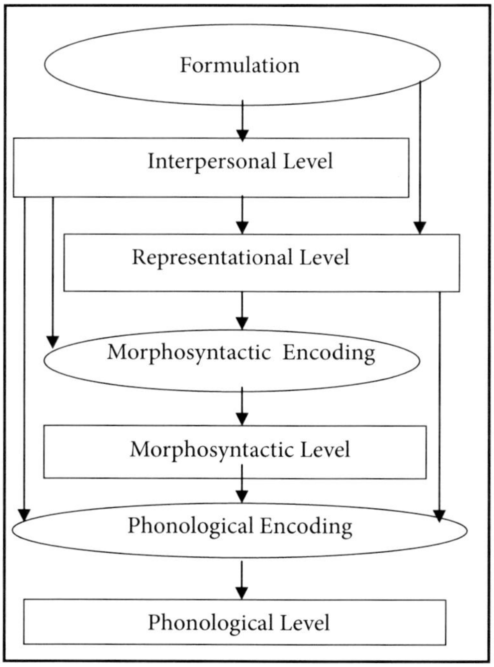

Figure 1. The grammatical component of FDG

Table 1. The language sample

Language	Family (based on Ethnologue*)	Genus (based on WALS**)	Source(s)
Kambera	Austronesian	Central Malayo-Polynesian	Klamer 1998
Samoan	Austronesian	Oceanic	Mosel 1992 Mosel & Hovdhaugen 1992
Santali	Austro-Asiatic	Munda	Neukom 2001
Imbabura Quechua	Quechuan	Quechuan	Cole 1982
Kayardild	Australian	Tangkic	Evans 1995
Turkish	Altaic	Turkic	Göksel & Kerslake 2005, Kornfilt 1997, Lewis 1967, Schroeder 2004
Ma'di	Nilo-Saharan	Maru-Ma'di	Blackings & Fabb 2003
Lango	Nilo-Saharan	Nilotic	Noonan 1992
Abun	West Papuan	North-Central Bird's Head	Berry & Berry 1999
Abkhaz	North Caucasian	North-west Caucasian	Hewitt 1979, 1987
Georgian	Kartvelian	Kartvelian	Hewitt 1987, 1995, Cherchi 1999
Basque	Basque	Basque	Saltarelli 1988 Hualde & Ortiz de Urbina 2003
Pipil	Uto-Aztecan	Aztecan	Campbell 1985
Berbice Dutch	Creoles and Pidgins	Creoles and pidgins	Kouwenberg 1994
Alamblak	Sepik-Ramu	Sepik Hill	Bruce 1984
Hdi	Afro-Asiatic	Biu-Mandara	Frajzyngier with Shay 2002
Tamil	Dravidian	Southern Dravidian	Asher 1982, Lehmann 2005
Mandarin Chinese	Sino-Tibetan	Chinese	Li & Thompson 1981
Garo	Sino-Tibetan	Baric	Burling 2004
Nivkh	Nivkh	Nivkh	Gruzdeva 1998 Matissen & Drossard 1998
Krongo	Nilo-Saharan	Kadugli	Reh 1985
Tuscarora	Iroquoian	Northern Iroquoian	Mithun-Williams 1976, Mithun 2000

* Ethnologue = Gordon, Raymond G. Jr., ed. 2005. *Ethnologue: Languages of the world.* 15th Edition. Dallas, Tex.: SIL International. Online version: http://www.ethnologue.com.
** WALS = Haspelmath, Martin, Matthew S. Dryer, David Gil & Bernard Comrie, eds. 2005. *The world atlas of languages structures.* Oxford: Oxford University Press.

Two of the levels in Figure 1 are relevant to the purpose of our paper: the interpersonal and the representational levels. These will be discussed below in some detail. For a more complete outline of FDG we refer to Hengeveld (2005).

At the interpersonal level all relevant units of communicative behavior are analyzed in terms of their communicative function. For our present purposes, the relevant unit of analysis at the interpersonal level is the so-called 'communicated content' (C) expressed by the speaker, which may consist of a varying number (superscript N) of 'ascriptive subacts' (T) and/or 'referential subacts' (R), represented as a list (between square brackets) in (1).[3] Note that variables at the interpersonal level are given in capitals for ease of recognition. Note furthermore that the FDG formalism (at all levels of analysis) makes use of a colon to represent a restriction operation, and a 'closing variable' between brackets at the end of each of these restriction operations, to mark off its scope. Thus, the formula (C_1: …(C_1)) should be read as: 'a communicated content (1), such that ….'

(1) $(C_1\text{: } [(T_1)^N\ (R_1)^N\ \ldots](C_1))$

At the representational level of analysis, linguistic units are described in terms of their semantic category. The highest category at this level is the 'propositional content' (p): an idea or unit of knowledge about a real or imaginary world. Being a mental construct, it can be located neither in space nor in time. It can be evaluated in terms of its truth. It may contain one or more descriptions of a 'state-of-affairs' (e): an event or state that can be located in space and time and can be evaluated in terms of its reality. A state-of-affairs is characterized by a 'property', represented by a variable (f)[4] (in the representation in (2) below this is f_1). Properties have no independent existence and can only be evaluated in terms of their applicability, either to other types of entity or to the situation they describe in general. The property (f_1) is itself a configuration of units that may designate a variety of semantic categories, such as further properties (f_2, in (2)), individuals (x), spatial regions (l), and temporal regions (t). All of these can occur more than once, which is indicated by the superscript *n*. The hierarchical structure of the representational level is given (in a somewhat simplified manner) in (2) (where again colons and closing variables are used for every restriction operation):

(2) $(\text{p: } [(\text{e: } (f_1\text{: } [(f_2)^n\ (x)^n\ (l)^n\ (t)^n]\ (f_1))\ (e))^n]\ (p))$

Note that the representational level is purely semantic in nature, that is, linguistic units are described in terms of their designation. The communicative use that is made of these units, e.g. reference or ascription, is accounted for at the interpersonal level. We will elaborate on this point below.

3.2 Interpersonal functions and representational categories

Layers at the representational level may correspond to different interpersonal functions. Consider the example in (3), where each instantiation of a variable is marked with a unique subscript (capital) *I, J, K* at the interpersonal level, and (small print) *i, j, k, l* at the representational level. Notice that the alignment of the interpersonal and representational analyses is such that every interpersonal variable is positioned right above the corresponding representational variable.

(3)
$$\begin{array}{l} \qquad\quad T_I \qquad\qquad\quad R_I \;\; T_J \qquad\qquad\qquad\qquad T_K \\ (e_i\text{: } (f_i\text{: } [\ (f_j\text{: die } (f_j))\ (x_i\text{: } (f_k\text{: man } (f_k))\ (x_i)\text{: } (f_l\text{: old } (f_l))\ (x_i))]\ (f_i))\ (e_i)) \end{array}$$
'The old man died.'

Thus, this example says that at the *representational* level, there is a state of affairs (e_1), characterized by the property (f_i), which contains (between square brackets) a description of a property (f_j) 'died', and an individual (x_i). The latter is characterized by two further properties: (f_k) 'man' and (f_l) 'old'. At the *interpersonal* level (f_j) 'died' corresponds to an ascriptive subact (T_1) and (x_i) to a referential subact (R_1). The referential subact is in turn realized through two further ascriptive subacts T_J and T_K, which attribute the properties f_k ('man') and f_l ('old') to the referent.

It is important to note that there is no necessary one-to-one relationship between ascriptive subacts (T) and properties (f), and between referential subacts (R) and individuals (x). This is shown in the following examples:

(4) That man is *a carpenter.*

(5) I like *that color.*

In (4) a linguistic unit designating an individual, *a carpenter* (x), is used ascriptively (T), that is, it is being ascribed to *that man*. Thus, the relationship between the interpersonal and the representational levels is (T/x). In (5) the linguistic unit denoting a property, *that color* (f), is used referentially (R). Here the relationship between the interpersonal and the representational levels is (R/f).

3.3 Heads and modifiers

Each of the units that we have just introduced (C, T, R; p, e, f, etc.), both at the interpersonal and the representational levels, consists of an obligatory part, its head, and one or more (n) optional parts, the modifiers. This general format is represented in (6), where α stands for any variable, h for its head, and σ for a modifier, and braces indicate optionality:

(6) $(\alpha_1\text{: h } (\alpha_1)\text{: } \{\sigma^n\}\ (\alpha_1))$

Heads (h) may be lexical or compositional; modifiers (σ) can only be compositional, because they have their own head. This is captured in the following representations, where *lex* stands for lexical unit:

	head	modifier	
(7)	$(\alpha_1$: $\mathbf{lex}$	(α_1): σ	$(\alpha_1))$
(8)	$(\alpha_1$: $\mathbf{(\alpha_2: lex\ (\alpha_2): \sigma\ (\alpha_2))}$	(α_1): σ	$(\alpha_1))$
(9)	$(\alpha_1$: h	(α_1): $\mathbf{(\alpha_2: lex\ (\alpha_2): \sigma\ (\alpha_2))}$	$(\alpha_1))$

For the purpose of our argument, it is crucial to note that the *complex* unit $\mathbf{(\alpha_2: lex\ (\alpha_2): \sigma\ (\alpha_2))}$ in first restrictor position in (8) is regarded as the head of α_1. This is different from many other approaches, which would analyze the *lexical* head of α_2 as the head of α_1. Consider the following example and its analysis at the representational level:

(10) The man regrets that the boy will marry.

(11) $(e_i$: $(f_i$: [
$(f_j$: regret$_V$ $(f_j))$
$(x_i$: $(f_k$: man $(f_k))$ $(x_i))$
$(e_j$: $\mathbf{(f_l: [(f_m: marry\ (f_m))\ (x_j: (f_n: boy\ (f_n))\ (x_j))]\ (f_l))}$ $(e_j))$
] $(f_i))$ $(e_i))$

In FDG, the head of the state-of-affairs e_j is the complex construction printed in boldface in (11). This complex head corresponds to *that the boy will marry* in (10), and not to just the verb *marry*, which is represented as the lexical head of the property-description f_m, not of the state-of-affairs e_j.

This approach allows us to draw a parallel between a *lexical* and a *complex, clausal* filler of the head slot of a certain unit. Consider the examples in (12) and (13) and their representational analyses in (14) and (15), respectively:

(12) the marriage

(13) that the boy will marry

(14) $(e_i$: $\mathbf{(f_i}$: marriage$_N$ $\mathbf{(f_i))}$ $(e_i))$[5]

(15) $(e_i$: $\mathbf{(f_i}$: $[(f_j$: marry $(f_j))$ $(x_i$: $(f_k$: boy $(f_k))$ $(x_k))]$ $\mathbf{(f_i))}$ $(e_j))$

In both cases a state-of-affairs (e_i) is characterized by a property (f_i). In (12)/(14), the head slot of this property is filled lexically by means of the noun *marriage*, while in (13)/(15) it is realized through the complex unit between square brackets, corresponding to the complement clause '*that the boy will marry*'. Mackenzie (1990) proposes essentially the same analysis, using the framework of Functional Grammar.

4. Parts of speech

4.1 Parts of Speech in Functional Discourse Grammar

The distinction between heads and modifiers at the representational level[6], and between ascriptive and referential subacts at the interpersonal level constitute two parameters, each with two values, which may be combined to yield four possible functional slots, which may in turn be used to define the functions characteristic of lexical items. This is represented in (16)–(19) below.

	T		T	
(16)	(f_1: **lex**	(f_1):	σ	(f_1))
	T		T	
(17)	(f_1: lex	(f_1):	(f_2: **lex** (f_2))	(f_1))
	R T		T	
(18)	(α_1: (f_1: **lex** (f_2))	(α_1):	σ	(α_1))
	R T		T	
(19)	(α_1: (f_1: lex (f_2))	(α_1):	(f_2: **lex** (f_2))	(α_1))

Figure 2 indicates how examples (16)–(19) illustrate the possible combinations of the ascriptive/referential distinction and the head/modifier distinction.

A close look at the representations in (16)–(19) reveals that actually all lexical elements are the lexical heads of representational layers of the f-type: (f_1) in (16) and (18), (f_2) in (17) and (19). This is another way of saying that lexical items designate properties or relations. Only when used as the main predicate of a clause does this f-unit correspond directly to an independent ascriptive subact. In all other cases it corresponds to an ascriptive subact *within* a higher ascriptive subact (as in (17)) or a higher referential subact, within which it ascribes a property to the referent (as in (18) and (19)). Thus, the functions of the items in boldface in (16)–(19) may be defined as in (20) (i)–(iv):

(20) i. Head of an f-unit that is used as an independent ascriptive subact (16);
ii. Head of an f-unit that is a modifier of (i) (17)
iii. Head of an f-unit that is the head of a representational unit that is used as a referential subact (18);
iv. Head of an f-unit that is a modifier of (iii) (19).

	Head	Modifier
Ascription	(16)	(17)
Reference	(18)	(19)

Figure 2. Crossclassification of the Ascription/Reference and Head/Modifier distinctions

Functions (i) and (ii) cannot be used directly as unique definitions of word classes. For function (i) this has to do with the fact that in many languages various classes of words can be used as the head of an independent ascriptive subact. Compare the following Dutch examples:[7]

Dutch

(21) Jan **werk-t**.
J. work-PRS.3.SG
'Jan works.'

(22) Jan is **timmerman**.
J. COP.PRS.3.SG carpenter
"Jan is carpenter."
'Jan is a carpenter.'

(23) Jan is **ziek**.
J. COP.PRS.3.SG ill
'Jan is ill.'

(24) Jan is **net-jes**
J. COP.PRS.3.SG well.organized-ADVR[8]
'Jan is well-organized.'

Note that (22) illustrates the use of a bare nominal predicate in Dutch, which is different from the phrasal nominal predicate in (25) (as will be further illustrated in examples (38) and (39) below):[9]

Dutch

(25) Jan is [**een timmerman**].
J. COP.PRS.3.SG INDF carpenter
'Jan is a carpenter.'

The predicates (in boldface) in examples (21)–(24) are represented as (26)–(29):

	T:		T	
(26)	(f_1: **werk**-$_V$	(f_1):	σ	(f_1))
	T:		T	
(27)	(f_1: **timmerman**-$_N$	(f_1):	σ	(f_1))
	T:		T	
(28)	(f_1: **ziek**-$_A$	(f_1):	σ	(f_1))
	T:		T	
(29)	(f_1: **netjes**-$_{MAdv}$	(f_1):	σ	(f_1))

In sum, Dutch verbs (V), nouns (N), adjectives (A), and some manner adverbs (MAdv) can be used as the head of an independent ascriptive subact; yet they belong to different PoS classes, because in other functional environments they are not interchangeable. This means that the function in (20)(i) is by itself not sufficiently distinctive.

Verbs, nouns, adjectives, and manner adverbs also differ to a considerable extent in the kind of element that can go into the modifier slots in (26)–(29). Consider the following examples:

Dutch

(30) Jan werkt **hard**.
J. work-PRS.3.SG hard
'Jan works **hard**.'

(31) Jan is **voormalig** timmerman.
J. COP.PRS.3.SG former carpenter
'Jan is a **former** carpenter."

(32) Jan is **erg** ziek.
J. COP.PRS.3.SG very ill
'Jan is **very** ill.'

(33) Jan is **erg** net-jes
J. COP.PRS.3.SG very well.organized-ADVR
'Jan is **very** well-organized.'

Adjectival and adverbial heads may be modified by the same degree adverbs, but verbal and nominal heads mainly take their own classes of modifiers. This may be represented as in (34)–(37). Here DAdv stands for degree adverb; Adjf stands for adjective used for 'reference-modification' (operating at the f-level); and Adjx stands for adjective used for 'referent modification' (operating at the x-level) (Bolinger 1967):[10]

(34) T: $(f_1$: werk-$_V$ (f_1): T $(f_2$: hard-$_{MAdv}$ $(f_2))$ $(f_1))$

(35) T: $(f_1$: timmerman-$_N$ (f_1): T $(f_2$: voormalig-$_{Adjf}$ $(f_2))$ $(f_1))$

(36) T: $(f_1$: ziek-$_{Adjx}$ (f_1): T $(f_2$: erg-$_{DAdv}$ $(f_2))$ $(f_1))$

(37) T: $(f_1$: netjes-$_{MAdv}$ (f_1): T $(f_2$: erg-$_{DAdv}$ $(f_2))$ $(f_1))$

Notably, (35) shows that the use of the notion 'bare nominal predicate' for the predicate in (21) is not entirely adequate. *Reference* modification, as in (31), is still possible with these 'bare nouns', since this type of modification operates at the f-level. In contrast, *referent* modification, which operates at the x-level, is not allowed with bare nominal predicates, as illustrated in (38).

(38) *Jan is rijk-e timmerman.
J. COP.PRS.3.SG rich-AGR carpenter
'Jan is rich carpenter.'

Since the ungrammaticality of (38) is due to the fact that referent modification applies at the x-level, not at the f-level, this also explains why this type of modification *is* possible within phrasal nominal predicates, as shown in (39):

(39) Jan is een rijk-e timmerman.
J. COP.PRS.3.SG INDF rich-AGR carpenter
"Jan is a rich carpenter."

Finally, note that Dutch shows Adjective-Noun agreement in the case of referent modification (39), whereas agreement may be absent in the case of reference modification (31).

Let us return now to the functional specifications given in (20). The representations in (34)–(37) clearly show that the word class of the modifier of an f-unit depends on the word class of the lexical head of that unit. This means that the definition in (20)(ii), like the one in (20)(i), is not sufficiently distinctive.

In short, we have shown that the functions (i) and (ii) in (20) do not allow for a one-to-one correspondence between function and PoS class. For the first function this was already noted in Hengeveld's (1992) original proposal for the classification of PoS systems, and solved by using a specific 'only'-condition for verbs, indicating that verbs can be used predicatively *only*. For the second function the definitions of modifying PoS have to take into account the word class of the head that they modify. With these provisos, and taking the functions in (20) as the point of departure, Table 2 can be constructed:

The '+' in Table 2 represents the defining uses of the various lexical classes mentioned in the left-hand column; the '–' represents the excluded uses; and the '+/–' potential uses. Verbs have a unique use, while nouns, adjectives, and manner adverbs may have an additional predicative use, next to their basic non-predicative uses.

Hengeveld (1992) and Hengeveld et al. (2004) have shown that, cross-linguistically, the distributional possibilities of PoS classes may differ considerably. A basic

Table 2. The distributional possibilities of parts of speech.

	(i)	(iii)	(iv)	(ii)
Verb	+	–	–	–
Noun	+/–	+	–	–
Adjective	+/–	–	+	–
MannerAdverb	+/–	–	–	+

division can be made between classes of lexemes that are categorized for a single syntactic function, and classes of lexemes that can be used in more than one syntactic function without derivation. The first type of PoS is termed 'rigid', whereas the second type is called 'flexible'.

Cross-linguistically, lexical flexibility and rigidity come in different degrees. Flexible PoS classes may be usable in two, three, or all four possible slots. In the case of rigid PoS systems, not all languages have a lexeme class for each slot. That is to say: some languages can express certain slots(s) only by means of a non-lexical strategy. The specific possibilities with respect to lexical flexibility and rigidity are constrained by the parts of speech-hierarchy given in (40):

(40)	head of predicate phrase	⊂ head of referential phrase	⊂ modifier in referential phrase	⊂ modifier in predicate phrase

In Hengeveld (1992) and Hengeveld et al. (2004), this hierarchy was interpreted unidirectionally. It was claimed to predict that the more to the right a syntactic slot is positioned, the smaller the chance that a language will have a separate, specialized lexical class to express it. With respect to flexibility, this means that languages are most likely to have a PoS class that can be used for the two rightmost functions. Moreover, if a PoS class can be used as the head and the modifier in a referential phrase, the hierarchy predicts that it will also be usable in the function positioned further to the right, namely as a modifier in a predicate phrase. With respect to rigidity, the hierarchy predicts that a language is most likely to lack a PoS class for the rightmost function, i.e. modifier in a predicate phrase (that is, it is most likely to lack manner adverbs). Furthermore, if a language lacks a PoS class for a certain slot on the hierarchy, it is predicted to lack PoS classes for all functions further to the right in the hierarchy.

However, in view of new language data, it seems that the parts of speech hierarchy is better interpreted as the superficial reflection of a two-dimensional implicational map. This map is based on two parameters, given in (41) and (42):

(41) Ascription > Reference

(42) Head > Modifier

The parameter in (41) says that it is more likely for a language to have specialized word classes for the ascriptive than for the referential function; the one in (42) says it is more likely to have specialized word classes for heads than for modifiers.

In principle, the combination of these two parameters would permit many logically possible PoS systems. However, these possibilities are constrained in three ways. First, given the dependence of the lexical class of the modifier on the lexical class of the head illustrated in (34)–(37), we do not expect a language to have adjectives if it does not have nouns, manner adverbs if it does not have verbs, etcetera. Second, in view of this predominance of heads over modifiers, we expect the ascription-reference parameter to show up primarily with respect to heads. Third, in FDG the interpersonal level governs the choices at the representational level. Therefore, we predict that the ascription-reference distinction is primary, and the head-modifier distinction secondary. These three constraints are given in general terms in (43)–(45):

(43) If a language does not have a specialized class of heads, it does not have the corresponding class of modifiers. (Heads > Modifiers)

(44) If a language has a specialized class of nouns, it has a specialized class of verbs. (Ascription > Reference)

(45) If a language does not have separate classes for ascription and reference, it does not have separate classes for heads and modifiers. ((Ascription > Reference) > (Head > Modifier))

The parameters in (41)–(42) and the constraints in (43)–(45) are accounted for in the implicational map in Figure 3.

The implicational map in Figure 3 leaves us with a limited number of possible PoS systems, which are represented in (46)–(55) below. Notice that for reasons of space we represent the PoS systems (and later on the DC systems as well) in one-dimensional, 'flattened-out' versions of the two-dimensional map in Figure 3 below.

The predicted PoS systems are divided into flexible systems and rigid systems. Flexible systems are those that have at least one flexible PoS class, while rigid systems have only rigid PoS classes. The flexible systems are listed in (46)–(50) below. In these tables, the flexible PoS classes are represented by dark grey cells, whereas rigid classes are in light grey. The labels used for a number of flexible PoS classes are taken from Hengeveld et al. (2004): a 'contentive' is a completely flexible lexeme that can be used in all four functions; a 'non-verb' is a lexeme that can be used in all but the predicative function; and a 'modifier' is a lexeme that can be used as a modifier in both ascriptive and referential phrases. Apart from these, we use the names 'nominal' for lexemes that can be used in head and modifier function in referential phrases, and 'predicative' for lexemes that can be used in head and modifier function in ascriptive phrases, in systems (48) and (50). The latter two PoS classes were not predicted by earlier versions of the theory (Hengeveld 1992, Hengeveld et al. 2004).

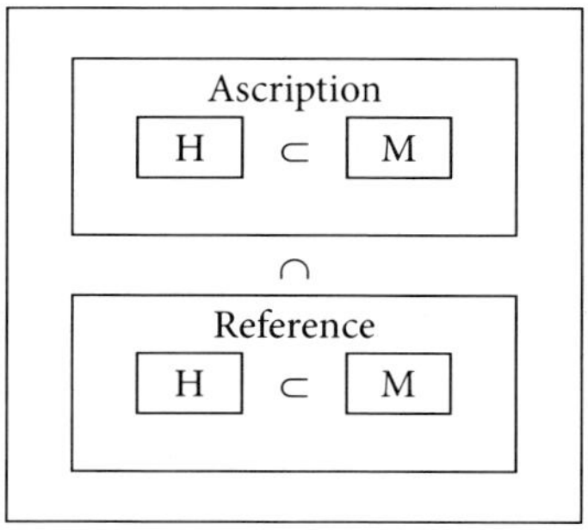

Figure 3. The implicational map for parts of speech

(46)

(i)	(iii)	(iv)	(ii)
contentive			

(47)

(i)	(iii)	(iv)	(ii)
verb	non-verb		

(48)

(i)	(iii)	(iv)	(ii)
verb	nominal		manner adverb

(49)

(i)	(iii)	(iv)	(ii)
verb	noun	modifier	

(50)

(i)	(iii)	(iv)	(ii)
predicative	nominal		predicative

The rigid PoS systems that we predict to be logically possible are listed in (51)–(55) below. Here, the rigid classes are also represented in light grey. In systems (52)–(55) one or more of the four functions cannot be filled lexically; the relevant cells remain white and are left unspecified.

(51)

(i)	(iii)	(iv)	(ii)
verb	noun	adjective	manner adverb

(52)

(i)	(iii)	(iv)	(ii)
verb	noun	adjective	–

(53)

(i)	(iii)	(iv)	(ii)
verb	noun	–	manner adverb

(54)

(i)	(iii)	(iv)	(ii)
verb	noun	–	–

(55)

(i)	(iii)	(iv)	(ii)
verb	–	–	–

It should be noted that there is not always a perfect match between the logically possible systems displayed above and the PoS systems actually encountered in the sample languages. As the data in the next sub-section will show, languages may display an additional PoS class from a 'neighboring' system (i.e. the one represented above or below it), or they may display additional closed or derived classes of rigid lexemes.

4.2 Part-of-speech-systems in the sample languages

The PoS systems of the languages in our sample are schematically represented in (56)–(77) below. As in the previous section, rigid PoS classes are represented in light grey, and flexible classes in dark grey. Furthermore, small, closed PoS classes are marked with a C,[11] and PoS classes consisting of only non-basic, lexically derived members are marked with a D. Languages with flexible PoS systems are represented first (in (56)–(64)), and are ordered from more to less flexible. They are followed by languages with rigid PoS systems (in (65)–(77)), which are ordered from those with four PoS classes to those with less than four PoS classes.

(56)

Samoan PoS	(i)	(iii)	(iv)	(ii)
Rigid	D Verb	–	–	–
Flexible	Contentive			

(57)

Kambera PoS	(i)	(iii)	(iv)	(ii)
Rigid	D Verb	–	–	C MAdverb
Flexible	Contentive			

(58)

Santali PoS	(i)	(iii)	(iv)	(ii)
Rigid	Verb	D. Noun	–	–
Flexible	Contentive			

(59)

Imb. Quechua PoS	(i)	(iii)	(iv)	(ii)
Rigid	Verb	–	–	C MAdverb
Flexible		Non-verb		

(60)

Kayardild PoS	(i)	(iii)	(iv)	(ii)
Rigid	Verb	–	C? Adjective	C. MAdverb
Flexible		Non-verb		

(61)

Turkish PoS	(i)	(iii)	(iv)	(ii)
Rigid	Verb	–	–	–
Flexible		Non-verb		
			Modifier	

(62)

Ma'di PoS	(i)	(iii)	(iv)	(ii)
Rigid	Verb	–	Adjective	D. MAdverb
Flexible		Nominal		
			Modifier	

(63)

Lango PoS	(i)	(iii)	(iv)	(ii)
Rigid	Verb	Noun	–	MAdverb
Flexible			Modifier	

(64)

Abun PoS	(i)	(iii)	(iv)	(ii)
Rigid	Verb	Noun	Adjective	C MAdverb
Flexible			C. Modifier	

(65)

Basque PoS	(i)	(iii)	(iv)	(ii)
Rigid	Verb	Noun	Adjective	MAdverb

(66)

Abkhaz PoS	(i)	(iii)	(iv)	(ii)
Rigid	Verb	Noun	Adjective	MAdverb

(67)

Georgian PoS	(i)	(iii)	(iv)	(ii)
Rigid	Verb	Noun	Adjective	MAdverb

(68)

Pipil PoS	(i)	(iii)	(iv)	(ii)
Rigid	Verb	Noun	Adjective	C. MAdverb

(69)

Berbice Dutch	(i)	(iii)	(iv)	(ii)
Rigid	Verb	Noun	Adjective	C. MAdverb?

(70)

Alamblak PoS	(i)	(iii)	(iv)	(ii)
Rigid	Verb	Noun	C. Adjective	C. MAdverb

(71)

Hdi PoS	(i)	(iii)	(iv)	(ii)
Rigid	Verb	Noun	C. Adjective	C. MAdverb

(72)

Tamil PoS	(i)	(iii)	(iv)	(ii)
Rigid	Verb	Noun	C. Adjective	C. MAdverb

(73)

M.Chinese PoS	(i)	(iii)	(iv)	(ii)
Rigid	Verb	Noun	C. Adjective	–

(74)

Garo PoS	(i)	(iii)	(iv)	(ii)
Rigid	Verb	Noun	–	C. MAdverb

(75)

Nivkh PoS	(i)	(iii)	(iv)	(ii)
Rigid	Verb	Noun	–	C. MAdverb

(76)

Krongo PoS	(i)	(iii)	(iv)	(ii)
Rigid	Verb	Noun	–	–

(77)

Tuscarora PoS	(i)	(iii)	(iv)	(ii)
Rigid	Verb	Noun	–	–

The majority of the languages of our sample have been analyzed for earlier studies (Hengeveld 1992, Hengeveld et al. 2004, Van Lier 2006). This is *not* the case for the following five languages: Kambera, Santali, Ma'di, Abun, and Hdi. For reasons of space, it is impossible to extensively document our classification of these languages' PoS systems. We will, however, briefly discuss two cases where our classification is slightly different from the one proposed in the relevant sources, due to the fact that for our definitions of PoS we do not take into account differences in the expression of certain morpho-syntactic categories associated with a specific function (such as TAM for the head of an ascriptive phrase or case for the head of a referential phrase).[12]

According to Klamer (1998: 91–115), in Kambera nouns and verbs can be distinguished on the basis of certain distributional characteristics, such as the possibility to combine with articles or adverbial modifiers. However, this is not relevant for our definition. What is crucial is that in terms of functional possibilities, there is no difference between nouns and verbs. This is illustrated in example (78) a,b, where the same lexeme is used as the head of an ascriptive subact and of a referential subact, respectively.

(78) a. Na ma-kaloru-nya na **manganga**...
ART REL.SBJ-arrange-3SG.DAT ART **steal**
'Who is engaged in theft,...' (Klamer 1998: 105)
b. Jàka **manganga**-ma-na-yna-i una,...
if **steal**-EMPH-3SG.GEN-3SG-DAT-ITER EMPH.3SG
'If he does steal again,...' (Klamer 1998: 105)

A similar case holds for the distinction between nouns and adjectives in Ma'di. According to Blackings and Fabb (2003: 106), they can be distinguished on the basis of their combinability with number inflection and determiners. Again, however, there is no difference between the two in terms of functional possibilities: notional adjectives can occur as the head of a referential phrase (as in (79)), and notional nouns as modifiers in a referential phrase (as in 80)):

(79) **ālī** rɨ̀ pɨ̄ ɛ̄-tʃá ádʒɨ́nɨ̄
short(PL) DEF PL.PRON (3)-VE-arrive yesterday
'The short ones arrived yesterday.' (Blackings & Fabb 2003: 106)

(80) Màɗí **ādrúpī** rɨ̀ ɔ̄ɗā rʊ̄ ɨ̀lɛ́-nɨ̄ kʊ̄
person **brother** DEF act REFL that-like NEG(NON-PST)
'A person who is a brother won't behave like that.' (Blackings & Fabb 2003: 304)

Further, Blackings and Fabb do not explicitly mention modifiers as a PoS class, but they state that there is a group of manner adverbs that can also be used as a modifier in a referential phrase. An example is *lɔ̄sɔ́* 'good/well', as in example (81) a, b:

(81) a. ɔ́pɨ́ nɨ̄ ɓārá **lɔ̄sɔ́** rɨ̀ ʔɨ̄
Opi PRON child **good** DEF FOC
'Opi is a good child.' (Blacking & Fabb 2003: 106)

b. ɔ́pɨ́ ɔ̄-sɔ̀ **lɔ̄sɔ́**
Opi 3-sew **good**
'Opi sewed it well.' (Blacking & Fabb 2003: 506)

With these clarifications we round off the section on parts of speech, turning to dependent clause constructions in the next section.

5. Dependent clauses

5.1 Dependent clauses in Functional Discourse Grammar

In terms of their functions, DCs may be defined in the same way as PoS. In this case, *complex, clausal* units substitute the *lexically* headed f-units in the overview below (both given in bold):

	T:		T	
(82)	(f_1: lex	(f_1):	σ	(f_1))
	T:		T	
(83)	(f_1: lex	(f_1):	**(f_2: lex (f_2))** **(f/e/p: [...] (f/e/p))**	(f_1))
	R: T		T	
(84)	($α_1$: **(f_1: lex (f_2))** **(f/e/p: [...] (f/e/p))**	($α_1$):	σ	($α_1$))
	R: T		T	
(85)	($α_1$: (f_1: lex (f_1))	($α_1$):	**(f_2: lex (f_2))** **(f/e/p: [...] (f/e/p))**	($α_1$))

Note that the head of the independent ascriptive subact in (82) cannot be substituted by a more complex, clausal unit, since it is lexical, not phrasal. Only f-units that are used as independent ascriptive subacts as a whole may be replaced by complex units, not their heads. The resultant construction is a predicate clause, as in example (86) and its representation in (87):

(86) To hesitate is to lose.

(87) T R

$(e_i: (f_i: [(f_j: \text{lose } (f_j))\ (x_i)]\ (f_i))\ (e_i))\ (e_k: (f_k: [(f_l: \text{hesitate } (f_l))\ (x_i)]\ (f_j))\ (e_k))$

Here (e_i) is used as an independent ascriptive subact, *not* as the head of that subact.

Consider now the lexically headed f-units printed in bold in (83)–(85). These can all be substituted by a complex f-, e- or p-unit, as we already showed in examples (12)–(15) in Section 3.3. In (88) and its representation in (89) an example is given of a complex f-unit replacing a lexically headed f-unit that is the head of a representational unit that is used as a referential subact (cf. (84) above), i.e. a complement clause.[13]

(88) The man regrets **that the boy is ill.**

R T

(89) $(e_i: (f_i: [(f_j: \text{regret}_V\ (f_j))\ (x_i: (f_k: \text{man } (f_k))\ (x_i))\ (e_j: \mathbf{(f_l: [(f_m: ill\ (f_m))\ (x_j: (f_n: boy\ (f_n))\ (x_j))]\ (f_l))}\ (e_j))]\ (f_i))\ (e_i))$

In example (90) and its representation in (91) a complex e-unit replaces the lexically headed f-unit that is a modifier within a referential subact (cf. (85)). This construction is called a relative clause.

(90) the man **who saw the boy**

R T T

(91) $(x_i: (f_i: \text{man}_N\ (f_i))\ (x_i): \mathbf{(e_i: [(f_j: see_V\ (f_j))\ (x_i))\ (x_j: (f_k: boy_N\ (f_k))\ (x_j))]\ (e_i))}\ (x_i))$

In example (92) and its representation in (93) a complex f-unit substitutes an f-unit that is the modifier of a lexical head of an f-unit that is used as an independent ascriptive subact (cf. (83)). This construction is called an adverbial manner clause.

(92) The man walked out stamping his feet.

T T

(93) $(e_i: (f_i: [\ (f_j: \text{walk.out}_V\ (f_j): \mathbf{(f_k: [(f_l: stamp_V\ (f_l))\ (x_i)\ (x_j: (f_m: feet_N\ (f_m))\ (x_j): (x_i)_{Poss}\ (x_j))]\ (f_k))}\ (f_j))\ (x_i: (f_n: \text{man}_N\ (f_n))\ (x_i))]\ (f_i))\ (e_i))$

Thus, these FDG analyses make clear how DCs can be compared to PoS, in terms of the functional slots that they are used in. Given this similarity, we may expect that, cross-linguistically, DC systems can also be characterized in terms of various degrees of flexibility or rigidity.

For instance, Turkish DCs with a verb form in *-AcAK*[14] are flexible to the extent that they can be used in functions (iii) and (iv), as shown in example (94) a and b:

(94) a. Orhan-ın bir şey yap-ma-**yacağ**-ı belliydi.
Orhan-GEN anything do-NEG-**NMLZ**-3SG.POSS it.was.obvious
'It was obvious that Orhan wouldn't do/wasn't going to do anything.'
(Göksel & Kerslake 2005: 423)

b. Fatma-'nın yarın gör-eceğ-i film
Fatma-GEN tomorrow see-NMLZ-3SG.POSS film
'the film that Fatma is going to/will be seeing tomorrow' (Göksel & Kerslake 2005: 442)

By contrast, DCs in Krongo with a verb form nominalized with the prefix *t-* are rigid. They can be used only in function (iii). An example is given in (95):

(95) nóoni àʔàŋ **t**-áfàrà kò-níimò kàtí m-íʔìŋ
know I NMLZ-IPFV:cry POSS-mother my GEN-he
'I know that my mother is crying about him.' (Reh 1985: 258)

In what follows, we predict a number of possible rigid and flexible DC constructions, in parallel with the various possible types of PoS classes that we predicted in the previous section. Then we classify the DCs of the languages of our sample (Section 5.2), and see to what extent the patterns of PoS and DCs are alike in each language (Section 6).

The possible flexible DCs are represented in (96)–(98); the rigid DCs follow in (99)–(101). The flexible DCs are named in parallel with flexible PoS, except for the first type, which is called 'multifunctional clause', because 'non-verbal clause' is clearly not a suitable term. Notice once more that we must disregard function (i) when looking at DCs, because the head of an independent ascriptive subact is always lexical. In (96)–(101) this slot is marked with an X.

(96)

(i)	(iii)	(iv)	(ii)
X	Multifunctional clause		

(97)

(i)	(iii)	(iv)	(ii)
X	Nominal clause		

(98)

(i)	(iii)	(iv)	(ii)
X		Modifier clause	

(99)

(i)	(iii)	(iv)	(ii)
X	Complement clause		

(100)

(i)	(iii)	(iv)	(ii)
X		Relative clause	

(101)

(i)	(iii)	(iv)	(ii)
X			Adv. manner clause

5.2 Dependent clauses in the sample languages

In this section we categorize our sample languages with respect to their DC system. Before providing the relevant data, however, we must define explicitly which criteria we use to distinguish between flexible and rigid DCs.

We classify as flexible those DC constructions that can be used in two or more functions, while using the same subordinator (i.e. no formal difference between complementizer/relativizer/adverbial subordinator), or the same special marking on the dependent predicate (i.e. no formal difference between nominalizer/participial marker/converbal marker). Notice that the second strategy includes constructions without a marker. In Santali, for instance, nominal clauses are characterized by the absence of the indicative marker *-a*, which is always present on predicates in main clauses.

As with our classification of PoS classes, we do not consider the expression of certain morpho-syntactic categories that are the consequence of using a certain DC construction in a certain function, rather than being inherent to the DC construction itself. In practice, this means that we will not take into account differences between (uses of) DC constructions in terms of the coding of Tense/Aspect/Mood, the usage of case markers and determiners, and the coding of arguments.

As an example of TAM-marking being irrelevant for flexibility/rigidity in DCs, consider once more Santali. As mentioned, its DCs are characterized by the lack of the indicative marker *-a*. Now, when such a DC functions as a relative clause or as a subject complement clause, TAM markers can be present. However, when functioning as an object complement clause, tense markers are disallowed, except when the main predicate is one of direct perception. In such cases we do not consider DCs with TAM-marking to be different from DCs without TAM-marking.

Second, to illustrate the irrelevance of case marking, consider Imbabura Quechua. In this language, a nominal clause takes an accusative case-marker when used as an object complement clause, but not when used as a relative clause. This difference is regarded as a direct reflection of the function of the construction in the main clause, rather than as a property of the DC itself.

The last type of coding that is irrelevant for the definition of flexible DCs is the manner in which arguments are expressed within the DC. Consider Kambera: this language has a nominal clause marked with *pa*, which can be used as a complement clause with co-referential subject, and as an object relative clause. In the former function the subject remains unexpressed in the DC, while in the latter function there is object-gapping.

In (102)–(123) we show the DC systems attested in the languages of our sample. The order in which the languages are presented is the same as in Section 4.2.[15]

(102)

Kambera DCs	(i)	(iii)	(iv)	(ii)
Rigid	X	Complement Cl.	Relative Cl.	Adv. Manner Cl.
Flexible		Nominal clause		

(103)

Samoan DCs	(i)	(iii)	(iv)	(ii)
Rigid	X	Complement Cl.	Relative Cl.	–
Flexible		Multifunctional clause		

(104)

Santali DCs	(i)	(iii)	(iv)	(ii)
Rigid	X	Complement Cl	Relative Cl.	Adv. Manner Cl.
Flexible		Nominal clause		

(105)

Imb. Quechua DCs	(i)	(iii)	(iv)	(ii)
Rigid	X	Complement Cl	–	Adv. Manner Cl.
Flexible		Nominal clause		

(106)

Kayardild DCs	(i)	(iii)	(iv)	(ii)
Rigid		Complement Cl.	Relative Cl.	Adv. Manner Cl.
Flexible	X	Multifunctional clause		
		Nominal clause		

(107)

Turkish DCs	(i)	(iii)	(iv)	(ii)
Rigid	X	Complement Cl.	Relative Cl.	Adv. Manner Cl.
Flexible		Nominal clause		

(108)

Ma'di DCs	(i)	(iii)	(iv)	(ii)
Rigid	X	Complement Cl.	Relative Cl.	–
Flexible		Nominal clause		

(109)

Lango DCs	(i)	(iii)	(iv)	(ii)
Rigid	X	Complement Cl.	Relative Cl.	Adv. Manner Cl.

(110)

Abun DCs	(i)	(iii)	(iv)	(ii)
Rigid	X	Complement Cl.	Relative Cl.	Adv. Manner Cl.

(111)

Basque DCs	(i)	(iii)	(iv)	(ii)
Rigid	X	Complement Cl.	Relative Cl.	Adv. Manner Cl.
Flexible		Nominal clause		

(112)

Abkhaz DCs	(i)	(iii)	(iv)	(ii)
Rigid	X	Complement Cl.	Relative Cl.	Adv. Manner Cl.

(113)

Georgian DCs	(i)	(iii)	(iv)	(ii)
Rigid	X	Complement Cl.	Relative Cl.	Adv. Manner Cl.
Flexible		Nominal clause		

(114)

Pipil DCs	(i)	(iii)	(iv)	(ii)
Rigid	X	Complement Cl.	Relative Cl.	Adv. Manner Cl.
Flexible		Nominal clause		

(115)

Berbice Dutch DCs	(i)	(iii)	(iv)	(ii)
Rigid	X	Complement Cl.	Relative Cl.	Adv. Manner Cl.
		Nominal clause		

(116)

Alamblak DCs	(i)	(iii)	(iv)	(ii)
Rigid	X	Complement Cl.	Relative Cl.	–

(117)

Hdi DCs	(i)	(iii)	(iv)	(ii)
Rigid	X	Complement Cl.	Relative Cl.	Adv. Manner Cl.

(118)

Tamil DCs	(i)	(iii)	(iv)	(ii)
Rigid	X	Complement Cl.	Relative Cl.	Adv. Manner Cl.

(119)

M. Chinese DCs	(i)	(iii)	(iv)	(ii)
Rigid	X	Complement Cl.	-	-
Flexible			Modifier clause	

(120)

Garo DCs	(i)	(iii)	(iv)	(ii)
Rigid	X	Complement Cl.	Relative Cl.	Adv. Manner Cl.

(121)

Nivkh DCs	(i)	(iii)	(iv)	(ii)
Rigid	X	Complement Cl.	Relative Cl.	–

(122)

Krongo DCs	(i)	(iii)	(iv)	(ii)
Rigid	X	Complement Cl.	-	–
Flexible			Modifier clause	

(123)

Tuscarora DCs	(i)	(iii)	(iv)	(ii)
Rigid	X	–	–	–

6. A distributional parallel between Parts of Speech and Dependent Clauses?

6.1. Lexical categorization and functional transparency

Earlier research (Hengeveld et al. 2004) has shown that the flexibility versus rigidity of PoS classes in a language has certain repercussions for the morpho-syntax of that language. More specifically, languages with a flexible PoS system need to 'compensate' for the functional ambiguity of their flexible lexemes on the morpho-syntactic level of their grammar, in order to secure functional transparency. In other words, since the lexical category of a flexible item is not sufficient to determine its function in a specific utterance, these languages have to mark the functional-syntactic slot in which the lexeme is used through other means. This can be done by using a fixed word order and/or specific function-indicating elements.

By contrast, in the case of a rigid PoS system, the lexical category of a lexeme does suffice to identify its function, because there is only one function that it is allowed to express.[16] Therefore, there is no need for morpho-syntactic function-marking, at least not in those slots for which a PoS class is available in the language. This does not mean, however, that such function-marking never occurs in languages with a rigid PoS system. There are actually many languages in the sample used by Hengeveld et al. (2004) that have both a rigid PoS system and syntactic function-marking through word-order restrictions. In short, languages with a flexible PoS system need morpho-syntactic function-marking, while languages with a rigid PoS system do not need morpho- syntactic function-marking, at least not in those functions that can be fulfilled lexically.

6.2 Hypotheses

Based on the parallel treatment of PoS and DCs in FDG as outlined in Sections 4.1 and 5.1, and the trade-off process involved in establishing functional transparency discussed above, we may hypothesize that the functional possibilities of a language's PoS system will be mirrored by the functional possibilities of its DC constructions (see also Van Lier 2006). Specifically, we expect that a language will use the same strategies to achieve functional transparency when a function is fulfilled by a *clausal* construction, as when it is expressed by a *lexical* item. This means that in languages with a flexible PoS system (and morpho-syntactic function-marking) we expect to find flexibility in the DC system too. Conversely, languages with rigid PoS systems are expected to use rigid DC constructions (at least in those functions that can be fulfilled lexically). Notice, however, that in the latter case we have to reckon with the above-mentioned fact that many languages with rigid PoS systems have morpho-syntactic function-marking, even though they do not need it. When such function-marking is indeed present, this would, at least from the point of view of functional transparency, allow a language with rigid PoS classes to have a flexible DC construction.

A third and final prediction that we make is in fact a non-prediction. It concerns those languages with rigid PoS systems in which two functions cannot be filled lexically or only with members of a small, closed PoS class. In the schemas in Section 4.2 this holds for the languages whose PoS systems are represented in (70)–(77).[17] Since there are no large open PoS classes to express these functions, there is also no basis to predict whether the DCs in those functions will be rigid or flexible. In those cases, we expect to find both patterns, as long as functional transparency is not violated.

6.3 Results

The hypotheses are largely supported by our data. First, we find that many languages with one or more flexible PoS class(es) also display flexibility in their DC system. This holds for Kambera, Samoan, Santali, Imbabura Quechua, Kayardild, Turkish, and Ma'di. There are three languages with a lexical class of flexible modifiers that do not have a corresponding flexible modifier clause construction: Ma'di,[18] Lango, and Abun.

It is noteworthy that in many cases (the multifunctional clauses in Samoan and Kayardild being the exceptions) the flexible DC construction in a specific language has a somewhat smaller range of use than the corresponding flexible PoS class in that language. More specifically, many flexible DC constructions can be used only in functions (iii) and (iv) but not in function (ii), i.e. they are nominal clauses, while the flexible PoS class in that language *can* be used in function (ii) and possibly also in function (i), i.e. they are non-verbs or contentives. For example, Imbabura Quechua has lexical non-verbs that can be used in functions (iii), (iv) and (ii), whereas its nominal clauses can be used only in functions (iii) and (iv).

Bearing this in mind, we may interpret the finding that the lexical modifier classes in Ma'di, Lango and Abun do not have flexible clausal equivalents as just another case of a DC construction being less flexible than its lexical counterpart: if a DC construction is 'one step' less flexible than a lexical modifier, then this amounts to a fully rigid construction, because there is only one function left. Moreover, we must take into account that all three languages have, apart from their class of flexible modifiers, a class of rigid manner adverbs. This may partly explain the absence of flexible DCs in these languages.

In fact, in all languages of our sample with flexibility in both their PoS system and their DC system, we have attested rigid DC constructions alongside the flexible ones. Notice however, that this finding does not contradict our hypothesis, since we predicted that flexible languages would allow flexible DCs, not that they would disallow rigid ones, since rigid DCs are functionally transparent by definition. A similar argument holds for the finding mentioned above, namely that flexible DCs often have less functional possibilities than flexible PoS. It means that those functions that cannot be expressed with the flexible DC must be expressed with a rigid construction, which is again by definition functionally transparent.

Turning now to the results concerning languages with rigid PoS systems, we find that, as expected, many such languages use only rigid DC constructions, at least in those functions for which a large, open PoS class is available. However, in four languages with fully rigid PoS systems — Basque, Georgian, Pipil, and Berbice Dutch Creole — we find a flexible DC construction, alongside the rigid ones. These languages all have a flexible nominal clause construction, (Basque even has two). We will discuss each of these constructions in turn.

In Basque, DCs with the conjunction *-en* can be used as the head and modifier in a referential phrase. In the former function the construction is normally used for interrogative or subjunctive complements. However, it can also be used as a complement clause with a factive meaning, mainly by speakers of western (mostly Bizkaian) Basque. In this latter function it is combined with a determiner, which ensures functional transparency (Hualde & Ortiz de Urbina 2003: 646).[19] The flexible use of the *-en* construction is illustrated in (124) a and b:

(124) a. Entzun dut Amaiaren neba hil d-**en**-a
hear AUX Amaia.GEN brother die AUX-**CONJ**-ART
'I heard that Amaia's brother died.' (Hualde & Ortiz de Urbina 2003: 646)
b. Pellok ekarri du-**en** dirua galdu dut
Peter.ERG bring AUX-**CONJ** money.DET lose AUX
'I lost the money Peter brought.' (Hualde & Ortiz de Urbina 2003: 764)

When used on a complement clause, *-en* can always be replaced by the complementizer *-ela*, but there is some pragmatic difference: the use of *-en* implies that the statement expressed in the complement is taken by the speaker as a true fact, while the same does not hold for a complement marked with *-ela*.

The second flexible construction in Basque is the so-called *bait*-clause, illustrated in (125a) (as a complement clause) and (125b) (as a relative clause):

(125) a. Hau da haren abanrailik handiena ez **bait**u
this is this avantage.PART biggest.DET not **CONJ**.AUX
ainitz xahutzen
much spend.IPFV
'That's the main advantage, that he doesn't spend much.' (Hualde & Ortiz de Urbina 2004: 648)
b. Landibarren badira lau kartier, **horiek**
Landibar.LOC *ba*.are four neighbourhood **those(RP)**
bait-ira Behaunem Dona Martine, Donoztia eta Azkonbegi
CONJ-are Behaune Dona Martine, Donoztia and Azkonbegi
'There are in Landibarre four neighbourhoods, which are Behaune, Dona Martine, Donoztia and Azkonbegi.' (Hualde & Ortiz de Urbina 2004: 816)

Two points are of interest here. First, as can be seen in (125b), when the *bait*-clause functions as a relative clause, a resumptive pronoun can optionally be used, in order to clarify the function of the construction. More generally, the use of *bait*-clauses for complementation is uncommon, while for relativization it is very common in present day spoken Basque, especially in eastern dialects (Hualde & Ortiz de Urbina 2003: 648, 816).

Georgian has a DC construction marked with the conjunction *rom*, which can also be used as a complement clause and as a relative clause. These uses are illustrated in (126a–b), respectively:

(126) a. **(is)** uk've še-v-a-mčn-i-e
(**that**(NOM)) already PREV-I-NV-notice-TS-AOR.INDC
rom es xalx-i sando ar ar-i-s
SUBORD this people-NOM trustworthy(NOM) not be-PRS-it
'I have already noticed that this people is not trustworthy.' (Hewitt 1995: 613)

b. gušin **rom** (beč'ed-I) m-a-čuk-e,
yesterday **SUBORD** ring-NOM me-LV-present-AOR.INDC
is beč'ed-I sad ar-i-s?
that(NOM) ring-NOM where be-PRS-it
'Where is that ring which you presented to me yesterday?' (Hewitt 1995: 607)

However, as can be seen in (126a), the *rom*-construction can be combined with a correlative element in the main clause when functioning as a complement. This is even obligatory when the complement clause is dependent on a postposition or functions obliquely (i.e. follows a verb that takes instrumental case). The correlative disambiguates the function of the dependent clause in a way similar to the resumptive pronoun in the Basque relative *bait*-clause. Moreover, the examples in (126) illustrate a contrast in terms of the position of the conjunction: very often, though not obligatorily, complement clauses start with *rom*, while in relative clauses *rom* avoids the first position. This is an additional way to differentiate between the two uses of a *rom*-clause.

Pipil normally uses rigid constructions for complementation and relativization: the former are introduced by one of the complementizers *ka(h)* and *ta(y)*, while the latter take a relativizer *te* or *ke*. However, the complementizer *ka(h)* can, 'at times' also introduce a relative clause (Campbell 1985: 128). The two uses of the *ka(h)*-clause are illustrated in (127a–b):

(127) a. Tesu ki-mati katka **ka** ne i-siwa:-w se: bru:hah
no it-know before **that** the his-wife-POSS a witch
'He didn't know before that his wife is a witch.' (Campbell 1985: 126)

b. Ni-k-miktih ne mistun **ka** ki-kwah ne tu:tut
I-it-killed the cat **that** it-ate the bird
'I killed the cat that ate the bird.' (Campbell 1985: 129)

The two functions of *ka*-clauses can be differentiated by means of constituent order: complement clauses are postverbal, and relative clauses always come after their head.

In Berbice Dutch Creole finite complement clauses and relative clauses are normally marked with *dati* and *wati*, respectively. Optionally, however, both the complementizer and the relativizer can be omitted. This results in a single flexible zero-marked construction, as illustrated in (128a–b):

(128) a. Ek glof ka o nin-te musu
1SG believe NEG 3SG know-PF V much
'I don't believe he knows much.' (Kouwenberg 1994: 242)

b. Di sem jermatoko eke pan-te ju abot
the same woman.child 1SG .tell-PFV 2SG about
'The same girl I told you about.' (Kouwenberg 1994: 268)

As in Pipil, potential functional ambiguity is resolved through fixed constituent order: object complements come after the main verb, and relative clauses follow their head.

To sum up, we have attested four languages that combine a completely rigid PoS system with a flexible nominal DC construction. In fact, this finding is not surprising, if we recall that many languages with rigid PoS classes also have morpho-syntactic function marking. Under the condition that function-marking is present, a flexible DC construction is allowed from the perspective of functional transparency. And in fact, this condition holds for all cases discussed above: the *-en* clauses in Basque are functionally disambiguated through the use of the determiner; the *ka(h)* clauses in Pipil and the asyndetic clauses in Berbice Dutch through word order. In the cases of Basque *bait*-clauses and Georgian *rom*-clauses, the ambiguity problem can be solved, as shown, through the use of resumptive pronouns and correlatives, respectively.

Finally, our last prediction, the non-prediction, is also borne out by the data: when a language has no PoS classes to fulfill the two modifier functions, then the DC constructions in those functions can be both flexible and rigid. Eight languages in the sample have the relevant PoS system. Out of these, two use a single, flexible modifier construction: Mandarin Chinese and Krongo. In these languages, functional transparency is achieved through various other means. Mandarin Chinese has fixed modifier-head-order in both referential and ascriptive phrases, in combination with a lexical noun-verb distinction. In Krongo relative clauses agree with their head noun in gender and number. Five other languages, namely Alamblak, Hdi, Tamil, Garo, and Nivkh, use one or more rigid construction(s). In Tuscarora, finally, there are no dependent clauses at all; this language uses independent clauses only.

7. Conclusion

This paper has shown how lexical and clausal constructions can be defined in the same way within the theory of Functional Discourse Grammar, in terms of the functional slots they may occupy. These functional possibilities were described and compared for the PoS classes and DC constructions of 23 languages. On the basis of our theoretical framework, combined with earlier research into the influence of lexical and morphosyntactic categorization on the establishment of functional transparency, we investigated whether and in how far the functionality of PoS classes in languages is related to the functionality of DC constructions.

On the one hand, we found preliminary evidence for such a correlation: many languages with a flexible PoS system have one or more flexible DC constructions, whereas many languages with a rigid PoS system use only rigid DC constructions in those functions for which they have a large, open PoS class. In those functions for which only a small, closed PoS class is available, or no PoS class at all, we find both rigid and flexible DC constructions. On the other hand, our data show that functional transparency can be reached through different strategies within a language system, and that more than one disambiguating strategy may be at work at the same time. This explains the finding that flexible DC constructions often do not cover the same range of functions as flexible PoS classes in the same language, as well as the fact that rigid DCs are attested alongside flexible DCs in languages with a flexible PoS system. Finally, it accounts for the fact that flexible DC constructions are also attested in languages with rigid PoS, as long as functional transparency is preserved.

Abbreviations

The following is a list of those abbreviations that are not included in the List of Standard Abbreviations of the Leipzig Glossing Rules.

ADVR	=	adverbializer
AOR	=	aorist
CONJ	=	conjunction
EMPH	=	emphatic marker
ITER	=	iterative
LV	=	locative version
NON-PST	=	non-past
NV	=	neutral version
PART	=	partitive
PREV	=	preverb
PRON	=	pronominal
REL.SBJ	=	subject relativizer
RP	=	resumptive pronoun
SUBORD	=	subordinator

TS	=	thematic suffix
VE	=	ventive

Notes

* We are indebted to Jan Don, Evelien Keizer, Lachlan Mackenzie, Gerry Wanders, and two anonymous referees for comments on an earlier version of this paper.

1. This section is partly based on Hengeveld & Wanders (2007).

2. Note that FDG is strictly a theory about grammar, although one that makes use of psycholinguistic evidence in its basic architecture.

3. There are a number of higher units of analysis at the interpersonal level, but these are mostly relevant to larger stretches of discourse, and we do not need to go into those here. One of these higher units is called 'Act', which motivates our usage of the term '*sub*act' for ascription and reference. Although this higher 'Act' does not play a role in the present paper and therefore the relationship with 'subact' is not obvious here, we use 'subact' in order to ensure compatibility with other work in the FDG framework.

4. Note that this is an innovation with respect to the publications on FDG mentioned earlier. The use of the f-variable for the complex property that is the head of (e) is similar to Cuvalay-Haak's (1997: 69) 'c' for the 'situational concept' (Vet 1990: 280), which serves as the description of an event. In Vet's (1990: 280) words: "By applying the predication [the situational concept, KH, EvL] to the time-space region e_i the latter becomes a 'conceptualized time-space region' (see Bartsch 1986, 1989) or 'situation'." We prefer to think of this unit as a linguistic rather than a conceptual one. By using this variable we arrive at a three-layered organization of event-descriptions ((e_1), (f_1), and (f_2)) as proposed in different forms and for different reasons in Dik (1997), Cuvalay-Haak (1997) and Rijkhoff (2002).

5. There is also the option of *the marriage of the boy*, but that is irrelevant to our argument here, because it still involves a phrase with a lexical rather than a complex head.

6. As explained in Section 3.3, the head-modifier distinction is also relevant at the interpersonal level, but this does not play a role in the definitions of the PoS classes that we are currently interested in.

7. Note that the predicative use of manner adverbs, as in (24), in Dutch is limited to just a few cases.

8. In most cases there is no distinction between adjectives and manner adverbs in Dutch. In other words, there is one class of lexemes that can be used as modifiers in both referential and ascriptive phrases (see the discussion on lexical flexibility further on in this section). However, Dutch also has a, relatively unproductive, process to derive manner adverbs from adjectives, namely with the suffix *-(t)jes*, as in this example.

9. For a recent discussion on the (generative) syntactic and semantic interpretation of bare nominals in Dutch, see De Swart et al. (2005).

10. See Hengeveld (2008) for a discussion of the distinction between reference modification and referent modification in the context of FDG.

11. In two cases, namely Kayardild in (60) and Berbice Dutch in (69), the C is followed by a question mark. This means that the status of the PoS class was not entirely clear from our sources. In Kayardild, the class of adjectives in quite large (about 100 items (Evans 1995: 238), but seems to be nevertheless of a closed nature. In Berbice Dutch, there are only two lexical items that seem to qualify as manner adverbs: *(so)so* 'like this, thus' and *gau* 'quickly' (Kouwenberg 1994: 112–113).

12. For a discussion about the theoretical and practical consequences of this approach, see Van Lier 2006, 2009.

13. Note that for reasons of simplicity we only indicate the relevant subacts in these and following representations.

14. The capital letters indicate which segments of this affix are subject to consonant-vowel harmony.

15. This means that the languages in (102)–(110) are the ones with flexible PoS systems, while the languages in (111)–(123) have rigid PoS systems. This ordering is maintained in order to facilitate the comparison of the PoS tables and DC tables.

16. Strictly speaking, as we saw in Table 2 of Section 4.1, for nouns, adjectives and adverbs there is no one-to-one relationship between lexeme class and syntactic function, because these PoS may also be used as the head of a predicate phrase. However, these PoS do have a single *defining* function.

17. The two relevant 'empty' or 'near-empty' functions are always the two modifier functions.

18. Note that Ma'di also has a flexible class of nominals, which *is* in fact reflected in the dependent clauses system: Ma'di has a flexible nominal clause construction.

19. Functional transparency is further promoted through relatively fixed word order: object complements tend to appear to the right of the main verb, whereas relative clauses mostly precede the head. The latter ordering is 'almost obligatory for many speakers of present-day Basque' (Hualde & Ortiz de Urbina 2003, 452, 765).

References

A. Descriptions of Sample Languages

Asher, Ron E. 1982. *Tamil*. London/New York: Croom Helm [Croom Helm Descriptive Grammars].

Berry, Keith & Christine Berry. 1999. *A description of Abun, a West Papuan language of Irian Jaya*. Canberra: Pacific Linguistics, Research School for Pacific and Asian Studies, Australian National University [Pacific Linguistics, Series B, No. 115].

Blackings, Mairi & Nigel Fabb. 2003. *A Grammar of Ma'di*. Berlin: Mouton de Gruyter [Mouton Grammar Library 32].

Bruce, Les. 1984. *The Alamblak language of Papua New Guinea (East Sepik)*. Canberra: Australian National University [Pacific Linguistics, Series C, No. 81].

Burling, Robbins. 2004. *The language of the Modhupur Mandi (Garo). Vol 1: Grammar*. New Delhi/Morganville, New Jersey: Bibliophile South Asia/Promilla & Co. Publishers.

Campbell, Lyle. 1985. *The Pipil language of El Salvador*. Berlin: Mouton de Gruyter [Mouton Grammar Library].

Cherchi, Marcello. 1999. *Georgian*. München: Lincom Europa [Languages of the World/Materials 147].

Cole, Peter. 1982. *Imbabura Quechua*. Amsterdam: North Holland Publishing Company [Lingua Descriptive Studies 5].

Evans, Nicholas. 1995. *A grammar of Kayardild*. Berlin: Mouton de Gruyter [Mouton Grammar Library 15].

Frajzyngier, Zygmunt with Erin Shay. 2002. *A grammar of Hdi*. Berlin: Mouton de Gruyter [Mouton Grammar Library 21].

Göksel, Asli & Celia Kerslake. 2005. *Turkish. A comprehensive grammar.* London/New York: Routledge.

Gruzdeva, Ekaterina. 1998. *Nivkh*. München: Lincom Europa [Languages of the World/Materials 111].

Hualde, José Ignacio & Jon Ortiz de Urbina. 2003. *A grammar of Basque*. Berlin: Mouton de Gruyter [Mouton Grammar Library 26].

Hewitt, Brian George. 1979. *Abkhaz*. Amsterdam: North Holland Publishing Company [Lingua Descriptive Studies 2].

Hewitt, Brian George. 1987. *The typology of subordination in Georgian and Abkhaz*. Berlin: Mouton de Gruyter.

Hewitt, Brian George. 1995. *Georgian: A structural reference grammar*. Amsterdam: Benjamins [London oriental and African language library, 2].

Klamer, Marian. 1998. *A grammar of Kambera*. Berlin: Mouton de Gruyter [Mouton Grammar Library 18].

Kornfilt, Jaklin. 1997. *Turkish*. London/New York: Routledge.

Kouwenberg, Silvia. 1994. *A grammar of Berbice Dutch creole*. Berlin: Mouton de Gruyter [Mouton Grammar Library 12].

Lehmann, Christian. 2005. Wortarten und Grammatikalisierung. *Wortarten und Grammatikalisierung. Perspektiven in System und Erwerb,* Clemens Knobloch & Burkhard Schaeder (eds.), 1–20. Berlin: Mouton de Gruyter.

Li, Charles N. & Sandra A. Thompson. 1981. *Mandarin Chinese: A functional reference grammar.* Berkeley: University of California Press.

Mattissen, Johanna & Werner Drossard. 1998. Lexical and syntactic categories in Nivkh (Gilyak). Düsseldorf: Heinrich Heine Universität [Theorie des Lexicons, Arbeiten des Sonderforschungsbereichs 282, No. 85].

Mithun-Williams, Marianne. 1976. *A grammar of Tuscarora*. New York/London: Garland Publishing.

Mithun, Marianne. 2000. Noun and verb in Iroquoian languages: multicategorization from multiple criteria, *Approaches to the typology of words classes,* Petra M. Vogel & Bernard Comrie (eds.), 397–420. Berlin/New York: Mouton de Gruyter.

Mosel, Ulrike. 1992. On nominalization in Samoan. *The language game. Papers in memory of Donald C. Laycock,* Tom Dutton, Malcolm Ross & Darrell Tryon (eds.), 263–281. Canberra: Australian National University [Pacific Linguistics, Series C, No. 100].

Mosel, Ulrike & Even Hovdhaugen. 1992. *Samoan reference grammar.* Oslo: Scandinavian University Press.
Neukom, Lucas. 2001. *Santali.* München: Lincom Europa [Languages of the World/Materials 323].
Noonan, Michael. 1992. *A grammar of Lango.* Berlin: Mouton de Gruyter [Mouton Grammar Library 7].
Reh, Mechtild.1985. *Die Krongo-Sprache (nìinò mó-dì). Beschreibung, Texte. Wörterverzeichnis.* Berlin: Dietrich Reimer Verlag [Kölner Beiträge zur Afrikanistik 12].
Saltarelli, Mario. 1988. *Basque.* London: Croom Helm [Croom Helm Descriptive Grammars].
Schroeder, Christoph. 2004. *Depiktive im Sprachvergleich Deutsch-Türkish. Eine konstrastive-typologische Analyse.* Habilitationsschrift, Universität Osnabrück.

B. Other References

Bartsch, Renate. 1986. On aspectual properties of Dutch and German nominalizations, *Temporal structure in sentence and discourse*, Vincenzo Lo Cascio & Co Vet (eds.), 7–39. Dordrecht: Foris.
Bartsch, Renate. 1989. Tenses and aspects in discourse. *Theoretical Linguistics* 15, 133–194.
Bolinger, Dwight (Bolinger, Dwight 1967 Adjectives in English: Attribution and predication. *Lingua* 18: 1–34.
Cuvalay-Haak, Martine. 1997. *The verb in Literary and Colloquial Arabic.* Berlin: Mouton de Gruyter [Functional Grammar Series 19].
Dik, Simon C. 1997. *The theory of Functional Grammar. Volume 1: The structure of the clause.* 2nd edition, edited by Kees Hengeveld. Berlin: Mouton de Gruyter [Functional Grammar Series 20].
Hengeveld, Kees. 1992. *Non-verbal predication. Theory, typology, diachrony.* Berlin: Mouton de Gruyter [Functional Grammar Series 15].
Hengeveld, Kees. 2005. Dynamic expression in Functional Discourse Grammar. *Morphosyntactic expression in Functional Grammar,* Casper de Groot & Kees Hengeveld (eds.), 53–86. Berlin: Mouton de Gruyter [Functional Grammar Series 27].
Hengeveld, Kees. 2008. The noun phrase in Functional Discourse Grammar. *Noun phrases in Functional Discourse Grammar*, Daniel García Velasco & Jan Rijkhoff (eds.), Berlin: Mouton de Gruyter.
Hengeveld, Kees, Jan Rijkhoff & Anna Siewierska. 2004. Parts-of-speech systems and word order. *Journal of Linguistics* 40: 527–570.
Hengeveld, Kees & Lachlan Mackenzie. 2006. Functional Discourse Grammar. *Encyclopedia of Language and Linguistics,* 2nd Edition, Volume 4, Keith Brown (ed.), 668–676. Oxford: Elsevier.
Hengeveld, Kees & Lachlan Mackenzie. 2008. *Functional Discourse Grammar.* Oxford: Oxford University Press.
Hengeveld, Kees & Gerry Wanders. 2007. Adverbial conjunctions in Functional Discourse Grammar. *Structural-functional studies in English grammar*, Mike Hannay and Gerard Steen (eds), 211–117. Amsterdam: Benjamins.
Lier, Eva van. 2006. Parts-of-speech and dependent clauses: A typological study. *Folia Linguistica* 40, 3/4: 239–304.

Lier, Eva van. 2009. *Parts-of-speech and dependent clauses.* (LOT dissertation series no. 221). Utrecht: LOT Publications.

Mackenzie, J. Lachlan. 1990. Let's get our heads together: a reply to van der Auwera. *Working with Functional Grammar: Descriptive and computational applications,* Mike Hannay & Eveline Vester (eds.), 133–144. Dordrecht: Foris.

Rijkhoff, Jan. 2002. *The noun phrase.* Oxford: Oxford University Press.

Swart, Henriëtte de, Yoad Winter & Joost Zwarts. 2005. Bare predicate nominals in Dutch. In: Emar Maier, Corien Bary & Janneke Huitink (eds), *Proceedings of SuB 9,* 446–460. Nijmegen: Nijmegen Centre of Semantics.

Vet, Co. 1990. Aktionsart, aspect and duration adverbials. *Unity in diversity: Papers presented to Simon C. Dik on his 50th birthday.* Harm Pinkster & Inge Genee (eds.), Dordrecht: Foris.

Authors' address

Kees Hengeveld / Eva van Lier
Department of Theoretical Linguistics
Faculty of Humanities
University of Amsterdam
Spuistraat 210
1012 VT Amsterdam
The Netherlands

P.C.Hengeveld@uva.nl, E.H.vanLier@uva.nl

Language Index

Subject index

In the series *Benjamins Current Topics (BCT)* the following titles have been published thus far or are scheduled for publication:

28 **GULLBERG, Marianne and Kees de BOT (eds.):** Gestures in Language Development. *Forthcoming*

27 **DROR, Itiel E. (ed.):** Learning Technologies and Cognition. *Forthcoming*

26 **SHLESINGER, Miriam and Franz PÖCHHACKER (eds.):** Doing Justice to Court Interpreting. vi, 239 pp. + index. *Expected September 2010*

25 **ANSALDO, Umberto, Jan DON and Roland PFAU (eds.):** Parts of Speech. Empirical and theoretical advances. 2010. vi, 291 pp.

24 **ARBIB, Michael A. and Derek BICKERTON (eds.):** The Emergence of Protolanguage. Holophrasis vs compositionality. 2010. xi, 181 pp.

23 **AUGER, Alain and Caroline BARRIÈRE (eds.):** Probing Semantic Relations. Exploration and identification in specialized texts. 2010. ix, 156 pp.

22 **RÖMER, Ute and Rainer SCHULZE (eds.):** Patterns, Meaningful Units and Specialized Discourses. 2010. v, 124 pp.

21 **BELPAEME, Tony, Stephen J. COWLEY and Karl F. MACDORMAN (eds.):** Symbol Grounding. 2009. v, 167 pp.

20 **GAMBIER, Yves and Luc van DOORSLAER (eds.):** The Metalanguage of Translation. 2009. vi, 192 pp.

19 **SEKINE, Satoshi and Elisabete RANCHHOD (eds.):** Named Entities. Recognition, classification and use. 2009. v, 168 pp.

18 **MOON, Rosamund (ed.):** Words, Grammar, Text. Revisiting the work of John Sinclair. 2009. viii, 124 pp.

17 **FLOWERDEW, John and Michaela MAHLBERG (eds.):** Lexical Cohesion and Corpus Linguistics. 2009. vi, 124 pp.

16 **DROR, Itiel E. and Stevan HARNAD (eds.):** Cognition Distributed. How cognitive technology extends our minds. 2008. xiii, 258 pp.

15 **STEKELER-WEITHOFER, Pirmin (ed.):** The Pragmatics of *Making it Explicit.* 2008. viii, 237 pp.

14 **BAKER, Anne and Bencie WOLL (eds.):** Sign Language Acquisition. 2009. xi, 167 pp.

13 **ABRY, Christian, Anne VILAIN and Jean-Luc SCHWARTZ (eds.):** Vocalize to Localize. 2009. x, 311 pp.

12 **DROR, Itiel E. (ed.):** Cognitive Technologies and the Pragmatics of Cognition. 2007. xii, 186 pp.

11 **PAYNE, Thomas E. and David J. WEBER (eds.):** Perspectives on Grammar Writing. 2007. viii, 218 pp.

10 **LIEBAL, Katja, Cornelia MÜLLER and Simone PIKA (eds.):** Gestural Communication in Nonhuman and Human Primates. 2007. xiv, 284 pp.

9 **PÖCHHACKER, Franz and Miriam SHLESINGER (eds.):** Healthcare Interpreting. Discourse and Interaction. 2007. viii, 155 pp.

8 **TEUBERT, Wolfgang (ed.):** Text Corpora and Multilingual Lexicography. 2007. x, 162 pp.

7 **PENKE, Martina and Anette ROSENBACH (eds.):** What Counts as Evidence in Linguistics. The case of innateness. 2007. x, 297 pp.

6 **BAMBERG, Michael (ed.):** Narrative – State of the Art. 2007. vi, 271 pp.

5 **ANTHONISSEN, Christine and Jan BLOMMAERT (eds.):** Discourse and Human Rights Violations. 2007. x, 142 pp.

4 **HAUF, Petra and Friedrich FÖRSTERLING (eds.):** Making Minds. The shaping of human minds through social context. 2007. ix, 275 pp.

3 **CHOULIARAKI, Lilie (ed.):** The Soft Power of War. 2007. x, 148 pp.

2 **IBEKWE-SANJUAN, Fidelia, Anne CONDAMINES and M. Teresa CABRÉ CASTELLVÍ (eds.):** Application-Driven Terminology Engineering. 2007. vii, 203 pp.

1 **NEVALAINEN, Terttu and Sanna-Kaisa TANSKANEN (eds.):** Letter Writing. 2007. viii, 160 pp.